Curricula for Teaching Children and Young People with Severe or Profound and Multiple Learning Difficulties

Curricula for Teaching Children and Young People with Severe or Profound and Multiple Learning Difficulties offers a range of compelling arguments for a distinct and separate pedagogical approach to the learning needs of the most educationally challenging pupils. This book, written in accessible, common-sense and non-academic language, provides an easy-to-follow alternative curriculum specifically designed to enhance and enrich the learning of children with profound and multiple learning difficulties. Chapter by chapter, guidelines and support are offered in key curriculum areas, some of which include:

- cognition
- language, literacy and communication
- mathematical
- physical
- sensory
- creative
- care
- play
- problem-solving.

This highly practical resource is essential reading for educational professionals, parents, school governors, teachers, teaching assistants, therapists and indeed anyone involved with maximising the educational opportunities of those with profound learning difficulties.

Peter Imray, now a freelance trainer and advisor, has been a teacher of children, young people and adults with special educational needs since 1986, mostly at The Bridge School in Islington, North London. He was part of the SCAA working party that published its findings on Profound and Multiple Learning Difficulties and the National Curriculum in 1996 and has been active in the continued development of learning difficulties pedagogy and curricula since then. His first book, *Turning the Tables on Challenging Behaviour*, was published by Routledge in 2008.

Viv Hinchcliffe has held an interest in SLD and PMLD curriculum since his involvement on *In Search of a Curriculum*, published by Rectory Paddock School in 1983, and this has continued unabated. He has published widely on issues as varied as language and communication, self-advocacy, drama and leadership, is a regular speaker at conferences and has been a member of a number of DfE and DoH committees. Viv has recently taken up the post of Head of Drumbeat School and ASD Service, the new flagship specialist ASD School of the London Borough of Lewisham.

National Association for Special Educational Needs (nasen)

nasen is a professional membership association that supports all those who work with or care for children and young people with special and additional educational needs. Members include teachers, teaching assistants, support workers, other educationalists, students and parents.

nasen supports its members through policy documents, journals, its magazine *Special!*, publications, professional development courses, regional networks and newsletters. Its website contains more current information such as responses to government consultations. **nasen's** published documents are held in very high regard both in the UK and internationally.

Other titles published in association with the National Association for Special Educational Needs (nasen):

Brilliant Ideas for Using ICT in the Inclusive Classroom
Sally McKeown and Angela McGlashon
2011/pb: 978-0-415-67254-2

Language for Learning in the Secondary School
A practical guide for supporting students with speech, language and communication needs
Sue Hayden and Emma Jordan
2012/pb: 978-0-415-61975-2

ADHD: All Your Questions Answered
A complete handbook for SENCOs and teachers
Fintan O'Regan
2012/pb: 978-0-415-59770-8

Assessing Children with Specific Learning Difficulties
A teacher's practical guide
Gavin Reid, Gad Elbeheri and John Everatt
2012/pb: 978-0-415-67027-2

Using Playful Practice to Communicate with Special Children
Margaret Corke
2012/pb: 978-0-415-68767-6

The Equality Act for Educational Professionals
A simple guide to disability and inclusion in schools
Geraldine Hills
2012/pb: 978-0-415-68768-3

More Trouble with Maths
A teacher's complete guide to identifying and diagnosing mathematical difficulties
Steve Chinn
2012/pb: 978-0-415-67013-5

Dyslexia and Inclusion
Classroom approaches for assessment, teaching and learning, second edition
Gavin Reid
2012/pb: 978-0-415-60758-2

Provision Mapping
Improving outcomes in primary schools
Anne Massey
2012/pb: 978-0-415-53030-9

Promoting and Delivering School-to-School Support for Special Educational Needs
A practical guide for SENCOs
Rita Cheminais
2013/pb 978-0-415-63370-3

Time to Talk
Implementing outstanding practice in speech, language and communication
Jean Gross
2013/pb: 978-0-415-63334-5

Curricula for Teaching Children and Young People with Severe or Profound and Multiple Learning Difficulties

Practical strategies for educational professionals

Peter Imray and
Viv Hinchcliffe

LONDON AND NEW YORK

First published 2014
by Routledge
2 Park Square, Milton Park, Abingdon, Oxon OX14 4RN

and by Routledge
711 Third Avenue, New York, NY 10017

Routledge is an imprint of the Taylor & Francis Group, an informa business

© 2014 Peter Imray and Viv Hinchcliffe

British Library Cataloguing in Publication Data
A catalogue record for this book is available from the British Library

Library of Congress Cataloging in Publication Data
Imray, Peter.
    Curricula for teaching children and young people with severe or
    profound and multiple learning difficulties: practical strategies for
    educational professionals/Peter Imray, Viv Hinchcliffe.
    pages cm – (David fulton/nasen)
    1. Learning disabled – Education. I. Hinchcliffe, Viv. II. Title.
    LC4704.I47 2013
    371.9—dc23
    2013018916

ISBN: 978-0-415-83845-0 (hbk)
ISBN: 978-0-415-83847-4 (pbk)
ISBN: 978-1-315-88329-8 (ebk)

Typeset in Galliard and Gill Sans
by Florence Production Ltd, Stoodleigh, Devon, UK

Printed and bound in Great Britain by
TJ International Ltd, Padstow, Cornwall

Contents

Acknowledgements

If we acknowledged everyone who has been instrumental in the writing of this book, the list would take up another book. A combined seventy plus years' worth of pupils, students, their parents and siblings, their teachers, teaching assistants (TAs) and therapists, working at Rectory Paddock and Riverside Schools in Bromley, South London, Drumbeat School in Lewisham, South London and Rosemary and The Bridge School in Islington, North London takes up an awful lot of space. And this is without mentioning the countless academics, from whose writings we have learned so much.

If you're in any of these groups, we thank you, but specifically we feel that we have to acknowledge the advice, help and support given by Mandy Hadfield on mathematical thinking and problem solving; Penny Lacey on thinking and problem solving; Mark Roberts on cognitive development; Tom Andrews on sex and relationships education; Sally Paveley on ICT; Keith Park and Nicola Grove on narrative and storytelling; and Diego Gasquez Navarro and Lana Bond on all things PMLD. We would also like to thank Barry Carpenter who initially set us to work together writing some of the training materials for the Teacher Development Agency (TDA) for teachers of children and young people with severe, profound and complex learning difficulties (www.education.gov.uk/complexneeds).

Abbreviations

ADHD	Attention Deficit and Hyperactivity Disorder
AISI	Adult Interactive Style Intervention
ASC	Autistic Spectrum Conditions
ESBD (sometimes referred to as SEBD or BESD)	Emotional, Social and Behavioural Difficulties
ICT	Information and Communications Technology
ISE	Individualised Sensory Environment
MAP	Multi-Agency Profile
MAPP	Mapping and Assessing Personal Progress
MLD	Moderate Learning Difficulties
MSI	Multi-Sensory Impairment
NC	(UK) National Curriculum
NT	neuro-typical
OT	occupational therapist
PIMD	Profound Intellectual and Multiple Disabilities
PMLD	Profound and Multiple Learning Difficulties
P Scales	Pre Level 1 (of the UK National Curriculum)
PSHE	Personal, Social and Health Education
QfL	Quest for Learning
RfL	Routes for Learning
SCRUFFY (targets)	Student-led, Creative, Relevant, Unspecified, Fun For Youngsters
SEN	Special Educational Needs
SIB	Self-Injurious Behaviours
SLD	Severe Learning Difficulties
SMART (targets)	Specific, Measurable, Achievable, Realistic and Time-bound
SRE	Sex and Relationships Education
TA	Teaching Assistant
TDA	Teacher Development Agency

Introduction

In 1996, Peter Mittler wrote of work completed in England by the Special Educational Needs Training Consortium (SENTC) funded by the English Department for Education (DfE) to *'review the systems currently in place to review the training of teachers'* (Mittler, 1996). Addenda to that body's 1996 publication, noted twenty recommended competencies for SLD teachers that carry significantly greater resonance today than they did in 1996, simply because (at the time of this book's publication in 2014) so few teachers have any formal training in learning difficulties, never mind severe and profound learning difficulties. Mittler (1996) quotes surveys conducted by the DfE which indicated that, at that time, only just over fifty per cent of teachers possessed specialist qualifications, a figure which Mittler thought worrying then, but might be viewed as nirvanic now. It is interesting to note a number of additional facts; first, the working party was not short of significant SLD/PMLD specialist input in for example Peter Mittler, Jean Ware, Barry Carpenter, Judy Sebba, Jill Porter and Viv Hinchcliffe; second, the SEN recommendations were published as addenda to the main findings; third, they were not acted upon. Perhaps it was seen that there was *no need* to have separate competencies for teachers who taught those with severe learning difficulties (SLD) or profound and multiple learning difficulties (PMLD) because every teacher in the UK taught the same thing, the National Curriculum. Work might be needed on differentiation, so we got the P Scales in 1997, but once these were got right, everything would be fine. Except that it wasn't.

This idea of teachers not needing to have specialist qualifications was around before the 1990s. Indeed, the report of the Advisory Committee on the Supply and Education of Teachers (ACSET) on Teacher Training and Special Educational Needs (1984) was instrumental in closing the specialist courses for trainee teachers who wanted to work with children with SLD in the UK. All these Initial Teacher Training (ITT) courses finished around 1995. The second author was SLD course leader in one of the last remaining training institutions and ironically was one of the first to be trained in the new B.Ed ESN(S)[1] just after children with SLD in the UK first entered the education system in the late 1970s from Health (previously, they were not included in the education system, but remained in Social Education Centres and Hospitals). The ACSET report supported a generic approach to initial teacher training:

> We are convinced that all initial teacher training courses must prepare their students to meet the needs of the full range of pupils in ordinary schools. This range encompasses a significant number of children who from time to time will have special educational needs, but will not experience a change of school setting, and responsibility for meeting those needs is not an option, but an integral part of the job.
>
> (ACSET, 1984; para 6)

While there is some mention in the report of the positive impact of specialist Initial Teacher Training for teachers of children with SLD, to fill jobs created by the reception of those children newly transferred into the education system, the report adds:

> It would, in our view, be quite inappropriate for courses of initial teacher training, leading to Qualified Teacher Status, to concentrate on producing teachers for this highly specialist and very limited field of employment.
>
> (ACSET, 1984; para 14)

How wrong could they be? The closure of specialist ITT courses in the education of children with SLD and PMLD in the middle 1990s has, arguably, had a catastrophic effect on schools up and down the UK, where the supply of well-prepared teachers qualified to teach children with SLD and PMLD soon dried up. Apart from a smattering of postgraduate courses, teachers have generally had to learn on the job. Further, with the political and academic consensus of the time leaning heavily towards a completely inclusive UK education system, there was little appetite for more radical thought (Hinchcliffe, 1997).

Since both authors were teachers of those with SLD and PMLD when the UK National Curriculum first came into being in 1988, we have lived under its shadow for a considerable amount of time. We are not suggesting that it is a bad curriculum model, we are perhaps not qualified to make such judgements, but we are suggesting that it is not, and never has been, a suitable model for those with SLD and PMLD. Nonetheless, we have had to live with it and like every teacher of those with SLD and PMLD throughout the United Kingdom, we have had to sculpt and cut and mould and shape and trim to try to make it into something it was never intended to be.

During all this time, there has been an ever-decreasing amount of time and energy given over to training teachers in the education of those with SLD or PMLD, either for teachers already in the profession or about to enter the profession. This is not the fault of the universities, merely an indication of where, on the list of priorities, specialist knowledge in SLD and PMLD came. Further, an increasingly significant role has come to be played by Teaching Assistants (TAs) and we doubt that it is an exaggeration to state that the whole of the UK special needs sector would probably grind to a halt without them. Their education, in terms of the specialist knowledge they need to maximise the educational opportunities of those with SLD and PMLD, is, needless to say, also largely ignored.

With these considerations in mind, therefore, we have set out to make a start at exploring pedagogic and curricula models that might be suitable for those with SLD and PMLD. We do not regard these models as merely suitable for school-aged children; they are, we believe, equally applicable to students of whatever age.

We have also tried very hard to ensure that this book is not totally UK-centric, or, as the UK is made up of England, Scotland, Wales and Northern Ireland, all with their own Departments of Education, even Anglo-centric. It is perhaps inevitable, however, that the book will have a UK flavour. There is a strong tradition of considerable knowledge among UK academics and practitioners, and we are naturally more familiar with their writings. Nonetheless, we wish to reach out to other parts of the world because the sharing of knowledge and the cross-fertilisation of ideas is clearly key to a dynamic education system that seeks to stretch and challenge.

We have divided the book into three clearly distinct but very inter related sections. The first, Chapters 1 to 4 have a broadly theoretical bent and deal with the issues of definition, difference, pedagogy, inclusion, assessment, progress and personalisation. The second and third sections, covering Chapters 5 to 9, and Chapters 10 to 15, take each of the strands that we might view as making up broad, balanced and relevant curriculum documents for the education of children, young people and adults with PMLD and SLD, respectively. We would like you to read this book as you want to, taking whatever bits interest you first and moving on from there. You can even read it from front to back, because we believe that this also makes sense, but we did not actually write it this way. We wrote the practical bits first and the theoretical bits afterwards, not because we were not interested in the theory, but more because we are both essentially practitioners; it is where we have come from. This is important, because it was the fundamental differences involved in the practice of teaching children young people and adults with SLD and PMLD that made sense to us first; the theory followed on from that.

We have tried to reference as much as possible, because while teachers, especially experienced teachers, often have the practical understanding and knowledge, they probably don't have the academic knowledge. This is not because they don't value it, but because the UK education system doesn't value it. Knowledge is, we believe, a good thing in itself, because it gives confidence to the practitioner and forms a sound base on which to both question current practice and search for better practice. There is also, however, in the UK at least, another, more Kafkaesque reasoning:

> Currently, and too often, we have a situation in which schools struggle to manage imposed, ill-conceived and impractical policies. As well as having to spend energies that would be better focused on helping the pupils, as well as having to devise procedures for themselves, head teachers and teachers find themselves having to justify their actions to uncomprehending authorities. Schools really should not have to be responsible for educating government, but that is effectively what they find themselves doing when they are made accountable for practices which have had to be created locally and despite statutory policy.
>
> (Blanchard, 1999; p. 19)

This may not be (and we sincerely hope that it is not) the case in other countries, but in the UK, school leaders of children who have SLD or PMLD are held accountable for the success of their charges while being judged against a curriculum model and assessment and progress models that are entirely inappropriate. School leaders and teachers therefore find themselves in the unenviable position of having to know considerably more than the people who are sent to judge them. They are, as it were, educating government.

This position has come about because there seems to be no real understanding within government and the civil service institutions that organise and monitor education, such as the Office for Standards in Education (Ofsted), that those with PMLD or SLD learn entirely differently to neuro-typical conventionally developing learners, and as such we are bound to teach them differently and teach them different things. The central tenet of this book is that the curricula models suitable for those with PMLD and SLD have been arrived at despite the system, not because of it, and that intellectual debate has been largely stifled. Even worse, pedagogic models have hardly been addressed at all, from whatever quarter, with the (we believe) mistaken assumption that all children face various learning difficulties across a continuum, seemingly holding sway. We have tried to address this deficit.

In doing so, we have deliberately not limited ourselves to recent books, articles, points of view and developments, but have made a number of stretches back in time to the 1970s, '80s and '90s. We do not believe this to be a weakness of the book; it is rather a reflection of the fact that PMLD and SLD pedagogy has a lot of catching up to do.

There are some areas we have missed out, most notably ICT, a physical curriculum for those with SLD, and a specific area on autism. There are different reasons for these omissions. The pace of change in ICT, especially with the continued development of iPhones® and smartphones, iPads® and tablets, and all the apps that go with them, is so astonishingly rapid that any musings we might have could well be out of date by the time we finished the chapter, never mind published the book. We believe that effective teaching is about using the tools that work for you and your pupils; for some people this includes ICT and for others it does not. As facilitators of the educational process, we should be doing everything we can to encourage and support those teachers who do want to develop their use of ICT further and we must try to make sure all teachers are aware of the ICT tools that any school has to offer. There is, further, a band of teachers and other practitioners who spend hours creating fantastic resources using PowerPoint®, Notebook®, Clicker® etc., and who are usually exceptionally generous with those resources. We have only to go to Priory Woods School at www.priorywoods.middlesborough.sch.uk and The Whiteboard Room at www.whiteboardroom.org.uk to check them out and there are, we know, many others.

Clearly we are preparing our pupils to live in a world where ICT plays a significant part and the 'life skills' aspect of ICT is something that we must offer our pupils if we are to do that properly. The questions for educators must relate to what our pupils need to know and be able to do, to become responsible consumers of ICT products and services that will enhance their lives. We have addressed some of these issues in various chapters throughout the book, but recognise that more knowledgeable others will need to flesh this out as the technology changes and develops over time. There are numerous references to the assistive technology aspect of ICT throughout the book, especially in the sections related to communication, since clearly this is something that we must consider for those of our pupils who are unable to access conventional equipment or communication.

The absence of any specific chapter on physical activity for those with SLD is more down to our joint lack of specialist knowledge of this field. We have included reference to dance, and though there is an extraordinary dearth of research or other written material on dance for those with SLD or PMLD, there is even less on physical exercise (PE). This, along with many other areas that we have looked at in this book, is clearly an area that needs researching.

There is little reference to Autistic Spectrum Conditions (ASC) in this book, despite the fact that the dual diagnosis of SLD/ASC, and less often PMLD/ASC, is an increasingly common phenomena in both special and mainstream UK schools. There are, however, a plethora of books and articles relating to ASC and we are primarily concerned with the educational goals of those with SLD and PMLD, whether those children, young people and adults have an additional ASC or not. While there may be changes to how one teaches there should be no reason to change what one teaches.

Finally, this is not a prescriptive model, in the sense that through reading this book you will discover what you must be teaching. We believe in teachers, whether they be school leaders, teachers, TAs, therapists, parents, carers, mealtime supervisors, bus escorts or anyone else who comes into regular contact with those with SLD or PMLD. Moreover, we believe in the professionalism of these teachers. We believe that they are capable of making their own decisions based on what motivates their charges and what motivates them as people.

Some of you may take up some of the ideas and thoughts outlined in this book; some of you may take up none, and some all. Education is a two-way process of discovery – there is a lot to be discovered.

Note

1 ESN(S) – Educationally Sub Normal (Severe) was the precursor of Severe Learning Difficulties. The changing language of special educational needs is discussed in Chapter 2, *Dilemmas of Difference*.

Part I

Pedagogical questions

Chapter 1

Setting the scene

This book is an attempt to argue a case that has been bubbling around in the UK for a considerable time, but many of the arguments are by no means confined solely to the UK, since they affect all children, young people and adults wherever they are in the world, with severe learning difficulties (SLD) and profound and multiple learning difficulties (PMLD).

Working towards a definition of SLD

The definitions of these two descriptive learning conditions are particularly UK based and need explaining. Such explanations could take up a book in themselves if we were to do the subject full justice, though (like the rest of the book) we will try to be brief and to the point. The UK definition is largely based on observation of broadly definable (group) characteristics that practitioners understand as defining SLD. These characteristics have been noted by Imray (2005) as being difficulties with communication, understanding abstract concepts, concentration, and moving things from the short-term memory to the long. Lacey (2009) has noted that this group of learners typically have inefficient and slow information-processing speeds, little general knowledge, poor strategies for thinking and learning, and difficulties with generalisation and problem solving. These difficulties may well be compounded by considerably higher than usual incidence of sensory, motor and health difficulties (Porter, 2005b); an additional Autistic Spectrum Condition (ASC) diagnosis (Jordan, 2001; De Bildt *et al.*, 2005); and the considerably higher than average chance of having attendant challenging behaviours (Emerson, 1995; Harris, 1995; Male, 1996; Allen *et al.*, 2006). Interestingly, Carpenter (2010) has noted an increasing complexity of learning difficulties since the turn of the twentieth-first century, an observation also noted by a recent UK Special Educational Needs and Disabilities (SEND) Review, which reported special school headteachers' comments on this issue (Ofsted, 2006).

While it may be that, as Fujiura (2003) has suggested, definitional problems have rendered any search for a true number of persons with developmental disabilities a largely futile exercise, we can at least bring some common notions to bear and have some common understanding as to what is meant by PMLD and SLD throughout this book. Outside of the UK, and especially in the USA, defining children, young people and adults as having a severe learning difficulty or disability has tended to be done within IQ terms and using different terminology. The 1973 revision of the American Association of Mental Retardation (AAMR) definition of mental retardation reduced the IQ diagnostic criteria from 85 to 70 (Grossman, 1973) with current US definitions remaining essentially unchanged to date (Schalock *et al.*, 2007). The USA has only recently given up the term mental retardation[1] and it would appear that the UK definition of SLD equates broadly to this (Porter, 2005b; Stoneman, 2009) or more accurately, the new terminologies of severe intellectual disabilities, significant cognitive disabilities or low-incidence intellectual disabilities, which Browder *et al.* (2009) consider to form a maximum of one per cent of the general population. This percentage would more or less equate to the number of school-aged children classified as having a severe learning or profound and multiple learning difficulty in the UK, whether in mainstream or special schools. Emerson *et al.* (2010) note that there is no definitive record of the number of children of school age in the UK, as the presence of learning difficulties is not recorded in the decennial census of the UK population. Emerson *et al.* estimate, however, that over 200,000 children in England have a primary SEN associated with learning difficulty. Of these, four out of five have a moderate learning difficulty, and one in twenty have PMLD. The American terms 'learning disabilities' or 'high-incidence disabilities', seem to relate broadly to a UK definition of 'moderate learning difficulties' (Tartaglia *et al.*, 2009).

Describing a range of difficulties by using a framework of normative Western intellectual development (IQ tests) is of course fraught with problems, but it is difficult to see how else one may come up with a common and useful definition. There have been other attempts to define SLD in normative terms, especially relating cognitive functioning to conventionally developing children. This has a long and distinguished tradition with Lev Vygotsky classifying children's cognitive functioning into broad, age-related groupings that we might now associate with PMLD in the zero to two years range, and SLD in the two to seven years range (Rieber and Carlton, 1993). An early American estimate came from Yesseldyke (1987) who proposed that those with SLD were unlikely to progress beyond the level of an average seven or eight year old, while a more recent UK attempt by Imray (2005) suggests they are functioning cognitively below, usually considerably below, that of a conventionally developing six year old[2].

The latter definition owes a great deal to the UK National Curriculum (NC) that has been in operation in England and Wales since 1988, which starts at Year 1 (five to six years old) and expects averagely performing neuro-typical (NT) children to be working comfortably within Level 1 in at least English and Maths at around six years old. Prior to 2000 all UK schools, statutorily required to indicate where all of their children were working within the NC, could only note with a 'W' that children who had not yet reached Level 1 were 'working towards it'. This naturally led to much complaint that children with SLD and PMLD (about half of whom are educated in separate 'special' SLD Schools) were excluded from comparators applicable to the rest of the whole school population. As a result the P scales (QCA, 2001) were brought in (where P stands for pre-Level 1), which gave eight levels from P1 to P8 that could be reached prior to Level 1. These have been subsequently revised (QCA, 2004; QCA, 2009) but remain essentially the same in principle.

The fact remains that the norm for the school population who are currently described as having SLD or PMLD is to be working at or below P8 for the whole of their school lives, that is, in the UK, up to the age of nineteen. There may be a number of pupils and students with SLD who achieve Level 1 of the NC and beyond in some areas, especially those who may have an additional autistic spectrum condition (ASC), but these will often be in areas where rote learning can be applied, as for example with reading and numbers; that is, the skill may have been gained but the understanding may well lag far behind.

Using the P scales as an aid to a definition of severe learning difficulties

It might be useful for UK readers to remind themselves of the upper limits of the P scales, since this also offers the opportunity to introduce the concept to readers from outside the UK. English is sub-divided into reading, writing, speaking and listening. Maths is sub-divided into number, shape, space and measure, using and applying. For the sake of space we have quoted in full only P7 and P8 from 'reading' and 'number', but they give a more than adequate flavour of the nature of the P scales.

English (Reading)

P7 Pupils show an interest in the activity of reading. They predict elements of a narrative, for example, when the adult stops reading, pupils fill in the missing word. They distinguish between print or symbols and pictures in texts. They understand the conventions of reading, for example, following text left to right, top to bottom and page following page. They know that their name is made up of letters.

P8 Pupils understand that words, symbols and pictures convey meaning. They recognise or read a growing repertoire of familiar words or symbols, including their own names. They recognise at least half the letters of the alphabet by shape, name or sound. They associate sounds with patterns in rhymes, with syllables, and with words or symbols.

(QCA, 2009; p. 11)

Maths (Number)

P7 Pupils join in rote counting to 10, for example, saying or signing number names to 10 in counting activities. They can count at least 5 objects reliably, for example, candles on a cake, bricks in a tower. They recognise numerals from 1 to 5 and understand that each represents a constant number or amount, for example, putting the correct number of objects (1 to 5) into containers marked with the numeral; collecting the correct number of items up to five. Pupils demonstrate an understanding of 'less', for example, indicating which bottle has less water in it. In practical situations they respond to 'add one' to a number of objects, for example, responding to requests such as add one pencil to the pencils in the pot, add one sweet to the dish.

P8 Pupils join in with rote counting to beyond 10, for example, they say or sign number names in counting activities. They continue to rote count onwards from a given small number, for example, continuing the rote count onwards in a game using dice and moving counters up to 10; continuing to say, sign or indicate the count aloud when an adult begins counting the first two numbers. Pupils recognise differences in quantity, for example, in comparing given sets of objects and saying which has more or less, which is the bigger group or smaller group. They recognise numerals from one to nine and relate them to sets of objects, for example, labeling sets of objects with correct numerals. In practical situations they respond to 'add one' to or 'take one away' from a number of objects, for example, adding one more to three objects in a box and say, sign or indicate how many are now in the box; at a cake sale saying, signing or indicating how many cakes are left when one is sold. They use ordinal numbers (first, second, third) when describing the position of objects, people or events, for example, indicating who is first in a queue or line; who is first, second and third in a race or competition. Pupils estimate a small number (up to 10) and check by counting, for example, suggesting numbers that can be checked by counting, guessing then counting the number of: pupils in a group; adults in the room; cups needed at break time.

(QCA, 2009; pp. 21/22)

What is interesting here is that the P scales are framed in terms of what pupils and students can do, or more accurately are in the process of learning to do, since they operate on the basis of 'best fit'. That is, a pupil assigned to the level of P7 has achieved all or most of the descriptors and may also be working within the next level up, P8. This 'can do' definition touches on a number of concerns with 'labeling' as being essentially detrimental to the child being labeled (Ho, 2004) and pre-dates Terzi's (2010) call for us to adopt the 'language of capability' rather than the language of deficit when describing the nature of special educational needs. While the nature of the 'identification dilemma' (Norwich, 2008) is explored more fully in Chapter 2, we can at least reflect that the P scales are entirely based on the language of capability, though they are of course also based entirely on the language of (i) conventional development and (ii) academic, intellectual functioning.

From this perspective it might also be useful to turn to the P scale definitions of Personal, Social and Health Education (PSHE), which along with Maths and English constituted the original P scales written in 1998 by a group of English special school headteachers (Ndaji and Tymms, 2009). PSHE also possibly represents the least academic subject within the UK National Curriculum and therefore might give a more accurate reflection of someone with SLD, who will, by whichever definition one chooses, naturally struggle within an academic framework. Here then, are the P scales 4 to 8 for PSHE and Citizenship.

PSHE and Citizenship

P4 Pupils express their feelings, needs, likes and dislikes using single elements of communication (words, gestures, signs or symbols). They engage in parallel activity with several others. Pupils follow familiar routines and take part in familiar tasks or activities with support from others. They show an understanding of 'yes' and 'no', and recognise and respond to animated praise or criticism. They begin to respond to the feelings of others, for example, matching their emotions and becoming upset.

P5 Pupils take part in work or play involving two or three others. They maintain interactions and take turns in a small group with some support. Pupils combine two elements of communication to express their feelings, needs and choices. They join in discussions by responding appropriately (vocalising, using gestures, symbols or signing) to simple questions about familiar events or experiences, for example, 'What does the baby need?'

P6 Pupils respond to others in group situations, playing or working in a small group cooperatively, for example, taking turns appropriately. They carry out routine activities in a familiar context and show an awareness of the results of their own actions. They may show concern for others, for example, through facial expressions, gestures or tone of voice, and sympathy for others in distress and offer comfort.

P7 Pupils communicate feelings and ideas in simple phrases. They move, with support, to new activities which are either directed or self-chosen. They make purposeful relationships with others in group activities and attempt to negotiate with them in a variety of situations, for example, if other pupils wish to use the same piece of equipment. They judge right and wrong on the basis of the consequences of their actions. They show some consideration of the needs and feelings of other people and other living things, for example, offering food to a visitor or watering a classroom plant.

P8 Pupils join in a range of activities in one-to-one situations and in small or large groups. They choose, initiate and follow through new tasks and self-selected activities. They understand the need for rules in games, and show awareness of how to join in different situations. They understand agreed codes of behaviour which help groups of people work together, and they support each other in behaving appropriately, for example, while queuing in a supermarket. They show a basic understanding of what is right and wrong in familiar situations. They can seek help when needed, for example, assistance in fastening their clothes. They are often sensitive to the needs and feelings of others and show respect for themselves and others. They treat living things and their environment with care and concern.

(QCA, 2009; p. 33)

Working towards a definition of PMLD

Profound and Multiple Learning Difficulties (PMLD) was first coined as a term by Evans and Ware (1987) and has been generally accepted across the UK as being an apposite term for that very small group of learners who are functioning at the very earliest stages of intellectual development and who have additional (and multiple) physical and sensory impairments. Some have sought to challenge this terminology, notably Hogg (1991) with his Profound Intellectual and Multiple Disability (PIMD) on the grounds that the disabilities experienced by this group are beyond mere 'learning difficulties' and permeate every area of life. While we have sympathy with this view, Ware's conjecture that 'in an educational context, what is important about disabilities and difficulties, however caused, is their impact on learning' (Ware, 2005, p. 67) carries a great of deal of weight as far as this book is concerned. Various other terms are used in various other countries, for example, MSID (Most Severe Intellectual Disabilities) in Australia (Lyons and Cassebohm, 2012) alongside the term PIMD, which also has considerable use in northern Europe. Those seeking a rounded and established definition of PMLD should immediately turn to *Routes for Learning* (WAG, 2006) from Wales, or its sister publication *Quest for Learning* (CCEA, 2006) from Northern Ireland. Written under the guidance of Jean Ware and Verity Donnelly, *Routes* is constantly referred to in this book and we would very strongly recommend it as being essential reading for anyone entering the world of PMLD for the first time. At around sixty pages it is concise, readable and academically rigorous, which are considerable tricks in themselves.

Given that the *Routes* definition of PMLD is concise and academically rigorous at sixty pages, it is clearly beyond the scope of this introduction to reduce that even further. We might note, however, that Imray (2005) has suggested that those with PMLD are likely to be pre-intentional communicators and will generally (unintentionally) communicate for needs/wants only, have extreme difficulties conceptualising abstract concepts, have difficulty learning though imitation, be (often totally) physically reliant on others and have a limited understanding of cause and effect.

The Qualification, Curriculum and Assessment Authority for Wales has suggested that those with PMLD are likely to display at least one or more of significant motor impairments, significant sensory impairments, and/or complex health care needs (QCAA Wales, 2003). Ware (2005) has pointed to the often missed effects of poor behavioural states, poor behavioural rates and significant difficulties in information processing, even when compared to other groups with learning difficulties, never mind NT learners. The behavioural state (readiness to learn) may well be severely impaired, with Guess *et al.* (1990) suggesting that less than half of the average PMLD pupil's time at school is spent in a state where they are fit to learn because of such conditions as sleepiness, pain, discomfort, distraction, etc. Behavioural rate refers to the average number of voluntary behavioural actions per minute, less than five behaviours per minute on average according to Ware (1987) and considerably less than NT children. When put together with the suggestion that the abilities of those with PMLD to process information is only comparable with very young NT infants (Kahn, 1976; Remington, 1996), we can see that such conditions will have 'profound implications for learning and thus potentially for teaching strategies' (Ware, 2005, pp. 69–70).

In our quest for a common understanding of the term PMLD, we may also borrow a shortened version of *Routes* to describe the main difficulties likely to be encountered. *Routes* gives in total forty-three possible milestones that the pupil with PMLD may encounter as she progresses, seven of which are classified as 'key milestones'. These milestones are not linear and may not all be relevant to all children, but they reflect earlier work carried out by other writers (Goldbart, 1994; Brown, 1996 for example) and are likely to broadly represent the cognitive and communication goals for someone with PMLD over the course of their life in school and beyond.

The *Routes for Learning* seven key milestones (WAG, 2006) are:

- notices stimuli
- responds consistently to one stimulus
- contingency responding
- contingency awareness
- object permanence
- selects from two or more items
- initiates actions to achieve desired result (exerting autonomy in variety of contexts).

British readers will be familiar with understanding the term PMLD within the P Scales as falling within levels P1 to P3 and it might be useful to quote QCA (2009) in its definition of P3(i) and P3(ii) as an indication of the upper cognitive levels normally associated with the term PMLD. It should also be noted that the lower P scales (P1 to P3) are generic – that is, they are not split into subject areas – and were further sub-divided in P1(i), P1(ii), P2(i), P2(ii), P3(i) and P3(ii) in 2001 (QCA, 2001a). This sub-division was almost entirely to do with assessing pupil progress and is discussed further in Chapter 3.

P3(i) Pupils begin to communicate intentionally. They seek attention through eye contact, gesture or action. They request events or activities, for example, pointing to key objects or people. They participate in shared activities with less support. They sustain concentration for short periods. They explore materials in increasingly complex ways, for example, reaching out and feeling for objects as tactile cues to events. They observe the results of their own actions with interest, for example, listening to their own vocalisations. They remember learned responses over more extended periods, for example, following the sequence of a familiar daily routine and responding appropriately.

P3(ii) Pupils use emerging conventional communication. They greet known people and may initiate interactions and activities, for example, prompting another person to join in with an interactive sequence. They can remember learned responses over increasing periods of time and may anticipate known events, for example, pre-empting sounds or actions in familiar poems. They may respond to options and choices with actions or gestures, for example, by nodding or shaking their heads. They actively explore objects and events for more extended periods, for example, turning the pages in a book shared with another person. They apply potential solutions systematically to problems, for example, bringing an object to an adult in order to request a new activity.

(QCA, 2009, p. 8)

It needs to be noted that the majority of those designated as having a profound learning difficulty in this book will (probably) not achieve the heights described in P3(ii) above, and will be working at cognitive levels below this (and usually well below this) for all of their school lives, but clearly this is by no means an exact science. The phenomena of fractured learning and spiky profiles are well established (Carpenter, 2010) and some pupils may be working at P1 or P2 for some areas, yet above P3 in others, especially in the areas of personal and social development for example.

Are the terms Severe Learning Difficulties and Profound and Multiple Learning Difficulties of any worth?

As we argue in Chapter 2, the terms SLD and PMLD are only of use if they can tell us something worthwhile about the child so designated. Labels, groupings and categorisations are useful in general terms because they aid understanding of the broad parameters of expectation. As a teacher, one would want to know who it is one is teaching, as well as the broad range of abilities in the class, because such knowledge can aid preparation, ensure that teaching is pitched at the right level and acts as an indicator of learning (and therefore teaching) potential. Critics will argue that such labels may also limit potential (Hobbs, 1975; Ho, 2004) because they act as pre-determined ceilings – if the definition confines the child to certain intellectual or physical parameters, why try going outside of these? Some go further, to argue that any attempt to label axiomatically produces 'ableism',

> a network of beliefs, processes and practices that produces a particular kind of self and body (the corporeal standard) that is projected as the perfect, species-typical and therefore essential and fully human. Disability then, is cast as a diminished state of being human.
>
> (Campbell, 2001, p. 44)

When this ableism is combined with a marketisation of education with schools competing for pupils and the best being defined in terms of exam passes and high academic achievement, it is not surprising that any ideal of an inclusive education system that would automatically abandon labels and permanent separation is put under extreme pressure (Runswick-Cole, 2011).

While we would not want to deny the marketisation of UK schools (though there are positive benefits to this as well as negative) the ableist arguments are more contentious. Such interpretations may well have existed, but (at the time of writing at least) attitudes towards disability seem to be changing; thanks largely to the paralympic's movement from strength to strength, disability is now seen in a much more positive light. To be disabled is not limiting, is not a 'diminished state', but rather an opportunity to overcome adversity, with labels allowing for a more level playing field in competing on equal terms. There is no point in refusing to recognise disability, as though by denying the term it will miraculously disappear; disability exists, says the Paralympics, and it exists in numerous forms. Moreover, these numerous forms are not comparable to each other and are not comparable to the able-bodied.

Having the 'label' of being disabled is only 'stigmatic' (Minow, 1990; Norwich, 2008) if success outside of the defined labeled parameters is actually achievable. Our arguments in this book stem from being as certain as we can be that, for those with SLD and PMLD, success within a mainstream pedagogy and curriculum designed for neuro-typical (NT) children is rarely achievable and access to that curriculum is therefore not compatible with any definition of equity. The fact that some children will have some success does not alter the argument. The reason we are discussing this at all arises from the mistaken assumption that treating everyone as the same constitutes equity. It does not; it constitutes blindness. It is a blindness that is derived from an extremely well-meaning and liberal base, but it is blindness nonetheless, and relates directly to Martha Minow's 'dilemma of difference' (Minow, 1990), which argues that we are stuck between a rock and hard place in our desire to treat everyone the same and everyone differently at the same time. In educational terms, having a different curriculum and pedagogy for some might be seen to be discriminatory, but an equally deleterious outcome might be an insistence on a curriculum open to all children on the grounds of non-discrimination.

Ann Lewis and Brahm Norwich (Lewis and Norwich, 2000; Norwich and Lewis, 2005) examine the relationship between categories of special educational needs, specialised provision and specialised teaching, and Norwich (2008) considers whether categorisation has any relevance to the development and implementation of teaching programmes. By developing a model that distinguishes between 'unique', 'distinct' and 'common' pedagogic needs, Norwich advocates a move away from the stereotypical models that have long persisted in education to a greater focus upon those needs that can be conceptualised in individual terms and more closely associated with actions to support learning. Norwich and Lewis (2005) are clear that there is a difference between pedagogy and curriculum:

> In asking whether pupils with special educational needs require distinct kinds of pedagogic strategies, we are not asking whether pupils with special educational needs require distinct curriculum objectives. We are asking whether they need distinct kinds of teaching to learn the same content as others without special educational needs.
>
> (Norwich and Lewis, 2005, p. 7)

As such they see three alternative positions to take with regard to pedagogy, which they delineate within Figure 1.1 below.

Lewis and Norwich (2000) separate out the knowledge required by the teacher to teach 'exceptional or unusual' groups of children on the basis that there may be specific knowledge about pupils in the exceptional range that is required in addition to the common

PEDAGOGIC NEEDS

Figure 1.1 Pedagogic positions: General versus unique difference positions
Norwich and Lewis, 2005, p. 3.

strategies used by all teachers to teach all children. But this implies that all specific knowledge is common to all, whereas there are extremely strong arguments for suggesting that it is not.

Such arguments come from the very real differences that exist in the teaching styles, strategies and, most fundamentally, the entirely different knowledge base that is required to successfully teach those with SLD and PMLD. This book is an argument in support of the supposition that 'the reason this specific knowledge and these specific techniques are required in the first place is precisely because those with severe and profound learning difficulties learn differently from less 'exceptional' children' (Imray and Hinchcliffe, 2012, p. 151). Interestingly, Norwich and Lewis argue that this applies to the whole of special educational needs (SEN), and this we believe is a major weakness in their position. Since the Education Act of 1981, special educational needs has come to mean something very different in the UK from that which exists elsewhere. That is, SEN defines around twenty per cent of the whole school population, the vast majority of whom might be reasonably expected to function within the broad parameters of a common teaching philosophy and curriculum. There are reasons behind this huge number, largely related to the ability (or rather the inability) of the UK mainstream education system to engage and inspire a significant proportion (the twenty per cent) in the business of education, but such considerations are well beyond the scope of this book.

Perhaps a more accurate reflection of the number of school-aged children with SEN in the UK would be the 2.7 per cent of children currently identified as deserving of a Statement of Special Educational Need[3], thus qualifying for automatic additional local government funding. But even this is hugely problematic because there are currently four categories and eleven sub-categories of SEN (DfES, 2003) who might qualify for such a statement. These are

1   Cognition and learning needs

   • Specific Learning Difficulty (SpLD)
   • Moderate Learning Difficulty (MLD)
   • Severe Learning Difficulty (SLD)
   • Profound and Multiple Learning Difficulty (PMLD)

2   Behavioural, emotional and social development needs

- Behavioural, Emotional and Social Difficulty (BESD)

3   Communication and interaction needs

- Speech, Language and Communication Needs (SLCN)
- Autistic Spectrum Condition (ASC)

4   Sensory and/or physical needs

- Visual Impairment (VI)
- Hearing Impairment (HI)
- Multi-Sensory Impairment (MSI)
- Physical Disability (PD)

To suggest (Lewis and Norwich, 2000; Norwich and Lewis, 2005), however, that the groups above are comparable and that what fits the many must fit all, is not convincing. Although they have attempted to differentiate all of the above categories (and more) by asking various writers to form an opinion (based upon research available at the time of publication in 2005), it is only the opinion of these individual writers, however eminent they may be. Norwich (2010) readily accepts that such opinions must, by their very nature, be 'politically' driven, and indeed politically resolved; and as Norwich and Lewis acknowledge, those driven by an inclusionist agenda are bound to promote ideas that centre on a common pedagogy for all. 'Indeed, it would be rather odd to adopt a common pedagogy and still argue for separate schooling' (Norwich and Lewis, 2005, p. 4).

Ware (2005), talking specifically about PMLD, believes that the very definition of PMLD 'implies a group/general differences position' (p. 69) but also states that it is possible to conceptualise the specialised teaching techniques necessary as 'lying at the high intensity extreme continua of strategies' (p. 77). Jordan (2005) adopts a more certain group/general differences approach for those on the autistic spectrum, though Porter (2005b) is more circumspect on whether those with severe learning difficulties learn differently as a group and seems reluctant to be drawn on a decision one way or the other. Wishart (2005), however, in discussing those with Down's syndrome, asks the question 'when does a continuum become a series of related but distinctive pedagogic strategies and when do these individually become so differentiated as to become specific to the group of learners with whom they are used?' (Wishart, 2005, p. 91.)

Norwich and Lewis's response to this question is to firmly plump for the 'unique differences' position – as are the responses noted by Norwich (2008) and Norwich and Nash (2011). This recognises pedagogic needs that are either common to all or unique to the individual (Norwich and Lewis, 2005) but rejects the concept that there might exist a group (or groups) who are definable and learn in a fundamentally different way from the norm, which is the view that the authors of this book are taking. Norwich and Lewis's view is that there is a 'continuum of difference', ranging, one must assume, from pupils who are the farthest end of PMLD right through to pupils who are 'labeled' as outstandingly intellectually able. Such a position no doubt figures in the logic behind the UK's attempt at measuring on a common scale the assessment and progress of every single pupil of the 8.2 million children who are currently a part of the UK statutory education system. The table is re-produced as Table 1.1 below.

Table 1.1 P scales point scores and conversion tables (DfE, 2009)

Level of academic ability	Points scored
GCSE A*	58
L7 of NC	45
C grade GCSE	40
Level 4 of NC	27
Level 2c of NC	13
Level 1c of NC	7
P8	6
P4	2
P1(i)	0.5

The desire of the UK Department for Education (DfE) to create a seamless progression from the lower reaches of the P Scales to the upper reaches of GCSE A* grades (the highest achievement level for exams taken by NT learners at age sixteen) is understandable but not logical, because it takes 'academic ability' as the sole criterion of assessment and progress. Yet academic progress is, by definition, the one thing that those consistently working within the P Scales do not achieve, otherwise they would not be consistently working within the P Scales. Table 1.1 shows that the most academically able children will achieve fifty-eight points of progression during their time at school and the least academically able (that is, those children consistently working within the P scales) will achieve (at the very best) six points of progression; most with severe and all with profound learning difficulties will make considerably less than that. There is nothing anyone can do about this. This is not automatically a result of poor teaching or poor scholastic provision or lack of ambition. The fault lies in adopting the same academic assessment system for all pupils, whether they achieve academically or not. It is rather like measuring a parrot against a carp by seeing which flies the farthest. Why would one do that? Such comparisons are neither helpful nor justifiable, and do nothing to further an inclusive society. The question should also be asked about whether such a table is insulting to those who do not easily academically achieve, and perhaps the less academically able they are the more insulting this type of comparison becomes.

The fundamental principle around which this book is written is to argue in the strongest possible terms for a 'general differences position' with regard to SLD and PMLD. This recognises that some pedagogic needs are common to all[4], some are unique to the individual but also some are specific to those with severe learning difficulties and some are specific to those with profound and multiple learning difficulties. We contend that pupils with profound and multiple learning difficulties are highly unlikely to learn to communicate, eat, reach out, make choices, proactively engage with others effectively, unless 'distinct kinds of teaching' are used. Pupils with severe learning difficulties are highly unlikely to learn to think and problem solve, play co-operatively, achieve sexual independence, achieve theory of mind, value self-determination, etc., unless 'distinct kinds of teaching' are used. It is not sufficient just to adopt and adapt teaching techniques that are common to all, because not all of these will work with children, young people and adults with such severe and profound difficulties in learning. This book is an attempt to delineate such distinctive teaching techniques.

Notes

1 The American Association of Mental Retardation (AAMR) changed its name to the American Association of Intellectual and Developmental Disabilities (AAIDD) in 2010.

2 Imray (2005) also suggests that those designated as having PMLD are functioning cognitively below, usually considerably below, that of a conventionally developing eighteen month old. There is naturally considerable suspicion among practitioners toward those who would equate cognitive ages to children, young people and adults with learning difficulties on the grounds that this may well demean the individuals labeled as being childlike, and therefore they would be treated like a child. This is not the intention, which is more to give a 'common-sense' view of the way in which a person with severe or profound learning difficulties might themselves view the world.

3 This figure has hovered between two and three per cent for a number of years (Ofsted, 2010).

4 One might assume, for example, that the pedagogic needs expounded by Maslow (1973) in his *Hierarchy of Needs* would encompass all learners as well as Mary Warnock's (2010) common goals of *'independence, enjoyment and understanding'* (p. 16).

Chapter 2

Dilemmas of difference

This is not a book (or even a chapter) about the inclusion of pupils and students with SLD and PMLD into mainstream education. This is an extremely interesting subject, but we do not have the space to do it justice here and so we won't try. We do wish however to approach the topic from the dilemmatic approach, that is, recognising that there are dilemmas of difference at work and that these need to be both addressed and resolved. The term 'dilemmas of difference' was first coined by Martha Minnow in her studies relating to the American legal system. She succinctly placed the dilemma in perspective by asking 'When does treating people differently emphasize their differences and stigmatize or hinder them on that basis? And when does treating people the same become insensitive to their differences and likely to stigmatize or hinder them on that basis?' (Minow, 1990, p. 20.)

The dilemma of identification

Both Minow and Brahm Norwich (the latter being someone we'll turn to constantly in this chapter) argue that such dilemmas are driven by stigma, in that difference is directly linked to deviance (from the norm) and the danger of stigmatisation in the form of low expectations, low value and a sense of inevitability that the difference is, ultimately, insurmountable. That is, the stigma in the field of special educational needs is not necessarily in a direct form where society as a whole thinks less of someone with learning difficulties because of their difference, though this may be the view held by some individuals, but more in the form of stereotyping potential for present or future achievement as less than the norm. Weinberg and Brumback (1992) have, for example, suggested that pupils with an ADHD diagnosis will constantly use their ADHD as an excuse for their behaviour (and adults will allow them to). We have probably all overheard (or even thought ourselves) 'Oh, he can't do that, he's got severe learning difficulties', and we can see that such a dilemma is not a million miles from learned helplessness (Seligman, 1975) or the enormous potential for damage that has.

Indeed, the whole nature of the language used within SEN is indicative of this dilemma – profound and multiple *disabilities*, severe learning *difficulties*, autistic spectrum *disorders* – especially where the defining conditions of such children are termed in deficit questions; what can the child *not* do? 'Difference is linked to stigma or deviance and sameness is a pre-requisite for equality. Perhaps these assumptions must be identified and assessed if we are to escape or transcend dilemmas of difference' (Minow, 1990, p. 50).

Dyson (2001) has identified a basic contradiction within liberal democracies 'between an intention to treat all learners as essentially the same and an equal and opposite intention to treat them as different' (p. 25), and this, Norwich (2008) notes, is interesting for its emphasis on recent UK developments. Norwich suggests that Dyson 'identifies resolutions that emphasise commonality as having become dominant, perhaps because of their adoption by governments, as then leading to backlashes that emphasise difference' (Norwich, 2008, p. 27). Perhaps this book represents one of those backlashes!

Of course recognising that there is a dilemma is only half the battle since a resolution to the dilemma(s) is equally important, though Norwich (2008) regards the concept of perfect solutions (or nirvanas) as only delusory, or leading to a 'conceptual dead end'. We need, he argues, to acknowledge that recognising the diversity of interpretations is just part of the challenge, as a response will be required should these interpretations be incompatible.

Ho's (2004) answer is to do away with stratifications and labelling and concentrate on the uniqueness of the individual, and Terzi (2010) takes this one stage further by urging us to move away from the negative language of disability into the positive language of capability. Taking her position from the writings of Amartya Sen (2001), Terzi argues the current classification systems, in whatever country, lead us inevitably to 'a relational definition of learning difficulties and disability in terms of limitation of capability' (Terzi, 2010, p. 150). She wants us to turn this on its head and embrace the conceptual gain of concentrating on the positive potential of an individual so that an understanding of the capabilities of the child, rather than the deficits, becomes the central theme agencies can work towards. This reflects the seminal work of Nicholas Hobbs (Hobbs, 1975a and 1975b) and the use of labels as a means of control, thus establishing two important principles. First, that labelling of children can only be justified if it can be shown to bring benefits to the individual and second, that these individual needs should take precedence over those of service delivery systems. The development of provision, he argued, should be focused upon the needs of the child rather than being contrived to fit the individual to inadequate systems.

Three things here: first, Terzi's analysis implies that a positive philosophy towards children with SEN does not already happen, but we would suggest that, at least in the UK, and when agencies are working together reasonably well, it probably does. Generally speaking, the desire to be positive and work in the child's best interests is there and those who are good at what they do are nearly always positive. Changing the language might make those who are not good at what they do think harder about being positive, but it won't make them any better at achieving it. Second, using the language of capability is inevitably very individualised and, rather like Ho's 'uniqueness of the individual' line, faces the same problems. As Warnock (2010) has so succinctly pointed out, a 'nasty child [will always] taunt another child', that is, those who wish to stigmatise always will, label or no label. We may well now recoil at the terms 'maladjusted', 'sub-normal', 'retarded', and these words certainly carry concepts of being less than normal, whatever that is, but as far as we are aware other terms of playground abuse like 'spastic' or indeed 'special needs' are just descriptive words, used to indicate a specific or general condition.[1] The 'labelling cycle' (Hastings *et al.*, 1993) comes into play to ensure that they become terms of abuse, but the words themselves are not intrinsically bad. The point here is that even if we did adopt Loretta Terzi's language of capability and, for example, celebrated a student's making his way to school independently every morning, how long would it be before we heard 'Oi, you, independence' sneered in the playground?

Finally, part of our humanness is to group; it's what we do to make sense of the world; it's part of our basic mathematical instinct. To deny our natural predilection towards grouping in order to avoid some people stigmatising others is understandable and even laudable, but quite probably doomed to failure. Stigmatising or not stigmatising the group, or members of the group, does not alter them as a group, or members of that group. One might stigmatise a bus as a poor version of an automobile when compared to a racing car, but it does not alter the fact that it is a bus. We do not, however, talk about a bus in deficit terms in the same way as talking about someone with SLD. A bus is described in terms of what it can do rather than what it cannot do, but a bus is designed to do these things. A human being is not designed to have severe learning difficulties. In other words, we need a point of reference to group, and what are our terms of reference for someone with severe learning difficulties using the language of capability? This is a child who can learn to be independent – yes, but so can everyone else. This is a person who can learn to communicate effectively – yes, but so can everyone else. Using such 'lesser' aims, however positively framed, also indicates by comparison what people cannot do, and those who wish to think in negative terms will continue to do so. The reality is that the person with SLD or PMLD will need greater levels of support in both areas and the point of reference for this group has to be their difficulties in learning.

We will have references to capability in general learning intentions (the UK P Scales are, for example, written entirely in capability terms) and we hope that this book is a positive celebration of the potential in all pupils with SLD or PMLD, but these will not tell us what a child cannot do and it may well be essential that we know this. One of the defining characteristics of someone with severe learning difficulties is the extreme difficulty with understanding abstract concepts (Imray, 2005) and it is imperative that teachers and teaching assistants (i) understand what this means in real terms and (ii) do not use abstracts when teaching. This is not just a question of knowing what works; we also have to know what doesn't work. So many of the problems with the UK National Curriculum applying to those with SLD and PMLD have arisen because the assumptions of learning style are based entirely on linear NT progression, yet we know this cannot be correct. This means pupils will get stuck at a certain level and teachers will not have any automatic strategies for moving them on, because, apparently, we all learn in the same way. Mark making is a perfectly acceptable rung to work on in the ladder of writing and should be encouraged in children who are at that level as much as possible; but this concept becomes ridiculous if we are encouraging mark making for fifteen years simply because some children with SLD are unable to get to the next level. Teaching phonics to a beginning reader is an important step in their development of early reading skills; however, for a child with severe learning difficulties, it may be an unhelpful starting point on which to dwell for any length of time.

The point about categorising, or labelling, or grouping (call it what you will) is that it is a functional activity. It tells us something, as teachers, TAs, therapists, about the range within which the child is working. It gives us a base so that we are not constantly evaluating and re-evaluating. It makes sense to do this. Again, Mary Warnock, who talks with a great deal of plain common sense, writes of her 1978 committee's determination to be rid of limiting and debilitating labels by bringing all categories into the broad umbrella of special educational needs; trying as she says to 'simultaneously . . . make them the same as and different from the rest. Clearly this was an impossible task' (Warnock, 2010, p. 125). Inevitably, new categories emerged and although learning difficulties is somewhat better than educationally sub-normal, it is still a category. Words are ever changing in our understanding of their meanings and can mean what we want them to mean. 'Gay' can mean lots of different things in lots of different situations from entirely positive to entirely negative, but rarely is it used in its original sense. Similarly 'disabled' has meant lots of different things to lots of different people over the years, but seems currently to be experiencing a turnaround in fortunes largely thanks to the Paralympics or *Disability Games.* Perhaps the answer is to work harder at abling rather than disabling certain words, like 'learning' and 'difficulties'.

The placement dilemma

The identification dilemma is only part of the problem. We also need to consider the dilemmas of placement and curriculum[2] (Norwich and Gray, 2007; Norwich, 2008; Norwich, 2010). Our views on the curriculum are stated throughout this book, and although we will re state them here, we will look first at the placement dilemma. In any event, the two are inextricably linked.

Norwich and Gray (2007) and Norwich (2010) see the resolutions to the dilemmas as having multiple options, ranging from a position of a high degree of commonality to a high degree of differentiation in what they refer to as the 'model of flexible interacting continua of provision'.[3] Within the placement options, four broad stances are identified:

A   Separate school (special school) and unit/class linked to ordinary school.
B   Same school: part-time withdrawal to separate special school/unit.
C   Same school and class (varying degrees of class withdrawal).
D   Same class (varying learning groups: no withdrawal).

The more commonality-oriented the stance, the more provision will veer towards options C and D, and vice versa for a more differentiated stance, steering more towards B and A.

It may seem that this book's strident calls for a separate curriculum and pedagogical models for those with SLD and PMLD would automatically put us in the camp that veers off Norwich and Gray's scales altogether (perhaps this is the Alpha option). But although our natural inclination is to plump for option A above, arguing for a separate and distinct pedagogy and curriculum does not automatically imply a separate and distinct placement. There is no reason why such provision could not take place in a mainstream school, any more than high-intensity subject specialisms taught at university should automatically mean separation. The students can still be on the same campus, still mix socially, still have common areas of interest such as sports and the arts, and there would still be natural opportunities to meet and interact; they just would not be studying the same things. 'Though inclusion can be defined in terms of participating in the common enterprise of learning, it can also be defined in terms of participating in common institutions (i.e. local common schools)' (Norwich, 2010; p. 82). We would have to work hard to ensure that peer relationships and friendships were given every opportunity to develop, and there would need to be a recognition that this takes time, and such time would probably have to be taken from the normal school day. The will on all sides would need to exist, and there would have to be some guaranteed protection of funding, but this is entirely possible. Difficult, but possible.

What would not be possible is 'part-time withdrawal to separate special school/unit' since this is placing the actual curriculum and pedagogy on offer to those with severe and profound learning difficulties as secondary and inferior to the curriculum on offer to their NT peers. It is as bizarre as suggesting that mainstream children ought to receive their education through a specifically designed SLD or PMLD curriculum and then undergo 'part-time withdrawal to a separate unit' for the rest. Why is it acceptable to assume that the mainstream curriculum is superior to the special? Isn't this discriminatory? What is clear (in the UK at least) is that there has been much fine talk about inclusion but very little action for those with SLD and PMLD (Male, 2001; Hodkinson, 2012). For inclusive education to work, there would have to be a genuine commitment by all interested parties to both respect and give time to diversity. 'Inclusive education is based on the principle that local schools should provide for *all* children, regardless of any perceived difference, disability or other social, emotional, cultural or linguistic difference' (Florian, 2008, p. 202; author's emphasis).

Inclusion is about helping all teachers to accept responsibility for the learning of all children. It is about giving time to diversity, respecting individual differences and accepting that the outcomes of learning can be different for us all. But as Peter Mittler warns, if by inclusion we mean educating more children with severe or profound learning difficulties in mainstream schools, then inclusion will remain nothing more than an ideology unless schools are seen to change both their culture and organisation to ensure greater access and participation for all pupils (Mittler, 2000). We have seen very little evidence of this over the past twenty-five years of the UK education system.

Inclusion isn't about placing children in mainstream schools; it's about changing schools to make them more responsive to the needs of all children, changing schools' existing systems, their curriculum, organisation, pedagogy, grouping, assessment and values. A much earlier, but still very relevant, quote from Mittler comes to mind when talking about protecting the best interests of some of the most vulnerable children in the education system:

> Special education wherever it is provided is a form of positive discrimination in favour of the handicapped child. It makes available on his behalf a favourable pupil–teacher ratio, teachers with special training, classroom assistants, specially adapted physical conditions, and a concentration in one building of specialists such as speech therapists, physiotherapists, occupation therapists, and sometimes also, social workers and psychologists. If handicapped children are to be educated in ordinary schools, this element of positive discrimination must be preserved.
>
> (Mittler, 1979, p. 97)

Inclusion is about not taking leave of one's senses; inclusive practice should be thought through carefully, perhaps on a child-by-child basis, looking at the needs of the individual. We recognise that inclusion and participation are essential to human dignity and to the enjoyment and exercise of human rights, but we have to work much, much harder about putting it in place than we have up until now. Other nations may feel that they have done a better job than the UK towards the inclusion of children, young people and adults with SLD and PMLD, but again, there is very little evidence of this.

> The endless debates and the streams of publications about 'integration versus segregation' for a minority of children have been overtaken by a new agenda, which is about human rights and about the kind of society and the kind of schools we want for our children.
>
> (Mittler 2000, p. vii)

We are clear that, for us, it is a fundamental human right for a child with SLD or PMLD to receive a high-quality education, to be taught by expert special educators using specialist resources, working on pedagogic and curriculum objectives that are tailored to meet individual needs that are necessarily different from the mainstream, in a caring and secure environment, with direct access to essential multi disciplinary professionals and specialist resources. If that can be achieved in an inclusive setting, so much the better, but let's not put the cart before the horse.

Simmons and Bayliss (2007) have an interesting take on this in their arguments relating to the inclusion of pupils with PMLD in the general classroom life of one special school designated for children with SLD in England. Inclusion here is defined as 'the extent to which the children with PMLD engaged with their social and educational environments' (p. 20). Their study suggests that the efficacy of special schools to educate children with PMLD is not established, and they point to the fact that staff of one special school in the south-west of England seemed to have no real understanding of what it meant to have PMLD. They noted a culture of continued isolation of those with PMLD while staff 'dealt with' more physically active and challenging children. There was also a seeming deep-rooted inability to differentiate teaching, one numeracy lesson being exampled where a largely SLD class explored numbers between one and nine, with children checking the correct numerals on a number fan. For the one child with PMLD, the TA would 'find the number for the child, put the fan in the child's hand and help the child raise the fan to show the teacher' (p. 21). While this could have been an isolated incident, Simmons and Bayliss suggest, through the evidence of numerous classroom observations and interviews with teachers and TAs in this school, that this non-understanding of the 'profound' part of PMLD permeated the school. Their conclusions on the base cause for this lack of understanding were lack of training opportunities in matters related to PMLD for both teachers and TAs. We would certainly echo any calls for improved specialist training in both SLD and PMLD; in the UK at least it is desperately needed. While we must hope that the introduction of Teaching Schools in the UK will significantly aid new teachers' knowledge, there are still many thousands of existing teachers and TAs who will not have access to such training on a regular basis.

Simmons and Bayliss went on to challenge the (untested) assumption that special schools are able to educate children with PMLD and to suggest that through using the principles of *'intersubjectivity'* (Trevarthen and Aitken, 2001) a mainstream education would do better. Trevarthen and Aitken (2001) cite

> evidence that even newborn infants, with their very immature though elaborate brains, limited cognitions, and weak bodies, are specifically motivated, beyond instinctive behaviours that attract parental care for immediate biological needs, to communicate intricately with the expressive forms and rhythms of interest and feeling displayed by other humans. This evidence of purposeful intersubjectivity, or an initial psychosocial state, must be fundamental for our understanding human mental development.
>
> (p. 3)

There may well be a 'purposeful . . . initial psychosocial state' with neuro-typical babies, but to make the assumption (as Simmons and Bayliss do) that such states are evident in children with PMLD because Trevarthen and Aitken note that children with certain syndromes (such as Rett) respond well to music therapy and intensive interaction is a huge leap and by no means even vaguely proven. To us, this seems insufficient evidence on which to base an argument in favour of fully inclusive classes. And there are other huge difficulties with the arguments put forward by Simmons and Bayliss:

- One school does not equal all.
- Ofsted are supposed to have the ability to recognise good from bad schools. There was no indication in the article of the status of the school from its latest Ofsted inspection and therefore it was hard to judge whether this was considered a good school (never mind an outstanding one) or not.
- The principles of lack of specialist training equalling poor specialist education apply in exactly the same measure to mainstream schools.
- The principles of teachers and TAs being too concerned with the demanding and troublesome in their classes to spend quality time with those with PMLD applies equally to mainstream schools.
- The school was chosen because it was 'highly regarded' by Ofsted and the Learning and Skills Council but it was only highly regarded 'for its "inclusive" provision for children with SLD and PMLD (that is, the children with PMLD are no longer located in a PMLD-specific class)' (p. 20).

One could equally make the point that this school no longer regarded the *education* of its pupils with PMLD as being sufficiently significant, in its difference from the SLD group, to warrant specialist knowledge and provision. It's hardly surprising therefore that it failed to live up to the authors' expectations. There is a huge and entirely unsubstantiated assumption that those with PMLD and those with SLD can and should be in the same (inclusive) classes. Why?

In a similar vein, Foreman *et al.* (2004) conducted a study on the relative behaviour states of eight matched pairs of school-aged students with profound and multiple disabilities for one full day in a segregated classroom and an inclusive classroom in Australian schools. Behaviour states were systematically observed and recorded, along with several contextual indicators including measures of communicative behaviours, activity, and social grouping. Despite the absence of significant differences in most observed student behaviour states between the two settings, the students observed in general (inclusive) classrooms in this investigation were involved in significantly higher levels of communicative interaction than their matched peers in special classrooms. Differences in the frequency of interactions between the communicative partners in the two settings were also observed. This is interesting for two reasons. First, although there were no significant differences between behaviour states, the levels and frequency of interactions were higher in the inclusive settings mainly through a significant increase in peer interactions. One must assume that such an increase in interactions will produce significant benefits on the quality of life of those with PMLD (Lyons and Cassebohm, 2011) – not to mention the quality of life for their mainstream peers – and this must be applauded. We must work hard on extending the opportunity and ability for quality social interactions for those with PMLD who will naturally find such opportunities limited because of their profound communication difficulties. Second, however, we must not assume that quantity equals quality. There is a serious difference between peer interactions and interactions from a skilled, highly trained expert in PMLD (whether this person be a teacher, a TA, a therapist, a parent or A.N. Other) who has the ability and knowledge to recognise where pupils with PMLD are in their learning cycle and move them on from that point. The fact that such studies as Foreman *et al.* (2004) are often used to justify the argument for full- or part-time inclusion in mainstream settings for those with PMLD (or SLD for that matter) is an indication of how low the concept of experts able to provide real educational opportunities for those with PMLD and SLD has fallen. Leinhardt and Pallay (1982) note tellingly that the 'setting itself is not the primary issue of importance, rather it is what happens in the setting' (p. 574). They go on to note that a setting does not eliminate or guarantee the presence of effective instructional practices, as most important variables can occur in most settings.

These thoughts have been largely borne out in the US where a literature review on the academic success of pupils with LDs (broadly equivalent to MLD in the UK) by McLeskey and Waldron (2011) draws the conclusion that

> those who were optimistic that the needs of all elementary students with LD could be successfully addressed in full inclusion classrooms have been largely disappointed. Well-designed inclusive classrooms provide a very good general education and meet many of the needs of students with LD, but have not proven sufficiently malleable to offer the high-quality, intensive instruction needed by most elementary students with LD to achieve desired educational outcomes.
>
> (p. 57)

And the level of practice required within the small area of academic learning – essentially revolving around the three Rs – is too great to be accommodated in withdrawal classes either. That is, children would spend more time being withdrawn than included, which largely defeats the object of the inclusive programme.

A similar (earlier) study in the UK provided similar results. Lindsay (2007) noted that

> the evidence . . . does not provide a clear endorsement for the positive (educational) effects of inclusion. There is a lack of evidence from appropriate studies and, where evidence does exist, the balance was only marginally positive. It is argued that the policy has been driven by a concern for children's rights. The important task now is to research more thoroughly the mediators and moderators that support the optimal education for children with SEN and disabilities and, as a consequence, develop an evidence-based approach to these children's education.
>
> (p. 1)

Returning briefly to the theme of a common campus, a few words of caution. We would not want to deny the real gains to be had from freely interacting with one's peers on a regular basis (Arthur-Kelly *et al*, 2008), since, when effort and time are put into this, it can be of considerable benefit to all parties. We do not, however, take a rose-tinted-spectacles view of this and, again, Mary Warnock's no-nonsense opinions resonate and should be read by all (Warnock, 2010).

There are very few studies on the quality of the short- and long-term friendships and peer relationships forged between those with learning difficulties and those without in inclusive school and college settings, and those that do exist are not particularly optimistic about their efficacy on a variety of fronts. Wendelborg and Kvello (2010) question their permanence; Carman and Chapparo (2012) note that those with learning difficulties are very likely to experience problems with group relations; Locke *et al.* (2010) contend that students with ASCs experience a greater degree of loneliness than their NT peers in a mainstream setting; Durkin and Conti-Ramsden (2007) point to a poorer quality of friendships than their NT peers for sixteen-year-old students with specific language impairments; all prompting Rotheram-Fuller *et al.* (2010) to suggest that a far greater emphasis needs to be given to improving the quality of the inclusive provision.

Perhaps from a curriculum perspective, quality is much more important than quantity; we therefore need to look at inclusion rather as we might look at any other subject, to be given x amount of time per week and to have no aims or objectives other than the inclusive experience. That is, the inclusion is the objective. Inclusive time needs to be carefully planned just like any other lesson, and though it may not lend itself to specific targets, being an intrinsically process-based activity, loose learning intentions for all pupils, both with learning difficulties and their NT counterparts, need to be carefully thought through. And, we would repeat, all this takes time and that time needs to be given up by the mainstream as well as the special school. If we are going to make inclusion work, there has to be a commitment to giving up that time from everyone: pupils, teachers, school leaders, inspecting agencies, parents, governments, society. It is *not* sufficient for the main burden of time loss to be placed on the learning opportunities of those with SLD and PMLD, and it is not acceptable that this should even be considered.

Of course for those with SLD and PMLD, inclusive times are about much more than just forging relationships with their NT peers, since they will need inclusive opportunities in the communities around them and with the people who inhabit those communities. Much of this will, however, come about as a natural side effect of travel training, shopping, attending the local swimming baths and leisure centres, visiting local libraries, etc. Inclusion for the mainstream will not come as a natural part of their curriculum; it has to be worked at.

The curriculum dilemma

Norwich and Gray's (2007) curriculum options cover the following:

A   Same general aims, different pathways/programmes, different levels in pathways and different (specialised) teaching approaches.
B   Same general aims, same pathways/programmes, different levels in pathways and different teaching approaches
C   Same general aims, same pathways/programmes, similar levels in pathways and different teaching approaches.

The more commonality-oriented the stance, the more curriculum design leans towards C and vice versa and, once again, Norwich and Gray have rejected as impractical the 'extreme' ends of the spectrum. Neither Norwich and Gray (2007) nor Norwich (2010) define 'general aims' or 'pathways/programmes', so we must make educated guesses about what they might mean. The general tenet of this book is to align itself broadly, and with some reservations, to option A above, assuming that the term 'general aims' can be agreed. Taking a rounded, broad perspective one might assume Mary Warnock's (2010) common goals of 'independence, enjoyment and understanding' (p. 16) as being reasonable, and certainly we would more than readily accept these as common to all children in all educational establishments within all pedagogies and curricula. The reservations are, however, related to two deep suspicions – that, first, such loose general aims, once openly espoused, would be deeply frowned upon by governments who need to be in control of the educational process. Arguably, it is why the UK National Curriculum was adopted in the first place – because the perceived state of the education system equals votes and national government needed to be in control.

Second, it is our deeply held belief, again borne out by the experience of being teachers and school leaders over the twenty-five years of a National Curriculum, that those with SLD and PMLD both deserve and need separate and distinct pedagogies. That is, it is not sufficient just to have different pathways and programmes (curriculum) without a distinct pedagogy, where pedagogy is defined as 'the broad cluster of decisions and actions taken in classroom settings to promote learning' (Norwich and Lewis, 2005, p. 7) because as Bennett (1999) notes, such decisions and actions directly interface with the process of learning; it is this process of learning that is so different from NT learners'. For those with PMLD, a mainstream type curriculum is not appropriate because

> they are learning the fundamental learning skills usually mastered by typical children in the first year or so of life. The subjects may be able to provide an interesting and challenging context for practising these fundamental skills but it is unhelpful to suggest that pupils with PMLD are learning English, Maths and Science.
>
> (Lacey, 2011, p. 5)

And of course for NT children, these *fundamental learning skills* are mastered with consummate ease well before they enter school, assisted by parents, siblings and carers who naturally give very little thought to the process of learning because it generally comes so naturally. Most importantly, these fundamental learning skills are not, in any real sense, taught to NT conventionally developing children; they are encouraged, enabled, allowed to grow and flourish. The process of learning for those with PMLD is entirely different and bears only a superficial relationship with the skills taught to teachers of NT children.

For those with SLD the challenge is similar, that is, to cast off the assumption that education for this group comprises of dumbing down what is already in place to fit learners who are operating developmentally at ages (often) well under a NT five or six year old. Teachers and other professionals will be used to seeing the term 'global developmental delay' ascribed to their children, and while 'global' and 'developmental' may well be apt broad descriptions, 'delay' is something else entirely. It assumes that children within this group will catch up, but children within this group will not catch up. The UK has recently adopted a well-written and highly promising Early Years Foundation Stage curriculum, which is discussed in Chapter 3 (Assessment and Pupil Progress), but it is completely fallacious to assume that this can be exported wholesale for those with SLD, with or without adaptations. As Rita Jordan remarks, 'an inclusive curriculum is about its applicability to all from its inception and not about adaptations and extensions to make a non-inclusive curriculum more applicable to excluded groups' (Jordan, 2005, p. 117).

Conclusion

We do not apologise for arguing vociferously that those with SLD and PMLD both deserve and need distinct and separate pedagogies, which in turn drive and inform distinct and separate curricula. We must get used to the idea that those with SLD and PMLD learn in fundamentally different ways from NT children, and we must therefore teach them in fundamentally different ways.

The drive towards an inclusive philosophy has been relentless, 'almost obligatory in the discourse of all right-thinking people' according to Thomas and O'Hanlon (2005, p. xi) and 'other' views for a separate and distinct pedagogy and curriculum are treated almost as though they ought to be a matter of shame.

The creation of special education as a separate system was in part a response to the exclusion of pupils with disabilities from mainstream schools. Thus, special education was an exclusive field of study originated in an act of discrimination which now supports a profession.

(Florian, 1998, p. 24)

But this assumes that we have the basic premise and balance of the idea of universal education right, and this is a big assumption.

Who says that the 'common entitlement' (which schoolchildren certainly never campaigned for) of the watered down Grammar School syllabus that represents the (misnamed) National Curriculum with its attendant inspection, testing and league tables is something which anyone in their right mind would wish to be included in?

(Lewis, 2000, p. 202)

Mere adoption of a common entitlement framework without sufficient thought about what that might mean for *all* children is not defensible. Perhaps we'll leave the last word, for now, to Richard Aird:

Rather than risk continuing to confuse the special education of SLD/PMLD learners, perhaps it is time to consider the need for a discrete National Curriculum in this sector, together with a meaningful framework of assessment, based on what teachers [of children, young people and adults with SLD and PMLD] really ought to be teaching their pupils. The current National Curriculum remains only a relatively small part of the taught curriculum for these learners and yet the DCSF [Department for Children, Schools and Families] maintains a distinct lack of interest in evaluating the quality of teaching and learning within the bulk of the SLD/PMLD whole curriculum.

(Aird, 2009, p. 12)

Notes

1   The term 'special educational needs' was introduced in the UK by the Warnock Committee (DES, 1978) specifically to change the negative connotation of labels, in that 'special' should be something to be wished for.
2   Norwich (2010) specifically advocates five areas to be considered in the continua of provision, namely (i) identification, (ii) placement, (iii) curriculum, (iv) participation, and (v) governance about educational provision, although we are only specifically addressing the first three of these, considering our views on the latter two to be implicit.
3   It is interesting to note that Norwich and Gray (2007) reject the extreme ends of total commonality and total differentiation represented in the placement debate by all children attending the same lessons in the same class in the same school to all children with identified SENs attending (separate) special schools, as being a *'futile pursuit of ideological purity'* (Norwich, 2010, p. 104).

Chapter 3

Assessment and pupil progress

> Not everything that counts can be counted, and not everything that can be counted counts.
>
> (Albert Einstein)

There is no doubt that assessment of pupil progress must go hand in hand with the curriculum being offered – if the curriculum is appropriate and meets pupils' needs, pupil progress should be clear, achievable and quantifiably measurable. If individual pupils do not make progress, it should be possible to work out why this is so and make the appropriate changes to rectify the problem. There may well still be a small number of pupils who struggle to make progress, there probably always will be, but when *all* pupils struggle it seems to us self-evident that something is (or some things are) very seriously wrong. At the very base, either the curriculum is wrong, or the assessment system is wrong, or the teaching is wrong; or quite possibly, as assessment and curriculum and teaching are inextricably woven together, all are wrong.

Table 1.1 (P scales point scores and conversion tables (DfE, 2009)), reproduced on page 13 in Chapter 1, is sufficient evidence to indicate that pupils with SLD (that is, in UK terms, those working consistently over time at levels at and below Level 1 of the NC) do not succeed and do not make progress within the National Curriculum. Those with PMLD (that is, in UK terms, those working consistently over time at levels at and below P4) do not succeed and do not make progress within the National Curriculum. It is not acceptable to state that some pupils are making some progress within the P scales because the P scales only measure what happens at the pre-curriculum levels, that is, before the curriculum is designed to start. Some may argue that the P scales have become an integral part of the UK NC, but how can they be when they're not measuring against the curriculum itself? And again, we repeat Rita Jordan's very apposite statement on the equity of such a system, that 'an inclusive curriculum is about its applicability to all from its inception and not about adaptations and extensions to make a non-inclusive curriculum more applicable to excluded groups' (Jordan, 2005, p. 117).

Using the P scales to assess progress under the NC for those with SLD and PMLD is rather like the old joke of the lost tourist asking directions from a local. 'Well' says the local 'I wouldn't have started from here.' Granted, we are where we are, but perhaps we really shouldn't have got here in the first place! Unfortunately, with regards to the education of those with SLD and PMLD at least, the UK education system has got itself into a bit of a muddle, simply in order to justify the continued primacy of a curriculum model (the

National Curriculum) that, for an admittedly very small percentage of the school population, is not fit for purpose.

Let us look, for example, at a case study from Ofsted (2004) from their publication *Setting targets for pupils with special educational needs*, which relates to one 3–19 years special school whose population consists almost entirely of pupils within the SLD/PMLD range:

> A three-year collation of pupil assessment data showed that there was underachievement in writing for all cohorts across the school. While most pupils worked between levels P4–P6, about 20 of the secondary pupils were working between level P7 and National Curriculum level 1. The reasons for this were not immediately clear. Did the pupils have insufficient time? Were teaching methods inappropriate or resources inadequate? Were expectations of pupils with poor fine-motor skills not high enough?
>
> An audit was undertaken and a new policy and scheme of work written. Age appropriate resources were provided, including ICT. Grouping arrangements were reconsidered. Lesson plans gave attention to writing in every lesson and were evaluated regularly. These plans were based on an approach to language development which used topics and themes to generalise the skills of reading, writing, speaking and listening. Grouping and individual profiles were used to measure progress and identify future targets.
>
> The impact of this development at individual pupil level is illustrated by the progress made by one pupil. In 2000, at Year 2, he was just beginning to understand that marks on a paper conveyed some meaning, for example, he could scribble alongside a picture. In 2002, at Year 4, he had progressed to differentiating between letters and symbols, copy-writing with some support, and was able to write his own name (as well as those of a few friends) legibly and with meaning. His most recent assessment indicates he can now correctly spell some high-frequency words.
>
> (Ofsted, 2004, p. 16)

If we spend some time analysing the above case study we might ask a number of critical questions: On what criteria are the P levels attained considered to be '*underachievement for all cohorts across the school*'? Does acceptance of the fact that this level of achievement might be considered to be perfectly normal for a specialist school for pupils and students with SLD and PMLD, automatically assume that '*expectations*' are '*not high enough*'? Are the three questions asked the only questions that could be asked? Could an alternative set of questions have been: Why do children with SLD and PMLD find writing difficult? Is the spread of achievement normal for a specialist SLD/PMLD school? Could it be that, like in many special schools, there is great diversity of pupils across the school and an individual cohort of learners can be a one-off, and reliably and justifiably cannot be seen as necessarily comparable historically to any other cohort in the school, or any other similar school? Why are all the higher achievers in the secondary department? Is this fact indicative of the time it might take to get a pupil with severe learning difficulties to the entry level (Level 1) attained by NT learners at age five or six? Is it a sound use of the school's resources to spend even more time on improving writing skills only to achieve between P7 and Level 1 by the time pupils get to Key Stage 3 at age eleven? Even if more time is spent on improving writing skills, will literacy skills rise to levels where pupils and students are fluent readers and writers? What will pupils who achieve Level 1 by the time they get to Key Stage 3 or 4 (aged eleven or fourteen) use their writing skills for? Are the writing skills (evident at Level 1, that is those displayed by a NT five or six year old) sufficient to allow a pupil to write fluently, or to write in any way that we might consider will add appreciably to their ability to be equal partners in society? Does the fact that some pupils can make some progress (the twenty mentioned above and the one pupil exampled above) indicate that all children with SLD and PMLD can achieve such progress? Even if achieved, is it sufficient progress to justify the time spent on achieving it?

Put more prosaically, the three questions could equally be:

1   Could the reason behind the *'underachievement'* (which was not immediately apparent!) have been the fact that this is a school for children and young people with severe and profound learning difficulties?
2   Is it legitimate to continue to teach subjects to children who continue to 'underachieve' and indeed in some cases, do not achieve at all?
3   What and how might we teach them, which would be a more constructive use of precious school time, and how we might measure both qualitative and quantitative progress?

Such children's widely acknowledged inherent receptive and expressive language difficulties (coupled with any number of other challenges to their learning such as information processing, memory, attention, motivation, etc.) may understandably lead to underachievement compared to non-learning-disabled peers. It may well be, therefore, that the problem of so-called underachievement for this group of children with SLD and PMLD is more to do with inappropriate comparisons to the progress, development and attainment of a non-learning-disabled children's peer group.

Ofsted are surely right to suggest that *'high expectations are key to securing good progress'* (DfE, 2009) but as Klaus Wedell has observed, even in the early 1990s,

> assessment . . . seems to have grown into a monolithic operation. As a result, it is easy to forget that assessment is no more than a means of obtaining answers to questions, and is justified solely by the meaningfulness of the questions asked.
>
> (Wedell, 1992, p. 161)

In this case the questions asked relate to progression within a linear-based and largely academic assessment scheme (the P Scales and variations of these such as Pivats and B Squared[1]), which a considerable number of writers have consistently argued are not suitable assessment and progression frameworks for children and young people with severe and profound learning difficulties (Barber and Goldbart, 1998; Robbins, 2000; Ware, 2003; Hewett, 2006; WAG, 2006; Lacey, 2009; Aird, 2009; Imray, Gasquez Navarro and Bond, 2010; Van Walwyk, 2011; Imray and Hinchcliffe, 2012).

Because Welsh schools have not been legally obliged (as English schools were and are) to report P scale scores, they were given the freedom to look at the whole issue of assessment and attainment afresh. Under the guidance of Jean Ware, Verity Donnelly, Phil Martin, Wendy Jones, Lynn Alton and Pauline Loftus and the auspices of the Welsh DfE's Qualifications and Curriculum Group in Cardiff, Welsh schools specifically worked on an assessment schema for those with PMLD. Their assessment guide, published as *Routes for Learning* (WAG, 2006) broke away from the idea of progress taking place through formal subjects and instead looked at key milestones that children with profound learning difficulties might go through. While these milestones are developmental in nature, the *Routes for Learning* (RfL) authors argue that the route learners take might not be, and suggest that 'pathways' through the 'routemap' could be individual and idiosyncratic depending on the interests, needs and abilities of the children concerned.

This first UK systemised attempt to break away from a linear developmental model for those with profound learning difficulties post-National Curriculum should be looked upon as a significant and perhaps seminal piece of work[2]. The idea that we might need to arrange the curriculum to fit the child rather than arrange the child to fit the curriculum was not a new one, even within the apparent constraints of the NC. In one of the first formal attempts to acknowledge the concerns with the relevancy of the subject-based UK National Curriculum to those with PMLD, the 1996 SCAA report noted that planning should start from the basis of needs, interests, aptitudes and achievements of the learners (SCAA, 1996). Further successive guidance documents issued by QCA and QCDA have consistently recognised that the NC might form only part of an appropriate curriculum delivery to those with complex needs and learning difficulties (QCA, 2001a, 2004a; QCDA, 2009). Nonetheless, the continued centrality of the NC has meant that few UK schools catering for those with severe and profound learning difficulties have felt able to venture beyond formalised subject-based teaching and develop a pedagogical framework around which a PMLD or SLD curriculum might be delivered. There may be a large element of tokenism, with schools in general and teachers in particular 'pretending' to teach what they do not actually teach in order to fit the model and, at worst, not making a very good job of delivering a watered-down mainstream primary National Curriculum.

The arrival in the UK of an Early Years Foundation Stage curriculum (DfE, 2012) for pupils up to the age of five has heralded a more user-friendly curriculum for conventionally developing NT infants that has some merits as a base for a primary SLD curriculum. But this should only be considered as a base since, once again, it is a NT curriculum model and was not written with learning difficulties in mind. It is, nonetheless, interesting to note that the inappropriate nature of a linear progression assessment tool, such as the P scales for learners who are learning at a pre-NC level, is formally recognised for developmentally young children:

> Assessment of [children within the EYFS Programme with SENs] progress should [recognise] that progress is not linear. We need to note, however, *that P scales do not relate to the EYFS framework and therefore, the P scales and EYFS are not compatible. P scales are not an appropriate assessment or monitoring tool for young children.*
>
> (DfE, 2010, p. 21; their emphasis)

It seems to us somewhat bizarre that the UK DfE can remark that the 'P scales are not an appropriate assessment or monitoring tool for young children' yet insist that they are an appropriate assessment and monitoring tool for those with learning difficulties who are working at academic levels equivalent to young children, and once again is indicative of the enormous muddle that the UK education system has got itself into.

In an attempt to ensure the fragile relationship between those with SLD and PMLD to the education system in the late 1980s, special needs educators and academics bought into the idea of a single National Curriculum applicable to all, even though it was perfectly clear that children with SEN were not part of the pedagogy or rationale behind the original curriculum model (Rose, 1998; Tilstone, 1999). A number also felt philosophically bound to the single curriculum concept and seemed determined to put inclusion at the centre of curriculum development for those with SEN (Byers and Rose, 1994; Evans, 1997; Sebba and Sachdev, 1997; Rose, 1998; Florian, 1998), of which those with SLD and PMLD were naturally a part.

Numerous attempts were made by writers to 'adapt' the National Curriculum for those with SLD and PMLD (Bovair *et al.*, 1992; Sebba *et al.*, 1993; Rose *et al.*, 1994, for example) and all special schools across the UK went into overdrive to ensure that they were teaching what they were supposed to be teaching; battleships and hospitals could have been built with the person hours involved in this adaptive process.

Virtually all pupils and students with SLD and PMLD still continued to fail under the system, registering a 'W' in the required reporting of NC attainment levels, indicating that these pupils were still 'working towards' the beginning. Finding this situation singularly un-inducive to an inclusive education system, a number of headteachers and academics came up with the P scales in the late 1990s. It should be noted this was not designed at that time to act as a scheme for assessing pupil progress (Ndaji and Tymms, 2009) but rather to indicate (especially to parents) where children broadly were in academic terms. Nonetheless, the powers that be saw this as an opportunity and integrated the P scales into the formal assessment methodology (QCA, 2001a) and have since compounded the problem by insisting on two NC levels of progression over each key stage for all children (DfE, 2010). This despite the real threat of a number of those with SLD plateauing in their academic progress for long periods of time (Imray and Hinchcliffe, 2012) and those with PMLD regressing due to their life-threatening conditions (according to Male, 2000, up to ten per cent). If taken literally, the two levels of progression scenario would mean that a pupil entering the formal education system at the age of six with an assessment of P5 (a middle range for a six year old with SLD) should have reached L5 of the National Curriculum by the age of sixteen and not only be taking, but comfortably passing, the national school-leaving (GCSE) exams. More muddle!

So in summary, the situation that we have in the UK in 2013 is that a curriculum model not designed for those with SLD and PMLD was introduced in 1988. Not surprisingly, pupils with SLD and PMLD failed to make the starting levels and so in 2001, a broad brushstroke system that was not designed to show progress was introduced in order to show progress. Perhaps those responsible for education in the UK ought to adopt the maxim of 'when in a hole – stop digging'.

The importance of specific and separate pedagogical frameworks for those with PMLD and SLD is central to the ideas and strategies held in this book. The imposition of a mainstream framework that is not fit for purpose relegates ideas that do not easily fit into the subject framework to the status of irrelevancy. As a result, they may become as easily forgotten as, for example, Individualised Sensory Environment (Bunning 1996; 1998) obviously has – see Chapter 9 (A sensory curriculum for pupils and students with PMLD) for an explanation of ISE. Significant ideas and interventions need to be openly discussed, tried out, tested, shaped, changed, incorporated and discussed some more. Such reflection gives status to teachers' questions and ideas drawn from working experimentally with children and this can be exciting and motivating for both teachers and learners. School leaders need to be confident in giving class teams the time for such experimentation, rather than run the risk of being castigated for not achieving short-term targets. Even lesser ideas need airing in order to discover that they might not work as well as originally thought, but we will not arrive at this stage unless and until the idea of specific pedagogical frameworks for those with PMLD and SLD is taken as seriously as it deserves to be.

It is worth quoting extensively from *RfL Additional Guidance* (WAG, 2006)[3] and noting that while the *Guidance* directly refers to the nature of assessment, the sentiments apply equally to curriculum development.

> Many linear or hierarchical assessments will be unable to detect the very subtle changes in behaviour shown by [learners with PMLD], regardless of how many 'small steps' are provided. In real life, children's development and learning is not compartmentalised. (p. 2)
>
> Assessment [should] celebrate the different abilities of learners with the most complex needs, rather than trying to fit them into an existing framework not developed with these needs in mind . . . Providing equal opportunities is about meeting individual needs – not treating everybody in the same way. (p. 3)
>
> It is now widely felt that over-reliance on pre-determined small steps from checklists may distort individual priorities and may narrow the curriculum taught. (p. 9)
>
> The quality of the teaching and learning is as important as the performance of the objectives. Teachers need a clear understanding of the *process* to be undertaken as well as the end point to be reached. (p. 9; their emphasis)
>
> Learners will not make sense of a fragmented curriculum, divided somewhat arbitrarily into subject categories. Tasks must be relevant and purposeful to maximise motivation and to help learners make sense of the world around them. Curriculum experiences need to be carefully mediated as unco-ordinated approaches, particularly those using different sensory pathways, can lead to a range of experiences that carry little meaning for learners. (p. 11)
>
> Our learners are entitled to access a curriculum and assessment framework which is fit for purpose and meets their specific needs – there is little benefit or increase in entitlement if they are included in structures which fail to do this. (p. 46)

Skills-based learning

Given that the nature of learning for those with PMLD and SLD[4] can never be guaranteed to be either linear or developmental (Barber and Goldbart, 1998; Ware, 2003; Imray, 2005; Hewett, 2006; WAG, 2006; Aird, 2009; Lacey, 2009; Carpenter, 2010; Van Walwyk, 2011; Imray and Hinchcliffe, 2012) it follows that a considerable challenge arises to our teaching methodology, which relates directly to a tendency towards subject-driven, target-centred, skills-based curricula models. Skills-based teaching and learning recognises that certain skills need to be acquired by much practice. A footballer will hone the skill of taking penalties by constant and repetitive practice. It is not necessary for this practice to take place within the context of a complete game of football, just as it may not be necessary for a learner to eat lunch in order to practise holding a spoon. The skill can be transferred to the relevant situations once it has been acquired, or even partially acquired, but (and it is a very big 'but') we run the risk of disassociating the skill from the practice with learners who will be poor at generalising skills. As Dee, Lawson, Porter and Robertson (2008) point out, those with SLD will 'need to spend time acquiring, consolidating and applying skills that other young people may take for granted' (p. 29).

A number of skills may actually be rehearsed and practised without the learner needing to know why the skill is being acquired. A pupil with SLD may rehearse and practise the skill of washing her hands, and we may even use a behavioural task analysis approach, so that each part of the skill is practised in small steps and then 'chained' together.[5] So the pupil learns to turn the tap on, wet her hands, take the soap, rub the soap on her hands, etc., until the whole chain of small step skills is acquired. Chaining them together gives the whole skill, but it is still not necessary for the pupil to understand what germs are, how they spread, why they are dangerous – she just needs to know what to do and when to do it. This does not mean that we are advocating teaching skills without understanding, quite the contrary; any skill is always improved, in terms of application especially, if it can be taught in context and the learner understands why. But we do recognise that a skill can be acquired without understanding and that this can sometimes be a useful teaching technique and a justifiable teaching and learning goal.

It is also the case, however, that the justification for using such skills-based learning approaches is considerably reduced for those with PMLD, and a useful general rule to adopt might be that the greater the degree of cognitive difficulties, the more cautious we must be about skills-based learning. This is because the pupil must, even with skills-based learning, have a motivation to go through the steps. When working with a pupil with SLD, it is possible to use instruction plus reward to engage a child in a task she might have no natural inclination towards, as in 'Wash your hands before you have dinner'. For some, especially those with an additional autistic diagnosis, the instruction itself without the contingent reward might be sufficient when it is part of the normal routine. Instruction, by definition, is not possible with someone with PMLD, and reward will very much depend on them having a refined understanding of cause and effect, which again, by definition, is not likely.

We might engage a pupil with PMLD in activities related to holding a spoon in order to practise that particular motor skill, but it is really important to adopt the philosophy of engagement in the actual activity itself, and not just because the pupil is practising the skill. That is, we cannot expect someone with PMLD to hold anything if she is not motivated by that particular activity. This then is where the group general differences position meets the unique differences position outlined in Chapter 1 (Figure 1.1, page 11) and personalisation of learning (discussed in Chapter 4). The group difference relates to an understanding that: (i) those with PMLD will not readily be able to generalise learning (that holding a thick wooden dowel to move a mobile can be equated to holding a built-up spoon handle to eat lunch); (ii) we cannot use instruction; (iii) we cannot use (an oblique) reward. The unique differences position (the personalisation of learning) relates to many things, but in this case particularly to an understanding of what the individual pupil might be motivated by to practise the motor skill – perhaps that might be a toy of some description, or grasping a wooden dowel to pull a mobile – but whatever it is, it must directly engage that particular pupil.

Skills-based learning is usually assessed using SMART[6] targets, with the theory being that the target is achievable within a set period of time (say one term). It is, however, probably true to say that the world of SLD and PMLD teaching is littered with discarded SMART targets that have never been achieved. Worse still, they are often repeatedly and endlessly rewritten and downgraded until they either become meaningless or translated into a skill that the learner already had in the first place (McNicholas, 2000; Van Walwyk, 2011). Teachers are also faced with the dilemma of deciding on the number of targets appropriate for each learner; too many makes it both very difficult to recall when recording and runs the real risk of compartmentalising learning. Now we are cooking and the learner has to reach out four times in the lesson; now we are interacting and the learner has to give two seconds of direct eye contact. If there are twenty or thirty other targets to remember, the learner's reaching out during interacting and giving eye contact during cooking may easily be overlooked. Fewer targets, on the other hand, tends to put tremendous pressure on success and might easily lead to all recordings just concentrating on those four, five or six targets for the term. There may be a myriad of other progresses in all sorts of other areas that are not recorded because the recorders are concentrating on the pre-set targets.

Again, as with the curriculum, this may well be related to the assumption that, just as all learners must benefit from subject-based learning, so all learners must benefit from SMART targets. Achievable and realistic may be reasonable; specific, measurable and time-bound may not. Dave Hewett puts it well in his 2006 article entitled *The most important and complicated learning: That's what play is for!* He argues that learning at this very early cognitively developmental level does not occur by laying one skill upon another to form a building block, but is adventitious, irregular and random, coming from all experiences in the holistic manner of young NT children learning through play. During pre-school playgroups, teachers will not have specific targets for children to achieve during play. They offer opportunities to play, tools to facilitate play, other children in the vicinity to play with; they will ladder and scaffold with children who might find it difficult and stand back with children who take to it easily; they will help to resolve difficulties and give problem-solving and thinking opportunities to children. They will do all of these things – but they will not set SMART targets! It is difficult to escape the conclusion that short-term SMART targets are insisted upon, not in order to ensure that pupils are learning, but to ensure that teachers are teaching, as though the fact that teachers are teaching automatically ensures that pupils are learning. It does not. Traditional approaches to teaching in schools tend to be highly structured with the teacher leading the activities in ordered sequential steps so that teaching and learning looks like Figure 3.1.

But when working with a child who is still at the earliest stages of communication, knowledge and learning, the immensely complex stuff that we wish to teach to her/him, looks more like Figure 3.2.

As Penny Lacey has remarked in her advocacy of SCRUFFY targets – **S**tudent led, **C**reative, **R**elevant, **U**nspecified, **F**un, **F**or **Y**oungsters – those with PMLD are 'poor consumers of SMART targets' (Lacey, 2010).

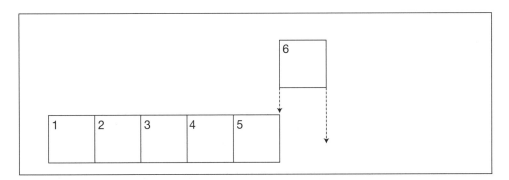

Figure 3.1 A linear developmental model of teaching (from Hewett, 2006)

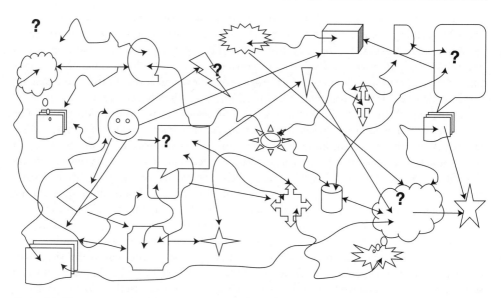

Figure 3.2 The complexity of communication learning (from Hewett, 2006)

A skill, in this quite tight SLD and PMLD pedagogical context, is therefore something that a pupil might practise and learn when understanding is not, strictly speaking, required. In this meaning it is extremely difficult to think of any 'skill' that might be appropriate to teach to someone with PMLD, because context and motivation for the task itself are always essential. We cannot, for those with PMLD, separate out the task and the motivation because we cannot instruct, and we must ensure direct and immediate stimulus responses. For children at very early levels of development, we can provide motivating contexts in which, for example, we can encourage a child to reach out and touch, but we cannot of course assume that they will want to do so. We can teach 'skills' to those with SLD because we can (mostly) instruct and we can introduce indirect rewards. A mobile is moved *because* she has pulled the wooden dowel; a dinner is not produced *because* she has washed her hands, although we can make this a prerequisite. Teaching and learning for those with PMLD will probably, therefore, mainly be process-based and the successful teaching of specific skills will always need to be contextualised.

Process-based learning

Process-based learning (Burden, 1990; Hinchcliffe, 1994; Collis and Lacey, 1996; Goddard, 1997; Hewett and Nind, 1998; Nind and Hewett, 2001; Hewett, 2006; Imray *et al.*, 2010) is a holistic approach that can be defined as the process of the teaching becoming the objective. Learning is taken as a whole rather than through teaching to specific individualised targets, largely because it encourages the teacher to structure planning around an open-ended philosophy. Intensive Interaction (Nind and Hewett, 1994) is perhaps the best example of process-based teaching and learning, where 'tasklessness' is at the centre of the interactive process. Interactors are urged to follow, celebrate and extend; 'tune in' to the learner and look for communication moments, creating the communicative flow being the objective of the session. Although the teacher may prompt and try different strategies to elicit progress, and the most skilfull and experienced teachers will have many strategies for achieving this, it is not up to the teacher to decide specific targets. The learner decides where the interactive process will go; the pace and direction of learning, and therefore the pace and direction of teaching, will be decided by the learner.

Taking this philosophy on to other areas of the curriculum with both PMLD and SLD opens up whole new parameters for learning, crucially giving elements of control back to the learner. Let's take two examples, one for a PMLD class and one for a SLD class. Both the age of the learners and the subject matter are fairly immaterial, but let's assume they are roughly in the middle of their school lives at aged ten, and both groups are involved in baking a cake. The PMLD class will be involved with baking a cake as a means of improving their exploratory abilities. The product really is unimportant; it is the process that is the key, and staff will ensure that pupils all have as much physical access to the materials as possible. The session might start with an object cue (perhaps a wooden spoon) being passed around the circle while a music cue (how about 'Animal Crackers in my Soup' by Shirley Temple?) is being played. Considerable thought will be given to individual seating and positioning, thus enabling and maximising free exploration; ensuring materials are easily accessible and identifiable – providing brown sugar so that it stands out from the white flour, presenting the flour and butter in a dark bowl and the brown sugar and dried fruits in a white one; giving plenty of time to independently explore each ingredient; offering opportunities for watching, tasting, touching, smelling, listening; making certain learners have the opportunity to mix ingredients and see, touch, taste, smell and listen to any changes as they happen. The skill of the teaching is to ensure that the process is motivating enough for each learner to independently explore as much as possible, that known motivating ingredients are placed just out of reach so that the learner has to work that little bit harder to get at them. The staff might reflect the process they are going through, perhaps making short pithy comments such as 'flour . . . soft . . . dry' or 'flour . . . butter . . . sticky!'. The staff will ensure that all pupils are as engaged and as active as they can be and record particular points of interest relating to engagement, enjoyment, rejection and general behaviour states and rates as they go along. It is, of course, vitally important that this is a really fun activity with lots of interactive moments, not only between staff and pupils but also between pupils and pupils.

The SLD class will be involved with cooking as part of the process of being as independent as possible; within that broad aim comes the process of learning how to cook independently; and within that, the firm establishment of the basic skills of cooking are central. Cooking for someone with SLD will therefore probably be a combination of skills and process. The skills will form the foundation of the learner's long-term goals (to be as independent in the activity of cooking as possible) and will cover such basics as how to be safe in the kitchen, how to follow a recipe, how to boil a kettle, how to use a microwave, how to use a cooker and hob, how to cut with sharp knife, etc. These skills, however, are not sufficient in themselves, since to be a truly independent cook one needs to be able and willing to learn through trial and error. What happens when the eggs fall on the floor and smash? What will happen to the cake if you put in too much flour? How do you bake a cake if you forget to buy the butter? What happens if you forget to turn the oven off? Too often, with those with SLD, we resolve the problem for them. This is not making the learner independent – it is making the learner dependent. This overarching issue must be addressed but cannot be taught as a skill is taught. It is a process, the pace of which will entirely depend on the individual learner and their relationship to their teachers and the subject area.

The key point about process-based teaching is that it recognises that those with SLD and PMLD need to learn within a whole continuum. When working within a curriculum designed for NT conventionally developing learners, teaching is compartmentalised as a matter of course; now we are learning maths, now we are learning science, now we are learning English. The pupil is required to make the connection about applying these compartmentalised experiences, and because they are NT learners they do. With process-based teaching, the maths and the science and the English are learned as a natural part of the process of cooking (or painting, or travel training or playing a game, etc.). Learning is always concrete and takes place in context. While generalisation is taught, it is taught from one concrete context to another, from, say, baking a cake to making a pizza, rather than an abstract non-contextualised (counting numicon bricks) to the concrete contextualised (counting bananas in a supermarket).

It may appear at first glance that the nature of process-based teaching and learning is relatively easy – no specific individual targets, set the process (of shopping or travel training or drama or music, etc.) in motion and see what happens. It is, however, anything but easy, since it requires a deep understanding of: (i) the nature of severe and profound learning difficulties; (ii) the individual strengths and needs of the pupils being taught; (iii) what motivates each individual pupil; (iv) how to motivate all pupils; and (v) the inherent risks involved. This is a high-risk methodology because what exactly will happen if the eggs fall on to the floor and smash? The teacher and the teaching team need to have a collective strategy that does not involve berating the pupil for her clumsiness, or cleaning up the eggs and magically producing some more, or abandoning the lesson, or suggesting what might be done. Working towards solutions involves a long-term commitment from the whole teaching team(s) to teaching in this way; this does not come overnight. It also means that the whole lesson might be about what to do when the eggs are lying in a broken mess on the floor, and you may not even have time to bake the cake.

Process-based teaching will probably mostly involve establishing order, structure, routine and certainty as a prerequisite and then gradually breaking this down. We will not get pupils to think unless we are prepared to accept that our pupils will probably only think for themselves if we don't think for them. We need to make it obvious that there is a problem in the first place and we need to teach trial and error. We need to get pupils used to the idea that the first solution is not always the right one, and even if it is the right one, it might not be the best one. We need to get pupils used to the idea the mistakes happen (all of the time!) and that this is a positive and natural process – it's how we all learn. All of this takes time and the greater the degree of learning difficulty, the more time it will take, but the potential rewards are huge – deep and meaningful learning and the ability to apply skills and generalise understanding.

The assumption of process-based teaching provides a platform for varied and disparate learning to take place, and individual progression may only be recognised in retrospect, at the end of each session, week, half-term, term and/or year (Imray et al., 2010). This retrospective target setting is legitimated by the tendency of objectives or target-based teaching to narrow the learning opportunities offered to those with PMLD and SLD.

A child, young person or adult at early developmental levels has much more chance of understanding and connecting the process, sequence and materials needed to wipe a runny nose if the learning takes place when she has a runny nose. The child, young person or adult with PMLD has much more chance of understanding and connecting the process and sequence of a story when a story is actually being enacted, and the learner is an essential part of that enactment (Park, 2010; Grove, 2010). All sorts of learning may take place here – sequencing, memory of events, anticipation, tracking, object permanence, emotional experience and understanding, contingency responding, contingency awareness, peer and adult interaction, sensory exploration, sensory tolerance, etc. – but limiting the recording of progress to one or two previously defined SMART targets is likely to produce, at best, limited opportunities to expand learning. At worst, target-driven teaching will lead teachers to teach to the next level as defined by various assessment documents, particularly those that break down normative developmental concepts such as the P scales into very small steps, whether the objective is appropriate for the individual pupil or not, and whether the target is of interest to the individual or not. Targets not achieved, because the pupil is not motivated to achieve them or because the target is too cognitively or physically challenging for the pupil to achieve, will be dropped or, more likely, linger on indefinitely in an increasingly diluted and meaningless form. This tendency applies equally to *RfL* and *MAPP* (*Mapping and Assessing Personal Progress* (Sissons, 2010)) and it is absolutely essential therefore, as both sets of authors take great pains to point out, that we do not confuse assessment with curriculum. Assessment documents such as *RfL* and *MAPP* will make suggestions as to the direction of travel; the curriculum will guide us to getting there. We must not make assessment the focus for teaching.

Recording and reporting on progress is absolutely vital to the success of process-based teaching and learning and it is strongly recommended that each teaching session ends with a plenary, where the whole class pauses the formal teaching process in order to celebrate success, record specific pupil progress, pick up areas of concern and inform the next lesson. At this vital time, the whole teaching team (teachers, TAs, therapists and anyone else involved directly in the lesson) reflects on what they have seen and heard, taking the lesson as a whole but, more importantly, each individual learner one at a time. More able learners can and must be directly involved in this process so that it becomes one of self-reflection with agreements on what they might work on next week, so the learning process is shared. Teaching is done 'with' learners rather than 'to' them. The class teacher must physically record success, maintenance or regress of each learner. Learner A may, for example, have tracked the teacher for five seconds or so during a sensory story and got very excited as it got closer to his turn to be tickled. Can we see if next time, Learner A will track for longer; at what point in the story does she start to get excited; will she get excited earlier in the story next time; does she show similar excitement for other parts of the story; will she next time? She may of course do none of these things – such is the fractured nature of the PMLD learning process – but she may at some time in the future; and again, we must be ready to record this when she does. This looser meaning of targets and objectives might be termed a 'learning intention' – we will offer the opportunity for progress in a certain way, and it is our broad intention to get there, but we must be prepared for the learner going somewhere else entirely.

Recording and reporting can be aided immensely by simple use of video. Setting up the video on a wide-angled lens and letting it run for the whole session enables staff to pick up on all sorts of things they might have missed. Viewing back such video evidence can provide an excellent focus for team meetings and, of course, can be legitimately used as evidence of progress for end-of-year reports. Looking out for differences of any form needs to become second nature for all members of the class team. Class teams need to get used to recording as they go along and using sticky notes to write a couple of words as an aide memoire ('John track 5 seconds', for example) can be a simple and effective system. There is an extremely strong case for suggesting that a static and permanent digital camera fitted with a wide-angled lens that can view the whole class constitutes part of the essential basic equipment for any and all classrooms involving pupils with SLD and PMLD. Apart from the obvious benefits for recording, reporting and assessing, it also might form an essential part of teacher, TA and other professional training, and be extremely useful in classroom action research projects.

While the P scales might form part of a legitimate assessment 'portfolio' for pupils and students with PMLD and SLD[7], this should probably form only a fraction of the indicators of progress across a whole range of areas, and the less academically able the pupil, the smaller this fraction might be. For those with PMLD, increasing interest is being shown in adapting the *Routes for Learning* pathways so that it can demonstrate progress, see for example the work being carried out by Claire Barnes at Willow Dene School (Barnes, 2010) and Lana Bond, Izanne Van Wyck and Diego Gasquez Navarro at The Bridge School (Bond *et al.*, 2011) and it seems logical to show the maps of individual pupils.

This is still very much work in progress, but there seems no reason why each learner might not have his or her progress shown by a graph indicating how many of the forty-three milestones have been achieved. It must be repeated that *RfL* does not rely on the idea of linear development, and the milestones achieved may be scattered. Nonetheless, indicating that a learner has achieved two milestones this year, for example, and sixteen in total, rather than the fourteen achieved up to the end of the previous year, is a legitimate indicator of progress. The progress may be scattered but it is progress nonetheless.

If we further sub-divide the milestones using the *Continuum of Skill Development* from *MAPP* (Sissons, 2010; see below) with its ten point markers showing the lateral progression within each milestone, we have a potential of 430 markers of progression. Another area where we might assess progress using numerical values is the original PSHE P scales with its subsections of: (i) attention; (ii) independence and organisation; (iii) interacting and working with others. Many schools have regarded these as being pertinent to those with learning difficulties for some considerable time and many with PMLD are able to show considerable progress over a number of years (perhaps getting as far as Level 5 of the fifteen) as long as we don't regard them as being developmentally linear. They are naturally divided into fifteen subdivisions and, again, many pupils with SLD working consistently within the P scales in the academic subjects seem able to achieve quite high scores in this area. So, with Mike Sissons' *Continuum of Skill Development*, there is a potential fifty or so markers for those with PMLD and as many as 150 for those with SLD.

Mike Sissons, from the Dales School in North Yorkshire, has written what is effectively a *Routes* for pupils with SLD entitled *MAPP – Mapping and Assessing Personal Progress* (Sissons, 2010). There is a quite deliberate homage paid to *RfL* in the structure and overarching philosophy of *MAPP*, in that it is non-linear in approach and talks of 'learning intentions' rather than targets. At the broadest level *MAPP* is made up of three main cross-curricular areas:

Communication   Thinking skills   Personal and social development

Each of these areas is then sub-divided to help provide a sharper focus on the needs of the individual learner. *Communication*, for example divides into the following seven sets:

Means of Communication: non-symbolic	Means of Communication: symbolic	Social Communication	Communicating Needs and Wants	Information and Concepts	Reading	Writing

These sets are then further divided. So, *Social Communication* is divided into:

Social responding	Conversational Turn-Taking	Imitation	Shared Attention	Initiating Conversation

Each set of subdivisions provides sharper focus and helps identify the current priorities for the learner.

So, for example, under *Signing* there are eight *milestones*:

Means of Communcation: Symbolic (cont.)

Signing

Milestones	Notes
Understands the link between a sign and the reference of the sign Signs coactively: tolerates adult help in physically shaping a sign Imitates signs Signs spontaneously Either gains attention before signing or directs sign towards an adult Increases personal repertoire of signs Links two or more signs Demonstrates an understanding of a sequence of signs	It is important learners are *aware that they are being helped to sign* and that they are not simply having their hands manipulated. The environment may be modified to encourage spontaneous use of signing. For example, an object the pupil likes *and for which s/he knows the sign* may be held in view but out of reach. Each sign should add to the meaning of the utterance. It is perhaps doubtful that 'please' and 'thank you' should count as additional signs if a pupil only signs to make requests. Where a pupil uses signing for more than one function and only tags 'please' and 'thank you' at the end of requests this may count as an additional sign.

Most importantly, although the milestone statements are set out in a broadly hierarchical sequence, there is no presumption that a given individual will work through all of them, or that they will work through them sequentially or that they will all begin at the same point. Using *MAPP*, the learner's pathway should be thought of as planning a route on a map (as in *Routes for Learning*) rather than climbing the rungs of a ladder. This approach acknowledges the differing strengths and needs of individuals and recognises the fact that some may need to spend far more time than others in a given area of learning. For some individuals, certain skills may always remain inaccessible and therefore need to be bypassed or replaced. In the manner of planning a journey, people may adopt different starting points and may visit different landmarks in travelling toward the same destination.

In the above example, the milestone statement is not selected because it is the next unchecked item on a list but because it is an important, relevant and realistic skill for that individual learner at that time. However, as the milestone statement is not being read off from a checklist, the accurate identification of priority areas and milestone statements has to be informed by accurate assessment of prior learning (including attainment and achievement) and by consideration of the learner's strengths, needs and aspirations. There is also, within the *MAPP* package, a Microsoft Excel spreadsheet that schools can use to give quantitative progress indicators for all pupils, and which may overcome the difficulties experienced in trying to make the P scales do something (indicate normative progress) for which they were not designed.

For pupils with SLD, *MAPP* itself covers a wide range of learning. There are something like 220 milestones (again, like *RfL*, without falling into the linear developmental trap) within the three broad areas of Communication, (Mathematical) Thinking Skills and Personal and Social Development, and the Continuum also works in the areas of fluency, maintenance and generalisation, as well as the *prompting* noted above. Just using prompting gives us a potential 880 levels of potential progress in a non-linear model.

MAPP represents an extremely interesting and indeed exciting development in the natural desire for those teaching children and young people with SLD to demonstrate that their charges can, and indeed do, make considerable progress throughout their school lives. *MAPP* has been published by Equals and is available for purchase at a nominal cost at www.equals.co.uk.

Finally, in our movement towards ensuring appropriate models of assessing pupil progress for those with SLD, we might look towards the process-based learning and the skills-based learning spoken of earlier in this chapter. It is questionable whether it is either desirable or practical to formally (quantitavely) assess process-based learning, since the process is not something that can easily be counted. It is a process – it can go off in numerous directions and come back to the beginning again to go off in another direction. It is how NT children learn when playing and may not be measurable in any formal sense. Learners will undoubtedly gain more by not being restricted to a specific (SMART) objective, although a loose noting of progress and interaction within a process may be possible with Erica Brown's (1996) 'Framework for Recognising Attainment' (Figure 3.3 below). This framework can very easily become an eighty scale approximate recorder by using the *Continuum of Skills Development* format. Such recordings might work in much the same way that a mainstream teacher might assess individual pupils' understanding of works of literature, which is also of course, a process.

The 'Framework for Recognising Attainment' was designed to be used in a wide variety of assessment situations with those with learning difficulties and is especially useful as a broad indicator of progress within process-based teaching and learning.

Skills-based learning for those with SLD is, of course, much more open to quantitative measurement. These might be in dressing/undressing, washing, showering, teeth cleaning, toileting, eating, drinking, sitting and attending, turn taking, appropriate behaviour, road crossing, money handling, shopping, cooking, independent living skills. Breaking down the acquisition of such skills through simple task analysis would provide many hundreds of 'measurements' as, for example, in the simple skill of washing one's hands:

1   go to washbasin
2   turn on tap
3   put soap on hands
4   rub hands together
5   rinse hands under tap
6   turn off tap
7   take towel/paper towel/turn on drier
8   dry hands
9   replace towel/dispose of paper towel
10   exit from the washbasin area.

A framework for recognising attainment

1   Rejection
    The learner is present in the session, but only because they have to be. There is an active rejection of another person's presence in their social space.

2   Encounter
    The learner is present in the session without any obvious awareness of its progression. It is sufficient that there is a willingness to tolerate a shared social atmosphere.

3   Awareness
    The learner appears to notice, or fleetingly focus on an object, person or event involved in the session. On the whole, however, there is still self-absorption.

4   Attention and Response
    The learner begins to respond, though not consistently, to what is happening in a session by, for example, showing signs of surprise or enjoyment.

5   Engagement
    The learner gives sustained and consistent attention to the supporting adult by, for example, looking, listening, following events with their eyes, etc.

6   Participation
    The learner is fully involved in the session for the whole period and occasionally, but not consistently, actively responds to the adult's lead. They will show enjoyment of the process through smiles and laughter.

7   Student initiation
    The learner is fully involved in the session for the whole period and *is clearly aware* of what is expected. They may well follow the sequence of the music and actions and will consistently offer as much pro-active movement as they physically can.

8   Imitation
    The learner is fully involved in the interaction for the whole period and will still largely be accepting physical support. The student will, however, *at least* occasionally, require no physical prompt or support to complete the movement sequences.

Figure 3.3 A framework for recognising attainment

Measuring progress within these ten 'sub-skills' through *MAPP*'s *Continuum* gives 100 measurements; what external inspector could not fail to be impressed by such demonstrations of progress? Again, the skill of making a slice of toast is also open to such a task analysis approach, since even though the kitchen and the equipment in it may change, the procedure is the same.

1   locate the toaster
2   place the toaster near to an electric socket
3   plug it in
4   switch it on at the socket
5   locate the loaf of bread
6   open the loaf of bread

7   take out one slice of bread
8   place it in the toaster at the appropriate angle
9   check the preset timer gauge is at an appropriate number
10   depress the lever to start the toaster
11   locate the butter
12   locate a knife
13   open the butter
14   locate a plate
15   place the plate, knife and butter on an even surface
16   wait for the toaster to pop
17   take the toast out of the toaster when it pops
18   switch the toaster off at the socket
19   take the plug out
20   spread the toast
21   slice the toast in half
22   eat the toast if desired
23   wash the plate and knife
24   dry the plate and knife
25   put the plate and knife away
26   put the toaster away
27   wipe down the kitchen surfaces used.

And when we extend this out against all the areas noted above, we can ensure that we are both making progress and recording it.

Conclusion

Assessment and progress is a perfectly legitimate way of demonstrating the effectiveness of the teaching and learning taking place in any educational establishment for any pupils. Furthermore, any external inspection system is justified in expecting a quantitative indication of such progress. Inspectors have enough to do judging the quality of the leadership team and the teaching, without having to wade through countless documents and reports noting qualitative progress as well. We are of the belief that inspections should be short and sharp and take the school as they find it, without prior notice, if they are to give a true reflection of the school's effectiveness. We also, incidentally, believe that inspectors grading the quality of teaching of those with SLD and PMLD, whether in special schools or mainstream schools, should be experts in SLD and PMLD with a strong teaching background in these fields. It is not sufficient to have a general 'special needs' background or understanding; teachers of children, young people and adults with SLD and PMLD need to be specialists, and as such, they deserve to be inspected by specialists.

To assess this effectiveness, however, individual pupil progress must directly relate to areas in which pupils can actually achieve. Those with SLD, and especially those with PMLD, are (by definition) unlikely to achieve academic success, and we must be prepared to challenge the view that persisting with an academic pedagogy and curriculum simply because it's what everyone else does is sufficient reason by itself. It is not. The UK system has proven over twenty-five years that a National Curriculum written for neuro-typical, conventionally developing learners is not fit for purpose for those with SLD and PMLD. If it were, such learners would not constantly be working at levels that are related to learning taking place *before* the curriculum was designed to start. Progress for those with PMLD and SLD will probably take place within either skills-based or process-based learning, and it is probably true to say that the more cognitively challenged the pupil the less they will be able to flourish in a skills-based learning environment. There are, nonetheless, numerous methods of assessment and assessing pupil progress in both areas, using both formal systems such as *Routes for Learning* (for those with PMLD) and *MAPP* (for those with SLD), but also with less formal systems based around the *Framework for Recognising Attainment* for process-based learning and a task-analysis approach for skills-based learning, especially when these are combined with *MAPP's Continuum of Skill Development.*

Notes

1   Both Pivats and B Squared are UK commercial variations of the P scales which, recognising the difficulty most children with SLD and PMLD have in achieving progress, break the P scales down into smaller, linear developmental steps. Pivats does this through five or so 'steps' between one P scale and the next; B Squared through considerably more.
2   Some readers may be more familiar with Quest for Learning (CCEA, 2006) the Northern Irish version of *RfL*. The two are almost identical and QfL openly acknowledges its debt to *RfL*.
3   It is also worth considering how closely these concerns also fit the teaching and learning of those with SLD.
4   A number of these writers, but not all, were specifically concerned with those with PMLD, although we would contend that the premise applies equally to those with SLD.
5   Other behaviourist techniques such as backward chaining, shaping and fading are also equally useful techniques for teaching specific skills, although they are not often taught to trainee teachers these days.
6   Specific, Measurable, Achievable, Realistic, Time-bound.
7   The fact that it is a legal requirement in the UK for schools to assess all pupils working below Level 1 of its National Curriculum against the P scales does not mean that it is legitimate; nonetheless it is a useful tool to ensure the legitimacy of the curriculum. Should a pupil be consistently scoring well above P8 and into the NC level indicators, it may be that she will need to be academically stretched more than a strictly SLD pedagogy and curriculum might be able to do.

Chapter 4

Personalised learning and engagement

In 2004, David Miliband, then Schools Standards Minister, put 'Personalised Learning' at the heart of the UK government's vision for education, defining it as 'high quality teaching based on sound knowledge of each child's needs' and emphasising that there must be,

> high expectation of every child, given practical form by high quality teaching based on a sound knowledge and understanding of each child's needs. It is not individualised learning where pupils sit alone at a computer. Nor is it pupils left to their own devices – which too often reinforces low aspirations.
>
> (Miliband, 2004, p. 3)

This book also espouses personalised learning; teachers of children with PMLD or SLD have to get to know individual children inordinately well in order to do the very best for them, and it is this deep knowledge of individual differences that steers teachers to provide meaningful contexts in which to really engage children. Of course, the UK government's vision of personalised learning nearly a decade ago was (and still is) inextricably linked to the view that you cannot tailor learning for individual children unless you have robust evidence of how they are progressing, and you cannot set individual learning intentions without a thorough assessment of and for learning. Assessment for learning is still therefore seen as an important tool to track children's progress and identify the learning style best suited to the individual. We doubt that there are many in special education who would disagree with this; much of our teaching has great precision and we want to build a robust evidence base of children's progress.

Unfortunately, one could be forgiven for thinking that personalised learning was a phrase grown out of politics, not education. The DCSF publication *Personalised Learning – A Practical Guide* (2009) talks about personalised learning as 'putting children and their needs first' so that no child 'should be left behind.' In this report, and many others of the time, there is much talk of '21st Century schools and systems being designed around the needs of children and young people'. However, despite its title, the report is about what it calls the 'pedagogy of personalised learning', which metamorphoses into more about target setting and exceeding national expectations in a competitive educational market than tailoring learning to meet children's individuals needs. 'The pedagogy of personalisation is distinguished by the way it expects all children and young people to reach or exceed national expectations, to fulfil their early promise and develop latent potential' (DCSF, 2009, quoted in Sebba, 2011, p. 206). It could be that putting such a slant on the term reflects more a position of nationalisation than personalisation!

Judy Sebba herself offers a definition where personalisation might mean 'how children and young people can have their needs met while being given greater control over their own learning and lives' (Sebba, 2011, p. 206), but goes on to question the views often expressed in UK special schools that personalisation is 'what they do'. Certainly many special schools would argue that they have been intimately involved with personalised learning for a number of years, especially with those pupils and students who have PMLD (Pollitt and Grant, 2008). Sebba, however, sees a confusion between the personalisation and individualisation of learning and insists that personalisation has everything to do with inclusion and as wide a concept of participation as possible. For the UK Central Government, achievement is the key – for those (like Judy Sebba) who hold inclusion dear, participation is the key. We would suggest that such political slants are not helpful. Personalisation is not about inclusion in the sense that we must get as many children doing as many things as their disabilities previously prevented them from doing, although this might be a side effect. Personalisation in learning is about ensuring that the curriculum is adapted to fit the child and not the child adapted to fit the curriculum.

Personalisation is, of course, a complicated and complex business for those with SLD and PMLD, and although Abbot and Marriot (2012) point out that it cannot merely be seen as a matter of handing over responsibility to the learner, the issue of control is a significant element of it:

> The biggest gains in terms of learning productivity will come from mobilising as yet under-utilised resources available to the education system: children, parents, families, communities. That is the ultimate goal of personalised learning: to encourage children to see themselves as co-investors with the state, in their own education.
>
> (Leadbeater, 2005, p. 4)

This view of enabling the learner to learn, of the teacher as facilitator rather than didact, of the 'teacher's expertise [residing] in their understanding of pedagogy [and no longer having] a monopoly on information' (DeFinizio, 2011, p. 216), of encouraging the learner to find their own pathways to learning, lies at the centre of the process-based learning model espoused in this book and is best summed up by Mel Ainscow:

> Learning is a personal process of meaning-making, with each participant in any activity 'constructing' their own version of that shared event . . . each pupil defines the meaning of what occurs in relation to their previous experience. In this way, individuals personalise the experience and, in so doing, construct forms of knowledge that may or may not relate to the purposes and understandings of the teacher.
>
> (Ainscow, 2006, p. 2)

The definition of personalised learning put forward by the authors of this book is simply spending quality time on things that really matter for children. What springs from really getting to know the children is focusing on those things that will have an impact on children's lives. Personalisation involves stripping away the less important areas of learning and focusing on the most important ones. We acknowledge how bold this sounds, but professional teams have a responsibility to prioritise learning for children with the most complex needs, and this type of decision making, particularly when done in partnership with parents and other professionals, is critical to making the best of what is precious and limited time in schools.

Generally speaking, for children with the most complex needs such as those with PMLD and some with SLD, we do not believe in a broad and balanced curriculum. Our view is that schools do not have time to offer all children an experiential curriculum – for the most complex children, let's focus on the things that matter. This is why we advocate a very different, personalised curriculum for some children, which might be broad and balanced when we can make it so, but above all, is relevant. Decision making about priorities for learning is a very individual thing. We propose that the intensity of personalisation depends on both the complexity and dependency of the learner. We choose to use 'intensity' rather than 'level' of personalisation because we think this captures more clearly the qualitative differences for different groups of children.

We would argue that a child with profound and multiple learning difficulties needs highly intensive personalised learning, using specialised teaching approaches, within a narrow range of curriculum areas that are concrete in form and that necessarily focus upon and respond to individual needs, physical needs, family needs and affective needs (including well-being and security). We shall turn to ways of organising this highly intense personalised learning below.

It is proposed that a less complex child needs less intense personalisation and a wider, more abstract and more experiential curriculum.

Figure 4.1 shows a direction of flow of personalisation from the more complex to the less complex child. This is a continuum and we are not proposing that children with PMLD are on one end of the curriculum and children with SLD on the other. The continuum is one of the complexities of children's needs, not ability. A child with SLD may have very complex needs, for example the child with SLD and severe self-injurious behaviour (SIB). The intensity of personalisation for a child with SLD and SIB will be very different from another child with SLD and would put him to the left of the continuum, where more intense personal learning needs have to be accommodated in order to find learning pathways.

Figure 4.2 is deliberately hypothetical and attempts to show the increased intensity of personalisation afforded to children with greater complexity of needs, the narrowing of the curriculum and how necessarily more concrete this curriculum should be in order to meet a more complex child's needs. We believe that all children benefit from personalised learning, but some children with the most complex needs should have richly intense levels of personalisation in order to find out their learning pathways and engage them.

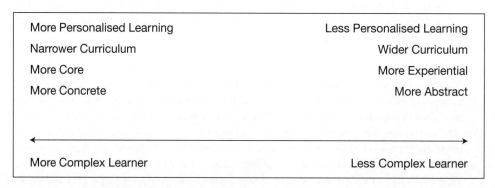

Figure 4.1 Direction of flow for personalised learning

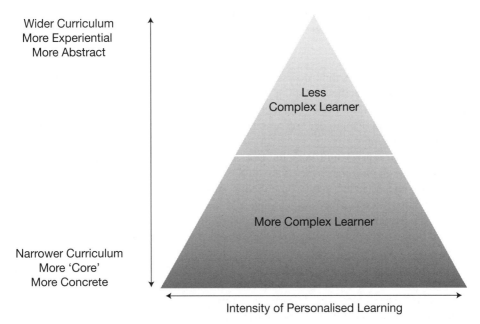

Wider Curriculum
More Experiential
More Abstract

Less
Complex Learner

More Complex Learner

Narrower Curriculum
More 'Core'
More Concrete

Intensity of Personalised Learning

Figure 4.2 Intensity of personalised learning

Engagement

The notion of personalised learning we are advocating, that is spending time on the things that really matter for children with SLD and PMLD and stripping away the less important areas of learning, is inextricably linked to children's levels of engagement. Finding out what motivates and engages children is key to personalised learning and the use of Engagement Scales (Carpenter, 2010; Carpenter *et al.*, 2010; Carpenter *et al.*, 2011) can offer valuable insights for class teams on maximising levels of engagement for each individual pupil.

Barry Carpenter and his colleagues in the Complex Learning Difficulties and Disabilities Project studied children's engagement in a number of special and mainstream schools in the UK. The project's definition of Complex Learning Difficulties and Disabilities (CLDD) is that:

> children and young people with Complex Learning Difficulties and Disabilities (CLDD) have conditions that co-exist. These conditions overlap and interlock creating a complex profile. The co-occurring and compounding nature of complex learning difficulties requires a personalised learning pathway that recognises children and young people's unique and changing learning patterns. Children and young people with CLDD present with a range of issues and combination of layered needs – e.g. mental health, relationships, behavioural, physical, medical, sensory, communication and cognitive. They need informed specific support and strategies which may include transdisciplinary input to engage effectively in the learning process and to participate actively in classroom activities and the wider community. Their attainments may be inconsistent, presenting an atypical or uneven profile. In the school setting, learners may be working at any

educational level, including the National Curriculum and P scales. This definition could also be applicable to learners in Early Years and post-school settings.

(Carpenter *et al.*, 2011, p. 2)

The CLDD research questions how these children learn, how they engage, and how teachers can personalise their learning pathways to engage them as learners. Further questions developed from these – namely, what are the principles, and the questions educators ask that lead them to develop strategies for teaching? Figure 4.3 shows the Project's definition of engagement.

The CLDD's Inquiry Framework for Learning is designed as a tool for educators in exploring and developing personalised learning pathways for children with complex learning difficulties and disabilities. It is described as supporting an approach that focuses on increasing children's engagement in learning in different areas of need, through a process of teacher discussion and reflection. Central to the research study is 'The Engagement Profile and Scale' (Carpenter *et al.*, 2011), a classroom tool developed through Carpenter and colleagues' research into effective teaching and learning for children with CLDD. The aim of the 'Engagement Profile' is to provide a snapshot of how the student demonstrates her engagement. It is described as allowing teachers to focus on the child's engagement as a learner and create personalised learning pathways, thus prompting student-centred reflection on how to increase their engagement, and in turn leading to learning.

Engagement, as described by the CLDD project, is multi-dimensional and encompasses:

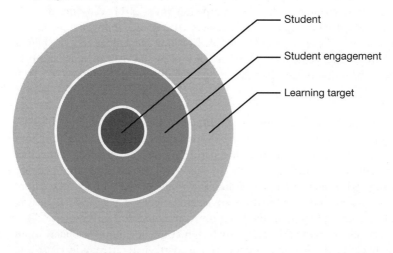

Engagement

Sustainable learning can only occur when there is meaningful engagement. The process of engagement is a journey which connects a child and their environment (including people, ideas, materials and concepts) to enable learning and achievement.

— Student

— Student engagement

— Learning target

Figure 4.3 Engagement

Taken from Carpenter *et al.*, 2010, p. 5.

- awareness
- curiosity
- investigation
- discovery
- anticipation
- persistence
- initiation.

By focusing on these seven indicators of engagement, teachers can ask themselves such questions as: 'How can I change the learning activity to stimulate [a child's] curiosity?' and 'What can I change about this experience to encourage [the child] to persist?' (Carpenter *et al.*, 2010, p. 5). The 'Engagement Profile' can be found at http://complexld. ssatrust.org.uk.

Children's engagement is key to personalised learning. It focuses teachers' attention both on what they teach and how they teach, but drills down further towards finding learning pathways that children respond to best. It seems to us that insufficient time is spent on looking at what really impacts on the lives of children with the most complex needs. Personalised learning is really the only way forward for children with the most complex of needs, many of whom are extremely difficult to reach. Their time is precious in schools and we know that they are unlikely to learn incidentally. Finding personalised learning pathways for children with complex needs through experimentation and being creative is exciting for both teachers and learners. It moves us into areas of action research, as encouraged by the CLDD project, where we ask ourselves what the best ways are of reaching children with the most complex of needs.

It seems to us self-evident that, with the extreme difficulty in realising effective academic research-based reasoning on which to base practice (Pring, 2004; Warnock 2010), teaching those with SLD and PMLD needs to be a classroom research-based and a classroom inquiry-based profession. In special education we need to encourage teachers to be reflective, take risks, try new things out. We want teachers to see value in applying personal questions. It is exciting to formulate ideas taken from work, to adopt an inquiry framework for teaching and learning. Seeing the importance and value in action research is motivating to teachers.

> There are no limits to what there is to learn about teaching pupils with special needs and there are no all-embracing formulas for successful teaching. If the quality of teaching and learning is to be raised in special schools, research needs to be done to investigate the best ways of helping children to overcome their learning difficulties and the best place for this research to be done is in a school.
>
> (Hinchcliffe, 1997, p. 121)

This was true in 1997, and it's still true today.

Really getting to know the children

Chapters 6 and 10 refer to a number of useful assessment guides to help teachers really get to know their children, for example the *The Pragmatics Profile of Everyday Communication Skills in Children* (Dewart and Summers, 1995) and *Individualised Sensory Environment* (Bunning, 1998), both of which focus teachers' attention on children's likes and dislikes.

At a more basic level, Box 4.1 shows some general questions that teachers and teaching teams may want to discuss to guide their decisions about prioritising areas of learning for children with complex needs.

Figure 4.4 is a Pen Portrait of a Lewis, a young child with PMLD. This example of how a team really got to know him is a 'Multi-Agency Profile' (MAP) (see Figure 4.5), written by Clare Chalaye, a teacher at Riverside School and Charlotte Parkhouse, Speech and Language Therapist. A MAP is a kind of 'Communication Passport' (Millar and Aitken, 2003). It shows a highly individualised approach to personalised learning by a team of professionals working in a multidisciplinary way. It shows the outcomes of such learning and helps everyone who comes into contact with the child know the child's likes, communication preferences, how best to physically manage the child, etc. The MAP is presented on a CD and information is provided simply, with video clips of how Lewis is learning to communicate intentionally, how he should be seated, etc. Video filming is, arguably, the best way to pass on essential information about a highly complex child, and we would certainly support the installation of fixed video cameras in classes to immeasurably aid such reflection and focus and improve training opportunities. Referring back to Figure 4.2, Lewis's MAP illustrates the high intensity of personalisation that is essential if his curriculum is to meet the high complexity of his needs.

Box 4.1 Questions for teachers about complexity

Discussion Points to a Class Team: Think of one of your more complex children – a child who may be difficult to reach, an enigmatic child, unpredictable, perhaps unfathomable.

How would you describe her?

On a good day, how does she relax?

What makes her most happy? Or what does she enjoy most?

With things is she interested in, and how long can she focus, concentrate or attend?

Speaking honestly, and only as a rough guide, what proportion of a 15-minute group lesson does she attend to?

What does she least like?

What ways have you found that were best for helping her to learn?

When does she concentrate, focus, get involved the most? What kinds of things do you do to help her to focus more?

What do you think and feel about how she is learning in school at the moment?

Is there anything that you would like to see added or changed in school to help her?

Are there things that we can learn from her family members?

What experiences during her schooling particularly stand out for you? Discuss both the positives and the negatives.

What are your main hopes for her education? Think of the short and medium term, as well as possible future outcomes.

What have been your happiest or favourite moments so far with her?

(Taken from Hinchcliffe, 2012)

Lewis's Pen Portrait

*Lewis is aged 5 years old.
Lewis has PMLD, including severe visual
impairment. He had infantile convulsions as a
baby and necessarily was prescribed Epillim
to reduce these at around 9 months old. This
had an impact on his responsiveness to
stimuli and made him sleep for much of the
day. In the last 1½ years he has been on a
Ketogenic diet which has dramatically
reduced his seizural activity and he now only
has one night time dose of a medication, that
doesn't induce drowsiness and lethargy.
Lewis lives with both his parents and his
sister, aged 15. Both parents work. Until
recently Lewis didn't show much response to
stimuli around him and self-stimulated with his
hands, pushing his eyes, exploring his mouth,
rolling his eyes back in his head and often
bringing his own feet to his face to feel with
his mouth. Lewis was tactile defensive and
was often reluctant to be touched or held by
adults, including personal care routines. Lewis
is able to sit independently but does not stand
or walk as yet.*

Figure 4.4 Pen portrait of Lewis

Lewis's
Multi-Agency
Plan
June 2011

Figure 4.5 A Multi Agency Profile (MAP) of Lewis

My Home Page

I'm Lewis. I am 6 years old and would like to tell you some things about me:

- My pen portrait
- How I communicate
- How I sit comfortably and travelling
- How I stand up and weight bear
- Other positions I like
- How I eat and drink
- If I am unwell
- Things I really like
- Things I don't like

(Click on the name of the page you want to see to go directly to it.)

How I communicate

- I can vocalise to get your attention. Often this is because I would like a drink.
- I smile if I am enjoying an activity.
- I press a big mack switch if this is placed in front of me, I like to see or hear the effect this produces.
- I reach out for objects that catch my attention (see video clip), sometimes to hold people's hands.
- I turn away or lean my head back if I do not want to start/ continue with an activity (you can see this in my painting photo).
- I am beginning to press a switch to request more.

Click here to see me reaching

Click here to see me pressing a big-mack to request 'more'.

Click here to return to My Home Page

turning away when finished an activity

Sitting comfortably and travelling

My class chair and tray

- I sit in my class chair with my lap strap and foot straps secured (though if you look very closely I have my feet loose in the video!)
- You must make sure my bottom is right back and my hips are square.
- My class-chair has a tray to help me work (see photo).
- I sit in a comfy booster seat with a back support when I travel (see second photo).

Click here to return to My Home Page

Me in my car-seat

Click here to see me in my class chair

How I stand and weight bear.

- I stand in my standing frame every morning. This helps me to strengthen my legs and also helps with my constipation.
- I also spend time in a pacer everyday. I go out to the playground in this. I move short distances by pushing back on my legs in this.
- I sometimes go in a lyco hoist to give me another opportunity to weight-bear. I really like this and play the musical keypad with my feet (see video clip).

Click here to return to My Home Page

Standing frame

Click here to see me in my pacer

Click here to see me in my lyco hoist

Other positions I like

- I like sitting in my buggy and going out to different places (see photo).
- I enjoy sitting up and playing with toys on the floor. I am very stable in a sitting position (see photo).
- I really like swimming and wear a special swimming jacket to swim independently (see video).

Click here to return to My Home Page

Click here to see me swimming wearing my special jacket

Sitting playing on the floor

My buggy

How I eat and drink

Click here to see me drinking

Click here to see me eating

- I am on a Ketogenic diet. This means that I can only eat certain foods.
- My Mummy sends in special dinners and a chocolate cake that she has made, every day.
- I sit in my class chair to eat. My food is soft and often has the consistency of scrambled egg. I need someone to give me my food using a plastic spoon (see video). I take about 5 minutes to eat.
- I have a drink after my meal and several other drinks throughout the school day. I drink squash and have this in a bottle with a teat. I can drink this independently (see video).

Click here to return to My Home Page

If I am unwell

- I like to sit in my buggy or class chair and have lots to drink. I sometimes get very upset if adults try to cuddle me and I want to be alone.
- I like to sit or lie still on a beanbag, if I am very poorly. I may even fall asleep.

- <u>My medication</u>

- I have emergency medication in case I have a seizure, but this hasn't happened to me for a long time now, due to my special diet.
- If I have a generalised tonic clonic seizure I am given emergency medication.
- My emergency medication is Buccal Midazolam and this is given to me after I have been in a constant seizure for 5 minutes.
- I may be very sleepy after I have had my medication so please find me somewhere comfy to lay down.

Click here to return to <u>My Home Page</u>

Things I like

- Mirror bells
- Musical instruments, especially the keyboard
- Swimming
- Trampolining with my friend (see video clip)
- People to say hello to me before they make physical contact. I am not so keen on surprises.
- Tickles with people I know well
- Spinning in a spinner with a friend (see video).

Click here to return to <u>My Home Page</u>

Click here to see me trampolining

Click here to see me in my favourite spinner

Things I am not so keen on

- I don't like lying on my back and sometimes get upset when my pad is changed on the changing bed.
- If I want to be left alone I do not like to be touched by adults, though this is becoming less and less as I mature.
- I don't really like riding on the i-joy (see video).
- I communicate that I am not enjoying an activity by crying, moaning and tipping my head back (see video)

Click here to see me communicating my dislike for an activity.

Click here to return to My Home Page

Thank-you for finding out more about *me*.

By Lewis!!

With a little help from Clare Chalaye and Charlotte Parkhouse

Click here to return to My Home Page

Personalised learning intentions

Table 4.1 illustrates Lewis's personalised learning intentions in three areas of his curriculum: cognition, communication and care/PSHE. The teaching methodology lends itself to formative assessment and over time a rigorous evidence base of Lewis's progress can be built up. Although such learning opportunities must always be contextualised, since Lewis will struggle to learn in a compartmentalised manner, the recording of the small developmental steps Lewis might take are necessary to build up his overall assessment and progress picture. While there are no specific SMART targets, the learning intentions that Lewis and the team can work towards are re-enforced by being directly related to Lewis's interests and motivations; the direction of learning is personalised. Any achievements can be recorded against his *Routes for Learning* (WAG, 2006) assessment profile and we can look to give this a numerical value over time, as noted in Chapter 3.

Table 4.1 Lewis's personalised learning intentions

Area of learning	Context to learning intention	Learning intention	How will my target be addressed?	Additional ideas for learning outside the classroom (including learning at home)
Cognition	Lewis often reaches for a particular toy when presented with two, such as the light up piano. We would like to extend Lewis's ability to show a preference for an item and to make a more deliberate choice, by regularly offering him a choice of an item he likes and one that is more neutral, e.g. a toy versus a blank switch pad.	I will consistently choose items that I like over a neutral item, when offered these two at a time.	1 I will be encouraged to choose one of two objects, one motivating toy/object and the other something I haven't shown interest in before (e.g. a writing tablet). If I choose the former I will engage in play activities with a member of Penguin class team, with the object I chose. The adult will roll, shake, throw, rattle the object to gain my attention and provoke a response from me. They will encourage me to look at them and the toy through making encouraging noises and physical prompts. 2 I will work on making choices for resources during cookery and art sessions where I will be introduced to a variety of different materials and encouraged to select one of two of these. The adult working with me will encourage me to explore these before making my choice, with one presented to my left and one to my right. I will be offered one more obviously stimulating item (such as bubble wrap) versus a piece of paper and be expected to choose the bubble wrap (for example). I will then access these and encourage them in shared exploration with an adult. 3 I will be offered two BIGmack switches, one with a song or poem recorded on this and the other switched off. I hope to be able to differentiate between these quite quickly and after a while consistently presses the switch that makes the sounds.	1 Please encourage me to make choices at lunchtime, offering me food in one hand or a toy in the other. It is suspected that I will consistently take the food item, as I am very motivated by food. Also offer me two types of food at lunchtime, e.g. bread or a spoonful of dinner. 2 Please encourage me to choose from two A4 photos for items I like e.g. of the oinking pig, the mirror bells and the keyboard. Give me the item I request immediately (as I reach for this) to reinforce my understanding that I have made a request in this manner. 3 Please give me opportunities to make choices when I am out on educational visits, for activities (from photos), for sensory resources purchased or for which adult I would like to work with.

| Communi-cation | Lewis is now showing more consistent responses to items than previously and particularly reaches for a sound and light infinity toy.

We would like Lewis to begin to use a BIGmack switch to make a consistent response for 'more' or to show a consistent more response in another way. | I will press a switch or use a consistent response to request more in a range of situations 1) to request another chocolate button, 2) to request more of a motivating activity and 3) to request further physical play e.g. tickles taps. | 1 Please encourage me to join in big engagement activities such as a parachute game or sensory song. Place a more switch in front of me and regularly pause the action in the story/song. If I press the switch start the action straight away. If not, please encourage me to hit this with physical prompts initially.
2 Please give me opportunities to use the choose and tell nursery rhyme programme and to press a switch (with 'More' recorded on it) for this to continue on to the next screen. This will encourage my understanding of cause and effect as well as of more.
3 I really like my juice and if I only have a little bit in my bottle can become quite cross. Please only give me a small amount of squash at a time and place a 'more' switch on my tray. If I press the switch, please put a little more squash in my bottle, if it has run out.
4 Please encourage me to explore activities or have physical interaction in burst/pause sequences. When you pause see what my response is and if I use this more than once interpret it as a request for more and give me another turn. Repeat this activity to see if I repeat the response again. | 1 At snack-time I really enjoy my chocolate buttons and will often hit a switch to say 'more'. Please avoid giving me another button unless I press the switch to consolidate my cause and effect understanding i.e. that if I press the switch I receive another sweet. Please give me this immediately after I press to reinforce the stimulus-response bond.
2 Please give me opportunities to show my own method of requesting more when learning outside the classroom. For example push me fast on the swing or the roundabout at the local park then stop this. How do I respond? If I make a response reward me with another turn immediately and write my response in my literacy book.
3 If I am having a snack off the school premises or at home and there is no BIGmack available for me to use, please encourage me to tap the table when I want another chocolate button or similar snack. If I do this give the next button/piece to me straight away and praise me for doing so. |

continued overleaf

Table 4.1 Continued

Area of learning	Context to learning intention	Learning intention	How will my target be addressed?	Additional ideas for learning outside the classroom (including learning at home)
Communi-cation. Intensive interaction.	Lewis has been exploring lots of different sensory media and is definitely less tactile defensive than previously. He also tolerates and even enjoys having physical interactions with adults more now. Lewis has shown a far greater interest in the world around him since his last IEP was set and he now reaches for people when they are near him. We would like him to begin to work on intensive interaction with an adult daily to further encourage his other awareness.	I will extend my reaching skills, my levels of eye contact with others and shared attention (for toys), in an intensive interaction/play situation from a baseline assessment carried out in June 2011.	1 I will sit facing an adult at a desk and carry out a five-minute intensive interaction session with them. During this session the adult working with me will mimic my every move and any sounds that I make. The adult working with me will record my interactions with them, particularly if I make eye-contact or reach towards them. 2 As I make progress with this target and begin to show increased other awareness the adult will continue with intensive interaction sessions, introducing a pair of objects such as shakers, balls, wheels or a set of bells. I will then be encouraged to explore the objects as the adult again mimics my behaviour e.g. ringing the bells as I do or dropping the shaker. 3 I will be encouraged to manipulate a sensory medium on the table in front of me, with an adult (such as water, jelly, cornflour, sand etc.) They will encourage me to attend to them and the medium by pouring the water over the back of my hand or encouraging me to try to pick up cornflour and water mixture. I will be encouraged to make eye contact with the adult at times during the session, demonstrating shared attention and to manipulate the media more purposefully with my hands throughout the course of this IEP.	1 At home, please sit opposite me, around 2 feet away, and copy my every move and sound I make. I enjoy this time and I think we will have fun together! 2 I would love it if I am given opportunities to explore sensory resources with you at home and share in fun activities such as row, row your boat and pat-a-cake and I often hold my hands up for this and find it funny! 3 When I am taking part in physical activities around the school, such as the trampoline room, swimming pool or during physio PE, please give me opportunities to interact directly with my peers or an adult. Carrying out these interactions in different sessions will help me to realise that my actions cause an effect wherever I am.

Care/PSHE			

Care/PSHE

Lewis has now had his multi-agency passport written, though this will continue to evolve as he grows and changes.
Lewis has made great progress with putting small food items in his mouth (if these are passed to him). We would now like him to start practising greater independence by using a spoon.

I will bring 3 spoons of lunch to my mouth per day using a spoon, with support only to load and pass this to me.

1 I will be given the opportunity daily to hold my spoon with the help and guidance from a member of Penguin's team, to eat my lunch after this has been cut up for me. If I am resistant to holding this the adult will gradually increase the number of times that they encourage me to do this over time (dependent on my progress). Eventually I will be helped to lift the spoon and the adult will remove their support as the spoon is approaching my mouth. As I become more confident with this activity the adult will let go of the spoon, as the spoon is further and further away.

2 At drinks and snack times I will be encouraged to bring pieces of biscuits, fruit etc. to my mouth from increasing distances, until I eventually pick this up from the table. An adult will initially guide me with this activity and will reduce the support offered as I begin progress.

3 I will work on fine motor activities across the curriculum. I will be encouraged to pick up stick, bricks, pens, bells and explore these with my hands. I will also be encouraged to play with spoons and other tools in sensory media, such as jelly, corn-flour solution and sand, to encourage me to scoop with these.

1 Please encourage me to independently load a few spoons of my evening meal, with hand over hand support initially, using my spoon to enhance my eating skills.

2 Please give me opportunities to pick up finger food items in my fingers and place these in my mouth. Please make these different sizes to help my fine motor skills.

3 Please hold food items that you are helping me to eat me at close proximity and pause briefly before continuing to move these to my mouth. This will encourage me to reach for them and manoeuvre them into my mouth, as I really like my food!

Part II

Curriculum issues for those with PMLD

Chapter 5

A cognition curriculum for pupils and students with profound and multiple learning difficulties

Cognition deals with the ways in which we gain information about the world around us, the conversion of this information into forms of knowledge our brains can deal with, the organisation of this knowledge and its use in directing and informing our behaviour. Learning involves relatively permanent changes in behaviour which come about as a result of experience.

(Barber and Goldbart, 1998, p. 102)

In many ways the idea of a separate strand for cognition within a PMLD curriculum is questionable since, by logical definition, all matters relating to learning must also be related to cognition, to the degree of understanding the learner holds. There are, by the very nature of PMLD, very few activities (if any) that might be considered to be skills-based in nature, that is, able to be learned without understanding. Juliet Goldbart makes this clear when she discusses the various stages of developing intentionality (cause and effect):

Intentionality is likely to be crucial for developing intentional communication as, until you realize you can affect the environment (*intentionality*), you are not going to realize you can specifically affect the behaviour of people in the environment (*intentional communication*).

(Goldbart, 1994, p. 20, her emphasis)

Within cognition we are therefore concerned with such areas as attention, perception, pattern recognition, learning, memory, concept formation, thinking, language and intelligence.

Conventional developmental lines for NT (neuro-typical) babies

Our understanding of cognition largely derives from Piagetian models of learning (Piaget, 1952) and subsequent re-workings and refinings of the first period of child development, the sensorimotor period, from writers such as Uzgiris and Hunt (1975) and Dunst (1980). This period lasts, in conventionally developing children, from birth to around eighteen months to two years. Figure 5.1 divides the period into a number of sub-stages and is a hybrid of the work of both Uzgiris and Hunt and Dunst. The table can, however, be seen to be immediately problematic as a developmental pathway for those with PMLD, simply because of the plethora of physical skills needed to advance along the months – grasping,

Behaviour	Age in months	Approximate description
Grasping	2	Reflex grasp of adult's finger or piece of dowel.
Holding	2	The baby holds object in hand for 15 seconds.
Mouthing	2–3	Mouths or sucks object (not sucking the hand itself).
Visual inspection	3	Baby visually fixates on the object held in the hand (or held in a fixed position for the baby) for several seconds.
Hitting	4	The baby bangs or hits an object on a table or other surface or hits the object with her hand.
Shaking	5	An object is waved or shaken by the baby.
Examining	6	A complex form of visual inspection. The object is rotated whilst fixated and its different sides are explored or manipulated.
Complex or differential	7	The baby shows behaviours which are differentiated according to the properties of the object, such as sliding a smooth surface, crumpling paper, rubbing cloth, knocking over a tower of bricks.
Dropping	8	The baby intentionally releases an object. This must include watching it fall, noticing where it ends up, listening for the noise of the impact.
Socially instigated	10	The baby's behaviour reflects an awareness of the social function of the object, such as building with bricks, drinking from a cup, 'driving' a toy car.
Showing	14	The baby shows an object to another person to instigate a social interaction.
Naming	18	Labeling an object, person or action with a 'baby name' – demonstrating an understanding of object names is not enough.

Figure 5.1 The sensorimotor period
From Uzgiris and Hunt, 1975; Dunst, 1980.

Table 5.1 Cognitive development in the sensorimotor period

Sub stage	Age	Label	Description
1	0–6 weeks	Reflex	Engages mainly in exercise of reflexes e.g. sucking, rooting. Some selective looking. Change in activity level on seeing a visually presented object.
2	6 weeks to 4 months	Primary Circular Reactions	If infant does something with her own body that she finds pleasurable e.g. sucks her thumb, she learns to repeat the action. Undifferentiated schemes e.g. looking, holding, mouthing.
3	4–8 months	Secondary Circular Reactions	If infant does something external to himself by chance e.g. makes a mobile swing, he learns to repeat the action. This is the first stage of intentionality. Differentiated schemes e.g. tearing, sliding.
4	8–12 months	Coordination of Secondary Schemes	Establishes goal prior to initiation of activity therefore intentionality fully established. Infant can coordinate previously unrelated actions to produce interesting results or solve simple problems. Functional use of objects e.g. cup, shoe.
5	12–18 months	Tertiary Circular Reactions	New means of achieving ends through experimentation. Exploration of container-contents relationships. Showing and giving objects. Relational then self-pretend play.
6	18–24 months	Beginnings of Thought	New means of achieving ends through mental combinations. Predicts cause-effect relationships. Decentred then sequenced pretend play.

Goldbart, 1994, p. 19.

holding, visually fixing, shaking, rotating, etc. may be impossible for someone with cerebral palsy and/or fine and gross motor difficulties and/or learning difficulties and/or visual impairments and/or hearing impairments. Golbart (1994) (see Table 5.1, above) has adapted the scales to elicit more of a general idea on potential developmental steps.

Explanation of the (Goldbart, 1994) stages of cognitive development in the sensorimotor period

1   **Simple reflexes** are evident from birth to six weeks old and are exampled by activities such as sucking and rooting – a reflex seen in newborn babies, who automatically turn their face toward the stimulus and make sucking (rooting) motions with the mouth when the cheek or lip is touched. The rooting reflex helps to ensure successful breastfeeding.

2   **First habits and primary circular reactions** occur from six weeks to around four months old. During this time infants learn to coordinate sensation and two types of scheme (habit and circular reactions). A primary circular reaction is when the infant tries to reproduce an event that happened by accident (for example, sucking her own thumb).

3   **Secondary circular reactions** occur when the infant is four to eight months old. At this time they become aware of things beyond their own body and are more object oriented. They might accidentally shake a rattle and continue to do it for sake of satisfaction thus strengthening their understanding of cause and effect.

4   **Coordination of secondary circular reactions** is from eight months to twelve months old. During this stage they can do things intentionally. The principles of contingency awareness are fully established and they can now combine and recombine schemes in order to reach a goal (for example when using a stick to reach something). They also understand object permanence during this stage. That is, they understand that objects continue to exist even when they can't see them.

5   **Deeper exploration of objects** occurs from twelve to eighteen months old. During this stage infants explore new possibilities of objects; they try different things to get different results.

6   **Symbolic thinking**, occurring between eighteen and twenty-four months old, sees a shift to an increased understanding of abstract concepts.

It should be noted that there is no particular expectation that those with PMLD will make any significant movement into either stage 5 or 6.

There is no doubt that these explanations of broad cognitive development are tremendously useful for those working with children, young people and adults with PMLD, since they give an outline of a possible cognitive 'programme of study'. It must, however, be remembered that development for those with PMLD may well not be along these linear lines but may be fractured and idiosyncratic depending upon the individual nature, difficulties, interests and motivation of the learners.

More about the earliest levels of development

Section 6 (pp. 55–68) of *In Search of a Curriculum* (Staff of Rectory Paddock School, 1983) is in the authors' views one of the most comprehensive accounts ever written on children's earliest stages of development as related to the education of children with severe and profound learning difficulties. Staff of Rectory Paddock School critically examined Uzgiris and Hunt's scales of psychological development in each of the following areas:

- visual pursuit and permanence of objects
- means of obtaining desired environmental events
- vocal Imitation
- gestural Imitation
- operational Causality
- object relations in space
- schemes for relating to objects.

In Search of a Curriculum went on to look at Carl Dunst's *Clinical and Educational Manual* (1980), which uses the Uzgiris–Hunt scales to provide a system for detailed assessment of a child's sensorimotor development. Table 5.2 below shows Dunst's summary of sensorimotor development, the vertical columns representing the seven Uzgiris–Hunt scales and the horizontal rows representing Piaget's six stages of sensorimotor development.

Gillespie and Roberts (1987)[1] used Uzgiris-Hunt and Dunst as a basis to write teaching programmes for children and young people at the very earliest levels of development. Part of the *Scale 1 Visual pursuit and permanence of objects scale* has been reproduced at the end of the chapter in Box 5.1 to show a developmental framework for teaching a child at very early levels to understand object permanence. As has been acknowledged earlier, youngsters with profound physical and sensory difficulties may not easily progress through this sequence of developmental objectives; however, the objectives offer a useful guide. As an aside, considering the objectives were written in the late 1980s, they represent an interesting example of how teachers were using such approaches in special education at that time and trying to break down learning into small achievable steps. Such a model is similar in style to that used by *Routes for Learning* (WAG, 2006), although *Routes*, perhaps mindful of the dangers of slavishly following the 'next prescribed target', looks to offer a more open-ended pathway. *In Search of a Curriculum*, a book written by teachers, was one of the first attempts by a special school to publish its developmental curriculum, in order to encourage schools to share their practice and learn from each other.

Creating a responsive environment

In *Creating a Responsive Environment*, a major piece of work that preceded *Routes for Learning*, Jean Ware posits that it is not simply about where the learner is on her journey towards cognitive understanding, but very much about different interpretations staff, parents, care workers, etc. might put on the behaviours of those with PMLD that might be radically different to their non learning-disabled peers (Ware, 2003):

1   **Differential understanding.** Those with PMLD might, for example, be dependent upon an 'understanding' from adults that someone with profound learning difficulties will not respond as readily as someone without, which may then become a self-fulfilling prophecy.

2   **Differential response.** The child with PMLD may have a different response to the non-disabled upon hearing a familiar voice, which might not be recognised as a response, in that she may, for example, relax rather than vocalise.

3   **Unconventional response.** They may exhibit unconventional behaviours such as tongue thrusting when food is smelt, which are less likely to be responded to when compared with smiling or vocalising (Downing and Siegel-Causey, 1988).

4   **Delayed or infrequent vocalisation.** A child with PMLD may not vocalise as readily or as frequently and, even when responded to by an adult, may well delay in interacting.

5   **Consistency of approach.** Use of switch-operated cause and effect toys to compensate for problems with movement and coordination may cause their own difficulties, such as mechanical and electrical faults not providing the necessary consistent feedback, switches moving position, learners becoming quickly tired by the extra effort involved, etc.

6   **Consistency of vocalisations and responses.** A child may produce few interactions with long pauses in between, making it difficult for another person attempting interaction to get a feel for any rhythm. The opposite may also be true in that the over-stimulated learner may produce too many interactions with no pauses.

Table 5.2 Selected characteristics of the attainments of the sensorimotor period

Stages (Age in months)	Domains of sensorimotor development						
	Purposeful problem solving	Object permanence	Spatial relationships	Causality	Vocal imitation	Gestural imitation	Play*
Use of reflexes (0–1)	Shows only reflexive reactions in response to external stimuli	No active search for objects vanishing from sight	No signs of appreciation of spatial relationships between objects	No signs of understanding causal relationships	Vocal contagion: cries on hearing another infant cry	No signs of imitation of movements he/she performs	No signs of intentional play behaviour
Primary circular reactions (1–4)	First acquired adaptations, coordination of two behavioural schemes (e.g., hand mouth coordination)	Attempts to maintain visual contact with objects moving outside the visual field	Reacts to external stimuli as representing independent spatial fields (e.g., visual, auditory) rather than as a spatial nexus	Shows signs of pre-causal understanding (e.g., places thumb in the mouth to suck on it)	Repeats sound just produced following adult imitation of the sound	Repeats movements just made following adult imitation of the action	Produces primary circular reactions repeatedly in an enjoyable manner
Secondary circular reactions (4–8)	Procedures for making interesting sights last: repeats actions to maintain the reinforcing consequences produced by the action	Reinstates visual contact with objects by (a) anticipating the terminal position of a moving object, and (b) removing a cloth placed over his/her face. Retrieves a partially hidden object	Shows signs of understanding relationships between self and external events (e.g., follows trajectory of rapidly falling objects)	Uses 'phenomenalistic procedures' (e.g., generalized excitement) as a causal action to have an adult repeat an interesting spectacle	Imitates sounds already in his/her repertoire	Imitates simple gestures already in his/her repertoire that are visible to self	Repetition of interesting actions applied to familiar objects

Stage						
Coordination of secondary circular reactions (8–12)	Serializes two heretofore separate behaviours in goal-directed sequences	Secures objects seen hidden under, behind, etc. a single barrier	Rotates and examines objects with signs of appreciation of their three-dimensional attributes, size, shape, weight, etc.	Touches adult's hands to have that person instigate or continue an interesting game or action	Imitates novel sounds but only ones that are similar to those he/she already produces	Imitates (a) self-movements that are invisible (e.g., sticking out the tongue), and (b) novel movements comprised of actions familiar to self	During problem-solving sequences, he/she abandons the terminus in favour of playing with the means. Ritualization: applies appropriate social actions to different objects
Tertiary circular reactions (12–18)	Discovers 'novel' means behaviour needed to obtain a desired goal	Secures objects hidden through a series of visible displacements	Combines and relates objects in different spatial configurations (e.g., places blocks into a cup)	Hands on object to an adult to have that person repeat or instigate a desired action	Imitates novel sound patterns and words that he/she has not previously heard	Imitates novel movements that he/she cannot see self-perform (i.e., invisible gestures, and that he/she has not previously performed	Adaptive play: begins to use one object (e.g., doll cup) as a substitute for another (e.g., adult size cup) during play with objects
Representation and foresight (18–24)	'Invents' means behaviour, via internal thought processes, needed to obtain a desired goal	Recreates sequence of displacements to secure objects: secures objects hidden through a sequence of invisible displacements	Manifests the ability to 'represent' the nature of spatial relationships that exist between objects, and between objects and self	Shows capacity to (a) infer a cause, given only its effect, and (b) foresee an effect, given a cause	Imitates complex verbalizations. Reproduces previously heard sounds and words from memory; deferred imitation	Imitates complex motor movements. Reproduces previously observed actions from memory; deferred imitation	Symbolic play: uses one object as a 'signifier' for another (e.g., a box for a doll bed). Symbolically enacts an event without having ordinarily used objects present

* The Schemes for Relating to Objects scales on the Uzgiris and Hunt assessment instrument parallels the achievements of the Play domain as explicated by Piaget (1945).

(Reprinted from Carl J. Dunst's 'Clinical and Educational Manual', 1980, with acknowledgements and thanks to the author and to the publishers, University Park Press, Baltimore)

7   **Predictability of vocalisations and responses.** Conducting a review of interactive literature relating to those with profound learning difficulties, Spiker *et al.* (2002) found that the signals and cues of children with disabilities were less consistent and predictable than their NT peers and that even those who knew them well, including parents, might have difficulty in reading the signs and signals and engaging responsively.

8   **Consistency of interactive approach.** Wilcox *et al.* (1990) noted that inconsistencies in interactions between the disabled child and various adults with whom they might come into contact may well cause additional confusions and uncertainties. An interesting experiment conducted by Murray and Trevarthen (1986) noted that the quality of interactions between NT children and their mothers decreased when responses from the child were delayed and inconsistent. The authors equated this to interactions between caregivers and intellectually disabled children, which they noted contained more commands and negatives than would otherwise have been the case with their more NT peers.

A practical way of creating a responsive environment could possibly involve 'stretching' (Lyons *et al.*, 2011), which like all the best ideas is very simple, but demonstrates how much we (as people who largely control our own lives) take for granted and often fail to apply to the teaching of those who are not in control of their own lives. 'Stretching' in this sense is not the physical movement, but more a cerebral activity that we do all of the time when engaged in activities we really enjoy. We 'stretch' by thinking about them before they happen, we make plans for the happening, we talk about our plans to others (collaborative 'stretching') and engage in daydreams about how much we'll enjoy the activity. Of course, 'stretching' also occurs after the event when we take pleasure from memory, reminisce with others, relive moments through photographs or music or just sharing narratives, and generally maximise our pleasure ready for the anticipation of it happening again. Lyons *et al.* (2011) demonstrate how this might be done in practice with some personal stories; here's Jenna's:

> Jenna is a 12 year old girl with PMLD. She is very much a 'girly girl' and since she was little has loved having her hair done up and makeup put on. Her mother Julie says she is blessed because so many other mothers have a hard time just trying to get their kids' teeth cleaned. Jenna doesn't struggle with daily pain so doing her hair and makeup are a real pleasure for her and Julie.
>
> Despite a busy daily schedule, Julie makes time to do Jenna's hair and makeup every week, sometimes twice a week, and makes a ritual of it. She lays out the equipment on the kitchen table the night before; the shampoo, conditioner, blow dryer, hair gel, eye shadow and lipstick. Jenna gets so excited. She makes a little crowing sound and her hands move backwards and forwards. She knows exactly what's going to happen in the morning!
>
> Julie knew Jenna loved getting her hair done from when she was little. She used to just tie it up but discovered Jenna wanted more so she kept brushing and started using bobby pins. She also found Jenna loved the hand mirror and wanted to watch. Julie soon bought a bigger desk mirror and Jenna wouldn't let her start until she was in front of it with her hand mirror in her lap. Jenna was very young when Julie first started applying lipstick but her responses made it clear that she felt like 'the queen of the castle' when the lipstick went on; and of course out came the hand mirror!

The first time Jenna's Nana took some photos using her phone Jenna was so excited. Now the family takes photos each time her hair and makeup get done, and sometimes even record a short video. Jenna's Dad loads these into the television and the family sits and watches the whole show the next day. Jenna gets the greatest enjoyment when the family plays that little video over and over and they have since bought a photo frame that changes pictures every minute or so. The family believes that Jenna feels just like a film star!

(p. 11)

Lyons *et al.* (2011) note that there are five basic 'generic steps':

1   Identify a favoured, preferred or enjoyed activity, experience or event, preferably a more frequent/regular daily or weekly activity.
2   Develop a plan to 'stretch' this activity so that the focus person has the opportunity to spend more time thinking about the activity – both before and after. Stretching before the activity aims to increase time spent in positive expectation and anticipation of the event. Stretching after the activity aims to increase time spent in positive reflection and reminiscence about the event. The potential efficacy of collaborative stretching can be enhanced through the active participation of other key support persons.
3   Implement this plan and monitor its impact on levels of enjoyment, happiness and subjective well-being: (a) during the 'stretched' periods before and after the activity; (b) during the activity; and (c) overall (say daily).
4   Encourage the individual towards 'independent stretching' i.e., to anticipate, expect, reflect and reminisce about this and other favoured activities.
5   Apply 'collaborative stretching' to other favoured activities to broaden its potential positive impact.

This 'independent stretching' could be facilitated by utilising the social scripts recommended by Musselwhite and Burkhart (2001) with the aid of a step-by-step type VOCA (Voice Output Communication Aid). This is explored more fully in Chapter 10, ('A Language, Literacy and Communication Curriculum'), since the principles of using the step-by-step as a medium for social scripts applies equally to both SLD and PMLD pupils and students.

Learned helplessness – how and why it can become a major obstacle to learning

Piaget (1952) argued that during the sensorimotor period children will increasingly acquire:

1   object permanence – the realisation that objects continue to exist, even if you can't see them;
2   a reduction in profound egocentrism – which allows babies to realise that they are distinct and separate entities and that there are different others in the world;
3   a refined understanding of imitation;
4   an improved understanding of cause and effect.

An adaptation of Vygotsky's 'zone of proximal development' (1978) for those with physical and intellectual disabilities might show three levels of learner activity, namely:

1   Participatory – during which learners perform activities with considerable physical assistance, which may include (i) physical manipulation or partial assisted movement and (ii) assistive technology such as switches, adapted utensils, etc.
2   Supported – during which learners perform activities with guidance and support, which may include (i) physical prompts – including cues such as object cues or music cues, etc; (ii) verbal prompts (iii) visual prompts – colour coding, icons or symbols, pictures, etc; (iv) assistive technology such as BIGmack switches (v) supervision, from occasional inspection to continuous observation.
3   Independent – the final level where learners should be expected to perform the activities on their own.

The 'zone of proximal development' can be simply described as the distance between the actual developmental level as determined by independent problem solving and the level of potential development as determined through problem solving under adult guidance or in collaboration with more capable peers (Vygotsky, 1978). The adult creates ladders and scaffolds – lays down supports for the learner – which are gradually taken away as the learner 'learns' to be more independent and solve problems on their own. The difficulty for those with both severe and profound learning difficulties is, unfortunately, that we often forget to take these props away; that is, we continue to offer ladders when our children, young people and adults should be challenged to climb on their own.

As the vast majority of learning will be through the interventions and with the assistance of adults, it is vitally important that we recognise the difficulties those with PMLD are likely to face and try to overcome them. This is especially important when considering the additional, if unwitting, tendency of adults and others to 'teach' those with learning difficulties to be 'helpless'. 'Learned Helplessness' was a term originally coined by Martin Seligman, an American psychologist, who at the time was studying the behavioural conditioning of dogs. Seligman (1975) noted learned helplessness to be a psychological condition in which a human being (or animal) has learned to act or behave helplessly in a particular situation – usually after experiencing some inability to avoid an adverse situation – even when it actually has the power to change its unpleasant or even harmful circumstance. Those who are consistently and routinely put in a position of having things done to them and for them, whether they want these things to happen or not, will not readily be able to change these circumstances and will come to accept the status quo as being 'unchangeable'. Seligman saw a similarity with severely depressed patients and argued that clinical depression and related mental illness came in part from a perceived absence of control over the outcome of a situation. Other writers such as Barber, 1994; Wilkinson, 1994; Smith, 1994; Collis and Lacey, 1996; Hewett and Nind, 1998; Ware, 2003; Imray, 2008 have argued strongly that addressing these issues of control is 'difficult for the teacher, but vital for the learner' (Ware, 2003). A number of the issues around control for those with PMLD are discussed further in Chapter 8 ('A Care Curriculum').

Forgetting to take the props away is sometimes about the need to control learners – for example to stop them making a mess that we have then got to clear up – and sometimes because we do not believe that learners are able to do things on their own; but it is perhaps more often that it is 'easier' (for us) if we do it ourselves. We've probably all been there with children of our own! Even if we can overcome this tendency, and all good teachers should strive to do this, one of the key reasons for learned helplessness continuing to be a major problem within the fields of severe and profound learning difficulties is time.

It really cannot be overstated that the perceived lack of time is one of the major reasons for so many instances of learned helplessness. Unfortunately, we have, as teachers, and as managers of teachers, and as inspectors of teachers, become obsessed with a particularly mainstream concept of breadth and balance. This demands that the whole of a prescribed curriculum is fitted into every single week so each learning opportunity is limited by the time it is allocated on the weekly schedule. The adoption of a subject-based curriculum model has resulted in a tendency towards teaching facts rather than the ability to think and act independently. We have become a short-term, 'results'-driven industry. As a consequence, we are always rushing to finish English or maths or history so that geography or RE or science can have its allotted time. For those with severe or profound learning difficulties this can cause immense problems. For those with severe or profound learning difficulties this will probably only ever lead to an inability to problem solve and attain deep, rather than surface, learning. For those with severe or profound learning difficulties, deep learning takes time, and often a considerable amount of time. This error may, incidentally, be equally apparent even if the PMLD curriculum 'subjects' became Communication, Cognition, Community, Creative, Physical, Sensory and Care. The idea that an Intensive Interaction session must be finished by 11.00 so the toileting can be followed by a sensory story with lunch at midday is not helpful to the promotion of deep learning. You may broadly plan it that way and indeed it may happen, but the fact that it may not should not be of overriding concern. Of course we do have to ensure breadth and balance, as long as it is not at the expense of work focused on meeting individual needs, but rigidly squeezing this into every week, rather than taking a longer view, is not helpful.

Learned helplessness – what we can do about it

We can reduce learned helplessness by adopting a number of clear and unambiguous strategies that are regularly discussed and agreed by whole-class and whole-school teams.

Here are twelve of the best:

1 **Building healthy attachments that allow for independent development,** or put even more simply, recognising that any working and/or social relationship that does not actively encourage independent development is axiomatically, unhealthy.
2 **Having high expectations**. This does not mean they have to be unrealistic, but having the high expectation that a learner might do an action on her own (for example, bringing the spoon to her own mouth without physical support) will mean giving extra time and may well result in additional work for the adult – for example cleaning up the mess when the learner drops the spoon.
3 **Recognising the desirability of failure**. There is nothing wrong with failing, it is how we all learn, through our mistakes. However, we do often try to shield our most fragile learners from failure and 'pretend' that they've succeeded when they haven't, much as we might let a small child win a race. Encouraging persistence means we are giving learners the opportunity to succeed on their own. It is imperative that staff work with learners to ensure there is a deep and abiding understanding that making mistakes is perfectly normal.
4 **Providing predictable environments**. The most profoundly disabled will not be able to learn if they are worried, anxious or fretful about what is happening, with whom and for how long, etc. Rather like working with learners with autism, it is vital that we

provide routine, order, structure and certainty before we can look to stretch learners into new ways of working and risk taking.

5   **Rewarding independent behaviours** with positive and entirely encouraging responses, and with immediate and successive opportunities to repeat the behaviour(s) in question, and indeed, extend them.

6   **Communicating with learners at their level**, not just physically by working with learners on the floor or kneeling down if they are in wheelchairs, but also remembering that language can be a means of control (by those who have it and against those who don't) if we use it too much and without thought.

7   **Recognising, responding to and reinforcing learners' initiations** requires a major area of detailed thought for each individual learner. Those looking to extend their knowledge in this quite complex area would be strongly advised to spend some quality time with Jean Ware's *Creating a Responsive Environment for People with Profound and Multiple Learning Difficulties*, published by David Fulton. It is designed to be an interactive book with staff teams encouraged to go through it chapter by chapter during successive team meetings. Equally, class teams might also look at Barry Carpenter and his colleagues' 'Engagement Scales' (Carpenter *et al.*, 2010). Broadly related to the Leuven Scales (Laevers, 1994), although much more related to how a child, young person or adult with PMLD might engage, Carpenter and his team extol the virtues of detailed observation so that specific scores might be given for the seven areas of Awareness, Curiosity, Investigation, Discovery, Anticipation, Initiation and Persistence. Carpenter *et al.* (2010) argue that such observations should not occur in a vacuum, and that observers need to have some idea of what a fully engaged learner might look like. They therefore suggest as an essential base, that pupils need to be observed engaging in at least one activity that they personally find highly engaging and at least one activity they personally find highly un-engaging. It may also be that those working with the learner will be able to utilise known motivators in all sorts of interesting ways to settle learners and increase their engagements in areas that they might previously have rejected.

8   **Fading prompting** as early as you can will allow the learner the opportunity to try doing things on her own. It may well (will probably) result in failure, but this is merely another opportunity to learn. Supporting adults need to think about the amount of assistance given to learners every day, and every part of every day, and look to pause before the assistance is given just to see if the learner makes an independent movement. Sometimes the pauses may need to be quite long, say tens of seconds, although this will of course depend on the individual learner's reaction and response levels.

9   **Providing real choices** – as opposed to superficial choices – which includes the power to say no and be listened to when they say no. This is discussed in considerable detail within Chapter 8 on 'The Care Curriculum'.

10 **Identifying what the learner is interested in and using that as a basis for working with them**, since we can now bring in a motivation to learn and extend independent behaviours. Those interested in developing this more might refer to Karen Bunning's (1996 and 1998) work in ISE referred to in Chapter 9 on 'The Sensory Curriculum'.

11 **Taking risks** and encouraging learners to not be frightened of new experiences. This means that adults will need to build in lots of order, structure, routine and certainty within the existing way of working before introducing something new. Staff will need to build in considerable caution and take things very slowly if learners are to be encouraged to take risks. A long-term approach with many opportunities to experiment,

built around having fun, may well be the best option. So for example, a learner who is tactile defensive of cold, wet, slimy materials such as paint or wallpaper paste might need many opportunities of relaxing into an art session where the touching of such materials is not required. Once relaxed, you might bring in warmed up wallpaper paste for her to touch, but only for the briefest moment before carrying on with the relaxing and safe activity. Gradually, over what might become an extended period of time, perhaps several months, staff may encourage a more open and adventurous response.

12 **Giving the learner time to succeed** is paramount in all of the strategies noted above. This is not only in terms of the lesson or session itself, but in recognising that learning timescales for those with PMLD may be vastly different to that of the rest of the school population, including those with SLD. Some things may take many months and maybe even many years of constant practice to even partially achieve. And of course, once you've given the learner time to succeed, you then have to get used to the idea of . . .

13 **Giving the learner more time!**

Establishing a cognitive learning profile

Routes for Learning (WAG, 2006) sets out the milestones that *might* mark out the cognitive learning profile of a person with profound and multiple learning difficulties as:

- notices stimuli
- responds to very obvious stimulus
- demonstrates brief memory from previously presented stimulus
- responds to range of stimuli
- supported one-to-one turn-taking with adult
- responds consistently to one stimulus
- briefly follows moving stimulus
- shows behaviour that can be interpreted as rejection to some stimuli
- responds differently to different stimuli
- anticipates repetitively presented stimulus
- participates in aided exploration of the environment
- anticipates within social routines
- redirects attention to second object
- random activities cause effect
- looks briefly after disappearing object
- action on reactive environment
- contingency responding
- purposeful action on everyday environment
- changes behaviour in response to interesting event nearby
- contingency awareness
- intentional exploration of the environment
- 'looks' backwards/forwards between two objects (knows two objects are present)
- perseveres by repeating action for reward in social game
- repeats action when first attempt unsuccessful
- object permanence
- does two different actions in sequence to get reward
- selects from two or more items

- modifies action when repeating action does not work
- shared attention
- expresses preference for items not present via symbolic means
- early problem solving – tries new strategy when old one fails
- initiates actions to achieve desired result (exerting autonomy in variety of contexts).

It should be noted that *RfL* takes in both communication and cognition milestones, but such is their interconnection that is often extremely difficult (and probably rather pointless) to separate out the two. Nonetheless, we have tried to do this here so readers may think about the essential interrelationship between cognition and communication. It is, however, essential that working practice puts the two areas back together again.

The seven *key* milestones are identified as:

- notices stimuli
- responds consistently to one stimulus
- contingency responding
- contingency awareness
- object permanence
- selects from two or more items
- initiates actions to achieve desired result (exerting autonomy in variety of contexts).

Although *Routes* suggests forty-three milestones in total, it recognises that there may well be unlimited 'sub-milestones' along the way. The milestones will not necessarily be achieved in numerical order (or through linear progression) as many routes ('pathways') to each milestone are possible. All learners will go through the key milestones, although the routes they use to get there may vary according to the individuals' physical, sensory and learning needs. The whole of *Routes* is process based and the assessment does not provide a summary score because 'the complex behaviours of someone with PMLD cannot be described by a single number'. *Routes for Learning* seeks to establish that learners with PMLD have 'unique abilities and ways of learning'; learning for PMLD pupils is best done holistically rather than through the teaching of isolated skills. *Routes* argues that assessments should take into account:

- preferred learning channels and ways of processing information – visual, auditory, tactile, kinaesthetic etc;
- ways of integrating new experiences with prior learning;
- ways of communicating;
- the ability to remember and anticipate routines;
- approaches to problem-solving situations;
- the ability to form attachments and interact socially.

Routes argues that there are key principles for effective learning. These are:

1   **Learners under stress will not learn effectively.**
    Learners must:

    i)   Feel secure with the people around them
    ii) Feel safe

iii) Be positioned comfortably
iv) Not be overloaded with stimuli
v)   Not be overly thirsty, hungry, tired, etc.
vi) Be calm, as much as is possible to know – what do we know and what can we find out? Learners need to be aroused but not too aroused.

2   **The brain needs a high level of sensory stimulation.**
    This involves:

    i)   Working through a limited number of sensory channels
    ii) Being aware of all seven of the sensory channels[2]
    iii) Assessing preferred positioning
    iv) Assessing preferred or dominant sensory channels
    v)   Assessing sensory difficulties, e.g. touch defensiveness.

3   **Input needs to be related to prior learning and experience.**
    This involves an understanding (in both teacher and learner) of the difference between:

    i)   contingency responding – understanding an action makes an effect but not realising the one-to-one association, i.e. that *one* action has *one* effect. It is most notable that the learner has understood the principle of contingency responding rather than contingency awareness when she, for example, presses a switch repeatedly to get a picture on the screen when she only has to press it once for the same effect.
    ii) contingency awareness – knowing that one action causes one particular response – as in pressing a switch once to get a picture on the screen.

4   **Object permanence needs to be established.**
    The process for learning this starts as soon as the learner is able to track an object moving across her visual field (and eventually disappearing) and as such starts with the very first milestone on the *Routes* map – notices stimuli.

5   **Learners need immediate and consistent feedback in their responses.** The authors suggest that for those in the contingency responding phase, memory spans are likely to be 'shorter than seven seconds'!

6   **We need to be aware of the possible continued existence of early reflexes** such as asymmetric tonic neck reflex and moro (startle) reflex and seek multidisciplinary advice on these.

7   **Transfer, or generalisation, of skills often requires specific attention** so that the 'ability to generalise skills will represent real progress for many learners with PMLD'.

Conclusion

The individual cognitive abilities of all those with PMLD will vary enormously from one learner to the next. Learning itself is unlikely to be smooth or automatically progressive along a straight (linear) pathway, but will be fractured and spiky, because of the nature of individual intellectual, physical and sensory difficulties and disabilities. We can take some instruction from studies of conventionally developing children in Piaget's sensorimotor period of development, although we must treat these studies with considerable caution. *Routes for Learning* describes what is currently the definitive example of a routemap of cognitive development for those with PMLD. We should spend some time familiarising ourselves with both the milestones and key milestones and adapting their suggestions to the learners in our classes. However, we must be cogniscant of the fact that *RfL* is an assessment protocol, not a curriculum document. If we just teach the next step on the list, we will be repeating the mistakes of working through the P scales and variations of them such as Pivats and B Squared. Curriculum ideas are addressed in more detail in the chapters that follow. Finally, much caution also needs to be exercised by all working with children, young people and adults with learning difficulties to ensure that we are not, however inadvertently, teaching our charges to be helpless.

Notes

1   For readers who would like to see the teaching objectives for all seven scales, please write to Dr Vivian Hinchcliffe at Drumbeat School and ASC Service.
2   The seven sensory channels of Visual, Auditory, Olfactory, Tactile, Gustatory, Proprioception and Vestibular are explored more fully in Chapter 9 on 'The Sensory Curriculum'.

Box 5.1 Developmental core curriculum from staff of Rectory Paddock School (1983)

Scales of development

Scale I: The development of visual pursuit and the permanence of objects.

Phase I

Procedure for objective A:

(1)   Sit the child on a chair
(2)   Use any bright object that attracts his attention and makes a sound when moved.
(3)   Hold the object about 8–10 inches in front of the child's eyes and shake it to attract his attention.

Objective A:
The child will fixate on the object momentarily either each time it is shaken or when his visual gaze moves across the object.

Sources: Dunst, scale step E1. (Corresp. to Piaget's stage I).

Procedure for objective B:

(1)   Sit the child on a chair.
(2)   Use any bright object that will NOT make a sound when moved.
(3)   Hold the object about 10 inches in front of child's eyes until he focuses on it.
(4)   Move the object slowly through a lateral arc of 180°.

Objective B:
The child will visually follow the object smoothly through the complete arc.

Sources: Dunst, scale step 1. Uzgiris and Hunt, 1d. (Corresp. to Piaget's stage II).

Procedure for objective C:

(1) Sit the child on a chair.
(2) Use any bright object that will NOT make a sound when moved.
(3) Hold the object about 10 inches in front of the child's eyes until he focuses on it.
(4) Move the object slowly to one side and away from the child making it disappear (behind him) and bring it back in front but slightly above the child's eyes on the opposite side. Always move the object in the same direction and make it disappear at the same point.

Objective C:
The child will linger with his glance at the point where the object disappeared.

Sources: Dunst, scale step 2. Uzgiris and Hunt, 2c. (Corresp. to Piaget's stage III).

Procedure for objective D:

(1) Sit the child on a chair.
(2) Use a bright object attached to a string that does NOT make a sound when moved.
(3) Stand behind child and suspend the toy in front of him about 18 inches from his face.
(4) When the child focuses on the object move it in a slow circular trajectory around the child so that it disappears and re-appears on 3 occasions.
(5) On the 4th trajectory, move the object around the child to the side opposite the point of disappearance but slightly behind the child so as not to be visible.

Objective D:
The child will turn his eyes, head, and/or body toward the side of the object's disappearance looking for the vanished object.

Sources: Dunst, scale step E2. (Corresp. to Piaget's stage III).

Procedure for objective E

(1) Sit the child at a table.
(2) Use an object the child is interested in, e.g., toy animal, car, doll.
(3) When the child focuses on the object place it on the table and cover it with a cloth so that a small portion of the object remains visible.

Objective E:
The child will obtain the object by either pulling it out from under the cloth, or removing the cloth and picking up the object.

Sources: Dunst, scale step 3. Uzgiris and Hunt, 3c. (Corresp. to Piaget's stage III).

Procedure for objective F:

(1) ⎫
(2) ⎪
(3) ⎬ As in objective D
(4) ⎪
(5) ⎭

Objective F:
After several presentations, the child will return his glance to the starting point or the point of re-appearance (slightly above normal eye level) before the object has re-appeared.

Sources: Dunst, scale step 4. Uzgiris and Hunt, 2d. (Corresp. to Piaget's stage III).

Procedure for objective G:

(1) Sit the child on a chair.
(2) Use a bright object attached to string that does not make a sound when moved.
(3) Stand behind the child and suspend the toy in front of him about 18 inches from his face.
(4) When the child focuses on the object move it in a slow circular trajectory around the child so that it disappears and re-appears on 3 occasions.
(5) On the 4th trajectory, move the object around the child to the side opposite the point of disappearance but slightly behind the child so as not to be visible.
(6) Repeat several times, varying the side to which the object is made to disappear.

Objective G:
The child will either a) turn in the direction of the trajectory but failing to find the object, reverse his searching to the opposite side to find and/or anticipate the re-appearance of the object or b) turn directly to the opposite side once the object moves out of his visual field in anticipation if the re-appearance of the object.

Sources: Dunst, scale step E3. (Corresp. to Piaget's stage IV).

Procedure for objective H:

(1) Sit the child at a table.
(2) Give him a favourite toy to play with.
(3) Place a cloth over both the object and his hand, making both invisible.

Objective H:
The child will either a) withdraw the object from beneath the cloth, or b) with his free hand will remove the cloth impeding visual contact.

Sources: Dunst, scale step E4. (Corresp. to Piaget's stage IV).

Procedure for objective I:

(1) Sit the child at a table.

(2) Use an object the child is interested in e.g., toy animal, car, doll.

(3) Encourage the child to reach for the toy but cover it completely with a screen (cloth). Bunch the cloth up so that the contours of the toy do not show through.

(4) If the child immediately lifts the cloth on the first presentation – move the table to one side and repeat.

Objective I:

The child will pull the screen off to obtain the object. NB: Make sure the child is not lifting the screen just to handle or play with it.

Sources: Dunst, scale step 5. Uzgiris and Hunt, 4d. (Corresp. to Piaget's stage IV).

Procedure for objective J:

(1) Sit the child at a table.

(2) Use an object the child is interested in.

(3) Have two cloths.

(4) Following the child's successful retrieval of an object hidden under a single screen (Objective I), place a second cloth next to the first one.

(5) Hide a toy under the first cloth (A) three times. Then switch to the second cloth (B).

Objective J:

The child will search for the object hidden under cloth A on all 4 occasions, even following the object's displacement under cloth B. NB: If the child does obtain the object from under cloth B this hiding counts as the first presentation for Objective K.

Sources: Dunst, scale step E5. Uzgiris and Hunt, 5b. (Corresp. to Piaget's stage IV).

Procedure for objective K:

(1) Sit the child at a table.

(2) Use an object the child is interested in.

(3) Have two cloths which are dissimilar in appearance.

(4) Hide the object under each of the two cloths alternately, covering the object completely each time.

Objective K:

The child will search correctly under each of the cloths.

Sources: Dunst, scale step 6. Uzgiris and Hunt, 6c. (Corresp. to Piaget's stage V).

Procedure for objective L:

(1) Sit the child at a table.
(2) Use an object the child is interested in.
(3) Have three cloths which are dissimilar in appearance.
(4) Hide the object under each of the 3 cloths, selecting the cloth to be used on each presentation at random (sample order: 2nd, 1st, 3rd, 1st, 1st, 3rd, 2nd).

Objective L:
The child will search directly under the screen where the object disappeared.

Sources: Dunst, scale step 7. Uzgiris and Hunt, 7c. (Corresp. to Piaget's stage V).

Procedure for objective M:

(1) Sit the child at a table.
(2) Use any object the child is interested in.
(3) Use 3 different opaque screens, e.g. cloths or cups.
(4) Hide the object successively under each of the three screens by moving the hand holding the toy in a path from L–R (or from R–L), so that the object becomes hidden under one of the screens, then re-appears in the space between, and again becomes hidden as the hand passes under another screen. Make sure the child attends to the complete hiding procedure i.e., the complete series of object appearances and disappearances.

Objective M:
The child will search directly under the last screen in the path.

Sources: Dunst, scale step E6. Uzgiris and Hunt, 8c. (Corresp. to Piaget's stage V).

Procedure for objective N:

(1) Sit the child at a table.
(2) Use any object the child is interested in.
(3) Use 3 screens (2 opaque and 1 small cushion/pillow).
(4) Place the object on the table. Cover it with one screen, then cover it with a second screen, and cover the second with a third. Arrange the screens so that the child cannot remove them all with one 'swipe' (e.g., use the cushion as the middle screen).

Objective N:
The child will remove all the screens and find the hidden object.

Sources: Dunst, scale step 8. Uzgiris and Hunt 9c. (Corresp. to Piaget's stage V).

Procedure for objective O:

(1) Sit the child at a table.
(2) Use a small object that will fit inside a box deep enough to make the object invisible to the child once it is lowered into it. Use a large opaque piece of cloth as a screen.

(3) While the child watches, lower the object into the box and then hide the box under the cloth. Turn the box over under the screen leaving the object hidden and remove the empty box. If the child hesitates show him that the box is empty.

Objective O:
Either a) the child will check the box and then proceed to find the object under the screen where the box disappeared, or b) the child will search for the object directly under the screen where the box disappeared.

Sources: Dunst, scale step 9. Uzgiris and Hunt, 10d, 10c. (Corresp. tp Piaget's stage V).

Procedure for objective P:

(1) Sit the child at a table.
(2) Use the object and box as in step 2 of objective O but have two large (and different) screens.
(3) Hide the object as in step 3 of objective O but under the second screen (B).
(4) Do this twice more (i.e., 2nd screen) (B).
(5) Hide the object as above under the first screen (A) (i.e., B twice and then A once).

Objective P:
The child will search correctly under the screen where the box disappeared.

Sources: Dunst, scale step 10. Uzgiris and Hunt, 11c. (Corresp. to Piaget's stage VI).

Procedure for objective Q:

(1) Sit the child at a table.
(2) Use an object and a box as in objective O but have TWO large cloths.
(3) Hide the object, using the box to produce the invisible displacement, under one of two screens, alternately. Place the empty box in the centre between the two screens.

Objective Q:
The child will search directly under the screen where the box disappeared.

Sources: Dunst, scale step 11. Uzgiris and Hunt, 12c. (Corresp. to Piaget's stage VI).

Procedure for objective R:

(1) Sit the child at a table.
(2) Use the object and box as in objective Q but use a third screen and obviously different piece of cloth (or a pillow/cushion).
(3) Using the box to create the invisible displacement by first lowering the object into it, make the box disappear under one of the three screens at random, leaving the object hidden under the screen each time.

Objective R:
The child will search directly under the correct screen where the box disappeared.

Sources: Dunst, scale step 12. Uzgiris and Hunt, 13c. (Corresp. to Piaget's stage VI).

Procedure for objective S:

(1) Sit the child at a table.
(2) Have an object small enough to be hidden in the palm of the hand.
(3) While the child watches, place the object in the palm of one hand and hide it by closing the hand.
(4) Move the hand in one direction making the hand disappear under the first screen, re-appear, disappear under the second screen, etc. Do not open the hand between screens. Leave the object under the last (3rd) screen and show the child the hand is empty.

Objective S:
The child will search under all 3 screens in the same order and find the object under the 3rd screen.

Sources: Dunst, scale step 13. Uzgiris and Hunt, 14c. (Corresp. tp Piaget's stage VI).

Procedure for objective T:

Repeat steps 1, 2, 3 and 4 of objective S.

Objective T:
The child will search directly under the LAST (3rd) screen in the pathway rather than going through the order of hiding.

Source: Dunst, scale step E7, Uzgiris and Hunt, 14d. (Corresp to Piaget's stage VI).

Procedure for objective U:

Immediately following success with objective T repeat the process of going under all three screen but leave the object under the FIRST screen.

* In order to remember to stop momentarily under the last screen open the now empty hand there also.

Observe the child's actions – does he:

(1) search only under the last (3rd) screen and give up
(2) search haphazardly under all 3 screens.

Objective U:
The child will search systematically from the last screen through the MIDDLE screen to the first – i.e., following an inverse of the order used in hiding.

Only if he goes to the middle screen in the reversed series without the object having been hidden there will it imply that the child holds a reversible image of the whole series of places where the hand holding the object disappeared.

Sources: Dunst, scale step 14. Uzgiris and Hunt, 15c. (Corresp. to Piaget's stage VI).

Chapter 6

A communication curriculum for pupils and students with profound and multiple learning difficulties

> Communication with people with the most complex needs is most successful with familiar, responsive partners who care about the person they are communicating with.
>
> (Goldbart and Caton, 2010, p. 1)

At the very essence it might appear that communication with those with Profound and Multiple Learning Difficulties is a very simple process. After all, if those with PMLD are operating at the very earliest developmental levels, common sense strategies utilised by every mother with her baby ought to be appropriate. But strangely, it is the apparent simplicity of the process that makes successful communication with those who really struggle with it so difficult. There may be a number of reasons for this:

1 We get tied up with targets that are based on how conventionally developing children learn, which are often too specific and too demanding. NT children learn with such astonishing speed and with such amazing fluidity and ease that using their pathways as a guide can be confusing, because they may be entirely different to the pathways that may be taken by children, young people and adults with PMLD. Nonetheless, the paucity of rigorous research means that often we have little else on which to base best practice.

2 Because we ourselves have learnt to communicate with such ease and such fluidity and generally do it so successfully, we don't *think* about the process from the very start. It might be compared to the fact that the best managers of top-class football teams are often not those who have been brilliant footballers themselves, because brilliant footballers do it all *without* thinking. This concept comes up again and again within this book (in Chapter 13, 'A Problem-Solving and Thinking Curriculum', for example) and is one of the major reasons for arguing for a distinct pedagogy for both PMLD and SLD. We can't always use common sense solutions, since teaching those with PMLD particularly, often sits outside of common sense.

3 We often don't allow sufficient time for communication because we're too busy doing other things. For those who struggle with communication, as all those with PMLD will, there is nothing that is more important. It may well be perfectly justifiable, therefore, especially for younger learners, to spend the vast majority (and perhaps even all) of their school week working on communication. Breadth and balance are excellent aims, but if they mean giving insufficient time to establishing

the communicative process, they may be counter-productive in the long term.

4   We don't spend enough time on the bigger, long-term picture, especially with communication. In the UK at least there is an obsession with short-term targets and with teachers teaching to those targets, as though this was the only and indeed the best way of demonstrating that children are learning. Learning to communicate for someone with PMLD is a long, slow, holistic process that will not necessarily progress along straight, even or predictable lines and will not necessarily give up its secrets to short-term targets.

5   We sometimes forget that communication is a two-way process that involves us as well. Effective communication 'is about two or more people working together and coordinating their actions in an ongoing response to each other and the context' (Bunning, 2009, p. 48).

This means that we have to work as hard as the person with PMLD on every single communication we have.

What we might need to work on

Given these issues and the difficulties listed below, it may seem contradictory to argue for the simplicity of communication, but it is important to remember that communication is basically a very simple process. Goldbart (1994) suggests that there are only four essential minimum conditions required for communication to take place. That is, *both* people (or all people if there are more than two) will need: (i) a means of communicating; (ii) a motivation to communicate; (iii) someone to communicate with; (iv) the time to communicate. In the event of a breakdown in the communicative process, it is very likely that one or more of these four precepts will need repairing.

Pupils with learning difficulties may face many problems in becoming effective communicators:

- they may have visual disabilities;
- they may have hearing impairments;
- they may experience sensory difficulties and confusions;
- the learner may not have reached a developmental level that can process and understand speech, signing and/or symbols;
- they may have uncertain abilities to interpret non-verbal and paraverbal communications;
- they may lack motivation within certain or most communicative opportunities;
- they may have idiosyncratic communicative patterns;
- the learner's communications may be brief and/or delayed, and so get overlooked;
- adults may find it difficult to interpret a communication;
- adults may be unable or unwilling to engage with learners' communications, especially if those communications come in the form of challenging behaviours;
- they may have poor powers of concentration;
- they may not trust others in all or certain situations and have a standardised rejection response to most communications.

As a result, and at a very general level, it may be that the following will represent the basic communication skills that might be worked on with all those who have PMLD:

- emotional engagement;
- attentional skills – person and time;
- turn taking – reciprocity;
- using and understanding non-verbal communication – eyes, face, body language;
- being close enough to a communicative partner – proximity;
- receiving and giving touch;
- responsiveness to vocalisations.

Dewart and Summers (1995) divide the pragmatics of communication into four sections, and these also seem reasonable broad areas to work on. The four are:

1   **Expression** – ability to request, ability to reject, ability to gain attention, intent, other means of initiation.
2   **Comprehension** – response to [name], response to verbal commands in context, response to gesture and Makaton signs.
3   **Social interaction** – ability to joint reference with significant other, turns taken after a model and/or prompt, number of times significant other needed to prompt.
4   **Behaviour** – ability to express pleasure, ability to express distress.

On a more specific level, *Routes for Learning* (WAG, 2006) suggests that those teaching and working with children, young people and adults with PMLD might look to work on the following communication milestones, where the learner observably:

- reacts to close contact with familiar adult;
- responds to familiar voice or other personal identifier;
- allows supported one-to-one turn-taking with adult;
- responds to own name;
- terminates interaction with adult;
- objects to termination of interaction;
- anticipates within social routines;
- communicates 'more';
- communicates 'more'/'no more' through two different consistent actions;
- attracts attention;
- initiates social game;
- communicates choice to attentive adult;
- deliberately gains attention of another person to satisfy need;
- engages in shared attention;
- expresses preference for items not present via symbolic means;
- initiates actions to achieve desired result (exerting autonomy in variety of contexts).

It should be especially noted that these milestones are not linear, and will not necessarily follow the same pathways for all pupils and students. Further, *RfL* is insistent that learning for those with PMLD is an holistic process, and we recognise that separating out the communication from the cognitive milestones (as above) is a paper exercise. We are most definitely not recommending compartmentalising learning.

The process-based nature of communication

When working with learners who are at a very early developmental level it is almost impossible to separate out the learning of communicative skills from the actual process of living and, to this degree, communication can be seen to be perhaps more than any other area of development an almost entirely process-based activity. There are of course specific skills involved in the art of communicating that we can attempt to teach, such as pressing a BigMack in order to indicate the desire for something, or looking at a preferred object to indicate choice, but the success of this will undoubtedly be entirely dependent on the motivation of the child (to gain the 'something'), the context of the activity (is it familiar enough, rewarding enough, with people she knows and trusts enough?) and of course the ability of the pupil to understand cause and effect in a refined manner, and to be at least contingently responsive.

Specific strategies for communicating with those with PMLD

Communication passports have been around a while but are perhaps still underused, at least according to Goldbart and Caton (2010). They are short, easily accessible, easy to read booklets that will give the maximum amount of information about the individual to anyone who can give five minutes to read it – and five minutes is probably the maximum time it should take to read a communication passport. Therefore they need to be displayed in a prominent place in the classroom and all new staff directed to read them before starting work. Strictly speaking they are not about the person with PMLD communicating directly, but the indirect benefits of improving the knowledge of adults and gaining a commonality of approach can be considerable. Ashcroft (2002) identifies a communication passport as a personalised form of practical information about a person with communication impairments who is unable to 'tell their own story', in order to help themselves, their carers and the staff working with them. It thereby provides a 'passport' to the 'getting to know you' stage that we all go through when we meet someone new for the first time. A communication passport aims to:

- provide practical information about communication and personalised needs;
- achieve consistency across contexts;
- considerably ease and support continuity in transitions;
- help guide other people's behaviour;
- present information clearly and accessibly;
- empower (through the imparting of *accurate* knowledge) the person with PMLD and the people who work with them;
- provide a shared history;
- give information on how communication systems are used;
- reduce stress and frustration for all involved;
- hasten development of positive relationships;
- ensure smooth integration of new staff and consistent management.

Communication passports promote positive interactions by helping to inform communication partners what to expect and how to interpret a person's different behaviours. They can give ideas about how to create opportunities to communicate, what means of communication the person uses and the vocabulary she understands, and of course really importantly, what she likes and is motivated to communicate about. The very making of them (although time consuming) can be tremendously useful as an opportunity to bring about communication among key people, create changes in attitudes, increase the confidence and sense of value for both the person with PMLD and her family and, by the very nature of so many working collaboratively, can offer new insights and solutions.

Ashcroft (2002), Russell (2002) and Millar and Aitken (2003) all suggest that the style of the communication passport should be written from the personalised perspective of the individual themselves with 'chapters' containing a page or two that might include information on:

- All about me
- Things I like and don't like
- Things you can do to help me
- Important people in my life
- How I eat and drink and what I like to eat and drink
- How I listen and hear, see and perceive
- Any special additional sensory issues I might have
- How to talk to me
- Things I am working on
- Important medical information
- Positioning information.

This written information might be additionally supported by photographs of family, friends, favourite objects, activities, foods, and we might also use ICT and particularly video of the individual in action, as suggested in the example of Lewis's Multi-disciplinary Action Plan in Chapter 4. Indeed, it might not be long before such documents are held on an iPad or tablet owned by the child, young person or adult with PMLD.

Intensive interaction

Intensive Interaction (Nind and Hewett, 1988, 1994, 2001, 2006; Hewett and Nind, 1998; Kellett and Nind, 2003; Caldwell, 2005, 2007) has proved to be one of the most significant advances over the past thirty years in the development of an effective communication curriculum for those with complex learning and communication difficulties. Intensive Interaction was essentially developed from two independent but very much related ideas. Gentle Teaching, originated by J. J. McGee and colleagues in New Zealand (McGee *et al.* 1987) argued that those with severe learning and communication difficulties need to be taught how to have a relationship (we might interpret this as being taught how to love and be loved) before we can expect them to learn other skills; Gentle Teaching was, in fact, essentially a reaction against the behaviourist, skills-based teaching pedagogy prevalent at that time. On the other side of the world in the UK, Gary Ephraim was arguing for an holistic communication tool that echoed the natural ways mothers interacted with their very young babies (Ephraim, 1979).

Much has been written about Intensive Interaction and it is strongly recommended that those interested in developing their skills read at least Nind and Hewett's 2001 *A Practical Guide to Intensive Interaction* published by BILD. There is also the Intensive Interaction website at www.intensiveinteraction.co.uk, an exceedingly accessible DVD produced by Dave Hewett that is excellent as a staff training guide and you can get information regarding whole school and individual training opportunities by contacting Dave Hewett at www.davehewett.com.

As a brief guide, Intensive Interaction (which is widely used in the UK at least, across both child and adult services with people often described as pre-verbal, pre-linguistic, pre-intentional and/or difficult to reach, often those with PMLD or ASC) is designed to foster early communication skills. It is based on conventional parent/infant models of interaction and largely follows the communication process from birth involving a shared two-way enjoyment. We become the flexible and responsive partners – reinforcing the child's engagement and her ability to understand that she can affect the actions of those around her. Meaningful engagement with a more competent partner reinforces skills.

The core principles are those of tasklessness, that is, a deliberate lack of agenda or any specific target or objective. Adults follow the child's lead, celebrate any action or vocalisation as an intentional act of communication – whether it is or not – and try (in the long term) to extend knowledge and understanding of communicative interactions. The adult therefore needs to 'tune in' to the learner and look for communication moments, so that the act of creating the flow becomes the objective of the session.

At its best, Intensive Interaction is done all the time as a matter of course, but to get to that state it is advisable to give it at least one regular discrete weekly slot on the timetable for all PMLD groups, and perhaps as often as several times a day for some younger learners. There may on occasion be a few learners, especially those who are at the earliest stages of communicative development and/or who are exhibiting extreme challenging behaviours, with whom it is necessary to use Intensive Interaction techniques almost exclusively (Imray, 2008), at least until those challenging behaviours reduce significantly.

Intensive Interaction is fundamental, not only as a primary means of fostering meaningful communicative opportunities with those who might otherwise be considered impossible to reach, but also as one of the best exemplars of the process-based teaching approach. As a series of broad brushstroke rules, Intensive Interaction is likely to work best when the interactor:

- allows the learner to take control and for the most part, lead the session;
- is seen by the learner to enjoy the experience of the interaction;
- gives his/her total attention to the learner;
- treats all actions and vocalisations made by the learner as positive attempts to communicate;
- uses as little language as possible – often hello and goodbye are sufficient for those with PMLD;
- does not give up too early, either in the session itself or over time – it may take many years to maximise a learner's communicative abilities;
- gives the student time – pauses, when nothing is apparently happening, are really ok;
- use pause–burst–pause sequences during periods of nothing happening to give the learner time and opportunity to respond;
- documents changes – using recording sheets and videoing sessions with a static wide-angled lens;
- talks to his/her colleagues and shares experiences in a general plenary involving the learners after every discrete session.

There have been several research studies done on the efficacy of Intensive Interaction (for example, see Leaning and Watson, 2006; Samuel *et al.*, 2008) and certainly it would be difficult to find many (if any) experienced practitioners not convinced of its potential power. Indeed Mary Kellett argues that 'for children at early levels of development, perhaps we should be contemplating the need for Intensive Interaction or 'Social Communication' Co-ordinators, in the same way we consider having Maths or English Co-ordinators' (Kellett, 2000, p. 171).

As noted above and elsewhere in this book, Intensive Interaction is one of the classic process-based ways of teaching and learning and shies away from the behaviourist skills-teaching approach. In the words of Dave Hewett and Melanie Nind;

> We would argue that there are practical reasons for using behavioural approaches. They are effective for some skills learning. We would also argue that there are practical reasons for using alternatives to behavioural approaches. These centre around their inadequacy for teaching complex areas like sociability and communication and the comparative power of interactive approaches to facilitate these important and complex developments. Intensive Interaction was developed for this very practical purpose. We are also aware however, that Intensive Interaction fits with a certain way of seeing the world, that to operate within its principals and to use its methods requires us to think in certain ways. It is because of this respect for the individual with learning disabilities for what they are, this willingness to work with them rather than do things to them, that makes a conflict with behavioural approaches somewhat inevitable.
>
> (Hewett and Nind, 1998, p. 176)

The use of language

One of the most notable areas of Intensive Interaction is its non-dependence on language. With the notable exception of active, fun, learning times, such as will be enjoyed during drama, poetry, storytelling, etc., language needs to be used with the greatest possible caution. Language and the ability to communicate fluently and widely across a whole range of subjects to a whole range of people is a fantastically powerful tool, but it can also be used as an instrument of control over those who don't have it. Consider how you might fare in a foreign country with no understanding of the language – all your learning and skills would count for nothing. The lesson this teaches us is that we must use language selectively and wisely. As a general rule, in exactly the same way as we use language to support signing, less is most definitely more.

Let's take the example of Edward going out to play. Edward is five years old, is cognitively functioning on the cusp of PMLD and SLD, is ambulant and has been given a small red ball as an object cue for the playground. Here the member of staff could easily have drowned Edward out by constant, though no doubt well-meaning, verbal descriptions:

> 'OK Edward here's the shiny, hard, red ball. We're going outside now because it's time to play. Come on, up you get, swing your legs around that's it. Oh, don't drop the ball you butterfingers! Let's help you to pick it up again, and off we go into the playground, through this door . . .'

Instead he says:

> 'Edward, we're going outside. Outside Edward. We're going outside. Outside.'

The important words are 'Edward' and 'outside' with the latter being supported by the object cue and all other words are unnecessary obfuscations. It is essential good practice for all teaching teams to conduct regular *language audits* for all sessions throughout the day. Are we using language wisely; does it have to be said; what are the key words? When using language with those with PMLD, we might need to constantly ask ourselves the three questions: Why am I saying this? What do I hope to achieve? Am I making a difference?

Musical interaction

An interesting variation of Intensive Interaction has also developed through the work of Wendy Prevezer (2000) and especially Margaret Corke (2002, 2011) in the form of Musical Interaction. This is strongly based on the principles of Intensive Interaction and music therapy with its exponents arguing that it allows and encourages valid musical experiences; allows and encourages personal interactions; is a motivational communicative tool; is suitable for all learners (PMLD, SLD or ASC) who are at the earlier stages of communicative development; and does not require musical ability on the part of the teacher.

Musical Interaction does require:

- **interactors** – through face, body language and voice;
- **social interaction games** – such as burst–pause; anticipation games; rough and tumble; give and take; physical activities (clapping, tickling, rocking, rowing, peek-a-boo, hide and seek, throwing things backward and forward);
- **music** – although not necessarily what we might consider to be conventional music with recognisable tunes; anything that makes sounds, including voices, is sufficient.
- **structure to the lesson** – all round in a circle; a musical introduction; an (age appropriate) hello song; time for small group and peer interactions; time for one-to-one interactions; an (age appropriate) goodbye song.

Corke (2002, 2011) argues convincingly that a voluntary, active input from the learner is absolutely essential for growth and learning to take place. She argues for a move away from the traditional music sessions where only conventional tunes are played (and where music is sometimes done to children rather than with them) and a move towards sessions where we use music to teach interactive and communicative skills. Musical Interaction then becomes a means of allowing and encouraging valid musical experiences, a means of allowing and encouraging personal interactions, and a motivational communicative tool.

The use of high-tech communication aids

One of the weaknesses of Intensive Interaction might be perceived to be the fact that such interactions are largely in the control of supporting adults. That is, unless we can teach someone with PMLD to begin a conversation, communication or interaction, they will always be dependent on the whim, mood or time available to supporting adults. One of the ways of doing this might be through the use of high-tech communication aids such as micro-switches, which the pupil with PMLD can press to gain attention, perhaps with the message 'Come and talk to me please' recorded onto a BigMack. To be successful at this, of course, the pupil would have to have an understanding of cause and effect, or more specifically, she would have to be contingently aware (see Chapter 4 for an expanded discussion on this).

If those with PMLD are not in control of the ability to initiate interactions, we may never get to the stage of moving pupils on to declarative communications and there is a strong case (Camaioni, 1993) for arguing that broad communication targets need to involve declarative, rather then merely the imperative communications before such communications can truly be considered to be intentional.[1] Ware (2011) points out that shared attention is a critical step in the development of intentional communication and notes that research with typically developing children suggests that children begin to communicate intentionally in order to share information by around ten months of age. This is interesting because *Routes for Learning* (WAG, 2006) places the deliberate gaining of attention of another person to satisfy a need and engaging in shared attention as quite late milestones for someone with PMLD; they are nonetheless legitimate long-term (holistic) targets for all learners with profound intellectual difficulties.

The use of micro switches to act as communication aids and gain attention has long been established (Shweigert, 1989; Schweigert and Rowland 1992; Lancioni *et al.*, 2006; Lancioni *et al.*, 2009) but there may be a tendency (especially as switch use is so open to the setting and achieving of short-term SMART targets) for us to regard cause and effect as an end in itself. In an excellent article on the use of technology with those with PMLD, Sally Millar asks a very pertinent question:

> What are we actually trying to achieve beyond the 'magic' gateway of cause and effect? Surely it is the child's acquisition of intentionality, both in communication and in cognition. Communication intentionality develops through interactive social routines and joint shared attention. Technology use should therefore be part of a programme aiming to increase participation and interaction, not to replace these. Cognitive intentionality develops gradually through the experience of exploring and learning to control the immediate environment.
>
> (Millar, 2009, p. 15)

Once again, Millar points to the absolute imperative of working with those with PMLD through an holistic process with learning taking place over time. Isolating and compartmentalising learning does not sit well with this group of learners.

Once we've taught the pupil that an adult *will* come to her *immediately* upon her pressing a switch, we then need to teach her that communication is actually a two-way process (Bunning, 2009) and it may be neither possible nor convenient to have a conversation at that point in time, although perhaps we could do this later. This then brings in a whole new range of potential cognitive and communicative learning – when exactly is later, for example?

Generally speaking, and we do recognise that this is a broad generalisation, the use of high-tech communication aids involving computer technology, VOCAs and switches, needs to be treated with some caution and we would advise keeping it simple (Millar, 2009). Information technology is moving at such a fast pace that we need to be careful we're not spending years teaching isolated skills where a learner presses one switch in one setting for one stimulus. We need to be clear why we're doing what we're doing. Having said that, the communicative potential of such devices as iPads® and tablets for those with PMLD is undoubtedly enormous and those interested would be well advised to keep a constant check on developments through such user groups as the SLD Forum. Membership of this forum is open to anyone engaged in all and any things related to the education of those with SLD and PMLD and is a source of constant information. Type 'SLD Forum' into a search engine for interactive access.

The use of cues

Underpinning the delivery of all communicative activities throughout the day will be the extensive use of cues. These essentially fall into the category of Alternative and Augmentative Communication (AAC) and will include touch cues, sound cues, object cues, signing, symbol use and photographic cues.

Object cues come from Objects of Reference (OoR) which were originally pioneered by the RNIB for use for with very young visually impaired pupils as a precursor to Braille (Ockelford, 2002). Ockelford argues that OoRs themselves need to be personalised to suit the motivation and interests of the user in much the same way that we might personalise a symbols book, and there is a great deal of sense to this. As a first step towards symbolic understanding it may well be that objects will be easier to relate to language than line drawings or photographs, but it is also likely that the cognitive abilities necessary to make such a symbolic breakthrough will be beyond the majority of those with PMLD. *Routes for Learning* (WAG, 2006) notes the skill of being able to express a preference for items not present via symbolic means as being number forty-one out of forty-three on their list of milestones.

Jones *et al.* (2002), recognising the practical, day-to-day difficulties involved in individualising objects of reference, recommend a generic, standard set of objects, not least because it represents a first step on the ladder of an individualised communication system and their use both instructs and motivates staff. Therefore, it is more likely that everyday use of objects of reference as communicative tools will, for the vast majority of learners with PMLD, come within a generic set of object cues (rather than OoR that are personalised) that can be used in two very useful ways:

a) As an introduction to *every* discrete teaching session on the timetable, *before* the session starts, where for example, a wooden spoon might indicate a cookery session, a chlorine-smelling towel might signify hydrotherapy. This directly assists PMLD learners to make sense of a world where everyone but themselves is in control. There is after all *no* guarantee that PMLD learners can understand what we are saying. We make assumptions that they do – but who is to know for certain? Object cues are therefore acting like a timetable (or at least a now and next timetable) where, indeed, the object cue supports the word.

b) As an introduction to set routine times of every day – toileting, drinks, playtime, lunch, etc. These object cues might be held in large bags attached to wheelchairs or be in a fixed and very accessible position of the classroom for ambulant users. The ultimate aim for these object cues is that learners will offer them to staff independently as an indication that they would like a drink *now*, or the toilet *now*; in other words, display intentionality. This is perhaps a long shot for most developmentally early learners, but if we don't give them the option, we won't get the result. Object cues are designed to be concrete representations of abstracts (words) and therefore should represent as near as possible the actual event. For some things (such as lunch or drinks) this is relatively easy, but for others (such as Interaction) this is going to be very difficult, and to some degree we are going to have to go with an abstract concept. Schools need to be sure they are talking to as many relevant carers and professionals as possible to get continuity throughout the learners' lives, and be especially mindful of transitions.

Touch cues are very simple additional physical cues to the PMLD learner that again might help them to make sense of their world. It is very difficult to overemphasise the *total* lack of control that the developmentally early learner has over her life, and we therefore have an obligation to give any additional help we can give. Jean Ware (2003) makes for interesting reading in this respect. At the simplest level, touch cues are physical assists to understanding, so that a couple of taps on the back of the leg to an ambulant PMLD learner indicates that you are asking them to sit down, or brushing both arms in a downward motion simultaneously is an indication (as a physical mirroring of the *finished* sign) that the session/activity has ended. But this concept can easily be extended into all areas of the school day, from a tap on the right shoulder to indicate that you are turning a wheelchair to the right, to inventing a touch cue to support the object cues that are already in place.

Sound cues are usually pieces of music but logically could be any sound that can be played to indicate the start and/or end of a particular event or activity. For example, we might play 'Perfect Day' (Lou Reed) as learners come into the classroom from the bus; *Scheherazade* (Rimsky-Korsakov) to indicate the start of a storytelling session; 'Must I Paint You a Picture?' (Billy Bragg) at the start of the art sessions, etc. The piece played is not important, as long as the same piece is played every time for a short time (say thirty seconds). It is really important that we don't continue to play music beyond this introductory time, because it may then become intrusive, especially to learners who have difficulty in integrating their senses, and rather than aiding learning will become obstructive to learning.

Smell cues operate on the same principle as sound cues, but of course they linger for much longer and therefore need to be used with care. A smell for the day might however be a useful additional cue – it's fish and chips so it must be Friday.

Symbol cues. It is probable that the majority of those with PMLD will be cognitively unable to recognise symbols, but it may well be pertinent for the more able, that is those who might be considered to be on the cusp of SLD. They are probably best used as aids to developing choice making by, for example, laminating on to switches to indicate which switch operates the somersaulting pig and which operates the CD player.

Signed cues. Again it is not clear if the majority of those with PMLD will understand signing, but it remains inherently good practice to sign as much as we can to everyone in the school, whether they need it to communicate or not. All teachers should take responsibility for signing so learners can pick it up if they want to and are able to.

Assumptions

One of the most intriguing elements of teaching and working with children, young people and adults with PMLD is that one is never entirely sure that what one has been trying to teach has actually been understood, since so much is down to interpretation. Porter *et al.* (2001) make the very valid point that in interpreting a particular action, inaction, vocalisation or silence as both meaningful and having a specific meaning, we do so when one of the communication partners (the person with PMLD) is not in a position to correct misunderstandings. Such misunderstandings can therefore go on indefinitely and indeed be extended through being passed on from one staff member and one report to every staff member and every report. They recommend validating communications and information with those who are most significant in the life of the person with PMLD, that is, those who know them the very best. Hogg *et al.* (2001) also point out that assumptions carry some weight in the estimation of the positive or negative responses offered by service users with profound intellectual and multiple disabilities. That is, a particular response was seen as more positive (by staff) when it was contextualised as a stimulus, which the client was assumed to like. This is understandable, as long as we're *absolutely* sure that the client really did like the stimulus.

The degree of certainty is taken up by Grove *et al.* (1999) who point out that in a social and political climate that encourages active participation in decision making by people with learning difficulties, the onus is often on practitioners, carers and advocates to represent the wishes and interests of individuals. The issue of the validity of their interpretations is then foregrounded. Grove *et al.* (1999) argue that

> meaning should be viewed as the negotiated outcome of interactions, always involving inference. Validity of interpretation is thus a continuous rather than a categorical variable, and needs to be supported by the systematic collection of evidence from a range of sources.
>
> (p. 190)

Such evidence should allow for information derived from subjective, intuitive insights to be combined with information obtained through observation and testing, but it is really important we remember that we are often only guessing. It may be a very good guess based on all the evidence we can muster from all the sources available, but it may still only be a guess. Teaching those with PMLD is the only area of teaching where the best answer we can give to the question 'Has the pupil learned this?' is 'I think so.'[2] We get carried away by certainty at our peril!

Literacy and the PMLD learner

It is difficult to overestimate the importance of the writings of Nicola Grove and Keith Park – both together and independently – on both the theory and practice of the teaching of literacy to those with learning difficulties. Anyone with the slightest interest in working in the fields of drama, storytelling, poetry and/or literature with learners with PMLD (and other LDs for that matter) is strongly urged to go directly to their work for both theoretical and practical advice. *Odyssey Now*, the story of Odysseus 'translated' for the direct participation and active involvement of those with any (or no) learning difficulties of any age and first published in 1996, remains one of the classic works of learning difficulties literature and inclusion, and there are many others published by the pair since then.

More than any other writers, they have brought to life the idea that those with PMLD, with all of the attendant problems and difficulties associated with cognition and communication noted above, can not only experience and enjoy language that they may not initially (or indeed ever) directly 'understand' in the sense we understand language, but can also gain meaning and fulfilment from its richness. They are insistent that 'the best literature has a power that goes beyond words . . . literature is too important to restrict to those who can read' (Grove, 2005).

Park (2010) posits that the principles of interactive storytelling recognises the 'music of words' and that 'apprehension precedes comprehension'. He argues that we should 'see it feelingly' and 'read with the ear' so we, and those we are working with, engage directly with the 'affect' (emotion) of the words, which can be directly translated through the affect of the teacher's voice and manner. He quotes extensively from works of great literature such as Samuel Taylor Coleridge's *Kubla Khan* and James Joyce's *Finnegan's Wake*, and notes that even though their meaning is opaque, the pattern, rhythm, affect and emotion strikes at a deep and central part of our humanity.

Park encourages us to read out loud a verse of Coleridge's *Kubla Khan* and challenges us not to be moved by its beauty and power, even though the verse's exact meaning may escape us:

> I would build that dome in air,
> That sunny dome! Those caves of ice!
> And all who heard should see them there,
> And all who cry, beware! Beware!
> His flashing eyes, his floating hair!
> Weave a circle round him thrice
> And close your eyes with holy dread
> For he on honeydew hath fed
> And drunk the milk of paradise.

Again, in Nicola Grove's words, 'Narrative and poetry are fundamental to our emotional and cognitive functioning, providing the means by which we make sense of our experiences and relate to those of others' (Grove, 2005).

Park (2010) notes that it is not sufficient for the teacher to merely read out the words, but it is essential learners are as fully involved as they can be both in and within the experience. To this end he has resurrected the ancient art of call and response and applied its principles to the teaching of literature to those with learning difficulties and disabilities. By mastering the basic rules of this simple yet extremely effective technique, we can deliver everything from one-word poetry to complex speeches from Shakespeare and all that's in between. Learners are directly involved through being an essential part of the rhythm and beat of the words and lines repeated back by their supporting staff; they may use communication aids such as a BigMack for example to call or respond to specific words or lines; staff may assist rhythmic movements through encouraging and supporting rocking, stamping, clapping, banging, vocalising, using VOCAs, laying learners on sound boards and enjoying, in any way they can, the process of being part of the rhythm of the group; feelings and emotions can be acted out by staff through facial expression and body responses directly to the learners involved.

Nicola Grove and Keith Park's work is discussed in further detail in Chapter 10 ('A Language, Literacy and Communication Curriculum for SLD').

Sensory stories

The use of sensory stories for those with PMLD is a long-established method of delivering literacy, and sensory stories are excellent vehicles for delivering whole school or class thematic topics in an interesting, exciting and wholly developmentally sympathetic manner.

There are (almost literally) countless numbers of stories that can be adapted and they don't just have to be confined to the standards like *Handa's Surprise* and *The Bear Hunt*. These are both brilliant stories for delivering in a sensory story mode, and it is the elements of these (their laying down of one basic scene varied and repeated through several episodes, which builds to a climax) that can be remodelled for other stories. It is perfectly possible for them to be delivered to older students, but they are essentially for younger learners and we need to recognise this. Nonetheless, the elements of the stories that make them such a success can, with a few additions, be condensed into the 'ten essentials' noted in Chapter 9 ('A Sensory Curriculum for PMLD').

Once devised, the same story should be repeated weekly for *at least* half a term (and probably longer) so learners have a real opportunity to become familiar with it and so practise their sequencing, turn taking, anticipatory and memory skills – all essential base elements of communication. There is no reason why secondary-aged students should not be involved in sensory stories. They don't need to be childish – you can make them as gory, disgusting and rude as you like! Pete Wells from Portland Academy in Sunderland has an excellent website at www.petewells.co.uk where you can download lots of free secondary PMLD PowerPoint® slides. There is no reason why you couldn't adapt these for a non-Power-Point® presentation if you preferred to work in this way. It is advisable to permanently store new stories so you are not always re-inventing the wheel, and a major order of clear plastic lidded boxes that are clearly labelled, not interfered with and always returned to the appropriate storage space is strongly urged!

Notes

1 Declarative communications (Bates *et al.*, 1975) are communications for the sake of themselves, as in for example 'Isn't it a lovely day'. They are not meant to gain anything from the recipient other than joint attention and acting as a point of contact, but are essentially social communications, expressed for the sake of communicating. Imperative communications are primarily based on meeting specific or general needs and wants and when used by those with PMLD may be considered to be mainly pre-intentional (Goldbart, 1994).

2 This 'fact' is also likely in the teaching of many with SLD. It is one of the principal reasons for adopting a group differences position for both PMLD and SLD in the separate pedagogy debate.

Chapter 7

A physical curriculum for pupils and students with profound and multiple learning difficulties

It is fairly evident that motor and/or perceptual disabilities can severely limit the possibilities for communication (Bullowa, 1979; Coupe O'Kane and Goldbart, 1998). It only takes a short reflection on the relationship of physical dexterity to conventional child development in terms of the ability to reach, grasp, maintain a hold, manipulate, explore, turn towards, turn away from, move towards, move away from, etc., to ascertain that detailed models of very early child development (Uzgiris and Hunt, 1975; Dunst, 1980) will probably not strictly apply to those with physical (and intellectual) impairments.

Aitken *et al.* (2000) take the point even further and suggest that the whole learning process is endangered by physical disabilities:

> [Since the 1980s] a wealth of evidence has accrued to show the positive effects which come when children, even young infants, have a chance to gain control over their environment, and how that control is severely impaired in the non-ambulant child.
>
> Even though they have fewer chances to decide and control their experiences, non-ambulant children can still learn by them. However, those experiences are much more likely to be of frustration and failure. At this point, a second difficulty arises, because experiences gained in one setting can carry over to other settings. Expectation of failure learned in one setting make the learning of new activities much more difficult. The person who is non-ambulant may be 'turned off' the learning of new tasks and activities. Rather than learning that they can be successful they have learned that there is little point even in trying.'
>
> (Aitken *et al.*, 2000, pp. 30–31)

Clearly, the physical well-being of the pupil with PMLD is of paramount importance and, depending on the needs of the individual, may take up a considerable percentage of curriculum time; a point we will return to later. Goldsmith and Goldsmith (1998) posit that the main aims of encouraging movement in those who have physical difficulties should be

- to increase independence
- to protect body shape and
- to improve general health and morale.

They go on to suggest that within this framework it is imperative we ask a number of key questions on behalf of those who probably cannot effectively voice their own views on the subject. Physical 'management', rather like 'care', constitutes a part of the curriculum that can be done *to* the individual, whether the individual likes it or not. Complaints from the individual can be met with arguments around 'no pain, no gain' and what is in the 'best interests' of the pupil, but as Aitken *et al.* have pointed out above, it is imperative that this is done sympathetically. The questions Goldsmith and Goldsmith propose are as relevant today as they were in 1998; namely, is the individual

- well enough?
- rested enough?
- willing enough?
- comfortable enough?
- old enough?
- young enough?

And is the activity

- easy enough?
- and promoting a normal, symmetrical body shape?

It is not a matter of whether the individual is well, comfortable or willing, but are they well *enough*, comfortable *enough*, willing *enough*? This simple additional condition carries a welter of meaning. Goldsmith and Goldsmith also ask whether the individual is 'old enough' or 'young enough' – a highly pertinent point since it seems likely that few major gross motor physical improvements are likely to take place beyond the age of seven or eight for those with mild cerebral palsy (CP), and often much younger (perhaps aged three) for those with the severest forms of CP.

In a significant longitudinal study involving 657 children between the ages of one and thirteen, representing the full spectrum of clinical severity of motor impairment in children with cerebral palsy, Rosenbaum *et al.* (2002) demonstrated that: (i) the estimated limit of development decreased as severity of impairment increased; and (ii) there is a tendency for children with lower motor development potential to reach their limit more quickly, and for those with the most severe forms of CP this may well be as young as three.

They were, however, insistent that this study should not be interpreted as a reason for abandoning physiotherapy or other physical programmes:

> It is extremely important that parents, physicians, therapists, program managers, third-party payers, and other decision makers do not assume further therapy is unhelpful or unnecessary when the curves [demonstrating upward linear progress] appear to level off. Continuing efforts should be made to address ways both to increase independent activity and to promote participation of children with disabilities, as well as to address secondary impairments that may arise. It should also be remembered that the children in the present study were receiving a range of contemporary developmental therapy services that we believe are representative of the therapies provided in the Western world. It is likely that as new therapies emerge, patterns of motor development in children diagnosed as having cerebral palsy may change and modifications to these models will be needed.
>
> (Rosenbaum *et al.*, 2002, p. 1362)

Therapy may well be needed to try to maintain the levels of movement the child has to attempt to ward off the inevitable deterioration as the child with CP gets older. The need is, therefore, to strike a balance between what the child needs from a purely therapeutic/ medical perspective, what the child is able to tolerate at any particular time and the promotion of independent activity and physical participation. The key to bringing these together lies in ensuring both engagement and motivation (Carpenter *et al.*, 2010). As Michael Mednick puts it, for those with PMLD their,

> disability often renders them helpless, without the opportunity to make real choices about what affects them. We need to give them back as much control as possible, even though most tasks require adult intervention and support. In this way they will start to believe in themselves.
>
> (Mednick, 2002, p. 1)

In support of this, Ware (2003) notes the importance of fully involving the pupil in physical activities such as physiotherapy within an interactive and engaging framework and suggests keeping oneself in a position where we are able to observe any responses with consistent pausing to encourage such responses. This line comes back to the *Routes for Learning* (WAG, 2006) assertion that effective learning should be holistic in nature – learning must be grounded in relevant and meaningful everyday experiences and activities.

Measuring motor function outcomes, Bower *et al.* (2001) argue that however much therapy helps to maximise motor abilities, these are not likely to be maintained in the long term if they are not used in daily activity, and this very much lends weight to the general premise noted by Scrutton (1984) that clinical experience points to the conclusion that the effective parts of treatment are those which become part of the child's life.

Ensuring physical education is an everyday part of the child's life

Aird (2001) suggests that the Physical Curriculum (in his terms, the management of mobility) might cover the development of:

- eye/hand coordination and fine motor control
- posture
- spatial awareness
- orientation and movement.

Dividing the curriculum into these sorts of areas can be a useful tool for ensuring we are covering all the bases. But Aird is also insistent that practising (for example) eye/hand coordination in isolation may not be an entirely effective way of working. These need to be worked on through other activities that are motivating to the individual. There is no point in expecting someone with PMLD to pick up a pen and start drawing because they will not be at that intellectual level and, even if they were, might not be motivated by the activity. Nor is it either sufficient or acceptable to offer hand-over-hand support, since this is merely doing the activity for them and encouraging learned helplessness. They may, however, want to explore art materials such as paint, clay, fabrics, leaves, plastics, etc., on the basis that any material can be an art material. It is not the production of an artistic work that is important here, but the grasp, manipulation, feel, taste, visual image through the motivation to do some or all of these activities. It is the exploration and the physical practice that's important and the skill of the teacher lies in their ability to make that exploration exciting to the individual. The same might apply to a number of other activities such as cooking.

Other opportunities to practise fine motor movements will come through switch work and through the manipulation of any materials and objects that are motivating to the pupil, whatever they are. Karen Bunning has done some very interesting work here through an intervention, termed 'Individualised Sensory Environment' (ISE). Although this was initially developed for use with adults with profound and multiple learning disabilities (Bunning, 1996), the principles equally apply whatever the age. The aim was to reduce the level of non-purposeful engagement, characterised by stereotypic actions, self-injury and neutral behaviour, and to increase the levels of purposeful interaction with people and objects. The results showed that the clients (adults with PMLD) emitted high levels of non-purposeful behaviour at baseline, but an increase in purposeful interactions and a reduction of non-purposeful engagement after ISE intervention[1] (Bunning, 1998).

Physiotherapy

Use of regular and routine physiotherapy and hydrotherapy is always a good starting point for the Physical Curriculum. There is probably not a school in the whole of the UK that believes they have sufficient physiotherapists – therefore, working with those you have in a team approach is absolutely essential. It is likely that a number of physiotherapy teams will use the Bobath approach. Named after wife and husband team Bertha and Karel Bobath, the therapy explores ways of encouraging more natural movement patterns that can be integrated into everyday life. It is not a rigid regime of exercises and is very much dependent on (i) the strengths and needs of the individual pupil and (ii) skills and expertise of the therapist. The Bobath concept insists on a trans-disciplinary approach involving occupational therapy, physiotherapy, speech and language therapy, teachers and parents, and is therefore ideal for both school and home settings. Goals need to be realistic according to the client's potential and appropriate to the environment encountered during daily life (Mayston, 2000). It is unfortunate that there do not appear to be any empirical studies demonstrating the efficacy of the Bobath methodology over conventional methods, and certainly a number of non-Bobath-trained physiotherapists would claim that the principles applied are merely good practice.

If you are interested in a goal-directed approach within physical movement you may wish to make reference to *The Profound Education Curriculum*, published by St Margaret's School (2009).

Positioning

As a general rule it is always good to organise regular positional changes throughout the day for all and any pupils with gross motor disabilities, and you will need to work with your physios to ensure that body postures remain symetric. Try sitting in a chair for twenty minutes without making any gross motor movements – keeping your trunk and legs still – then imagine having to sit in the same position for several hours at a time! The overall and obvious benefits of physical activity do not cease to apply simply because one has gross motor difficulties. Studies have demonstrated improved sleep patterns and consequently improved alertness in school time when children were physically active for many parts of the school day (Low, 2004), and weight bearing activity three times a week for twenty minutes over eight months improved bone mineral density in children with spastic cerebral palsy (Chad *et al.*, 1999). There are also bound to be associated benefits in helping to keep children's airways clear and preventing chest infections through them assuming a more vertical posture.

All of this brings in, once again, the hugely problematic issue of time, because it does take time to make these positional changes, and the older and heavier the child, the more time it takes. However, we must not under any circumstances make a shortage of time an excuse for not doing this. These issues – problematic for both teachers and managers – are discussed more fully within Chapter 8, 'A Care Curriculum'. It makes sense to make these 'exercise times' fun occasions by perhaps singing an 'exercise song', call and responding to an 'exercise poem' – you could turn this into an age-appropriate activity for older students by using a version of American GI's marching songs (Park, 2010) – or using it as an opportunity for a more informal Intensive Interaction session.

Besides stretching and moving positions, using standing frames needs to be considered and, as these can sometimes be quite traumatic occasions, it is especially important to make it as much fun as possible. There are bound to be some pupils for whom a standing frame is seen to be something of an instrument of torture, and again it is imperative that we are sympathetic to the potential considerable discomfort being experienced.

Massage

Massage can be an extremely useful activity to blend in with stretches and positional changes, as long as this is not seen as a 'throw-away' activity. Besides being an excellent way of loosening muscles and easing stiffness, massage can be used as a means of teaching whole body understanding and proprioception (Bluestone, 2002) and is an excellent medium for teaching – Flo Longhorn for example, gives a detailed example of teaching maths through massage (Longhorn, 2000).

Movement

Movement to music sessions are an excellent way of building muscle memory and improving both gross and fine motor control. At its simplest this might take the form of an aerobics session where a particular piece of music – 'Bonkers' by Dizzee Rascal for example – indicates a particular movement, say rocking back and forth or swinging arms from side to side. At first this movement would need to be very heavily physically supported by an adult and indeed there may be an element of considerable resistance, to which the adult would need to be sympathetic. Over time, however, we would be looking for a deeper understanding of what might be required, less resistance, moving towards passive co-operation, to active co-operation, to independent movement. This area relies heavily on the work carried out by Chris Knill in the 1980s and 1990s (Knill, 1992) and although his work is currently out of print a variation of the idea is supported by 'Holistic Music for Children'. This latter programme covers the four areas of body awareness, moving sounds, discovery, and singing and learning. Further details of this approach are available at www.holisticmusicforchildren. co.uk.

Drama and dance

Aitken *et al.* (2000) note the efficacy of drama and play activities through the use of rhymes, rhythms and songs as an excellent way of promoting gross body movements, but the whole issue of dance and PMLD is one that is notable for its lack of research and published practice (Lamond, 2010). Again, there is a tendency to think of dance and PMLD as the practice of pushing wheelchairs to music, and while this may well have some beneficial effects if done sympathetically, it is another example of things being done to the person, rather than with the person. The work of Veronica Sherborne is relevant here (Sherborne, 1990) but will need some adapting to accommodate PMLD students (especially those who are older) and while Sara Bannerman-Haig's work in a special school with both SLD and PMLD pupils primarily reflects on dance and movement as central means of delivering psychotherapy, it nonetheless gives some interesting ideas on the possibilities open to both teachers and physical therapists (Bannerman-Haig, 1997; Bannerman-Haig, 2006).

Mobility

The distinct possibility that early ambulance in children with gross motor difficulties will not be maintained in later life (Bottos *et al.*, 2001) makes maximising children's mobility potential all the more pertinent. Much work has been done on the whole issue of movement, mobility and independence by MOVE (Mobility Opportunities Via Education), which can be accessed via www.disabilitypartnership.co.uk. By focusing on sitting, standing, walking and transferring, the trans-disciplinary MOVE team attempts to create repeated opportunities for the meaningful practice of functional skills as a part of daily life. Considerable emphasis is placed on providing opportunities for weight bearing, muscle and bone strengthening, fitness and overall participation.

Health and safety issues

As with all gross motor activities, you will need to look after yourself. Back problems are endemic in the education and care of those with PMLD. Although much lifting equipment is available, however sophisticated that equipment is, there are bound to be many manual handling situations on a daily basis. It would be wise to ensure that you look for some training in this area with regular updates if you are working with pupils with PMLD.

Note

1   ISE is discussed in considerably more detail in Chapter 9 on 'The Sensory Curriculum'.

Chapter 8

A care curriculum for pupils and students with profound and multiple learning difficulties

> While medical conditions do not necessarily imply SEN, medical conditions have to be managed for effective education to take place.
>
> (Farrell, 2006, p. 82)

A question to be thinking about

What is most important – teaching the pupil to say 'yes', or teaching the pupil to say 'no'? What are the hazards in teaching both?

Care as an educational concept

It may seem strange to include the issue of care as an essential feature of a curriculum document, since for many years before (and indeed immediately after) the advent of the National Curriculum in the UK in 1988, those with PMLD were often taught in 'Special Care' classes that critics argued both marked them out from the education that was going on elsewhere and downgraded the concept of a separate PMLD curriculum (Byers and Rose, 1994). Since then the issue of care within the educational process seems to have been largely ignored. Unfortunately, if we continue to treat care as a necessary but largely time-wasting educational by-product, something to be got over with as quickly as possible so we can get back to the important issue of education, we will never be able to develop a pedagogical case for care *within* the curriculum rather than an addendum to it. It is the authors' strong belief that for those with PMLD, care is far too important to be relegated to a side issue.

It is an undeniable fact that many with profound learning difficulties will require a great deal of care throughout their lives. The 'M' in PMLD (Evans and Ware, 1987) refers directly to the considerable liklihood of multiple disabilities attending the intellectual impairment implied by the word 'profound' (Kiernan and Kiernan, 1994) and the nature of the care needed will directly affect both learning and teaching style (Goldsmith and Goldsmith, 1998; Miller, 1998; Aird, 2001; Farrell, 2005).

In 1990 only twenty per cent of babies born weighing less than 2lbs would have survived. The figure for 2011 is eighty per cent. We are now able to save babies at twenty-three weeks gestation (2nd Trimester) – Marlow *et al.* (2005). But there is approximately fifty per cent chance of some degree of disability. And the baby might be in intensive care for several months. Nonetheless, improvements in neonatal and paediatric care have undoubtedly led to an increasing number of children with PMLD surviving into adulthood (Barr, 2009) with the number of children in the UK living with complex health needs increasing (DoH, 2004). This means that we are now seeing a generation of children and young people with complex health needs, who may require high levels of support and whose conditions may be life threatening and/or life limiting (Barr, 2009). Zijlstra and Vlaskamp (2005) found, in a Dutch study of forty-eight children with PMLD, that eighty-five per cent had epilepsy, eighty-one per cent had visual impairments, thirty-one per cent had auditory impairments, sixty-seven per cent had gastrointestinal problems and thirty-eight per cent had pulmonary problems.

Such studies point to the fact that multiple disabilities will not just be confined to the visible such as paraplegia, quadriplegia and asymmetric body postures, since there is an equal likelihood of 'internal' difficulties such as scoliosis, aspiration, hip and arm joints loosening over time for those who are not weight bearing and/or have limited use of limbs, problems with internal organs, especially the liver, kidneys and heart. Those with cerebral palsy are likely to experience extremes of spasticity (hypertonia), while at the opposite end of the scale Rett Syndrome girls are more likely to experience severe hypotonia. Those with PMLD will have a considerably increased chance of experiencing epileptic episodes (Ayers, 2006), with Johnson and Parkinson (2002) noting that epilepsy is a symptom of an underlying problem in a person's brain that can effect learning.

On a more basic level, the physical function of the intestines and lungs is designed to work best when people are ambulant and upright for a reasonable percentage of the day so the natural forces of gravity can play their part. Those who are not – those for example who spend most of their waking lives in wheelchairs – will be prone to constipation and chest infections, and anyone who has ever experienced the effects of these will attest to their debilitating consequences.

Goldbart and Caton (2010) point out that a person's health, their sensory skills, and sensory difficulties, will critically affect their communication and their ability to communicate effectively. As such, these will need regular assessment and monitoring, and it is not sufficient to do this occasionally. Regular formal sensory assessments should be part of the education process for all those with PMLD (as well as those with an ASC diagnosis) besides of course the ongoing checks that will apply in every classroom. Indeed, the general issue of wellness brings to the fore the essential teaching truth famously propounded by Maslow (1954) in his 'Hierarchy of Needs', that learning is only likely to take place when the basic care conditions have been put in place (see Figure 8.1 below).

It is therefore absolutely essential that supporting adults, whether in school or out, actually do take care of such issues as pain, illness, hunger, thirst, cold, heat, discomfort, cramp, stress, uncertainty, confusion, anxiety, fear, tiredness, periods, epilepsy, diet and any other imponderables that might also be included.

The absolute imperative of collaborative working comes strongly to the fore here and Spargo and Northway (2011) put an exceedingly strong case for the primacy of the role of the school nurse. We would go further to suggest that the school nurse needs to be considered as part of the whole educational team around the child since they have an important role in developing a care understanding and how this is likely to affect learning. In addition, this could also include their potential to act as an important bridge between school, home and health services and between school and adult services during transition periods (Spargo and Northway, 2011).

Particular attention has to be given to knowing and listening to those with PMLD. Orr (2003) writes eloquently from the personal perspective of a person with complex needs and their basic human right to being as secure as possible in their sense of who they are and where they are at any given time. This involves a considerable amount of 'listening' on the

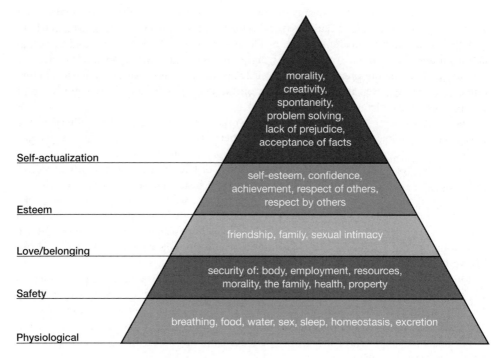

Figure 8.1 Hierarchy of need (Maslow, 1954)

part of supporting carers. Ware (2003) argues very strongly that it is not sufficient just to know the child, since there is a strong tendency in caregiver/child interactions for:

- the person with PMLD to be the passive partner;
- the caregiver to be the dominant partner;
- comparatively few responses to be received from their caregivers;
- clashes between the person with PMLD and the caregiver (i.e. where both are 'speaking' at once).

Listening as a part of enabling

Since those with PMLD were first formally involved in the education process in 1970, considerable time and effort has been expended on discussing pupil and student voice and involvement directly in the educational process. This has often involved ideas around student councils, as per the mainstream model, but this would clearly be entirely tokenistic if applied to those with PMLD. This does not mean, however, that we should not be listening to the voice of the student with PMLD and, equally importantly, acting upon that voice. Investing time in teaching those with PMLD to have a pro-active voice, be fully contingently aware in an interpersonal sense – my actions can have an effect upon you – and knowing the pupil as well as you can know him or her, is always time well spent, however much time that may actually take up. It must be remembered, however, that pupil and student voices should have the right to say no as well as yes – of which more below.

Carpenter (2010) warns of the increasing likelihood that the already recognised growth in the numbers of those born with a PMLD in the twenty-first century (Male and Rayner, 2009; Ofsted, 2010) will throw up as yet unknown care requirements, which will in turn undoubtedly directly impact upon learning styles. Curriculum models have tended to traditionally concentrate on MSI (multi-sensory impairment), particularly with reference to visual and hearing impairments, without too much reference to the multitude of other potential difficulties. Richard Aird, although warning against the primacy of care plans over learning in an educational setting (Aird, 2001) nonetheless recognises that care, and of course how that care is imparted, is an integral part of both the life and learning of someone with PMLD.

Considerable information on the nature of particular conditions and syndromes can be gained from the CaF Directory www.cafamily.org.uk and Wikipedia.

The centrality of routines

Also underpinning the delivery of the curriculum will be the extensive use of routines, a very much underrated and underutilised opportunity to teach and learn. The very act of going to the toilet (or more probably for someone with PMLD, going to the changing area) is a real opportunity to learn, provided *exactly the same routine* is used every single time by all members of staff. The same time(s) of the day, utilising the same changing areas, using the same language, the same object cues, the same verbal cues (of say *1, 2, 3, lift*) when changing pads, etc. Ensuring consistency in routines allows pupils to build upon previous learning experiences and have many hundreds – possibly many thousands – of opportunities to practise and learn over their lifetime in school. Other routine times that *must* be consistent if real learning is to derive from them will be arriving at and leaving school, lunchtimes, break times, assemblies, the start and end of the day, the start and end of lessons. Cues that might help with establishing these routines might include using music, smells, touch, objects, etc. Once the routine has been regularly established and constantly re-established there will be real opportunities for subtle interactive moments of sharing and being part of a collaborative process (Barber, 1994).

Taking control

It is likely that issues of PSHE (Personal Social and Health Education) will be addressed within the issue of care for those with a PMLD, although it is probably also true that this is less an issue of what is taught, but more an issue of how it is taught. It is worth quoting Chris Wilkinson at length when he argues that:

> principles [of curriculum development] should be based on a view of education which offers all pupils the chance of empowerment, esteem and autonomy as well as gratifying and pleasurable experiences. If people are empowered they can make decisions and, as a result have an impact on their culture, family and community. If they are esteemed and valued for what they are and not for what they might become, they will have status and their views will be taken into account at policy level. In this way they will not be considered to be second-rate citizens. If they have autonomy they will gain the skills, knowledge and understanding necessary to give them access to their culture, family and community. If they have gratifying and pleasurable experiences they are more likely

to remain intact at an emotional as well as a physical level. It is surely from these principles
that we offer an education that is meaningful and relevant.

(Wilkinson, 1994, p. 61)

Essentially Wilkinson is referring to issues of control, and for those with a PMLD it will be
necessary to teach how and when they might gain that control. This is especially and vitally
important for those who are, in the main, not in control of their own lives, but who by
necessity have others managing it (Barber, 1994; Wilkinson, 1994; Collis and Lacey, 1996;
Hewett and Nind, 1998; Orr, 2003; Imray, 2008). This will naturally involve a great deal
of sensitivity and reflection by teachers with the central question of 'Am I doing the right
thing?' always to the fore. Teaching those with a PMLD is particularly challenging simply
because it is so easy for the teacher to take control, to be didactic and to limit learning
rather than expand it.

Perhaps the easiest way to ensure we're not falling into that trap is to ask another question
'Have I taught my pupils how to say NO?' The ability to say 'no' and for that 'no' to be
acted upon is something that we all tend to take for granted. But can the same be said for
those with a PMLD? Again an extended quote, this time from Peter Imray discussing task
avoidance, highlights the point:

The bare facts of the matter are that even if those with severe or profound learning
difficulties are able to say 'No' they are almost *never* listened to when they do say 'No'.
As adults living in a relatively free society, we have the right to say 'No' and the reasonable
assumption that our 'No' will be listened to – if not, we have access to rational argument,
our freedom to take our physical selves and our labour elsewhere, and if the worst comes
to the worst, the law to uphold our claim.

As children living in a relatively free and child-friendly society, our children have the
right to say 'No' and the reasonable assumption that even if their wishes are not acted
upon, their case will be listened to, heard fairly and honestly by adults who are keen
to involve them in a decision making process, and if the worst comes to the worst,
there are at least others in the public purse – social workers, police, child welfare
organisations and of course, the law – who will listen to their arguments and rationalise
any decision.

Do SLD and PMLD adults and children have that same right? Unfortunately '*no!*'
Although the theory is that they do have that right, this is not borne out in practice,
because as professionals whose job it is to look after the disabled we generally judge
that they are not intellectually able to make such decisions. We therefore make those
decisions for them, and naturally we judge that it is right that six year old A will get
up at 7.00 each morning to get ready for school; ten year old B will not punch the
nearest person to him whenever he sits in assembly; teenager C will do Drama on a
Wednesday morning with the rest of her group; twenty-two year old D will have his
toenails cut.

And in many ways we are right to make such decisions, because by acceding to their
refusals we would be complicit in restricting experiences and learning opportunities.
We are after all teachers, parents, carers etc. and as such it is our duty to broaden
experience and teach about social conventions as much as possible. As such there is a
natural contradiction between our desire to be understanding and sympathetic to these
problems and our need to be practical. Life after all, goes on. It cannot wait for A to

wake up naturally – the bus for school will have left for the next pick-up. We all have to do many things we don't want to do – including drama and assemblies. There are painful consequences of failure to look after our personal care – including in-grown toenails. All of us, both with and without learning difficulties, have to cope with the less pleasant aspects of life and we're not going to help the individual by spoiling them and giving in to tantrums.

We are however, all individuals. The fact that the majority are able to accept the slings and arrows of outrageous fortune does not mean that everybody is able to. For some, the loss of self, the sense of powerlessness, the feeling of being totally out of control, is so strong that it takes over and sends them into a panic of violence. It would be like you being asked to eat a bucket of live cockroaches or drink a glass of vomit without the right to say no. What would you do?

(Imray, 2008, pp. 38–39)

This does of course go hand in hand with teaching contingency awareness, and the issue of control over the every day issues in life is a classic example of the holistic approach so strongly argued for in *Routes for Learning* (WAG, 2006). There are bound to be very many occasions when learners will not want to do things, touch things, taste things, be in certain places, and if we are to teach the ability to negate (to say 'no') it is *absolutely essential* that learners are listened to and that their 'no' is acted upon by the teacher (Rawlings *et al.*, 1995).

Making choices

Making choices is a complex issue for those with learning difficulties (Harris, 2006) and part of that understanding is that the choices made are sometimes inconvenient for those giving the choices. Unfortunately, we also might have to accept that this can have (sometimes extreme) deleterious effects upon the individual exercising their right to say no, for example, to healthy foods (Smyth and Bell, 2006). There is no doubt that such situations will test the educator to the full, especially when the issue of fully understanding consequences is so problematic. This does not, however, alter the basic premise of teaching negation, and having done this and ensured that the learner has understood the power of their own negation, we can then move on to one of the real arts of teaching, that of encouraging the pupil to experiment and explore the world around them to the full. This takes time, patience, knowledge of the pupil and a considerable degree of skill, but it can be done.

On teaching 'feeding'!

April Winstock made the point in the early 1990s that we really must get into the habit of calling the process 'supporting people's eating' (Winstock, 1994) as feeding is what we do to babies and animals rather than grown people. This is not just politically correct semantics, because if we're supporting their eating we're concentrating on making the process as independent as possible and with as many choices as possible. We are doing things *with* pupils and students rather than *to* them. Because eating is one of those things that we do without thinking (we might think about what we're eating but the process itself is fairly automatic) we tend to forget how complicated a process it can be. Orr (2003) offers some key tips:

- Make it easier by offering one texture at a time. Observe the eater closely so that opportunities to communicate are not missed.
- Name the foods being experienced.
- A refusal may be for a number of reasons. Offer it again another day.
- Allow time for the eater to indicate when she is ready for another mouthful. Watch the whole body for an indication – she may move her foot to say 'more please'.
- Try extending favourites. If peanut butter is a popular choice then vary it with cashew nut butter and other nutty or chocolate spreads and offer the jars as smells so that the person eating at least has the opportunity for indicating preferences.

(p. 54)

The centrality of touch

One area within the Care Curriculum not previously mentioned, but nonetheless absolutely essential to the whole process, is touch. Touch, as a process of education, is hardly referred to by academics in any literature relating to the education of those with PMLD[1], except perhaps by Flo Longhorn, in her advocation of massage (Longhorn, 1993). In what must be the seminal article entitled 'Do Touch', Dave Hewett lays down two essential arguments for the extensive use of touch (Hewett, 2007), first as a basis to learning communication routines through what Nind and Hewett (1994) refer to as the 'Fundamentals of Communication', and second as a warning that if we are not perceptive and thoughtful, we can put the pupils we are serving in a situation where the only physical interaction they get throughout the day is 'functional' or 'professional touch' (Brennan et al., 1998).

Hewett (2007) goes on to state that in practice this should mean members of staff will need to routinely touch students in order to:

- reinforce other communications such as when placing a hand on the shoulder while speaking;
- give physical support and guidance;
- give reassurance – communicate security and comfort;
- physically intervene and manage negative behaviours;
- play, interact;
- role model positive use of touch;
- respond non-verbally;
- direct or physically prompt;
- give personal care;
- give physical cues for participation or understanding;
- aid protection in hazardous situations;
- give therapy such as massage, physiotherapy;
- function as the main form of communication;
- respond to students' use of physical contact for communication and making social connections;
- reward and affirm;
- give them the opportunity of choice to lead the communication;
- communicate affection, warmth, a sense of mutuality, etc., and enable the student to learn understanding of these things and the ability to communicate them;

- deliberately and most sensitively teach some students who do not want or like touch, the enjoyment and benefit of physical contact;
- give graphic experience of the tempo of life and physical activity enjoyed by another person, such as when a member of staff communicates calm and stillness through physical contact.

General and eminently sensible 'safety' guidelines for touch are also covered within the article through looking to the following areas:

- Know why you do it. Be knowledgeable on the purposes of using physical contact by discussion, thought and by reading the pertinent psychological and developmental literature.
- Have consent from the person. Obey the usual conventions concerning making physical contact with another person. If you rarely get consent to touch, then go back a few stages and work toward obtaining willingly given consent. At the very least, physical contact may be necessary to carry out basic care.
- Be prepared to discuss and explain your practices. First and foremost by being knowledgeable, as above.
- Document – have it acknowledged in the school curriculum document or workplace brochure. The culture and working practices of the school or other workplace are acknowledged in the curriculum document or workplace brochure and this will include explanation of the use of physical contact and the purposes of it.
- Document – have it acknowledged in any individual programme for the person. Be assertive. If you are certain that use of physical contact is fulfilling the person's needs educationally or developmentally, then state this in the documentation drawn up to support work with that person.
- Have good teamwork, both organisational and emotional. Teamworking practices should literally facilitate staff working together in teams so that staff or students are rarely alone. The teamworking ethos should also include good discussions among staff concerning the emotional aspects of the work, including crucially, orientations toward the issue of use of physical contact.
- Use of physical contact should be discussed openly and regularly. There should be no sense of furtiveness or 'hidden curriculum'. This important aspect of teaching technique should tangibly be a matter of open discussion and study.
- Have others present where possible. The most basic safeguard for staff and students is to have other staff present in the room when in situations where physical contact is likely to be taking place. At the very least, ensure that all standard classroom and work area doors have clear glass panels built in and do not have internal locks on doors where changing/toileting is going to take place.

Quality of Life (QOL)

Gordon Lyons and Michael Cassebohm have posed a number of questions garnered from both an extended literature review on what QOL might mean for those with PMLD (in their terminology, PIMD) and a series of interviews over time with parents, carers and significant others (Lyons and Cassebohm, 2010). Through these questions, they have laid down a 'Grounded Theory' which reveals, they argue, potential implications for a diversity of policies, practices and research that relate to the lives of children with PIMD, and which might ultimately improve their life satisfaction and quality of life. First, the 'take home message' is that the life satisfaction of children with PIMD can be discerned. Second, the theory gives weight to widespread parental and carer claims that they generally know their children well enough to discern their life satisfaction – including their happiness, wants and preferences – despite a body of professional opinion claiming that this knowing is overstated. Third, it suggests that unfamiliar others, who often shy away from engaging with children with PIMD, can come to know them and can come to understand their inner states.

(p. 199)

However, this begs a number of other questions. What exactly is different about children with PMLD from other children? The writers suggest that those with PMLD have unique ways of expressing feelings, which are fundamentally different to conventionally NT children: 'There is now broad professional recognition of the diversity and validity of the idiosyncratic communicative behaviours used by persons with PIMD' (p. 192). They reference Arthur (1994) and Felce (1997) to support their claims.

This means one has to spend a long time in the company of those with PMLD in order to get to know them very well, far longer than children without PMLD, and this is undoubtedly true. But this is a continuum rather than a fundamental difference. It is, in other words, a difference of degree rather than a difference of approach. The strategies we use would be no different from the strategies that we use for getting to know unfamiliar babies; time, patience and love will be to the fore. If we therefore stated that (i) the life satisfaction of children can be discerned, (ii) parents and carers generally know their children well enough to discern their life satisfaction, and (iii) unfamiliar others can come to know them and can come to understand their inner states, would there be any gainsayers? Who exactly is arguing with them on these three points and where exactly is this body of professional opinion claiming that 'this knowing is overstated'? There are bound to be some saying that *not all* parents and carers know their children, but who would deny that 'generally' this is true. Whether they generally know *what is best* for their children is, however, another matter entirely, but again we would argue that this applies equally to all parents and carers and all children. With regard to education, they go on to say that,

> Children with PIMD, like all children, go to school to learn. Special education curriculum generally embraces a 'common' curriculum with a functional skills orientation. If a core goal of education is to empower individuals to pursue a better quality of life as a contributing citizen, is education for fun, not (just) education with fun, worth reconsidering?
>
> (p. 200)

This is worrying. Apart from the obvious rejoinder that 'isn't education for fun', not just education with fun, worth considering for everybody?, there is an underlying question about what exactly Lyons and Cassebohm are proposing. The word 'reconsidering' is interesting, and suggests that is has been thought of (or indeed enacted) at some time in the past, but has now been rejected. One can't reconsider something that has never been considered in the first place, which is why we couldn't 'reconsider' education for fun in the mainstream – it is after all far too important for that![2]

Education for fun is not strictly defined by the writers, although it is implied that it is having the freedom to do what they (the pupils with PMLD) find enjoyable at any particular time, based upon the advocacy of supporting adults who know the child intimately and can accurately interpret the individual child's expressions of feelings. Does this mean, however, that education for this group of learners should (uniquely) not challenge and not stretch? Does this mean that for this group of learners life should (again uniquely) be about just 'enjoying the craic'? Lyons and Cassebohm specifically mention a long list, primarily involving doing enjoyable things, being content and allowed to 'just take it all in', being happy, enjoying fun, playing with water, being free of physical pain, having communication partners who can respond to their wants, interests and preferences, having a feeling of 'belonging' within relationships, and living at home. All of these are excellent things to strive for as part of a rounded education, but to be the main focus leads us to the conclusion the authors do not actually believe that those with PMLD are able to learn. Lyons and Cassebohm are clear that children with PMLD 'go to school to learn' but there is an unwritten '*but*' hovering not too far from this statement, to the effect that if they're involved in a common curriculum with a functional skills orientation, they'd be much better off having fun.

The general inference about having fun being better than formal education for this group of children carries echoes of other writers who advocate a totally inclusive experience (in the same class with mainstream peers) such as Foreman *et al.* (2004), Simmons and Bayliss (2007) and Arthur-Kelly *et al.* (2008), who all suggest that the rate of peer interactions is of itself, sufficient education. Lyons and Cassebohm, perhaps recognising that quantity does not always equal quality, merely take this one stage further by arguing that given (one assumes) time, patience and love, peers of those with PMLD may take on the role of skilled interactive communicative partner and come to understand the inner states of those with PMLD.

We hope that there is sufficient evidence in this book of our commitment to the principle that teaching and learning has to be approached as a fun activity for those with PMLD (and SLD, and all learners for that matter). Why would you not aim to have fun? It is the very stuff of learning. We don't know of any good teachers who approach a lesson plan with the view of making it as boring as possible. We know of some less-than-good teachers who set up boring lessons, but that's not the same thing at all. Surely the antidote to a 'common curriculum with a functional skills orientation' and/or boring lessons is to have a highly specialist curriculum (an uncommon curriculum) that addresses the particular needs of both the individual and the group (those with PMLD) in an holistic fashion, and to have it taught by highly trained, highly skilled, multidisciplinary teaching teams. Above all, we would espouse Mary Warnock's (2010) observation of the broad common goals of education being about 'independence, enjoyment and understanding' (p. 16). No doubt enjoyment would take centre stage, but independence and understanding seem endangered. We're certainly not averse to a party or three, but to base an entire pedagogy on this principle is questionable.

Conclusion

There are a number of questions relating to the care of those with PMLD that need to be looked at critically, not just in the school, but also in the home and of course in all places where care needs to be imparted (for instance in respite centres, after-school clubs, etc.):

- What do we need to cover in the Care Curriculum and can we make this a real educational opportunity?
- How can we involve the learner in these? It is really important that care is something done *with* learners, not to them. There is a huge area of learned helplessness that is very easy to take for granted but which can have severely detrimental psychological effects upon all learners.
- Are we fully up to date with eating and drinking programmes and is there a consistency of approach across all settings?
- How are we tackling the vital issues of personal care through toileting, hoisting, lifting, etc? Are we ensuring that sufficient time is allocated to these vital areas? Are we building in regular routines for toileting, etc. that *all* follow so these vital times are real learning opportunities?
- Are we relating the Care Curriculum to the teaching of PSHE (Personal, Social and Health Education), especially addressing the issues of control and negation?
- Are we working as productive and cohesive teams across all the disciplines and therapies? Are we including parents in decisions?
- Do we have an advocate system?
- Are we having fun?

Notes

1   Ashley Montagu, who talks about the enormity of touch in the evolution of humans, believing that touch really is the '*mother of the senses*' (Montagu, 1986) is one of a number who celebrate touch as a general benefit to all, but there is a notable silence on the subject with regards to education of those with PMLD or SLD.
2   We've put two exclamation marks just to make absolutely sure all readers are aware we're making a joke.

Chapter 9

A sensory curriculum for pupils and students with profound and multiple learning difficulties

For those with PMLD, who are all working at the earliest levels of intellectual development, the senses will represent a major focus of the curriculum. Extending our understanding, use and control of our senses allows us fully to explore the world and come to an understanding of it, how we interact with it, and how we interact with each other. Teaching through the senses therefore takes on a major significance (Longhorn, 1988; Brown *et al.*, 1998; Pagliano, 2001; McLinden and McCall, 2002; WAG, 2006; Beckerleg, 2009).

The seven senses (rather than the five) encompass sight (visual), sound (auditory), touch (tactile), taste (gustatory), and smell (olfactory) as well as the kinaesthetic proprioceptive and vestibular senses. These latter two physical senses involve our understanding of how the various parts of the body connect to each other, where we are in space and our whole body understanding.[1] There is no doubt that our advances in understanding of the potential effects of sensory impairments have moved on considerably since the 1990s with the publication of accounts from people with autism. It is now well established that brain patterns and functioning, the information the brain receives and the interpretation of sensory messages to the brain, can be vastly different for those on the autistic spectrum and equally vastly different from one individual to another (Smith Myles *et al.*, 2000; Bogdashina, 2003; Grandin, 2006).

Our understanding of the effects of sensory confusion are naturally nowhere near as certain for those with PMLD, simply because they cannot tell us directly about their experiences, but it seems reasonable to assume that sensory understandings may be equally awry at least for some, and we must be extremely cautious about making assumptions that those with PMLD perceive the world in the same way neuro-typically (NT) conventionally developing people generally do. It is, however, probably safe to assume that there is a greater incidence of sensory impairment among people with profound learning disabilities (Bunning, 1998) and the degree of sensory impairment is also likely to be more severe in type as the learning disability increases (Kiernan and Kiernan, 1994).

An interesting study attempting to improve the reliability of a 'sensory checklist' to enable practitioners to determine the behavioural responses of children with PMLD to sensory stimuli was carried out by Vlaskamp and Cuppen-Fonteine (2007). The researchers made adjustments that should have increased reliability but, strikingly, the reliability decreased for all components after adjustment. The effect of familiarity of staff as raters was examined and the results showed that staff who knew the child well could interpret that child's behaviour more accurately than persons who were unfamiliar with the child. In other words, whatever the test, there is no substitute for deep and intimate knowledge of the child. This clearly comes about with time, steady observation, attention to detail, a multi-agency approach and hard work.

Lima *et al.* (2011) and Lima *et al.* (2012) conducted studies measuring the physiological reactions of pupils with PMLD to sensory stimuli through responsiveness in terms of motor movements, heart rate and electrodermal responses. These were then compared to observable indications of interest and, while they found pupils generally demonstrated consistent physiological reactions, their behavioural reactions were rarely consistent. The authors suggest that this may have implications for the development and the emotional well-being of individuals with PMLD in that it suggests that reactions to, and potential appraisals of, sensory stimuli may occur despite the lack of consistent observable behaviours.

Tadema *et al.* (2005) put together a questionnaire that they felt would provide a base information pack for pupils with PMLD, asking teachers what they know and what they still need to know before setting up an activity. These covered the areas of:

Vision – encompassing range of vision, position, contrast, reaction speed, incidence of light, amount of stimuli.
Hearing – pitch, volume, reaction speed, amount of stimuli.
Tactile sense – aversion, low susceptibility, hyper-sensitivity, amount of stimuli.
Olfactory sense – recognition. aversion, hypersensitivity, preferences.
Motor skills – grab, grasp, hold.
Preference – visual, auditory, tactile, specific stimuli.
Where – size of room, position of the room, group size, surrounding noise, posture.
How – ability, reaction time, duration of attention.
When – alertness, fatigue.

So for example, with regard to the learner's *tactile sense*, do you know what she is averse to or hypersensitive to? With regard to *where*, do you know what the best room size is for her, and the optimum group size to maximise her engagement.

Van der Putten *et al.* (2011) used this questionnaire to test the efficacy of Multi-Sensory Environments (MSE) often known as sensory rooms or Snoezelens, in assessing pupils' sensory characteristics, and found them to be (with some slight reservations) highly effective.

Multi-sensory environments

According to Pagliano (1998) a multi-sensory environment is a dedicated room (or space),

> where stimulation can be controlled, manipulated, intensified, reduced, presented in isolation or combination, packaged for active or passive interaction and temporally matched to fit the perceived motivation, interests, leisure, relaxation, therapeutic and/or educational needs of the user. It can take a variety of physical, psychological and sociological forms.
>
> (p. 107)

The key thing here is control of the amount of sensory stimulation, and it is really important that these spaces are thought about as learning opportunities, rather than just places in which to put children with all the lights and sounds blazing away at once. They are most useful when used properly, as a resource for sensory stories, or visual tracking work, or noticing stimuli (try beaming a UV light on something reflective), or indeed just as a room in which to chill out. Activities in these spaces therefore need to be really thought through; they are excellent resources but can be extremely expensive. We have an obligation to use them appropriately.

Of course multi-sensory environments can also include areas that are not rooms, as in for example, sensory gardens. Hussein (2010) notes the opportunities for all sorts of activities including play in such spaces but, again, cautions about using them as real learning opportunities where proper planning and forethought is essential. In this way schools might see such spaces 'as an extension of the school's indoor classroom rather than just as an outdoor space' (p. 31).

The senses

As a general rule we should always try to work through a single sensory channel and try to resist working on too many senses at once, if we can avoid it. There may be some times where we don't want to avoid it, such as when telling a sensory story, since here we may have sight, sound, touch, taste, smell and the kinaesthetic senses all working together, or at least quite close together. It is good to do this occasionally to give learners practice at organising and filtering in a highly motivating setting where everyone is having a great deal of fun, and where the story itself is repeated over and over again. This, however, does not alter the general rule of working on one sense at a time if we can, since too much indiscriminate sensory input is likely only to confuse and confound.

Again, as a general rule, it is probably always best to consider your knowledge of the pupil's personal learning style. What do you already know about the pupil and the way they engage best? Have you assessed their sensory functioning? Are you engaging in teaching practices that are designed to promote sensory and perceptual development? Are you using teaching methodologies that take pupil preference into account? Are these methodologies supported by specifically selected resources designed to maximise the specific learning you want to tackle? Richard Aird sums it up well:

> Rather than subject a pupil to a battery of sensory stimulants in the hope of striking lucky, a better starting point would be to begin with the pupil's personal learning style and provide a safe, secure and predictable learning environment into which sensory stimuli may be introduced gradually, their impact upon the pupil's personal learning style noted, and elements of good practice disseminated across the timetable into [other curricula] subjects.
>
> (Aird, 2001, p. 51)

Good practice

At the very least, there are key questions we need to ask and knowledge we need to obtain about every person with PMLD in our charge.

Sight

There are a wide variety of visual impairments (VI) and a considerable number of syndromes that have an impact on eye conditions (Sacks, 1998). Clearly specific visual impairments are a highly specialised field and advice can be sought from the medical staff at your school; it may be that your Local Education Authority (LEA) employs a VI peripatetic teacher. It should also be noted that vision and the other senses tend to work closely together and that vision can be described as the 'integrating' sense (McLinden and McCall, 2002). We will look to see where a noise has come from to put it in perspective; a smell of burning will visually direct us to its likely source; we will visually check the unexpected touch to our leg to see the cat brushing against it. Vision allows us to make sense of the other senses. This is not to say that vision is the most important sense, just that no one sense can fully compensate for the loss of another.

The basic questions to ask are:

- Is there is a visual impairment – if so, in which eye?
- What functional vision does the learner have?
- Does the learner have perceptual difficulties? If so, what form do they take?

Things to remember are:

- Never position the learner facing any light source – otherwise you may just appear as a glowing blur. Make sure the light source is behind the learner.
- Try to dampen the glare from desktops – reflected light can be a source of much confusion.
- Use dark objects on a light background and vice versa – so for example when cooking a cake, put the rice and sugar in dark bowls but raisins and chocolate in white bowls.
- An unfussy room is a focused room – of course have displays, but don't change them too often; keep your rooms tidy and simple; don't change the positioning of the furniture if you don't have to because it only confuses.
- We tend to think in terms of working facing learners, or if they have a visual impairment that is more pronounced in one eye (or a hearing impairment that is more pronounced in one ear) from the 'better' side. However, we might also consider working behind a learner, especially when we're trying to assist the learning of particular skills such as using implements such as a spoon or fork (Orr, 2003).
- Try to dress yourself in clear single colours and avoid changing how you dress – you want the learners to look at you not your clothes.
- Never assume the learner can see you clearly – they may be able to but if we assume they can't we will try to compensate by, for example, giving touch cues to our presence. These additional cues will only aid communication, interaction and understanding.
- There is sometimes a tendency to confuse ability with motivation. The fact that a pupil can spot a sweet from twenty paces does not mean the pupil has good vision, it might just mean that she's very motivated by sweets. I will often be driving along a dual carriageway and notice, without thinking about it and among the hundreds and probably thousands of cars travelling in the opposite direction, a particular car. It will always be a sports car, because I'm motivated by them. I do not consciously seek them out, but they're always in my consciousness.

Hearing

Again, detailed knowledge of hearing impairments (HI) is a highly specialist area and external advice may need to be sought. Your LEA may employ a peripatetic HI teacher and if you're in the UK you might be well advised to seek the services of SENSE for those pupils who have a dual VI and HI. They are very experienced with PMLD and can be contacted at www.sense.org.uk.

Basic questions to ask are:

- Does the learner have a hearing impairment? If so what kind? Like VI there are a considerable variations of specific condition and degree of impairment in hearing.
- Does the learner have problems with high-pitched noises or low-pitched noises? Usually it is low-pitched noises that are the problem and men might need to be conscious of enunciating clearly and slowly.
- Which ear is affected and therefore which is the best side to be if you are doing side-by-side work such as, for example, helping the learner to press a switch?

Things to remember:

- Just because the learner has a good bill of physical health in the areas of hearing and vision does not mean they can see and hear well, since they may have one or more perceptual difficulties. That is, as with those on the autistic spectrum, the message that goes through to the brain may get skewed, and/or they may have a particular sensitivity to light and sound. Remember that perceptual problems and visual impairment will also affect the hearing – particularly in one's ability to locate a noise.
- Sharp shiny surfaces will rebound noise just as much as they rebound light and soft surfaces help to pinpoint the noise better.
- Most importantly we must always be aware that most sensory confusion is caused by people!
- Speak clearly, slowly and *use as little language as possible.* Language must, of course, be used with developmentally early learners, but it must not be used without thought for the level the learners are at. Language is an enormously powerful tool that can be used for good or ill. At its worst, when it is used thoughtlessly, language can dominate and exclude those who do not have it or do not have access to it. It then stops becoming a communicative tool and becomes instead a significant barrier to learning (Biederman *et al.*, 1994; Orr, 2003). We must use language carefully and in moderation; we must use language that is appropriate to the situation and the pupil; we must use language repetitively so pupils have many opportunities to understand meanings in real and concrete ways. We might do this by (i) reminding each other not to talk unless it's in relation to the lesson – social chit chat between adults needs to be kept to social times not work times; (ii) using words in the way we would use signs and symbols with the more able – selectively. Use only the key words in a sentence so 'We're going to do some painting now and I want everyone to sit round the table and concentrate on the sensory feel of the paint, the primary colours and the effect they have on each other when mixed' becomes 'Now we're going to paint . . . wet . . . dry . . . red . . . yellow . . . orange'; (iii) using repeat phrases for stock occasions. It doesn't matter what these are as long as they are adopted by everyone; (iv) supporting key words with object cues, signing if possible and symbols if appropriate to the developmental level of the pupil; (v) using call and response as a language teaching tool in drama, storytelling and poetry.
- Most of all *don't cross talk* and
- *Don't make unnecessary or unfocused noise,* such as background music. Just because it might help us to concentrate on menial tasks does not mean it helps those who

may well have difficulties with concentration. By all means use music to introduce sessions, or use music when it is relevant to what you're teaching, such as a story or a music lesson, but remember the rule of working through a single sensory channel if you possibly can.

Touch

Basic questions to ask are:

- Is the learner touch defensive?
- If so where? We tend to just concentrate on the hands and of course these are vital tools of discovery, but there may well be touch sensitivity in other parts of the body that might restrict exploration and indeed might make the learner very nervous around people – just in case you touch them! Not liking people being close to you is not going to help with the learning process.

Things to remember:

- We need to be very sensitive to touch defensiveness and treat it as a phobia – in other words, desensitise very slowly and with sensitivity to the individual's aversions. This could be a major programme of work for those who are very touch defensive and could take a number of years to affect change. You may want to consult with an OT on the best way to do this.
- Firm pressure is usually much more acceptable than gentle touch, especially when desensitising.
- Wear something personal to you for learners to identify you by. It is always good to introduce yourself with a touch cue, such as your special bracelet, or your curly hair, or your beard, or your glasses, etc., which will support and enhance the visual and auditory cues naturally given.
- For some, such as those on the autistic continuum, touch can be really stressful.

Taste

Basic questions to ask are:

- Does the learner have an eating and drinking programme? If so, do all those who are likely to work with the learner know it inside out and backwards? Consistency of approach is key and you will need to work closely with your Speech and Language Therapist (SaLT) to ensure the correct approach and continued progress.
- What are their favourite foods and drinks? Detailed knowledge of likes and dislikes are excellent for teaching about choice making, since most learners are naturally very motivated by food.
- How can we overcome the gastrostomy problem? There is no doubt that the gastrostomy can be a major life saver and an extremely effective method of sustenance for those who have aspiration difficulties. The condition where food and liquids enter the lungs instead of the stomach is unfortunately a very common condition in those with PMLD, but nil by mouth is an extreme solution and we will need to work closely with

SaLTs and medical staff to ensure that learners can continue to taste as often and as widely as possible. Food and drink are natures breath fresheners; try going for a couple hours with nil by mouth – it's not nice! For those learners who are denied any tasters, there may be a considerable degree of overcaution at work, which may be understandable if one person is making the decision. Therefore this might be a classic case of spreading the responsibility by involving as many people as possible in the decision, including of course parents. We really do have to consider the pupils' quality of life.

Things to remember

- Strictly speaking, mouthing is part of tactile exploration, but the combination of taste and touch (through the tongue) forms a major part of early discovery (Mednick, 2002; McLinden and McCall, 2002). *The important thing is not to discourage mouthing.* Don't worry too much – within reason! – about learners eating things such as glue, paint, paper, materials etc., as long as you're sure about choking and general safety issues.
- It may be, however, that the desire to explore with the mouth can directly impede the learning process and learners may need to orally explore in order to concentrate, rather like a doodler needs to draw. There are various dummy-type alternatives and chewing toys on the market, or you might try 'chewelery', which hangs around the neck on a necklace and is always available when needed.
- Pica – the Latin word for magpie, a bird reputed to eat almost anything – is a medical disorder characterised by an appetite for non-nutritional substances such as stones, coal, sand, dirt, soil, faeces, chalk, paint, soap and just about anything else you care (or don't care) to think about. Those with pica will generally, but not always, not swallow the item and often seem to need the taste and feel of the object in their mouths.

Smell

Basic questions to ask are:

- Are you giving learners an opportunity to practise and refine their sense of smell in the same way as they might practise and refine their sense of touch?
- Are you giving learners the opportunity to practise smelling before they taste and eat?

Things to remember

- Smell is very closely related to taste and they should be used regularly in tandem, especially when supporting a pupil in their eating and drinking.
- Try to be consistent with your own scent, that is don't change your brand of perfume and deodorant. It can be an excellent additional cue as to who you are, especially for the visually or perceptually impaired.
- Smell is the most difficult sense to use selectively and should be used sparingly. Orr (2003) makes the very valid point that smells are often an imprecise source of information because of the 'artificial smells industry'; that is, when are the smells of pine or coconut or rosemary real, or things smelled via air sprays, shampoo or massage oil?
- Smells such as joss sticks, etc., cannot be withdrawn easily and can therefore 'hang around' for a while!

- However, smells can be useful for big cues; try for example, using a smell a day to cue students into each day of the week – 'mmm vinegar . . . (or indeed uggh vinegar . . .) it must be Friday'.

Kinaesthetic senses

Orr (2003) has observed that detachment from other people, through the use of buggies, pushchairs, wheelchairs, cots, playpens, etc., may well disorientate those who have sensory difficulties. This is especially so when travelling or in transition between one place and the next, even if you've stayed in the same room. He suggests four things the learner needs to know:

- Where am I?
- Who am I with?
- What's happening?
- What's happening next?

and we need to ensure that we have answered these questions *before* we do anything else.

Question

You have to lose one of your five main senses! Which one do you lose and why?

An answer

It is tempting to think that sight is the dominant influence because it is so central to our lives, but the senses all work together and are equally influential in helping us to make sense of the world. Be cautious about giving insufficient notice to the sense of smell since it works very closely with the sense of taste.

Activities for working on and with the senses

Sensory stories are excellent vehicles for delivering whole-school or class thematic topics in an interesting, exciting and wholly developmentally sympathetic manner. There are commercially available sensory stories such as Chris Fuller's 'Bag Books' at www.bagbooks. org and Pete Well's at Portland School in Sunderland has lots of free PowerPoint downloads for older learners at www.pete.wells.co.uk. Although Nicola Grove and Keith Park's stories – such as the fantastic *Odyssey Now* (a journey through the adventures of Odysseus) and *Macbeth in Mind* – are largely aimed at those with SLD, they are both excellent inclusion opportunities for a mixed SLD/PMLD group of any age from KS1 upwards (Grove and Park, 1996; 1999; 2001). Keith Park has also published an amount of PMLD/SLD versions of classic plays, poems and novels that can be easily adapted for sensory stories, especially if one uses his 'Call and Response' method of delivery (Park, 2010). Please refer to Chapter 5, 'A Communication Curriculum' for a fuller explanation of this.

The general principles of delivering a sensory story are much the same as any other story for those with learning difficulties and can be defined within the ten essential elements of storytelling:

1 **Give it a beginning** – introduce the story with an object cue and/or a musical cue for the story.

2 **It should have meaning to the participants**, although the meaning may be held in the interest and excitement generated, rather than the storyline. You might not have direct experience of a magic carpet, but you can revel in the wonder of it.

3 **Use repetition** – you just cannot get enough! Use repetition in the story itself through a strapline that's repeated at regular intervals, rather like a short chorus in a song. Use repetition in the delivery of the story – one story might take up an hour a week for at least half a term and quite possibly a whole term. Your learners will not get bored since the repetition is a recognition that learners will probably need very many opportunities to experience the story in order to understand and therefore enjoy it and gain learning from it. Teachers and teaching assistants must be prepared for the amount of repetition necessary and resist the temptation to switch off and just go through the motions – the more you put into it the more they'll get out of it.

4 **Keep the actual story/episode short** – and therefore easily remembered – although the telling of it may take half an hour or so by the time you've introduced props and time for each learner to be actively involved in the story. As a general rule resist the temptation to make the story too complicated; less is often considerably more. Think of the essential elements of the great children's stories such as *The Bear Hunt* and *The Gruffalo*. Look at the repetition held in both of them – they're both essentially one scene with several variations building up to a climax. Simple is *much* better than complicated.

5 **Use all and every means of communication** – signing, speaking, action, facial expression and props – but remember that the best storytellers primarily use their voices to paint the pictures.

6 **Use language selectively**. You may use difficult language, but only if it has relevance to the story. So you could make a sensory story from *Othello* and use the original Shakespeare as it has wonderful rhythmic quality, which makes poetry such a good base. Use call and response to bring out the rhythm (Park, 2010).

7 **Introduce sequences of dramatic events** and make it exactly the same every week in order to encourage anticipation of events.

8 **Make it exciting and dynamic**. Give it emotional content with at least one major high point in the story.

9 **Build in (and allow) as much audience participation as possible**. For those with PMLD this will mean opportunities to explore the props and have an interactive relationship with them. Staff supporting the session should act as 'secondary' storytellers – repeating the lines on a one-to-one basis, giving the story personal meaning to each learner, scaffolding understanding and generally hamming it up as much as they can! If you're working with a large group (say more than six learners) you might be best to have your staff seated between learners at regular intervals.

10 **Give it an ending** that is clear and supported by as many cues as possible – verbal cue, touch cue, music cue, etc.

Once devised, the same story should be repeated weekly for *at least* half a term (and probably longer) so learners have a real opportunity to become familiar with it and so practise their sequencing, turn taking, anticipatory and memory skills – all essential base elements of communication.

Don't worry too much about what is age appropriate – the film industry would have died years ago if they had just stuck to making films for grown-up people! Don't not tell sensory stories to students because they're of secondary age; just don't make them childish. They need to be about things that any teenager would find interesting like sex and death and rock and roll!

Cooking allows for an infinite variety of sensory exploration and experience for pupils with PMLD. For those wishing to equate traditional National Curriculum subjects to this document, cookery is a fantastic vehicle for mathematical thinking and scientific exploration. Depending on the cognitive abilities of the learner, just the process of baking a cake covers areas such as size, quantity, position, measurement, weight, structure of properties, temperature, sequencing, cause and effect, estimation, counting, addition and subtraction, fractions, division etc, etc. The state of the finished cake is neither here nor there – since it is the process of exploration through looking, tasting, smelling and touching, as well as mixing the ingredients and experiencing the change that occurs when flour is mixed with water, or when sugar melts, or when various spices go into a curry that is important. And of course we can always buy a cake or ice cream or a curry to eat for the end of the lesson!

Massage. Pupils with PMLD are likely to have very little awareness of their own bodies. They may not know how their body parts are connected (our proprioceptive sense) and may not know where their bodies are in relation to the space around them (our vestibular sense). These two kinaesthetic senses need to be worked on as much as the conventional five, and massage can be an excellent focus.

Massage is, however, too often used as a 'throwaway' activity to fill in time and is not given the importance it deserves. Massage sessions might

- concentrate on a particular area of the body per half-term
- last for at least twenty minutes
- use base oils but not essential oils (which may cause sensory confusion)
- be a quiet, calming and relaxing activity.

For lots of ideas on massage have a look at Flo Longhorn's *Planning a Multi-Sensory Massage Programme for Very Special People* (Longhorn, 1993).

Proprioceptive Massage (Bluestone, 2002) comes from the HANDLE Institute in America (the Holistic Approach to Neuro-Development and Learning Efficiency), under the direction of Judith Bluestone. She claims that this approach

1   organises mental processing
2   influences the body's biochemistry
3   helps mould the actual structure of the brain.

It may, or may not, do these things – we have not been able to locate any independent research to confirm or deny the claims – but in any event, the process makes sense for those who may find the conventional skin-on-skin massage challenging. Proprioception refers to the brain's unconscious sense of the whole body. The brain processes information from the other senses to give an understanding of its wholeness; to determine where our bodies are in relation to the environment around us and where the various parts of the body are in relation to one another – for example, where our knees are in relation to our thighs, etc. For students with damaged or incomplete sensory awareness (virtually all PMLD) this can be problematic and will undoubtedly need developing.

Massage of the proprioceptive sites of the body is carried out by using a small (tennis-sized) soft foam ball instead of the hand, avoiding skin-on-skin touch, which some may find extremely problematic. Always try and remember to:

- Work on the back of the body.
- Start and finish at the top of the spine.
- Apply firm and lingering pressure when you finish at the top of the spine.
- Roll the ball in the same direction and apply equal pressure throughout.
- Roll the ball slowly.
- Talk your partner through the massage – naming body parts in simple clear language helps to reinforce body awareness.
- Be sensitive to the communications of your partner.

Art clearly has the potential to be a major vehicle for sensory and cognitive development. Care needs to be taken to ensure that learners are participants rather than merely observers (of the adults making the pretty picture!) or, possibly worse, objects to do things to; making learners put their hands in paint in order to create a picture full of handprints, for example. We need to move away from the idea of conventional paintings and allow, encourage and facilitate our PMLD learners to make art for themselves. The key to teaching art is remembering that the process of undertaking the sensory experiences relating to the materials and the cognitive experiences derived from combining materials are far more important than the finished work. If it's artistically good enough for Kandinsky and Jackson Pollock, then it's certainly good enough for us.

Individualised Sensory Environment. Karen Bunning has done some very interesting work in an area that could have been put into practically any of the areas relating to PMLD Curriculum through an intervention, termed 'Individualised Sensory Environment' (ISE). Although this was initially developed for use with adults with profound and multiple learning disabilities (Bunning, 1996; 1998), the principles equally apply whatever the age. The aim was to reduce the level of non-purposeful engagement, characterised by stereotypic actions, self-injury and neutral behaviour and to increase the levels of purposeful interaction with people and objects. Bunning's (1998) study showed that the clients (adults with PMLD) emitted high levels of non-purposeful behaviour at baseline, but an increase in purposeful interactions after ISE intervention, although it was noted that the presence and positive interaction of others was a significant factor.

ISE operates on the principle that if the learner wants (an object) enough she will be very motivated to indicate 'more' in some way when the object is removed. The object (a tray of dried pasta, for example) is presented to the learner, who is then encouraged to interact with it. She may touch, taste or smell the pasta with (initial) support or not, for a period of time – say thirty seconds or so. When the tray is withdrawn, the presenter will observe the learner's reaction, assuming interest will be supported by a look, reach or a vocalisation to indicate that the learner wants more. The tray is re-presented to the learner and this may be repeated two or three times more. If initial interest is discovered, the pasta tray will be presented to the learner at other times of the day and week by other presenters to ensure that the motivation to engage with the object has some consistency of intent. Even if the tray is rejected or the learner shows disinterest, the presenter should try again at other times in case the rejection or disinterest was affected by some other external factor, such as too much noise in the classroom or general sleepiness on the learner's part.

ISE is immensely useful as a means of:

- discovering likes and dislikes
- structuring the environment to provide meaningful forms of stimulation to foster purposeful responses
- decreasing stereotypical self-stimulations
- using sensory stimuli to encourage the learner to engage in purposeful behaviours rather than non-purposeful.

This latter point is extremely pertinent when one considers the amount of 'down time' the average person with PMLD is likely to have throughout the course of their lives, not just at school, but also at home, at respite and at residential placements in adulthood. Rather than plonking someone in front of a television screen and assuming what you might like to do is what the person with PMLD might like to do, we can provide activities that engage the learner as much as playing a video game, reading a book, doing a crossword puzzle or watching a TV programme might engage others.

Although Bunning's original thesis primarily involved working through the tactile, proprioceptive and vestibular sensory channels, there seems no reason why other sensory channels should not be worked on and the list of objects you can use in a programme is really only limited by your imagination. Here are some examples: uncooked pasta; uncooked rice; uncooked beans; water (in all its forms – warm, cold, bubbled, iced, etc.); dough; various balls of all descriptions and sizes; seashells; jelly (again in all its forms of various solidity and consistency including raw); bubble wrap; non-mix paint in a sandwich of cling film sealed with gaffa tape; feathers; handcream; cornflour paste; jack-in-the-boxes; scouring pads; stickle bricks; mashed potato (again, in various levels of consistency and warmth); dry cereal; peek-a-boo with a blanket; spinning secretary's chair; rocking chair; swings; hoists; water-filled balloons; round and round the garden; fine water spray; bells; various mobiles; leaves; mirrors; slime pots; vacuum cleaner with nozzle attachment; latch-switch-operated fans; latch-switch-operated music; sand (dry, wet, half wet, etc.); clay; shaving foam; foot spa; vibrating cushion and other vibrating toys; bumble ball; sponges; various materials (e.g. felt, leather, satin, lycra, hessian, fur, etc.).

Teachers can use ISE as a means of discovering the sensory preferences because the programme demands feedback from the learners. It teaches us that even learners who we think we know very well may well have favourite things we don't know about, because *they* don't know about them yet either. It teaches us that we are all different and that we need to find the motivators if we are to engage learners successfully (Carpenter *et al.*, 2010). There is, finally, a strong argument for suggesting that teachers suspend the curriculum on a regular basis, for perhaps as long as a half a term at the beginning of every key stage, in order to check that the sensory preferences displayed at the beginning of the last key stage still apply. We may well find some changes; we may well find significant changes; if we don't ask the questions we won't get the answers!

Further reading

For practical day-to-day ideas, try Tina Beckerleg (2009) and anything by Flo Longhorn. Apart from *A Sensory Curriculum for Very Special People*, originally published in 1988, Flo self-publishes and all of her considerable output can be obtained from Amazon.

For a detailed exploration of PMLD and the senses look at Paul Pagliano (2001) and Michael Mednick (2002).

Conclusion

It is almost impossible to be certain that any pupil or student with PMLD does or does not have difficulties with sensory perception, and it is equally challenging to ascertain the degree of that severity if they do. These days the medical world may well be able to tell if there is a physical problem, with sight or hearing for example, but perceptual difficulties are another matter altogether. Given this, it seems reasonable to operate on the assumption that sensory difficulties are more likely than not and to lay out the curriculum in such a way that each pupil and student has many opportunities to work on their sensory understanding. Conducting regular sensory audits on each individual pupil is an essential prerequisite to ensuring that learning takes place.

Note

1 For those wanting a fuller explanation of the kinaesthetic senses, including a description of the functions of the Golgi tendon organs and muscle spindles, we would recommend a look at Pagliano (2001, pp. 42–43).

Part III

Curriculum issues for those with SLD

A language, literacy and communication curriculum for pupils and students with severe learning difficulties

Coupe O'Kane and Goldbart (1998) succinctly summarise the difficulties those with learning difficulties and communication impairments might have. They may:

- have skills as respondent but not as an initiator;
- not be able to identify the topic of conversation by establishing joint reference;
- not be able to maintain a topic leading to frequent topic changes;
- give insufficient feedback as a listener about continued interest, such as no head nodding or saying 'mm';
- give insufficient feedback to the speaker about understanding the content of communication. That is, there may be no requests for confirmation or clarification such as 'What do you mean?', 'Uh?';
- interrupt inappropriately in timing and in content;
- be unable to extend a communication after an initial turn as initiator and respondent;
- terminate conversations prematurely with terminations communicated ineffectively;
- be unable to recognise and repair breakdowns in communication.

For those with severe learning difficulties, whether or not they have an additional autistic spectrum disorder, effective communication is unlikely to come either easily or naturally. Therefore, it is imperative that those working with them put the conditions in place to maximise opportunities for spontaneous communication. It might be a good start to ensure that the following questions are always asked in every classroom, irrespective of the age or ability levels of the pupils: Do you know what motivates and interests your pupils? Do you know why your learners are likely to want to communicate? All of us communicate more freely about things that interest us. Learning intentions in communication need to be personalised if they are to be effective – you cannot have group learning intentions in communication. We must remember that *the motivation to communicate* is a key communicative necessity.

Are you having *lots* of fun? Making learning fun, so pupils don't even know they're learning, is a very simple way of ensuring that pupils stay motivated. Play lots of games, from very simple one-to-one games for younger learners, such as 'round and round the garden' and 'peek-a-boo', to more complex games such as 'Kim's Game' and 'Buckaroo' in the classroom, or (gentle) variations of 'British Bulldog' in bigger spaces. Make sure you give lots of opportunity for repetition of their favourites.

Are you using lots of exiting stories and poems? Storytelling is an extremely complex and difficult skill and pupils will need lots of active practice. If pupils can't tell familiar stories (such as fairy stories, for example) how are they going to tell their own stories about important, funny, scary, worrying things that happen to them?

Are you having discrete sessions of Intensive Interaction with your pre-verbal pupils? Intensive Interaction is not just effective with PMLD pupils but with any learner who is at the earliest stages of communicative development, and can be particularly effective with your learners who have an additional ASC.

Have you organised the classroom environment and structured it to ensure pupils know what is required of them? This helps pupils to stay calm, secure and ready for learning, and they will therefore be much more likely to concentrate on learning rather than worrying about what is going to happen next.

Have you discussed pupils' individual communicative learning intentions with your team; with other professionals (especially the Speech and Language Therapist – SaLT); with parents and carers; with others they see every day such as the transport team and mealtime supervisors? It is important to share the communicative learning intentions you might have for your pupils so everyone they see on a regular basis is working towards the same objectives.

Are you using too much language and are you assuming that your pupils can understand everything you say? Many children with learning difficulties develop strategies to make it appear as though they've understood, when they might not have understood at all. Learned echolalia (repeating the last word or words spoken to the pupil) for example, when responding with the word 'park' to the question 'Would you like to go to the park?' or the word 'orange' to the question 'Would you like blackcurrant or orange?' It could also be that the child can only process the last thing he or she has heard, that is, upon hearing two unrelated commands such as 'Take off your coat and bring me your book', the child may just bring you his book, or indeed only understand the word 'book'.

Are you giving your pupils as many opportunities to understand using a multi-communicative environment? That is simple, clear language *and* signing or symbol or picture or object cue. Remember, many children with severe learning difficulties really benefit from adults' visual clues supporting language, such as a Makaton sign or symbol to visually support the concept. A question 'Do you want a drink?' spoken and supported by the two Makaton signs 'you' (point) and 'drink' (tipping a cup to the mouth) is far clearer than just spoken words on their own.

Are you aware of each pupil's preferred communicative avenue? Does every pupil have *immediate* access to communicative opportunities? Do they have the (i) words either vocally or through a VOCA (voice output communication aid) such as an i-Pad or a 4-Talk-4 or a Step-by-Step, or (ii) the signs, or (iii) the symbols to hand through, for example a symbols keyring, or (iv) the photographs to talk about what interests them? Are pupils and/or staff unable to use these communicative avenues, because they are not immediately to hand but scattered around the room, or in a cupboard, or kept only in the classroom? We must remember that *the means to communicate* is a key communicative necessity.

Are you giving each pupil time to communicate with you or another member of staff on what interests them? Children may have learned to be quite passive (if things are provided for them, there's no need for communication). The focus is not to anticipate a child's needs, e.g., giving them a drink when you think they are thirsty, but to manipulate the communicative context – place a bottle of juice in a child's approximate environment – to encourage them to use the communicative abilities they have (signing for a drink, etc).

Are you making sure someone is around to talk to when *they want* to communicate? Can you stretch their ability to communicate with you by modeling and teaching more words and/or signs and/or symbols? Are you ensuring that schedules and timetables are used at regular intervals throughout the day? Some may be able to hold long-term information (the daily timetable) but most will need additional cues regarding much shorter periods of time such as now and next.

Are you asking your pupils to communicate twice when they only need to do it once? Sometimes we make it too hard by insisting that they hand over a symbol, for example, when they could far more easily point or lead us to, or just take something they're interested in. It won't help the communicative process if the extra communication we're asking for doesn't make sense to the pupil. The instruction, 'now say it again using your signs' does little for pragmatics.

Have you taught your pupils how to ask for help? When we are stuck for a solution to a problem, our natural inclination is to seek someone who knows what to do and ask for help. Problem solving and thinking skills will not come naturally to those with learning difficulties and the danger is that the pupil will see it as an insurmountable problem and not try; in many cases, adults will solve the problem *without* being asked. This means the pupil will not even have to work out that a problem exists in the first place! We have to be extremely careful that we don't instill learned helplessness.

Are you listening to behaviours? It is difficult, but we must remember that challenging behaviours are communications. They are poor communications, but they are probably the best the learner can do and we need to listen to what they are expressing. The pupil has developed these challenging behaviours because they are often effective in getting what the child wants or venting anger and frustration. It should not be our objective to control children, but give children an appropriate and acceptable means of control. That is, a communication that is listened to.

The key communicative necessities

The things one needs to communicate (Goldbart, 1994) are, therefore:

- A means (method) of communicating – through words, sign, symbol, pictures, gesture, object of reference or, equally likely, a combination of some or all of these things.
- A reason (motivation) to communicate – which might mean needs and wants but could equally be communicating about something that interests the person.
- Someone to communicate to – this will usually be an adult, because they are usually easier to communicate with for someone with learning difficulties.
- Time – which is always an excellent investment if it is allowing a pupil to be a proactive communicator, an independent, rather than a dependent, communicator.

Why should your learners want to communicate?

1   To socialise.
2   To negate.
3   To express feelings, emotions and attitudes.
4   To ask for help, request information.

5   To make real choices.
6   To make themselves understood.
7   To communicate about things that interest the individual.
8   Requesting needs and wants.

Let's explore these more fully:

Socialising

Socialising starts with Intensive Interaction (Nind and Hewett, 1994, 2001; Hewett and Nind, 1998; Hewett, 2011), which really should be at the cornerstone of all work being done with those at an early communicative level – those who are pre-verbal and/or whose communicative abilities are unrefined. Intensive Interaction is not just for those with profound learning difficulties and it is not just about 'teaching children to communicate' in the sense that we might teach children a series of skills. The core principles hinge on the fact that communication is about so much more than language or the words signed or the symbols handed over. Certainly, symbols systems such as the ASC-based PECS (Frost and Bondy, 1994) or Clare Latham's more SLD-based 'Communication Books' (Latham, 2005) can teach the skills needed to request needs and wants, answer questions, make choices, etc., but the real core elements of human communications – to be social – are not and cannot be addressed through skills-based teaching. This is very much a *process-based way of teaching*, where the process of the communicative interaction is the objective.

Interactors will be looking for shared enjoyment that is two way; they will be engaging as a flexible and responsive partner – reinforcing the pupils' engagements; engagement with a more competent partner reinforces the engagements of the learner with a view to reaching an emotional engagement that goes beyond skill. The process of engaging in effective Intensive Interaction will increase the learners' ability to attend, both to their communicative partner and by concentrating for longer periods of time on the interactive process; turn-taking skills and the ability to be reciprocal will improve. Learners will be able to extend their abilities to use and understand non-verbal communications through the eyes, face and through body language; they will be able to practise receiving and giving touch, be more ready to accept the proximity of others and extend their use of either or both vocalisations and verbalisations.

Negation

The practice of saying 'no' is explored more fully in Chapter 8 ('A Care Curriculum'). The general principles of teaching those with severe learning difficulties to say 'no' in an appropriate manner and most importantly to be listened to when they say 'no' in an appropriate manner, are the same as will apply to those with profound learning difficulties. For some with SLD, this process will be an essential element of their education towards being fully social beings. It is neither sensible nor functional to suppress it since, for some, not being listened to when they say 'no' will only drive them to saying 'no' in a way that has to be listened to – that is through exhibiting challenging behaviours. It has often been argued that such behaviours in such circumstances are both entirely understandable and entirely normal (Harris, 1995; Harris *et al.*, 1996, 2001; Hewett, 1998a, b; Imray, 2008).

Expressing feelings, emotions and attitudes

This is in many ways one of the functions of the Creative Curriculum, but in terms of a Language, Literacy and Communication section is an area in which literacy will feature highly. Games and play are also excellent ways of learning about one's own emotions as well as seeing them in other people and learning how to recognise them in others. Remember that having fun is a huge learning opportunity because children – whatever the level of learning difficulty – are always engaged when they're having fun. Remember that . . . games are not time out from real work; they are the most intensive developmental work you can do (Nind and Hewett, 2001, p. 66).

Playing games in and out of the classroom (Barratt *et al.*, 2000; Nind and Hewett, 2001; Delmain and Spring, 2003; Ludwig and Swann, 2007; Barron, 2008, 2009) should be an essential element of every SLD classroom, irrespective of the age of the students. There is a very strong case for suggesting that games, like play, should be discrete 'subjects' with as much importance as any other subject and be taught as a discrete session at least once a week, and for young children, probably a lot more often than that. It is certainly true that games should not (must not) just be limited to activities that happen at playtime or lunchtime (Collis and Lacey, 1996; Barratt *et al.*, 2000; Lacey, 2006).

Playing games is a classic example of process-based teaching. There will inevitably be lots of learning intentions, but the main thing is the process and enjoyment of the game itself. It is not advisable to set any specific individual objectives – play the games and see what happens – as retrospective recording assesses what has been achieved by each individual over time.

Melanie Nind and Dave Hewett suggest that games are an essential part of the SLD curriculum because of their key features:

> Games are joint activities with mutual involvement (which help to establish common references and shared meanings).
>
> Games involve repetition (which allows for repeated practice without boredom and provides predictable, secure activities).
>
> Games involve alternate turn-taking (which means opportunities for learning and practising one of the most fundamental rules of conversation – taking turns).
>
> Games are intrinsically motivating because of their intrinsic fun (which helps to ensure that they are played often with positive associations).
>
> Games provide opportunities for problem solving (which means opportunities for applying thinking skills, involving effort but not stress).
>
> (Nind and Hewett, 2001, pp. 55–56)

And we might add that games provide contact with other children in an atmosphere of expectation and fun; they make children, and the rich contexts we engineer for them, more appealing to other children, which increases the opportunities for contact. For example, we must not underestimate how enticing it will be for mainstream children visiting SLD classrooms during integration or inclusion, when they are paired with young children making pretend cups of tea and preparing dinner in the 'home corner'. Games have potential to be continued at break and lunchtime by the children themselves, once they have been played many tens or possibly many hundreds of times.

It is not necessary to spend hours making up new games for your pupils and students to play – just think of the games you played as a child and adapt them if necessary. You can make a whole host of games of or with anything – lycra for example (Taylor and Park, 2001) – and there are lots of books out there that will often need only slight adaptations to be eminently suitable for SLD pupils. Here are three games either taken straight or adapted slightly from Barratt *et al.* (2000):

1   Letters in your name game

- An adult is the caller.
- Children stand in a line about five metres away.
- Caller calls a letter of the alphabet.
- Children take a step forward if that letter is in their name.
- Letters are called out randomly.
- First one to reach the caller becomes the new caller.

Variations

- Letters are written (big) on twenty-six large cards.
- Names are written for each pupil.
- Use colours in clothing.
- Use colours or shapes or cartoon characters or members of staff on a board – each child has different board.
- There's a referee!

Educational benefits of the letters in your name game

- Knowing the letters of the alphabet.
- Knowing the letters in your own name.
- Concentration.
- Listening.
- Looking.
- Counting.
- Thinking.
- Remembering.
- Turn taking.
- Learning how to win.
- Learning how to lose.
- And we have a maths, English and PSHE lesson all rolled into one!

2   Balloon game

- Group sit on chairs in a large circle.
- Adult pats a balloon in the air and calls the name of a pupil.
- Child jumps up to pat the balloon and calls out another name.
- Object is to avoid the balloon touching the floor.

Variations

- If they're really good at this, use a beach ball and seat them on the floor.

Educational benefits of the balloon game

- Answering to your own name.
- Choosing.
- Attracting the attention of another appropriately.
- Co-operating within a group.
- Understanding and abiding by the group rules.
- Estimating time.
- Waiting.
- Listening.
- Looking.
- Concentrating.
- Turn taking.
- Acting quickly.
- Hand/eye co-ordination.

3   Run to the mat game

- Place a PE mat in one corner of the playground.
- Leader decides on a key phrase such as 'all aboard'.
- Leader instructs everyone to dance, hop, touch their toes, or spin on the spot in a very low-key voice.
- Leader calls 'ALL ABOARD' and everyone runs to the mat.
- Last one on the mat is out.

Variations

- Tell a story about going on a boat trip, it's a lovely sunny day, swimming in the sea, LOOK OUT, SHARKS! and ALL ABOARD!
- Change the story so that the key phrase ends up as SCRAMBLE or LET'S GO or RUN FOR YOUR LIFE.

Educational benefits of the run to the mat game

- Co-operating within a group.
- Understanding and abiding by the group rules.
- Listening.
- Concentrating.
- Remembering.
- Anticipating.
- Toleration of proximity.
- Taking the lead.
- Learning to win.
- Learning to lose.

Requesting information or asking for help

This is an area explored in depth within Chapter 13 ('A Problem-Solving and Thinking Curriculum'). The inability of those with SLD to ask for help is one of the basic elements making up learned helplessness and must be addressed as early as possible within a pupil's school life.

Making real choices

This is another area that is explored fully within Chapter 8 ('A Care Curriculum'). Again, the principle that applies to those with PMLD about choice making will equally apply to those with SLD, which is essentially that we need to ensure learners fully understand the consequences of making choices. We have a tendency to offer bland choices as a regular part of learners' experience, for example 'Do you want blackcurrant or orange juice?' or 'Do you want a plain crisp or a salt and vinegar crisp?' Here, unless the child has a real aversion to blackcurrant or plain crisps, the consequences of making the wrong choice are minimal. The child still has a drink and a crisp. What if we offered say a plain crisp or a slice of raw potato? What if we offered orange or freshly squeezed lemon juice or (non-alcoholic) beer?

Making themselves understood

Recent research suggests that at least from eighteen months, even when the main purpose of communication is to get something, NT conventionally developing infants see communication as about being sure that 'you understand what I mean', rather than simply being about being sure that 'I get what I want' (Grosse *et al.*, 2010). It is therefore really important that we identify the pupil's preferred communication system(s) and maximise her opportunities to confirm meanings when these might be initially unclear.

Communicating about things that interest the individual

This is again an essential area for all those working with children, young people and adults with severe learning difficulties to be concerned about, as it is, clearly, related to motivation. Teachers, TAs, SaLTs, parents, care workers and hosts of other professionals, such as mealtime supervisors and bus escorts who will have regular contact with learners, have the potential to seize the communication moment and are often in control of the means of expression through symbol, object cue, photograph, words and signs taught. If we are to encourage proactive rather then reactive communications it is absolutely necessary to work with and around learners' own motivations, although of course this shouldn't be an exclusive area.

Requesting needs and wants

This area may well be something that is open to sabotage – another issue explored in greater detail in Chapter 13 ('A Problem-Solving and Thinking Curriculum') – but essentially this is about deliberately creating opportunities to proactively communicate. Here you might adopt a number of strategies such as:

• Make favourite items inaccessible but visible (e.g. in transparent containers, on the top of a cupboard, etc) and assume an expression of incomprehension when they're pointed at.
• Give small portions (e.g. of food) to encourage a response for more – and remember 'more' and 'please' on their own are not acceptable.
• Set up motivating tasks that need help (e.g. a cutting activity without scissors).
• Pause in the middle of a highly motivating activity.

- Offer a real choice – especially the right to say 'no'.
- Offer something they don't like in order to encourage a protest – especially at snack time.
- Contradict expectations to encourage a request or comment (e.g. give the student the wrong coat at going-home time).
- Engineer a challenging situation. For example, blow up a physiotherapy ball so that is too big to get through a door and ask a pupil to deliver it to someone in a nearby classroom. Clearly, you would never compromise the dignity of a child or young person, and this is very much a case of exercising thinking skills and problem solving. It may be that you can ask two or three pupils to solve the problem, thereby encouraging them to work (and think) collaboratively.
- Encourage learners to ask for help – think ahead to make problems, not easy solutions.
- There are lots more – can you talk to your colleagues and make a list? Perhaps you can make it a task at a teachers/staff/class meeting.

Some points to remember

- Always give lots of time to answer.
- Always give non-verbal prompts and options whenever possible.
- You have to ensure an entirely predictable environment first – only then can you sabotage.

Using sign

Signing has long been established as an excellent supplementary to language with numerous advantages. It is very cheap (or relatively so once the school has bought in training and the necessary signing books); it's easy to use and fairly easy to learn (at least for supporting adults); it's very portable; it is an excellent supporter to verbal language – both receptive and expressive; it's very flexible as a teaching tool and can be taught in lots of fun ways such as stories and song. While one would hesitate to call them disadvantages, there are certain issues one needs to be aware of. Signing can be challenging for those with motor problems and/or processing difficulties; members of the general public and often members of the user's family will probably/may not understand, thus adding to the user's potential frustration; fluency is best, but hard to achieve; motivation can be a problem for ASC learners; older learners might not take to it automatically, so perseverance may be called for.

Signing works by drawing attention to the speaker and giving additional cues for the receiver. This is especially important when the person with learning difficulties is using it, since it can give a great deal of confidence that what has been said is what has been understood. Signing makes speech more concrete, especially for iconic words such as house or banana, for example; it is longer lasting than speech in that the sign can be repeated or extended or just left to hang; it simplifies and slows speech, especially when supporting adults use it. Anything that makes us speak slower and concentrate on key words must be useful. It can be tactile as well as visual and auditory, for example, using Canaan Barrie[1] signs or adapting Makaton signs such as 'finished' to a body sign by brushing one's hands down the arms of a pupil.

Essentially, pupils with SLD will need a number of attributes to be able to maximise their ability to sign, namely fine and gross motor control; the intellectual ability to understand the symbolic nature of language; a reasonable attention span, especially if they're going to use (and understand) more than single sign communications; the ability to process dual channel information; the motivation to communicate through signing; something to sign (communicate) about; someone to sign (communicate) to. Given all of these requirements it is undoubtedly best to introduce signing as early in the child's life as possible, and certainly well before they come to school.

Teaching signing is also not as straightforward as it might appear and there are certain principles that are best borne in mind:

- Establish a small group of useful and motivating signs.
- Teach one by one and in context, and remember that repetition is the key to learning.
- Try to extend the learner's lateral progression rather than just piling on more signs. That is, if the learner has a bank of twenty signs, can she sign them to different people, in different settings and in different situations?
- Have a sign of the week – remember that the staff have to learn before the pupils, and the staff must use the sign at every opportunity. The more we use it, the more likely the pupils will as well.
- Set up situations which encourage pupils to sign, especially fun activities such as stories and songs. Signing songs are brilliant for motivating both learners and supporting adults to sign, although you will probably need to pick ballads (they're slower) and be prepared to interpret some words. A popular signing song for example, is Carol King's 'You've Got a Friend', but a number of lines require the meaning to be signed, rather than a literal translation of the words. 'They'll take your soul if you let them' does not mean you'll be damned for eternity, but is a poet's phrase for letting you down, or breaking your heart. In these instances, it doesn't make sense to be literal.
- Reinforce at every opportunity.
- Get into the habit of signing – just because your pupils are not signing (yet) doesn't mean you shouldn't use it.
- Treat idiosyncratic and incorrect signing in the same way as you would mistakes in language. That is, allow but model the correct sign immediately.

In the UK and other English-speaking countries, signing for those with SLD has been supported by the use of Makaton and latterly, SignAlong. These are both sign-supported speech systems that use the word order and syntax of spoken language, as opposed to signing for the deaf, such as British Sign Language (BSL) or American Sign Language (ASL), which are separate languages in their own right, with their own syntax and word order. As such they are entirely different and must not be confused. However, using individual BSL (or ASL) signs to support Makaton or SignAlong should be perfectly acceptable, as long as it is taught on the principle of supporting the spoken word. Teachers should resort to BSL signs if there is no Makaton or SignAlong word, or equivalant word, available.

Using symbols

Task

Your team leaders/managers have asked you to make a number of generic symbol keyrings for (i) years 3 and 4, (ii) years 7 and 8, (iii) years 11 and 12 that can apply to most pupils in most situations. Write a list of words you might put on to the key ring at each level.

There are two ways these keyrings can work as very simple but effective interactive communication aids. First, a generic list of symbols can be put on the keyrings, which are worn by all members of staff and by as many pupils as will wear them, and/or second, a personalised group of symbols that are then immediately accessible to both the individual learner and to all members of staff. In either case it is likely that the number of symbols will be limited to twenty or twenty-five as a maximum, simply by the fact that any more would make the whole thing unwieldy.

It is very tempting to put a whole series of control words on these keyrings, such as sit, wait, dinner, home time, bus, playground, etc. Phrases such as 'good sitting' and 'good waiting' are equally staff controlling words and should be avoided if at all possible. The logic of the keyrings is to both encourage and allow for spontaneous communications in all sorts of situations (in other words providing both means and motivation). Pupils will not, however, be encouraged to wear them and use them spontaneously if staff utilise them as control mechanisms. I don't think I would want to be anywhere near a symbol keyring if I saw adults constantly bearing down on me making me do things I might not want to do!

It is therefore really important that communication systems:

- allow the learner to control rather than just being instruments of control;
- are learned in dynamic social situations;
- are constantly refined and decoded;
- allow pupils to be active participants in the process of learning to communicate.

PECS (Picture Exchange Communication System)

While it is recognised that PECS may well be an effective means of aiding needs wants communications for those with autistic spectrum disorders, it should be noted that PECS is *a* symbol system, it is not *the* symbol system. It may well not be suitable for those working at or below P6/7 because of the absolute necessity to be able to distinguish between a number of symbols. PECS may be extremely well suited to non-verbal, non-communicative, non-learning disabled autistic children, but this does not mean it is suited to all (non-verbal) children, especially when the desire to communicate is apparent, as it is with the vast majority of those with SLD (at least in those without additional autism). We need to ensure that we fit the system to the child rather than just fit the child to the system.

The use of PECS (Frost and Bondy, 1994; Bondy and Frost, 2001) was widely noted by Lacey *et al.* (2007) in their in-depth study of teaching literacy in special schools. Abbott and Lucey (2005) had recorded that some ninety-six per cent of SLD schools used symbols as a regular means of aiding communication and Lacey *et al.* noted the common use of PECS within that. Dawn Male has reported on two research studies (Magiati and Howlin, 2003; Carr and Felce, 2007) on the use of PECS, both using control groups and both reporting the clear efficacy of PECS for stimulating communicative and dyadic interactions between children and adults. However, both studies were criticised by Male (2008) for 'proving' nothing more than that a sustained intervention with additional specifically trained PECS intervenors resulted in an increase in the spontaneous use of PECS: 'when it comes to enhancing the communicative acts of children with autism, the PECS method is better than doing nothing at all. However, what we do not know is whether it is the *best* method' (p. 40; original emphasis). A trifle harsh perhaps, but based on the failure of studies to test comparatively with another intervention and the lack of longitudinal studies.

Although there are no studies that clearly indicate this, it would seem PECS is fast becoming the dominant symbols system in use in SLD schools in the UK, replacing the more traditional symbols books. Is this a true reflection of what is actually occurring and, if it is, is the widespread use of PECS justified for those who may not have autism?

Lacey *et al.* (2007) ask other questions relating to the use of symbols, notably whether their use aids reading. On the contrary, however, they found that,

> recent work by Sheehy and associates has suggested that teaching symbol systems (symbols under the words which are later removed) are no more successful than teaching words alone in gaining traditional reading skills. At worst, symbols interfere with the recognition of words. Sheehy and Howe (2001) suggest that the association between the picture symbol and the written word can actually make it harder for someone with learning difficulties to remember the association between the spoken and written words.
>
> (p. 151)

Another strategy to consider, which is heavily dependent for its success on identifying and utilising areas of interest for the learner, is 'Communication Books' (Latham, 2005). Clare Latham attempts to take the emphasis away from the noun (object) dominated format traditional within symbols books with her *Developing and Using a Communication Book*, available from The Ace Centre, Oxford at www.ace-centre.org.uk. Latham (2005) posits that many symbols systems fail as pro-active communication aids because they are essentially noun based with no room for verbs (action words). They therefore might show a symbol of a ball but not what the relationship is between the ball and the pupil. Is it something the child wants to play with now, later, at playtime? Is it a football, a tennis ball or a physio-ball? Does the child want to play on her own or with others? If the latter, whom? How can the child refine her conversation if there are no qualifying verbs? How can communication books become effective 'Alternative and Augmentative Communication' (AAC) aids if they do not allow language and communication to grow? In order to overcome these obstacles Latham has devised a split-page book, showing verbs on the left page and nouns on the right. There may be a number of noun pages (grouped according to genre) so learners have practice at generalising the use of verbs with a number of nouns.

Latham argues that there are a number of key 'requirements for success' if the symbols book is not to become just another failed system gathering dust in a classroom cupboard. She notes these as:

1   Nominate one person (or possibly two or three working closely together) willing to be the learner's communicative partner(s). This will need to be someone (usually a TA) who is liked by the learner and is with her for much of her day. It is interesting to note that Latham is insistent that this (or these) TA(s) take ownership of the book in the first instance, only gradually passing it over to the learner as the learner gains confidence and interest. Failure to use the book or forgetting to have it with her, or getting it torn, etc., are not the pupil's responsibility or fault. We (the supporting adults) need to make success in this as easy as possible in the first instance or it might never get off the ground.

2   Decide which symbols or photos are pertinent to the pupil and where they will be placed on the page.

3   Be consistent with both of these as you progress.
4   Build language through the constant repetition of the core vocabulary.
5   Concentrate on key words.

She is also clear about what not to do!

1   Don't test. Prove that the book can be useful for commenting.
2   Don't stop using the book, even when the learner isn't.
3   Don't make it a chore – *have fun.*
4   Don't rush the learner through the stages.

Latham also advises passing through clear set stages:

Stage One (this might equate in UK P scale terms to someone working at around P4 and
    upwards):

- The learner is communicating through gestures, taking you to items and pointing.
- Supporting adults take responsibility to get the book out; find time to chat about
  things the learner enjoys; point to the appropriate pictures as they are discussed.
- The learner watches and maybe points occasionally at the photos or symbols.

Stage Two (P4/5 and upwards)

- The learner is communicating single ideas through the pictures.
- Supporting adults introduce symbols for 'you', 'come' 'look' and 'want'.
- Continue to pause to allow the learner to point to a symbol while chatting.
- The learner might link a core vocabulary symbol with a topic symbol or picture.

Stage Three (P5/6 and upwards)

- The learner is using symbols to link two or three ideas and is using some core
  vocabulary.
- Supporting adults help the learner to get the book and find the right page;
  routinely use the book throughout the day; extend vocabulary and links.
- The learner begins to take responsibility for getting the book; links three or four
  ideas; uses the question, negative and describing symbols.

Stages 4 and 5 (P7 and P8 and upwards)

- Continue to expand the learner's independence.
- The learner is gradually encouraged to take responsibility and move away from
  dependence on one key member of staff.

Kossyvaki, Jones and Guldberg (2012) have established what they call the Adult Interactive
Style Intervention (AISI), the principles of which have been extracted from a wide variety
of interventions including Intensive Interaction (Hewett and Nind, 1998; Nind and Hewett,
2001), Musical Interaction (Corke, 2002, 2011), SCERTS (Prizant *et al.*, 2006), Options
(Kaufman B, 1994; Kaufman R, 2003) and Hanen (Manolson, 1992). All of these use the
transactional model of development, which argues that adults' behaviour shapes children's
development and influences their communication (Wetherby and Prizant, 2000).

Kossyvaki *et al.* (2012) note thirteen general principles and a further nine communicative opportunities (p. 177) with examples of how they might look in practice. You will observe that a number of these have already been elaborated on in this and other chapters, but they are such fundamental principles that they most definitely bear repeating.

General principles of AISI (with examples)[2]

Establish appropriate proximity/contact – The supporting adult (SA) notices that there is nobody sitting next to a pupil when he is finishing his biscuit and he is about to ask for another one. The SA moves next to the pupil, making sure there is no more than a metre distance in between them.

Show availability – The SA holds out her hand with vertical palm after realising the pupil will need help with an activity.

Gain child's attention – The SA chants 'What shall we do with Nathan now?' and pauses while sitting next to him in the sensory room.

Wait for initiations – The SA waits for the pupil to hand in the 'biscuit' symbol before prompting him to do so. The SA only prompts the pupil when it is obvious he is not going to initiate.

Respond to all communicative attempts – The SA shows the pupil his timetable saying 'It's time for work' when he tries to escape by pushing her away.

Assign meaning to random actions or sounds – In the sensory room, the SA sits in front of the pupil facing her and sings 'Row, row the boat' joining his rocking.

Imitate the child – The SA imitates Michael's vocalisations in the sensory room and pauses in anticipation for more.

Follow the child's lead/focus of attention – In soft play, the SA follows the pupil to the mirror once he had enough on the trampoline and starts a new game there related to the mirror.

Use exaggerated pitch, facial expression, gestures and body language – The SA is very animated while jumping on the trampoline with the pupil. The SA's tone of voice is gradually increasing before the end of each turn and she laughs once the turn is over.

Use minimal speech – During a sorting activity in work time, the SA speaks slowly and stresses the key words to the pupil: 'Find *same*'.

Provide time to process information – Before starting a new activity the SA shows the pupil his timetable and gives him time (up to ten seconds) to process the information.

Expand on communicative attempts – The SA says 'biscuit' when pupil A (with a verbal communication level of vocalisations) gives her the 'biscuit' symbol but says 'more blackcurrant' when pupil B (with a verbal communication level of occasional words) gives her the 'blackcurrant' symbol saying an approximation of the word 'blackcurrant'.

Use non-verbal cues – When the pupil stands up during work time the SA shows him the timetable, taps on his chair and guides him physically to sit down.

Communicative opportunities of AISI (with examples)

Offer choice – During work time, the SA moves the work box closer to the pupil and waits for him to choose the activity he wants. He has to do all the activities of the work box but can decide on the order he is going to do them.

Stop part way – During soft play, the SA sings to the pupil his favourite song, dropping the ending word and pausing so he will join in.

Give small portions – The SA gives just one piece of chocolate to the pupil every time he gives her the 'chocolate' symbol to prompt him to ask for more.

Make items inaccessible – In the sensory room, the SA puts the light curtain out of reach but in sight so the pupil will ask her to take it down.

Give material the child will need help with – Once the work box is put on the table the SA does not take off the lid but waits for the pupil to ask her to do so.

Contradict expectations – The pupil is staring into space and the SA steps in front of him to elicit a reaction.

Give non-preferred items – The SA puts some carrot on the pupil's plate knowing he does not like it to elicit protest.

Withdraw attention – In soft play, while jumping on the trampoline with the pupil, the SA gradually stops to make the pupil ask for more.

'Forget' something vital – The SA gives the pupil the yogurt he asked for but 'forgets' to give him a spoon so he will have to ask for it.

The communicative opportunities noted above can also be aligned to ideas held in Chapter 13 ('A Problem Solving and Thinking Curriculum').

You might also use a variation of 'Options' (otherwise known as 'Son Rise') or 'Floortime' (Greenspan and Weider, 2003), both techniques sharing a number of similarities with Intensive Interaction. Although they are also both developed for working with children on the autistic spectrum, it may be that they could be equally interesting techniques for those with SLD. Both are about finding a communicative pathway into those who struggle with social interactions by using the things that are highly motivating to the children themselves. These can be anything the child finds interesting from pieces of string to Thomas the Tank Engine toys to model dinosaurs; such choices are, of course, highly individualistic. The adult does not lead, but follows the child's lead, with the aim of entering into joint play, joint engagement and of course social interaction and communication. There is no reason to believe that these techniques would not work with hard-to-reach children with complex difficulties who have an understanding of declarative communication.

Literacy

In a two-fold study Lacey *et al.* (2007) conducted a literature review of literacy and severe learning difficulties and a study of practice in thirty-five schools in the East Midlands, observing 122 'literacy' lessons and interviewing sixty-one teachers. It is worth directly quoting their conclusions from their literature review on literacy in SLD schools:

1   National guidelines on teaching literacy assume that learners with SLD should be taught in much the same way as typical learners, although this is not based on any research evidence with this group.

2   Research on learners with Down syndrome shows that many can learn to read and write conventionally. It also shows that they are likely to use visual pathways to learning more effectively than auditory pathways. Further research is required to establish whether this is true for other groups of learners who have difficulties in the area of language and communication.

3   Learning symbols as a bridge to using text may not be helpful but learning to read symbols may be a useful skill in its own right. However, as yet there are few books for older learners that use alternatives to text such as symbols.

4   Although almost all schools for children with SLD use symbols, it is not known how many use them systematically for learning to read.

5   Despite the importance of pictures in emergent literacy for very young children, little is known about how to teach students with SLD picture 'reading' as a skill in its own right.

6   ICT provides useful media for learning about both conventional text and inclusive access to literacy, through computer software, digital photography, filmmaking and other technology such as CD players, mobile phones and iPods®. HMI suggest that schools may not be using these media very imaginatively.

7   Access to literature through means other than reading and writing (e.g., drama, television, video and storytelling) is important in its own right even if it does not lead to conventional literacy. The extent of the use of these inclusive literacies in schools for pupils with SLD is not yet known.

(Lacey *et al.*, 2007, p. 152)

Some points to tease out from this are:

1   We can probably draw an educated guess from point two above that those with SLD are likely to find learning new words through phonics decoding skills extremely difficult, and there is more on this below. Whole-word recognition and encouraging children to guess the meaning of words through context should always be the default starting position. By all means try phonics, but don't necessarily expect it to be effective for anyone with SLD. Generally speaking, if children are significantly delayed in their understanding and expression of language, they are going to find reading more difficult. In the initial stages, a personalised approach (selecting vocabulary that is within the child's experience) is going to be a useful starting point (Lock, 1999; Hinchcliffe, 2001).

2   The assumption that learning to read through symbols is a precursor to reading words is not founded on any evidence. Using symbols for pre-readers should probably be limited to (i) timetables and schedules, the reading of which can be an extremely useful exercise for ensuring structure and certainty to the pupil's day, and (ii) practising reading a variety of social sight symbols such as 'ladies' and 'gents', etc., which are often diverse enough to confuse even the most sophisticated reader!

3   It should be noted that point six above may already be outdated, such is the pace of technological change. More can perhaps be made of pictures, including moving pictures. It may well be that the considerable technological advances being made with iPads and iPhones, tablets and smartphones (as well as their inevitable reduction in price) will open up a whole new area of literacy for the SLD pupil and student.

As partly noted above, Lacey *et al.* (2007) suggest that there is a considerable tendency for teachers in UK SLD schools to follow 'normative' literacy lessons –structures for teaching literacy that might be found in mainstream schools. Lacey (2006) notes that literacy for teachers primarily means:

- traditional orthography including phonics sessions and handwriting, especially names;
- conventional literacy – especially going to the library and choosing books, whether the pupil can read or not and whether the pupil spends time with the chosen book or not;
- social sight recognition – such as 'Gents', 'Ladies', 'Exit', 'Look Left', etc., as a preparation for everyday living;
- reading with symbols including making books with symbols;
- non-conventional 'literacy' artefacts such as story sacks and bag books;
- communication – particularly the use of PECS.

The suggestion that pupils and students with SLD are ever likely to be fluent readers is, however, not borne out by the evidence or the research.

How conventionally developing children learn to read

Drawing an extensive map of the development of literacy in conventionally developing children, Linda Gibson suggests that literacy begins from a very young age with learning taking place through social interaction with adults and exposure to developmentally appropriate print such as picture story books and 'feely' books. Gibson (1989) goes on to identify four key stages:

Pre-readers – from birth to two years

- Through sharing books with adults, children develop book-handling skills, so the child becomes aware of the symbolic nature of books, especially responding to non-concrete objects – the pictures – rather than treating the book as just another object or toy.
- Towards the end of this stage, the child may recognise their own name in print, but the overall process is largely the same as the emergence of communicative skills.

Emergent Readers – from two to four

- The child starts to recognise the importance of print and engage in storytelling by talking through their games.
- They explore rhyming patterns in chants and nursery rhymes.
- The teacher must constantly coax collaborative learning from the child in order to help them make sense of what is read.

Early Readers – from four to five

- Children begin to know the difference between their own writing and drawing, and develop the key skill of writing their own name.
- They enjoy copying letters and exploring writing patterns.
- They develop an understanding of the alphabet and identify more and more words in a variety of contexts.
- They only now begin to understand sound correspondence and basic single letter phonics.

Fluent Readers – from five onwards

- Children start to become fluent readers who can process print details automatically.

- They begin to use a more sophisticated phonic understanding to tackle new and unfamiliar words, although this skill does not fully develop until later, probably after the age of six.
- Equally importantly, children are increasingly able to handle a variety of print forms.

The point about Gibson's arguments are that, while they apply to NT conventionally developing children, we can draw lessons from them for those who have severe learning difficulties, especially when we note that phonics skills are not likely to kick in until the age of six has been reached and passed. Some of those with SLD may well attain this cognitive level, but it is highly likely that the considerable majority will not (Imray, 2005).

How children with severe learning difficulties learn to read

Hinchcliffe (2001) proposes that when planning appropriate work for children with SLD, teachers need to bear in mind visual and non-visual approaches to teaching reading. Regarding the latter, Smith's treatise on the 'inside-out' approach to reading (Smith, 1985, 2011) is important. Smith emphasises the amount of information which, as readers, we project from 'inside our head' out on to the print: 'The basic skill of reading lies more in the nonvisual information that we supply from inside our head rather than in the visual information that bombards us from the print' (Smith, 1985). Let's take a paragraph chosen entirely at random from a children's classic, *Anne of Green Gables*:

> I should think she would better punish Diana for being so greedy as to drink three glassfuls of anything' said Martha shortly. 'Why, three of those big glasses would have made her sick even if it had only been cordial. Well, this story will be a nice handle for those folks who are so down on me for making currant wine, although I haven't made any for three years ever once I found out that the minister didn't approve. I just kept that bottle for sickness. There, there, child, don't cry. I can't see as you were to blame although I'm sorry it happened so.
>
> (Montgomery, 1985, p. 101)

The 'inside our head' understandings required for the comprehension of this passage are considerable. For example, what is cordial? What is currant wine? What does 'a nice handle' mean? Who is the minister and why might he disapprove? How has that concept changed over time since the nineteenth century in rural Canada? What does 'keeping a bottle for sickness' mean? None of the answers to these questions will be immediately apparent from the text; they require additional pieces of knowledge that 'are taken as read'!

According to the 'inside-out' view it can be assumed that many children with SLD will be disadvantaged since their difficulties with cognitive and linguistic skills will mean they will be approaching the reading task with less non-visual information than the non-learning disabled child. They will inevitably have difficulties utilising contextual information, that is, asking the right questions of the text.

As intimated earlier, children with SLD learning to read traditional orthography will also undoubtedly experience difficulty utilising 'outside-in' approaches to reading, which means using visual information to derive meaning directly from the print – for example, using phonics (decoding letters, letter clusters and whole-word approaches (recognising the shape of words) etc.). In reality, children with SLD can be expected to learn only a limited repertoire of word-attack skills. For more able children who demonstrate some ability in this area, the teacher may consider the following aspects of visual information in planning reading work: learning the sounds of individual letters ('a'); letter clusters ('st'); patterns or shape of words ('tap') and learning whole words ('said') with some high frequency words to be taught as sight recognition.

As stated, phonic skills have a major emphasis in accepted approaches to teaching literacy, through for example the UK National Literacy Strategy (DfEE, 1998), but there are bound to be limits as to how many letter-sound or cluster-sound correspondences pupils with SLD can retain. For more able children with SLD, it may be worth limiting the teaching (at least in the early stages) to all single letter sounds; consonant blends; a few digraphs, e.g., ch, sh, th, ee, oo ai (and possibly if they're very, very able, ou, ay, igh). These are clues to help readers identify words, words that must make sense in their context. The challenge is for pupils to be encouraged to use both visual and non-visual information in their reading: to recognise whole words (visual); to use simple phonic clues (visual); to use context to derive meaning (non-visual).

Lexical Access

Lexical Access is the chain of processes by which information from text is transmitted from the eyes to the word memory (or lexicon) in the mind as, for example, when the information we get from seeing the printed word 'cat' is transmitted to our mind, enabling it to get the meaning of the word. Two possible access routes have been proposed. One is that of direct visual access, as described above, by which the mind gets the meaning direct from the print; the other is the phonological encoding route, which involves the reader in speaking each word (either aloud or sub-vocally (under one's breath)) and then getting the meaning from this spoken word. Encoding is likely to be at a more abstract level for more experienced readers (more aligned to phonological representation), but children with SLD at the early stages of learning to read are likely to experience difficulty with phonological access routes and be more suited to visual access routes, for example, through learning to read the meanings of words in the context of their use by utilising a 'language experience' approach (see below).

The differences between spoken and written language

An appreciation of the differences between spoken language and written language is critical to teaching literacy. Donaldson (1978) wrote that very young children's language is embedded for them in the context, which is the flow of events that accompany it:

> The non-linguistic context of spoken language exerts a powerful influence on interpretation. In other words, children – and indeed adults much of the time – do not interpret words alone. What they are basically interested in is to understand what people mean, rather than what words mean. They interpret words in their setting – both the physical setting and the personal setting – to such an extent that we may speak of the language as being embedded in its context.
>
> (Donaldson and Reid, 1982)

Written language has to manage without the context offered in speech. Guppy and Hughes (1999) talk about readers being denied the flow of spoken language, the wealth of information to help them anticipate the author's meaning. Illustrations to the text, symbols, pictograms, etc., may help, but they cannot possibly offer the same wealth of non-linguistic context as speech does. The complexity of written language is easily overlooked; written language is not just speech written down, which is why learning to read is more difficult than learning to speak: 'Language written down is . . . cut loose – or disembedded – from the context of ongoing activities and feelings in which speech thrives. Once on the page, language is on its own' (Donaldson, 1989).

When children begin to learn to read, they make use of their existing knowledge of spoken language, its meaning and its structures (its semantics and syntax). They bring expectations about meaning to the text, approaching the text with certain questions in mind and selecting enough information to provide the answers. Teachers of children with SLD will have to help pupils in this; they will have to ask the questions and help the children find the relevant information.

So in the early stages of learning to read, children will need help to make inferences from limited cues, to guess unknown words according to meaning and context and apply whatever word level skills they have learned. This means that in the early stages of teaching pupils to read, teachers must ensure that whatever text they expect children to read will make sense to them. This means taking great care on the choice of material that is presented to the child, avoiding what Donaldson calls the 'language of books', written language that is different from the kind of language children hear or use.

Helping children with SLD to develop early reading skills

All pupils beginning to learn to read need to understand that writing carries messages, so they can bring their expressive language competence to bear on reading (Donaldson and Reid, 1982; Hinchcliffe, 1996b, 2001). Some essential points for consideration when teaching pupils with SEN to read are:

1   The teacher must ensure that pupils actually have the necessary receptive and expressive language competence. Too often we find children who are at very early levels of language development but have been taught to read quantities of single words without any reference to a meaningful context (Hinchcliffe, 1991). Lock (1999) writes about the risks of exposing children with SEN to written forms of words when they do not understand the spoken forms.
2   The teacher must (at least in the early stages) ensure that the written language represents the kind of spoken language they can understand. It seems pointless to confront them in print with language that they could not understand even in speech.

For children who have reasonable receptive and expressive language abilities, their language skills will provide the foundation on which they can begin to understand language in its written form, provided that this written language is similar in vocabulary and structure to the expressive language they use and know.

This relationship between the words and what is understood by the words is described in the 'Simple View of Reading' (Gough and Tunmer, 1986; Hoover and Gough, 1990) and indicates that reading skills and listening comprehension are components of reading comprehension. According to this model, reading comprehension is the product of two distinct components – decoding and listening comprehension – each of which makes its own unique and independent contribution (Savage, 2001). Both of these abilities are necessary, but neither is sufficient in itself to explain reading comprehension (Gough *et al.*, 1996). The model may be expressed by the formula r = dc, where *r* is reading comprehension, *d* is decoding (the words), and *c* is listening comprehension.

This emphasis on listening comprehension is key, because the theory emphasises that reading is not just about being able to understand the words we see in front of us; we need to recognise that a pupil's ability to comprehend meaning will depend on their ability to listen (to themselves reading). In other words, two distinct processes are at work here – reading skills and listening skills, and the learner must be competent in both.

To test this theory, Roch and Levorato (2009) conducted a study with a group of individuals with Down's syndrome (mean age = fifteen years and five months) and a group of typically developing children (mean age = six years and eight months) who were matched for their level of reading comprehension. The students with Down's syndrome were shown to be weaker in listening comprehension but more advanced in word recognition – their ability to read the words did not necessarily equate to their ability to understand the text because their general abilities with language (their listening comprehension abilities) were impaired. Roch, Florit and Levorato (2011) conducted a follow-up study that confirmed these findings:

> Three main findings emerged: (1) reading skills, on the one hand, and comprehension, both listening and reading, on the other hand, are independent; (2) the development of reading comprehension is determined mainly by listening comprehension, which in this study proved to be very poor [for those with Down's syndrome]; and (3) participants [with DS] improved their performances in all the abilities considered, except for listening comprehension which remained at the same level after a one-year period.
>
> (Roch *et al.*, 2011, p. 239)

When hearing a child read, the teacher must try to judge, at every stage, what meaning (if any) the child is constructing on the basis of the information in front of her. In other words, the teacher must stay one step ahead and predict where in the text the pupil will encounter difficulty. And when the child experiences difficulties in understanding, the teacher must provide extra information (scaffolding) where necessary, to help the child construct the meaning, if practicable. The teacher should also encourage children to use both visual and non-visual clues to obtain meaning.

Pupils with SLD may not become fluent readers because their cognitive level may be too low, especially in being able to contextualise the words they are reading. Reading is not just a process of interpreting the printed words since it also involves comprehension, and these two skills are independently achieved and may well not develop in pace with each other. This fact on its own, however, does not mean that those with SLD cannot learn to read, since an intellectual ceiling may be overcome if the child has long enough to practise, though it may well be that judgements will have to be made on the merit or otherwise of devoting the time to developing reading skills, if the end result is ineffective. Again, an extensive quote from Lacey *et al.* (2007):

Although students of all ages with severe learning difficulties (SLD) spend a significant amount of curriculum time in literacy lessons, most of them only learn the rudiments of reading and writing. Some may learn a sight vocabulary of common words and some individual phonic sounds but most will find it hard to generalise these skills beyond early reading scheme books or similar simple text. Some will find it outside their ability to learn even a few words and sounds, and for those with the most profound intellectual disabilities, conventional literacy could be seen as irrelevant.

(Lacey *et al.*, 2007, p. 149)

Nonetheless traditional literacy skills may still be worked on through:

- Setting up specific reading groups for those who are able or who have the potential – perhaps identified at around KS2. There are going to be problems with age-appropriate materials which progress at a slow enough pace and ensure lots of opportunity for repetition. There are, unfortunately, no extended commercially produced reading schemes which do this, and nor are there likely to be given the very small market.
- Ensuring *lots* of practice on reading for meaning – especially for ASC learners.
- Specific reading of 'social' words and signs in context, practised both in and out of the classroom.
- Use of ICT, especially PowerPoint® to make story books.
- Cutting and pasting key words into a book and supporting these with photographs or iconic symbols.
- Making picture books with key iconic symbols.
- Curriculum mapping literacy skills, e.g., recipe reading, shopping lists, TV guides, etc.

But we should also recognise that:

For pupils with learning difficulties, reading may be interpreted as any activity that leads to the derivation of meanings from visual or tactile representations, for example, objects, pictures, symbols or words (QCA, 2001a, p. 7).

- Taking literacy as purely the written word automatically excludes virtually all learners with either SLD or PMLD.

There is no doubt that learning to read effectively is a significant skill and mastery of it will considerably improve a young person's ability to be independent in the world. However, for pupils and students with SLD whose upper intellectual levels are likely to be the equivalent of a conventionally developing six year old, learning to read is an extremely complex business, and we must make judgements about how able they are likely to become. There is so much to learn and so little time to learn it for all those with SLD, that not to make such judgements, but to carry on with conventional reading schemes irrespective of the reading age attained, must constitute a failure to provide a relevant curriculum.

This is exactly Brahm Norwich's (2008) *dilemma of difference* writ large, because this is not a dilemma that is abstracted away to somebody else. Every single person who is involved with the education of a child, young person or adult with learning difficulties must constantly ask the questions: Why are we teaching this? What are we trying to achieve? Are we making a difference?

Continuing to teach assuming conventionally developing models is unlikely to be of benefit and continuing to teach assuming conventional development is destined to fail. We do our children no service by refusing to recognise these elemental truths. Resolutions to the dilemma will, one supposes, rest on educated assumptions as to how far each individual learner can take their reading given how far they've progressed by a certain age, and it might be that this ought to be initially assessed by the age of eight, nine or ten.

What might literacy become for the pupil with SLD?

There are extremely strong arguments for suggesting that for pupils and students with SLD, literacy needs to encompass the spoken word as much, if not more, than the written word. Clearly then, storytelling and the mastering the art of narrative becomes key. Apart from teachers and TAs reading story books to children, there are a number of commercial storytelling packages, such as Chris Fuller's *Bag Books* available at www.bagbooks.org and Nick Wonham's *Choose and Tell* stories available at www.chooseandtellseries.com. You might also want to look at Pete Wells' splendid PowerPoint stories aimed specifically at secondary-age students with SLD and PMLD, freely available at www.portlandcollege.org

Leading the way, however, as writers of significant importance in both the theory and practice of the teaching of literacy to those with learning difficulties, are Nicola Grove and Keith Park – both together and independently. *Odyssey Now* (Grove and Park, 1996) remains one of the classic works of learning difficulties literature and inclusion, and there are many others published by the pair since then (Park, 1998c; 2009b; 2010; Grove and Park, 2000; Grove, 2005; 2010; 2012). Park's take on literature is that even the most complex and abstruse can be made accessible to those with learning difficulties if we take care of the rhythm, make it interactive, give it meaning in the affect of our voices and, above all, impart emotion. Take 'Alas, Alice', a poem by Michael Donaghy (1993) as an example. This is how it appears on the page:

Alas, Alice
who woke to crows and woke up on the ceiling and hung
there fearing the evening's sweeping and looked down now
at her unfinished reading and loved by sleeping and slept
by weeping and called out once. The words were dust. Who
left late singing and signed up leaving and ran home slowly
afraid of sleeping and hated thinking and thought by feeling
and called out once but no one came,
who dreamt blue snow and froze in dreaming and spoke by
reading and read all evening and read by patterns of blizzards drifting and dared by waiting and waited taking and
called out once and called out twice and coughed grey clouds
and carved four coffins and took by thanking and thanked
by seeking and drifted bedwards and lay there weeping and
counted her tears and divided by seven and called out once.
The words were crows.

Now, with the inclusion of a one-second beat that might be gently foot tapped, or finger clicked, or beaten on a drum, and a slight adaptation and occasional repeats of lines, this can be 'called' – with staff and pupils responding by repeating each line – as follows:

Alas, Alice
Who woke to crows
And woke upon the ceiling
And hung there fearing
The evening's sweeping
And looked down now
At unfinished reading
And loved the sleeping
And slept by weeping
And called out once.
(pause)
The words were dust.
(pause)
Who left late singing
And signed up leaving
And thought by feeling
And called out once
But no one came.
(pause)
Who dreamt blue snow
And froze by dreaming
And spoke by reading
And read all evening
And read by patterns
Of blizzards drifting
And dared by waiting
And waited taking
And called out once
And called out twice
(pause)
And touched grey clouds
And carved four coffins
And took by thanking
And thanked by seeking
And drifted bedwards
And lay there weeping
And counted her tears
And divided by seven
And called once.
(pause)
And called out twice
(long pause)[3]
The words were crows.

And what does this poem mean? Who knows? One makes one's own meaning, but the words are beautiful in their rhythm and simplicity, and convey (for this reader at least) a deep sense of loss and despair. What better way to portray sadness?

Learners may use communication aids such as a BIGmack to call or respond to specific words or lines; staff may assist rhythmic movements through encouraging and supporting rocking, stamping, clapping, banging, vocalising, using VOCAs, laying learners on sound boards and enjoying, in any way they can, the process of being part of the rhythm of the group. Feelings and emotions can be acted out by staff through facial expression and body responses directly to the learners involved. Call and response can form the essential rock upon which drama and poetry for those with severe learning difficulties is founded.

Readers are strongly urged to beg, borrow, steal (or preferably buy) a copy of *Interactive Storytelling*, which gives 'scripts' ranging from A. A. Milne to William Shakespeare; all entirely suitable for all abilities and ages.

Call and response:

- is a simple method of encouraging fun communications;
- relies on the natural poetic rhythm and flow of language;
- accepts that these rhythms are innate;
- each line is kept deliberately short and rhythmic;
- works best when dramatic and conveying feeling and emotion;
- is naturally and automatically including rather than excluding.

Teaching our children to be storytellers

As Keith Park is to call and response, so Nicola Grove is to storytelling. She argues very cogently (Grove, 2005; 2010; 2012) that the art of narrative is a tremendously powerful and central part of our understanding of ourselves as social beings. But the art of narrative, the ability to tell stories, is not automatically given – it has to be learned, and for those with severe learning difficulties, this can be a long and slow process. It is nonetheless an essential process, one that is vastly underrated in a world of the written word, and one that teachers of those with learning difficulties must address.

Conventionally developing children start to listen to stories from a very young age, and begin to tell their own stories soon after they learn to talk. These skills are continually refined as the child grows up, particularly as they learn to write. Our own storytellers – novelists, poets, playwrights, actors, songsters – gain great status from their skills, and rightly so, and even in non-literate societies (or perhaps, especially in non-literate societies) the story carries enormous importance. Learning how to tell them is an essential way of learning about life.

What does a story do? A story has a beginning, a middle and an end; it has purpose and meaning to both the teller and the listener; it teaches us to listen carefully; it teaches us about structure, and about the natural rhythms and flow of language; it teaches us about emotions – fear, excitement, anxiety, heartbreak, happiness, love – in a safe and secure setting, not only other people's (the characters' in the story line), but also our own. Most importantly, however, our ability to tell stories both directly effects and affects our under-standing of our own humanity. As an example, think of something you have experienced over the last twelve months or so that has meant a lot to you. This can be happy or sad, exciting or full of pathos, thrilling or frightening, or maybe all of these things at once. What have you done with this information? Most likely, you have not kept it to yourself, unless it was *the most terrible secret in the world*! Most likely you have told someone, because that's what we do, it's part of what makes us social animals, it's part of what makes us human. Sharing our lives with others in this way allows us to relive the happy and exciting and thrilling, and gain enjoyment from the enjoyment of others. It marks us out as special, individual and unique. I have done this, I have value, I am important, I am me. Sharing the sad or pathetic or frightening experiences of our lives allows us to evoke others' sympathy and empathy, put our problems into perspective, receive back comfort of someone else's similar experience so we know we're not alone. I am me, but I'm also with others who love me and care enough about me to listen and share in my problems as well as my joys.

What does a story mean to those with learning difficulties? Children, young people and adults with learning difficulties also start listening to stories from a very young age; they possibly continue to listen throughout their lives; but when do they get to tell stories themselves? And when do they get to tell stories about themselves? Most often, the severe communication difficulties experienced by children with SLD and PMLD preclude the art of telling stories, and therefore preclude them from an essential part of becoming a social human being. Things, good and bad, happy and sad, still happen to them, but the knowledge of them, the relating of them, the sharing of them, becomes the property of those who can communicate effectively, parent, siblings, teachers, TAs, doctors, nurses, bus drivers, Uncle Tom Cobbly and all; everyone in fact, but the person themselves. The stories of the events that actually happened to the child, young person or adult with learning difficulties are not owned by them, they are owned by others. We've taken away their ability to tell stories by not spending enough time teaching them how to do it effectively. We're so busy teaching them how to read and write that we've forgotten to teach them how to communicate.

If we are to attempt to develop storytelling skills in children, young people and adults with SLD, the emphasis needs to be on very simple but dramatic stories, initially told by the teacher. Over time, learners are encouraged to take in not only the structure and essential elements of that particular story, but also the structure and essential elements of storytelling itself. They can then move on to the most important part – telling their own stories, telling their own lives. First of all, however, the learner must learn how to tell a story, and that is not as easy as it sounds.

Task

Here are two stories to be going on with, the first courtesy of Nicola Grove. Can you analyse what makes this a great story and write two more in a similar vein?

Story Number 1 – The Robber!

One day, I was walking home from school. It was cold and dark and rainy. SUDDENLY, I heard FOOTSTEPS. I looked behind me . . . but there was nothing there. I carried on walking home. It was cold and dark and rainy. SUDDENLY, I heard FOOTSTEPS again. I looked behind me . . . but there was still nothing there. I carried on walking home. Then the footsteps got LOUDER and FASTER and then a BIG MAN was standing over shouting 'GIVE ME YOUR MONEY!' I gave him all the money I had and he ran off down the road and I never saw him or my money again. That is the end of the story!

Story Number 2 – SNOT!

One day, about a year ago, I had a TERRIBLE cold. I was sneezing all of the time. AAAAACCCHHHOOOOOO. I went downstairs to have breakfast but I felt a sneeze coming on. AAAAACCCHHHOOOOOO. Oh no! White gloopy snot all in my brothers cornflakes. I felt another sneeze coming on. AAAAACCCHHHOOOOOO. Oh no! Green bits all on my mum's new dress. My dad was very cross and started telling me off but I felt another sneeze coming on. AAAAACCCHHHOOOOOO. Oh no! White and green snot all in my dad's hair. It was running down his face and everything! Here, said Mum, use a tissue! AAAAACCCHHHOOOOOO. That is the end of my story!

You may tell these stories as a raconteur would, or you may act them out. Here are the bare bones of 'The Spider in the Sandwich' (another Nicola Grove story), which can be initially acted out by two members of staff using props,[4] and then taken over by one or two pupils. We have deliberately not put a script here because it is REALLY important that these stories are told and not read. This means the words might occasionally change and that's OK because as with all communication it is the sense of the thing we have to convey, not the accuracy of recall.

One day . . . Person A makes a sandwich.

Person B wants a sandwich but is too lazy to make it. 'Make me a sandwich' 'No, make your own.'

A is distracted – a knock on the door, a tap on the window, the phone rings – and B (who has engineered the distraction) takes a bite from the sandwich.

'Who ate my sandwich?' 'Not me.'

This is repeated.

After the second time, A says, 'I'm going to make a fresh sandwich and it's just going to be for me' but A secretly puts a spider in the sandwich.

When the distraction occurs again, B takes a bite 'OH NO . . . THAT'S DISGUSTING.'

The end.

Things to do with the stories

- Tell one story at a time. The story must engage the learners and if it doesn't, drop it and tell another.
- Check out the top ten tips for writing and telling stories in Chapter 5.
- Note how the best stories are short, simple and involve lots of repetition. Look at what makes *The Gruffalo* and *The Bear Hunt* such great stories. These are essentially the same short scenario repeated several times and building up to a crescendo.
- Don't not tell stories to secondary-age students because you're worried about 'age appropriateness'. Any story can be age appropriate if you make it so. Try adapting *Little Red Riding Hood* for fourteen year olds – it's all about the irresistible and oh so dangerous 'wolf' that mothers don't want their daughters to marry. You can put sex and death and rock and roll into any children's story and it automatically becomes age appropriate, although of course cultural considerations may determine how much sex and death and rock and roll you can safely put in. And if you're still worried, just replace the wolf with a zombie!
- When you've told the story at the beginning of the session, encourage each pupil to tell the story themselves by sitting in the storyteller's chair. This is a 'special' chair that

confirms the authority and control of the person leading and should be given the appropriate amount of reverence by all. You'll need to help them a lot at first, but you can act as the 'response' to their 'call' by mirroring (scaffolding) what they say and encouraging everyone else in the group to do the same. Using this call and response method has a number of important functions:

- It confirms that the narrator is leading the speaking, rather than competing for a voice.
- It confirms that the narrator has successfully communicated what they want to communicate.
- It allows for major errors to be rectified as you go along (minor errors should be ignored as long as the core of the story is the same).
- It allows for 'affect' to be instilled (and thereby modeled) by the adult who is acting as the primary response.
- It confirms that the audience has understood.
- It confirms that the audience is listening.
- It slows the process down and gives the narrator a chance to gather their thoughts.
- It sets out a clear sequence of events.
- It gives an opportunity for gentle prompts if the narrator has forgotten the next line.
- It gives the narrator the chance to go 'off piste', especially as they get more skilled, and still take the audience with them.

- Repeat this format with the same story for several weeks, perhaps breaking up the sessions by making a picture book or PowerPoint or videoing scenes with your pupils as the actors.
- The aim here is to teach pupils that stories have a structure (beginning and middle and end), high points, a conclusion and an audience. This latter point is really important since the best storytellers take their audience with them and include them as part of the story.
- Non-verbal pupils can sign, or hold up pictures/symbols, or use a VOCA such as a Step-by-Step to aid the storytelling (Musselwhite and Burkhart, 2001). If using a VOCA try to get a child of roughly the same age and gender to record the voice. Staff and more able pupils can still 'respond' to their 'call'.
- As your pupils start to improve their storytelling skills, they can start to make up their own stories about real events that relate to them. They can, in other words, tell their own stories about their own lives.
- Once you've firmly established the basic storytelling skills through short, exciting, dramatic fictions (and this for most pupils with SLD could take several years) talk to learners' families (during parents' evenings, etc.) about special events and stories the family might relate at home.
- Take ownership of the everyday stories that are normally kept in the staffroom.
- Encourage staff to write down the events that happen to your students, especially if they carry emotion – funny, scary, dramatic etc.
- Start a 'Storytelling Box' to keep in the staffroom where stories can be posted.
- Involve the learners as much as possible in the writing of their own stories.
- Storyboard the stories into short books using real characters as much as possible. If you can support this with photographs, so much the better.

- Video two- or three-minute narrations to show at home in the same way that we might tell a favourite anecdote, and especially get your students to film using their mobile phones or iPads/tablets. This then becomes the equivalent of taking a book home.
- Share your performances at assemblies so they become owned by the whole 'culture'.
- Most of all – have fun being literate!

Notes

1 Canaan Barrie is a signing system developed initially for those who are deaf/blind and relies on touch. It is not commonly used with those with learning difficulties because it is (like British Sign Language) a language in its own right, although the principles may be adapted.
2 To make for ease of understanding, we have allocated female status to the Supporting Adult (SA) and male status to the pupil, for this section (on AISI) only.
3 The pause might be indicated by continuing with the beat (but no words) for four seconds and the long pause for eight seconds. It is amazing how powerful such 'silences' can be and, because the beat goes on, the pupils are held to the rhythm and tend not to lose concentration.
4 We must, however, try to ensure that we don't overuse props as we want to teach the skill and art of narrative rather than performance. Props, while handy for an initial dramatisation of the story, may well both detract and distract from the narrative.

Chapter 11

A mathematical thinking curriculum for pupils with severe learning difficulties

Question

Can you think about five activities that *do not* involve the use of mathematics in some form? The secret to successfully teaching mathematics may be to teach it through other areas, any areas, so mathematics is something that is 'interesting and relevant for pupils and enables all to participate and grow' (Higginson, 1999).

Both academics and practitioners alike argue that it is defensible to 'concentrate on the basics' for those who have a characteristically slow rate of learning, and that teaching maths in terms of practical, everyday situations makes it both relevant and understandable (Robbins, 2000; Stewart *et al.*, 2000).

The point about the above question therefore is that it should be impossible to think of anything we consciously do that does not involve maths in some way – even falling asleep involves shape, space and measure, since we have to work out where we are going to be comfortable enough to fall asleep, check that there's enough room and the best shape to put our bodies into. If mathematics is all around us, why not teach 'all around us'? There are of course principles that must be applied to ensure children have a chance to be successful in learning and be able to apply the basics in mathematics.

There follows an extended quote from the Cockroft Report of 1982, written well before the UK National Curriculum came into existence. The quote is discussing maths with conventionally developing children and is not concerned with those with learning difficulties; nonetheless it makes salutary reading:

> Mathematics is a difficult subject both to teach and to learn. One of the reasons why this is so is that mathematics is a hierarchical subject. This does not mean that there is an absolute order in which it is necessary to study the subject but that ability to proceed to new work is very often dependent on a sufficient understanding of one or more pieces of work which have gone before. Whether or not it is true, as is sometimes suggested, that each person has a 'mathematical ceiling' (and so far as we are aware no research has been undertaken to establish whether or not this is the case), it is certainly true that children, and adults, learn mathematics at greatly differing speeds. A concept which some may comprehend in a single lesson may require days or even weeks of work by others, and be inaccessible, at least for the time being, to those who lack understanding of the concepts on which it depends. This means that there are very great differences in attainment between children of the same age. A small number reach a standard which enables them to study mathematics at degree level but many others have time to advance only a very short distance along the mathematical road during their years at school.

Because of the hierarchical nature of mathematics these pupils do not reach a position from which they are able to tackle the more abstract branches of the subject with understanding or hope of success, though some can and do continue their advance after they have left school.

(DES, 1982, pp. 67–68)

What can we take from this and how can we apply it to those with severe learning difficulties?

Numeracy

Numeracy (number) is not easy to teach and certainly goes far beyond the ability to rote count or repeat words (numbers) in a particular order. The basic principles of understanding number were established by Gelman and Gallistel (1978). There are six principles in all, although for those with SLD we are really only concerned with the first three. These are:

The one-one principle – one and only one unique number tag must be assigned to each item counted – one is always one and two is always two.
The stable order principle – count words must be produced in the same order for each count – four always follows three, seven always follows six.
The cardinality principle – the final word of a count denotes the total number of items counted – indicating that the concept of a distinct group to be counted has to be established.

Gelman and Gallistel's theory is insistent on the cardinality principle being understood before the concept of number can be fully realised. Research with *typically* developing children in the UK shows that cardinality emerges a few months either side of the fourth birthday (Nye *et al.*, 2001). This fact alone will indicate that it will be very difficult for a good percentage of children with SLD to fully grasp the concept of number, especially as cardinality will get more problematic once numbers get above two or three (Staves, 2001; Porter, 2010). This does not mean that cardinality cannot be taught, just that we must move cautiously and individually through the gears. There is no point in moving an individual on to counting sets of five if he cannot consistently identify sets of three.

Staves (2001, p. 75) suggests that there may be numerous reasons for children failing to count correctly, since they may:

- fail to correspond pointing to individual objects;
- fail to correspond the sound to the pointing action;
- miss an object;
- itemise an object more than once;
- miss a number name;
- apply the same name twice;
- confuse the order of names;
- lose track of what has been counted and what remains to be counted;
- fail to stop the verbal sequence at the last object, keeping on because of the rhythm;
- not realise the last number is cardinal;
- miss some objects because they don't think they should be included in the count because of their colour, shape, position, etc.

McConkey and McEvoy (1986) make the very pertinent points that those with SLD find number difficult because the multi-dimensional sequence needed to count successfully – identify the items making up the set, recall the number names in the proper order, give each item in the set one (and only one) number name, remember the objects that have been counted and those that remain, realise that the last number named is the total for the set – has to be performed simultaneously *and* perfectly. They posit that games, because they are motivational, allow much repetition and are non-pressured (it's only a game), and especially games played with a single number dice, are an effective way of improving number skills.

Porter (1993) concurs with the concept that those with SLD, even when they can count, have considerable problems with cardinality because the difficulty of making the cardinal count transition is too great an intellectual leap.

> It is the significance of the last tag which eludes the child. Rather than its having meaning in terms of the properties of the set as a whole, the question 'how many?' is simply identical to the request to count the items.
>
> (p. 74)

As McConkey and McEvoy advise, therefore, play *lots* of number games and sing *lots* of number songs whenever and wherever you can; it doesn't have to be in a maths lesson! Recognise that a number of those with SLD may need literally thousands of rote opportunities to practise counting, and if children are going to count, be sure that they're counting something interesting and motivating to them (Staves, 2001; Weeks 2012). You will not necessarily guarantee that they can understand number, but they never will if they do not know (at least by rote) that four follows three. Games are also good for numeral recognition.

It is also important at this point to be very sparing with the whiteboard when working with number and SLD. Extensive use of whiteboards is a fairly typical trap that unwary teachers are likely to fall into, because there are so many programmes easily available (for NT learners) and because they seem lots of fun and have a high visual impact. However, they do work on the principle of normative development, where cardinality will be naturally established, or has already been established. This will not be necessarily so with children with SLD. Games, songs, stories and rhymes, etc., when shown on the whiteboard become abstractions and therefore difficult for someone with SLD (who will struggle with abstract concepts) to relate to in a concrete way. Games, songs, stories and rhymes that use *real* objects the child can handle and hold are much more likely to have an impact.

When matching and sorting, sets (to be counted) need to be clear and without dubiety. If counting cars, for example, the cars must be identical in size, appearance and colour. Once cardinality at a certain stage has been established it is advisable to generalise the skill learned by, for example, asking for three cars (of any colour) from a group of other toys, and then perhaps three cars of any colour and size from a group of other toys. In many respects, the true test of a child's ability to count is for him to successfully give you the correct number of cars from a bucket of lots of cars in response to the instruction 'give me three cars'.

When teaching children with SLD to learn to count groups of objects, it may be worth encouraging children to move items slightly with their finger to highlight the number tag. This helps prevent children missing an object, counting objects more than once or applying the same name twice.

It is a good idea to start working with *number lines* as early as possible so that pupils have a visual representation of 'more than' and 'less than'. Start with zero to ten and work up, personalising as pupils make individual progress.

If addition is to be taught we need to remember that children must be able to 'add on' using the first number in the sum. How many in this group? Now add one. How many now? Once that skill has been established they then need to recognise the largest number (of two) even if the numbers to be added are, say, two plus three. The assumption might be that we would teach pupils to put the two numbers together, but this is merely counting, as is evidenced by the sum two plus twenty-three. Even if the pupil had worked out the necessity to 'count on' it would be illogical to start that counting on from two. Subtraction works on the same principle, only in reverse.

Time must be spent recognising numerals as this will have significant impact on all pupils, irrespective of whether they learn to count or not. Just think of clocks and watches, telephone numbers, bus numbers, television channels, ovens, keyboards, game consoles, etc. It is only necessary to learn from zero to nine, and cardinality does not have to be established. Again, remember to generalise the skill by looking at numerals of differing typeface and size.

The language of mathematics

Comparisons. We need to very careful about language here because it very easy to add confusion. For example, which is the biggest number? 7 or 2? Which is the biggest coin, a 2p piece or a £1 coin? The influence of specific language skills (or quite possibly, the absence of them) should not be underestimated (Paterson *et al.*, 2006). Porter (2010) posits that this makes it even more important to use approaches to teaching that build on the pupils' strengths, especially using language and mathematical examples that are already familiar to pupils. Rather like language generally, mathematics will make much more sense when it is seen in context.

Number names themselves might be more difficult to understand for those who struggle as communicators. In English, for example, numbers from thirteen to nineteen are spoken 'back to front' compared with numbers from twenty onwards, so we say 'twenty-four' but 'fourteen' (rather than the much more logical 'teenfour'); the words 'eleven' and 'twelve' are even more irregular, especially when so much mathematical language is now based on units of ten rather than twelve.

It makes sense when teaching comparisons to be consistent in using specific comparative words across all areas of learning and all teachers (including home):

- number and capacity = more, less; holds more, holds less
- length = longer, shorter
- weight = heavier, lighter
- area = bigger, smaller
- time = before, after, now, next.

Words to explore within

- position – in, on, next to, outside, inside, over, under, above, below
- direction – *in front, *behind, opposite, apart, between, left, right, up, down, along, through, away from
- movement – slide, roll, turn, stretch, bend, forwards, backwards, sideways, through.

* Bear in mind the problems of deixis[1] when teaching 'in front' and 'behind', and avoid using teaching resources with fronts or backs, e.g., dolls, cars, etc. (Cox, 1991). With people and objects that have fronts and backs, you will run into difficulties when asking children whether things are in front or behind. For example, when asking a child whether a ball is 'in front of' or 'behind' a miniature plastic figure of a footballer, the visual perspective of teacher, child and footballer needs to be taken into account when determining the correctness of a child's answer. The skill and effectiveness of teaching such words is to recognise that these are all descriptive of things and events happening. This makes them perfect for teaching through games, drama, dance, PE, art, music, play, travel training, shopping.

Effectively, these are all concepts that lend themselves to process-based teaching. It is the process of the game, the drama or the music playing that is important and central. Children will learn the language of maths and indeed other concepts in maths because, as we've seen already, 'maths is all around us, and so the feeling grows; it's written on the wind, it's everywhere we go'! And they'll learn it all the better because they're having fun and are involved in activities that are pleasurable and therefore bear considerable repetition. As with all things SLD, repetition is very much the key to learning.

Other key concepts

Money. This is the classic case of never assuming that the rules for typically (conventionally) developing children and those with severe learning difficulties are the same. Because they're probably not! It is very easy to get confused as a teacher of children with SLD, because the linear developmental approach so necessary for mainstream children's mathematical learning dictates that we teach from the base – recognition of 1p, 2p, 5p and 10p coins, and so on. For those who are very likely to have extreme difficulties with number, however, it is best (as a basic and universal principle of functionality) to teach 50p and £1 first, and then £2, and for older learners, £5 notes. Once children with SLD have learnt the principle of recognising what motivating personal snack item they can buy for 50p, for £1, for £2, pupils can move on to working on two 50ps equalling £1, two £1s and four 50ps equalling £2 and various combinations equalling £5. Then, and only then, can we go down to the smaller denominations of 20p, 10p, 5p, 2p and 1p, in that order.[2]

It is probably unwise to use plastic or cardboard money if you're expecting learning to take place, and equally unwise to use photographs of coins for matching. Always use real coins (stuck to card if you're matching, loose if you're not), which means you'll have to organise a float and count the coins back in after a session. Money is a hard enough lesson to learn for those with SLD, without abstracting the lesson even further.

In the same vein it is always best to go and practise shopping for real if you possibly can, but if not, use real money when playing at shopping in the class. Why not have a permanent tuck shop where mid-morning snacks are bought for less than 50p or £1 and change given. It doesn't have to be the exact change for most learners, but it will give them opportunities to get used to the principal of exchange. They can also practise going to the bank (asking a designated adult) to get their money out, holding on to money, putting it in a purse or pocket and not losing it, putting it back in the bank (handing it back to an adult) at the end of the lesson – all key components of money. Remember also to have some items marked up as the exact amount (say 50p) so pupils get used to not receiving change for some items.

Estimation is best done in real situations so that it has meaning. How many stickers/biscuits/sweets/cups/balls will we need for everyone in the class to have one each? How long will we need to tidy up? How much paint do I need to complete my painting? How much can I carry when moving resources from one class to another?

It is really important to be positive about mistakes and accept Einstein's dictum that 'Anyone who has never made a mistake has never tried anything new'. Encouraging a spirit of adventure and risk is explored in greater detail in Chapter 13 ('A Prolem Solving and Thinking Curriculum'), but we need to accept that encouraging estimation carries considerable risk, in all sorts of areas. If, for example, after much previous practice, modeling, demonstrating and support, your pupil estimates that she only needs a single coin to buy an item that plainly costs much more, you must allow her go through with the process. The interim result will be no purchase at the shops, with the inevitable consequences that will ensue, but we mustn't hide from these consequences and we mustn't shield the pupil from these consequences. Otherwise we won't get to the end result – real and independent understanding from the learner.

Time. Clearly, telling the time accurately, even to the hour, is going to be a big challenge if learners have not established the cardinality principle, although this doesn't mean we shouldn't be teaching time. Areas that can be worked on are visual timetables; now and next; key passages of time and moments of the day such as lunchtime, playtime, home time; setting alarms to indicate short passages of time, especially useful for cooking, tidying up, warnings that sessions are about to end, etc.

Fractions and division may seem a strange element to work on without a firm grasp of number, but this is an important skill for sharing as well as problem solving. Encourage pupils to chop whole apples and segment whole oranges in halves first and then halves again. Halve sheets of paper for painting, clay or plasticine in art, cakes on birthdays and whole bars of chocolate for treats. It is *really* important that you get the children to carry out these tasks themselves, rather than doing it for them. Yes, they will make a mess and yes problems will occur – but if they don't try, they won't learn! Encourage your children to take responsibility to divide anything that can be divided, such as whole bags of crisps, whenever the opportunity arises. Mistakes will be made, but lessons will be learned through those mistakes.

The problem with maths?

Question 1

With regard to teaching pupils and students with severe learning difficulties, which position do you hold and why do you hold it?

1   We should teach mathematics through a differentiated approach to a National Curriculum and strategies that apply to all.
2   We should teach mathematics through other subjects.
3   We shouldn't teach mathematics at all.
4   Another position?

Question 2

Is mathematical literacy possible for those with SLD when mathematical literacy has been defined as:

an individual's capacity to identify and understand the role that mathematics plays in the world, to make well founded judgments and to use and engage with mathematics in ways that meet the needs of that individual's life as a constructive, concerned and reflective citizen?

(OECD, 2006, p. 1)

This is an interesting definition precisely because of the opening few words, viz 'an individual's capacity to *identify and understand the role that mathematics plays* in the world.'

Question 3

If the answer to Question 2 is no, should we be teaching mathematics as a discrete subject? The defining difficulties facing a person with severe learning difficulties makes for interesting reading in relation to mathematical thinking:

- *Communication* – numerous writers (for example Robbins, 1991; Staves, 2001; Paterson *et al.*, 2006; Porter, 2010) have pointed out that because so much of formal maths is related to linguistic ability, those with communication problems are very likely to be at a serious natural disadvantage in learning.
- *Difficulties in understanding abstract concepts* – virtually all of number (especially mental arithmetic) is abstract.
- *Difficulties in concentration* – especially in holding more than a single piece of information at a time and multi-tasking, a basic requirement of effective counting, addition, subtraction, etc., and most definitely a requirement of problem solving.
- *Information processing difficuties in moving things from the short-term memory to the long-term memory.*
- *Inefficient and slow information processing speed,* which carries additional problems when added to difficulties in concentration.
- *Little general knowledge* – requiring constant contextual referencing for learning to take place.
- *Poor strategies for thinking and learning*
- *Difficulties with generalisation and problem solving* – in the same way that context plays an essential role in aiding the understanding of specific words in particular and language in general (Locke, 1999; Hinchcliffe, 2001) so context is essential for mathematical understanding (Porter, 2010).

Other factors

Headteachers of SLD schools in the UK noted that 'average' ability levels had declined markedly over the last ten years, that is from 1996 to 2006. There was no firm research relating to this, but it was a common enough theme for it to be part of an Ofsted SEND Review (Ofsted, 2006).

A 'new generation' of children with learning difficulties, described by Barry Carpenter as Complex Learning Difficulties and Disabilities (CLDD) (Carpenter, 2010), are presenting with more diverse, fractured and complex difficulties; this is apparent across all sectors, both in mainstream and special schools. Co-morbidity is commonplace, especially in the areas of ASC and ADHD, but also in children who present with extremely spiky profiles, with often particular difficulties in mathematics.

The developmental approach

Maths is often represented as a process of linear progression, so specific skills are learned in a set order – in number it is counting first, then addition, then subtraction, then multiplication, then division, then fractions, etc. Because maths skills are based on establishing 'building blocks', we can't move on until the first block is learned. *But*, because those with SLD have (by definition) the problems noted above, many may never learn even the first block (cardinality). We often, therefore, end up teaching the *same thing* throughout the whole of a learner's education! How often when teaching shape, for example, do we fail to work on three-dimensional shapes because pupils have not mastered differentiating between simple two-dimensional shapes? Shape becomes a constant 2D square, circle and triangle, and number becomes a constant counting to five. We might vary the colours and size of the shapes (making it even more confusing in the process!) and we might vary what we count to five, but the essence is the same. Do we need to look further than the developmental approach in maths and recognise that a large percentage of learners with SLD will *never* get the concepts?

The Developmental Approach adopts 'traditional good practice' for SLD/PMLD teaching and:

- teaches to a maths curriculum;
- focuses on a specific objective;
- teaches one small step at a time with lots of opportunities for practice;
- uses the same equipment to avoid confusion;
- utilises rote learning.

But this approach may have had the effect of narrowing the maths curriculum in our desire to achieve *measurable success* against normative developmental markers (Robbins, 2000). Cutler (2000) argues that we may have lost sight of the broader picture and for numeracy, for example, we no longer concentrate on where numbers fit within the number system; the relationship between numbers, and the importance of pattern within maths. We might need to make sure that by compartmentalising maths in discrete sessions teaching to patterns of normative development, we don't neutralise other learning opportunities. (Robbins, 1996).

The primary/secondary split?

Perhaps we should try to establish as many basic skills as possible up to the age of nine, ten or eleven years of age. Developmental age is closer to chronological age and therefore more age-appropriate resources are available. After nine, ten or eleven we can establish a base line and stretch laterally. The difficulty here is that Maths (with a capital M) is generally regarded as a key and primary subject, along with Language and often Science. The argument goes that everyone has the right to be taught maths, and to deny that right is to diminish the breadth and balance of the curriculum as well as the basic rights to equal educational opportunities. Pupils may well achieve numeracy and many other areas of maths if they are given sufficient time. Who are we to deny that opportunity? Perhaps.

This issue is rather like the reading and writing dilemma; some pupils may get there to some degree given time, but how much time must we spend getting there? And is 'there' a place worth getting to given all the other learning that is not taking place while we concentrate on such narrow targets? Might it be that we get overwhelmed by the need to teach maths as a discrete subject when maybe it almost *demands* to be taught within other areas?

Questions

How much maths is in the art room? What mathematical concepts can we teach when painting?

Answers

- Large and small paper
- Different shaped paper
- Different quantities of paint – thick paint, thin paint
- Small brush, big brush
- Estimating quantity needed
- Problem solving if you run out of paper or paint
- How long do you need?
- Time to clear up
- What do you need to first, what second, what last, etc.?

Question

Where's the maths in the kitchen? What mathematical concepts can we teach when making a pizza?

Answers

- Size
- Quantity
- Position
- Measurement
- Weight
- Structure of properties
- Temperature
- Sequencing
- Cause and effect
- Estimation
- Counting
- Addition and subtraction
- Fractions
- Division

Question

Where's the maths out of school? What mathematical concepts can we teach when travel training?

Answers

- Estimation of distance, time, etc.
- Spatial awareness
- Speed of traffic
- Relative speed of different traffic
- Speed of walking at different times, for different purposes
- Direction
- Recognising bus numbers
- Reading bus/train timetables
- Direction/routes of buses
- Paying fares
- Counting bus stops
- Sequencing
- Past/next/after/full and other mathematical language

How have teachers got to teach maths?

According to the UK's Qualifications and Curriculum Authority (QCA, 2001b; QCDA, 2009) the organisation that largely advises the national inspecting body (Ofsted) on curriculum variations applicable to those with an SEN, teachers should (not might or can, but should) teach in ways that match and challenge their pupils' abilities. They can also:

- Work within earlier chronological key stages;
- Maintain, reinforce, consolidate and generalise;
- Focus on one or limited aspects of the age-related Programme of Study;
- Use everyday activities as a focus;
- Work within accredited Schemes of Work such as Equals and ASDAN for older (14+) learners.

The point being here that even within the statutory bodies there is a clear recognition that we (teachers) have to ensure our teaching is relevant to those we are teaching. The difficulty usually arises because the method of measuring progress, in the UK system at least, is at present entirely defined by models of normative development (the P Scales and the National Curriculum levels). And again, in much the same way as models of literacy, we are driven down roads that may be completely irrelevant to the way pupils with SLD learn, with the tail wagging the dog; that is, assessment and pupil progress driving what we teach.

What is progress? Part one

We are good at practising (usually developmental) skills in the classroom, but how good are we at encouraging children to apply those skills? If we're going to extend our learners' mathematical abilities, we have to be sure they can apply them; we have to be sure they understand maths in the context in which they're applying it. It is not necessary that they understand the theory; it is necessary they understand the practice.

This means we have to think very, very carefully about the individuals' abilities and potential so we can maximise their opportunities for independence. Let's take cooking as an example. At the low end of SLD (in UK terms, those who are working consistently between say P4 and P6) it may well be that independence is best achieved by enabling learners to follow a clear recipe, laid out in single words and/or symbols and/or photographs, to make a favourite simple dish – beans on toast, for example. Such learners will probably always need some level of adult support to oversee the completion of the task, but it is entirely possible, given time, that they would be able to achieve it entirely independently.

This in turn means that the long-term aim for such learners is the mastering of the following abilities *completely independently* without any physical or prompting support from the attendant adult:

- deciding what to eat for lunch;
- checking whether the resources are available;
- deciding what needs to be bought;
- putting a symbol/photograph shopping list together;
- ensuring sufficient funds are available;
- checking the weather;
- deciding on what outdoor clothing to wear;
- travelling to the shop;
- purchasing the needed items;
- carrying the shopping back;
- returning the change to the appropriate place or person;
- changing into indoor clothing;
- sorting out the correct recipe;
- washing hands;
- opening the can;
- heating up the beans;
- making the toast;
- sorting out the cutlery and plate;
- making a drink if required;
- washing the dishes and putting them away.

A number of points arise from this long-term aim. *All* of the above involves maths. Mathematics for the person with SLD is an holistic concept. Maximising independence must always be the long-term aim and we must always be ambitious, we must attempt to stretch. We need to tackle this stretching slowly. It is very possible that achieving this level of independence may take several years of regular (at least weekly) teaching sessions.

We have to accept that some learners will not achieve this level of independence, but that does not negate the long-term aim. Failure is OK, not trying is not. Maintenance of independence might well be regarded as a legitimate indication of progress for this group of learners. Achievement of a broad target must not mean that we cease to teach it, as skills can and will be lost if they are not regularly practised. For this group of learners, learning is not like riding a bike!

There is a product involved – eating the beans on toast – but the teaching of the 'skills' necessary to achieve the end is a process. Teaching them in isolation is possible, but runs the real risk of negating their meaning for the learner. We can teach most of the above as separate or sub-grouped concepts, but they all have to have real meaning for the leaner and must be taught in context. There's no point in checking the weather unless there's a reason to check the weather. What's the point of checking the weather unless you're thinking of going out?

Personalisation of the learning will follow the motivation of the learner, especially around favourite things to eat and drink, but we can group most of the teaching into more or less equitable ability groups. The process of going to the shops is the same for all, but our ambition for the level of independence achieved will vary from learner to learner.

What is progress? Part two

For more able learners, in UK terms those working at around P7 and above, the basic tasks might remain roughly the same, but our expectations of the degree of independence achievable will be very different and our expectations of the timescale taken to achieve that independence may be very different. We can also therefore concentrate on differentiating the maths in the tasks, for example by making the cooking more complex. If we expect these learners to progress from making beans on toast entirely independently to making a pizza from scratch, again entirely independently, we then make the shopping list, the shopping, the cooking and the tidying up more complex.

There is naturally a limit to the degree of creativity involved with making beans on toast apart from adding other ingredients to the beans, but making a pizza allows for all sorts of variations in the consistency of the dough, different toppings, different amounts, etc. Encouraging independence encourages mistakes to be made. This is a good thing since we are encouraging learners (teaching learners) to think and problem solve. What happens, for example, when a learner who has had lots of practice at making a pizza pours a whole packet of flour into the dough mix? We (teacher and TAs) would probably stop her. What happens if we don't; if we allow her to make and eat the pizza with ten times more flour in it than should be? She might say 'That was really delicious'! but she might also recognise that a mistake was made, and if we praise her effusively for having a go and we can help her to reflect on that mistake in a positive way, she might take a step towards achieving *real* independence.

Technically, within the UK National Curriculum model, we have to cover number; calculation; problem solving; shape, space and measure; handling data; algebra. All these areas can be covered in all of the other areas we might need to teach in a very (crowded) full SLD curriculum.

Mathematics, as much as any other subject, can be taught more practically, more contextually, more concretely, and much more motivationally, if it is taught as part of the process of shopping, art, dance, playing games, travel training, cooking, drama, or any part of life being lived.

Learning mathematical concepts is a different prospect for those with severe and profound learning difficulties. For this group of learners, it is perhaps the case that mathematics is best studied through 'careful and thoughtful adaptation of both the curriculum and the environment in which it is delivered' (Longhorn, 2000).

In any event we must avoid teaching maths in a shallow fashion, when the theory of maths takes precedence and the context is secondary. Perhaps maths might be best taught in exactly the converse situation. When the context is directly allied to the process so that deep and meaningful learning takes place.

Shape, space or measure?

Imagine a situation where you have taken a group of students shopping for their weekly cooking resources. It is quite a large shop involving goods that are heavy and light, large and small, fragile and robust. You have deliberately allocated only two students to pack the shopping and carry it back to school because this is an ideal opportunity to be involved in deep and meaningful learning that is entirely context bound, were students can practise their awareness of shape, sorting, matching, weight, tesselation, size and quantity. Activities could include:

1   Sorting the heavy and light items and different food items and/or packaging.
2   Deciding how many bags are needed to make the task easier, or do they need to take a bag/bags with them, and if so what type?
3   Sorting the bags out so they can carry them more easily?
4   Discussing what might happen if the bag is too heavy, what could they do?
5   Trying a range of containers – bags (plastic and paper) and boxes.
6   Experimenting on the difference each of these containers makes?
7   Trying out different methods of packing these containers?

In other words they need to think strategically, use mathematical knowledge and understanding, and respond to problems selecting the practical approach and mathematics that is required by the situation.

A critical analysis of the teaching of number and counting with children with severe learning difficulties

In the UK there has been an elevation of numeracy as the prime area for mathematical teaching with successive National Numeracy Strategies, and there is a naturally considerable interest in how this affects the maths curriculum in the typical SLD school and, indeed, for the typical child with SLD in a mainstream setting. For Robbins (2000) the original UK National Numeracy Strategy (DfEE, 1999): 'sets out to improve teaching but as yet there is no hard evidence that it improves learning, certainly not across the whole spectrum of ability. Furthermore we have no proof of its efficacy with children whose learning is impeded by disability' (p. 9). And more than a decade on, there is still no evidence.

Robbins goes on to suggest that adopting national strategies which, like the National Curriculum, give the 'clear impression' that the learning and involvement of those with SEN 'had not been given any serious consideration', are likely to only produce a tunnel-vision approach which may restrict learning. The elevation of numeracy as the primary objective in mathematics restricts the emphasis to a linear, neuro-typical methodology, and an insistence on dedicated maths lessons encourages compartmentalisation of the timetable. This in turn squeezes out the possibilities for teaching mathematics through other areas of the curriculum (Robbins, 2000).

In writing on whether developing numeracy is important to those with severe and profound learning difficulties, Jill Porter cites a number of studies of numerousness in animals and very young (neuro-typical) children which suggest number is not only important, but evident in their consciousness: 'Infants not only seem to have an *awareness* of numerical differences but it appears as if infants are able to construct mental representations of number as they are also able to *anticipate* the outcome of numerical change' (Porter, 2010, p. 5; her emphasis).

Such views are contentious; Mix *et al.* (2002), for example, argued that there is a great deal of difference between a general awareness of quantity and numerousness, and this still does not, of course, automatically indicate that those with learning difficulties have the same awareness. Nonetheless, an earlier study by Porter (2005a) drew on studies of typically developing children and investigated their application to three pupils with learning difficulties. She found that their responses to individualised learning contexts mirrored the progression suggested in the literature, namely from awareness of number to simple actions using number cues to problem-solving behaviour, and posited that responses from the SLD population to conventional mathematical tasks are often limited because they lack relevance and interest.

While the three pupils with SLD cited in her study are interesting, this work doesn't compare to her earlier study involving fifty-eight SLD pupils between the ages of seven and fourteen involving simple counting and error detection (cited in Porter, 2000). This study found that twenty per cent of the pupils understood the task and were able to detect the errors made; fifty-five per cent followed the counting but were unable to detect the errors; twenty-five per cent followed neither the counting nor the errors. In other words, eighty per cent of the sample had failed to master number sufficiently to count simple numbers effectively, since if one cannot detect a simple error, the 'skill' of counting is insufficiently well established and therefore ineffective.

Interestingly, Porter herself questions the validity of her own research in 'seriously underestimating pupils' potential capabilities' because, she surmises, SLD teachers did not (at the time of the original study) rate the acquisition of numeracy very highly, devoted comparatively little time to it (compared to mainstream nurseries, for example) and, crucially, failed to extend learning by producing counting strings just a little ahead of the child's actual competence (Porter, 2000). Or perhaps those with SLD have extreme problems in mastering numeracy?

A further study on the cardinality principle was conducted by Nye *et al.* (2001) on behalf of the Down's Syndrome Association. This followed the process of understanding number formulated by Gelman and Gallistel (1978), the first three of their principles being, as previously noted:

- The one-to-one principle – one and only one, unique number tag must be assigned to each item counted.
- The stable-order principle – count words must be produced in the same order for each count.
- The cardinality principle – the final word of a count denotes the total number of items counted.

Nye *et al.*, noting that research with typically developing children in the UK shows that cardinality emerges a few months either side of the fourth birthday, put to the test that those with Down's Syndrome (DS) develop academically (although not necessarily chronologically) in the same developmental sequence as conventionally developing children.

The study involved twenty-three DS who were all developmentally under four years of age (although chronologically between six and seven) matched with twenty conventionally developing (CD) children all under four. Their findings showed that:

- The scores were significantly better for the CD group for both the one-to-one principle and stable-order principle.

- In a test for accurately giving sets of (two or three) objects, however, there was no (statistically) significant difference between the two groups.
- The study reported that seven out of the twenty conventionally developing children had managed to demonstrate mastery of the cardinality principle, as had two out of the sixteen Down's Syndrome children. Unfortunately, seven of the Down's children had refused to co-operate with the test and were therefore ruled out of the results!
- Both groups made additional progress with adult support.

Are there conclusions to be drawn from both studies? Perhaps, perhaps not. What is clear, however, is that more large-group studies of this sort are needed if we are to draw firm conclusions on the ability or otherwise of those with severe learning difficulties to master number.

The final words (for now) go to Brian Robbins:

> Mathematics in particular is built on previous learning, and certain key elements of knowledge and skill are prerequisites to successful new learning . . . When faced with pupils who do not possess [mathematical] concepts in any way that enables them to apply them, we need as teachers to find strategies to enable them to understand and apply these essential tools.
>
> This is one example of the tensions that have been created for teachers who know that it is unrealistic to push their pupils towards unachievable targets and yearn for a more realistic and meaningful approach to mathematics teaching.
>
> (Robbins, 1996, p. 30)

Notes

1   Deixis refers to the fact that understanding the meaning of certain words and phrases in an utterance requires contextual information. Both parties have to know which 'he' and which 'car' you're referring to when you say 'He'll give you the car'.

2   Although we're referring to the pound sterling here, the same principles apply whatever the currency, although you may have the even harder difficulty of differentiating between notes rather than coins. This can be quite tricky when the notes are the same size for differing denominations and you might be uncertain about colour recognition, especially when note colours are often quite insipid. Identifying numerals may well therefore be key and will take a lot of work in establishing.

Chapter 12

A creative arts curriculum for pupils with severe learning difficulties and profound and multiple learning difficulties

Task

Take the story of *The Bear Hunt* and write down some ideas about how you might use the story as basis for a short drama with primary-aged pupils, and if you want to be really adventurous, secondary-aged students, and even more adventurous, adults. Think about how you might make *The Bear Hunt* suitable for secondary-aged and adult actors. What are the elements of a story that you think might appeal to secondary-aged students and adults? Can you elevate these in the story? Is there any language in *The Bear Hunt* that you think might be a bit too childish for those over the age of eleven? Can you transpose more adult words?

As this is about teaching pupils and students with severe learning difficulties, plan to spend at least an hour per week over at least a term, because we know that for those with SLD, repetition is the key to learning. And as this chapter is on the creative arts in general rather than drama in particular, think how you might bring in other elements of the arts such as dance, art and music, which will aid telling the story in a dramatic form. Finally, what do you think your pupils or students will gain from this?

Some answers

The Bear Hunt is one of those classic tales for children that has all the ten essential elements for a good story[1]; and it doesn't have to be told as a story (in the sense of following the pictures and words in a big book[2]) because it is very simple to adapt into a piece of drama. The drama becomes about *doing* and *being* rather than merely telling, with the pupils transformed into participants (actors) rather than audience. 'Surely learning (for those with severe learning difficulties) is most effective when it takes place in contexts which allow pupils to see the relevance and application of what they are learning: contexts which mirror reality as closely as possible?' (Byers, 1994, p. 88). In other words, what better way to learn about being part of group with a common goal, having a collective spirit of adventure, being looked after and protected, being frightened, going from danger to safety and then being kept safe. For those with severe learning difficulties learning is most effective when it takes place in situations that are actually real, or if that's not possible – and being chased by a real bear might be stretching risk assessments just a trifle too far – drama allows us access to contexts which 'mirror reality as closely as possible'.

For younger children you might actually go through tall, wavy grass, squishy, squelchy mud, a deep, dark forest, etc. You might actually go into a dark, dank cave and actually meet a bear, even though these are representations of reality with the grass and the forest being long strips of paper and branches and twigs suspended from the ceiling, the cave being the sensory room with all the lights off, the bear being one of the pupils dressed up. For younger pupils, those teachers lucky enough to live near the countryside might think of taking the classroom into a forest ('Uh-oh . . . What's behind that tree?'); for older students we might progress to being imaginative about the difficulties faced rather than making the props in art lessons – in other words, extending into thinking about other states of mind.

Drama, dance, music and art are merely more sophisticated extensions of both play and games playing, and it is not necessary to be strict about divisions. Lots of early developmental games such as 'The Farmer's in the Den', for example, can be made into full-scale dramas, so pupils can experience what it's like to be the farmer, the wife, the child and the dog. Any story is open to becoming a piece of drama, or something that can be translated into movement, music or art.

Leaders of schools especially, but also teachers and TAs, often get exercised by the concept of age appropriateness and consider it an essential part of their remit to move older (secondary-aged) pupils away from the childish. This is probably because many with severe learning difficulties naturally drift towards what they know and can be comfortable with in the arts, so the predilection towards childish songs and children's TV programmes and books might carry on well into adulthood. But their intellectual difficulties are likely to give them a view of the world that is in many ways equivalent to a very young child and it should not be surprising that they continue to find materials designed for very young children appealing.

Certainly we need to extend the learners' experience of new and more adult concepts, but we must be very careful not to alienate learners by our desire to push them into adulthood. In the arts, we may extend the adult elements of apparently childish stories (such as *The Bear Hunt*) so that we concentrate more on the unknown (giving a sinister tone to 'uh-oh' and a decidedly scared tone to 'we're not scared'); build up the tension as we enter the forest and especially the cave; enter into a deliberately darkened room so the students can't see what's in it, hang 'spiders webs' from the ceiling and place strange things like fridge-cold 'slime' strategically around the room. We might transform the bear into a werewolf or a zombie and one of the 'Uh-ohs' might be 'Bodies, masses of rotting bodies. We can't go over them. We can't go under them. OH NO . . . We have to go through them!' You could in fact do whole piles of rotting bits of torso ('Uh-oh. Legs!') or better still with the older students, let them decide what the 'monster' is and what the hazards are, so they are directly engaged in the process of imagination and other states of mind.

Equally, there is no reason why apparently adult artistic experiences, like *A Midsummer Night's Dream* or *The Tempest*, for example, shouldn't be introduced to quite young learners. Perceived adult themes and perceived childish themes are not mutually exclusive and we would do well to consider the part that magic, and the desire for magic things to happen, plays in all of our lives. Being adult should not be about losing the magic, a fact that Hollywood has long understood.

Another word of caution: performance is an excellent thing to do, especially as it is such an effective way of instilling self-confidence and a sense of self-esteem into our learners, but if you're only thinking of the product rather than the process, the learners may only get your ideas imposed upon them. This should not be about you (the teacher) being a great director, choreographer, graphic designer or musical arranger (or even a great teacher!), this should be about them (the learners) working as actors, dancers, artists, musicians and *in the process* thinking about what they're doing and taking control of their own learning. Above all – and this really ought to be printed in big capital letters and placed in a prominent position in every staffroom in the land – make sure you have fun. The arts, perhaps more than any other area of learning, give tremendous opportunities for having fun, and with fun goes learning. If you can build in a little bit of stretch from the previous week (and it doesn't have to be much) the very process of having fun will have much more of a chance of lodging in the memory and therefore stimulating learning.

Why it is so important to elevate teaching the arts to those with severe and profound learning difficulties

Cahill (1992) talks of the arts as being an excellent vehicle for raising children's self-confidence, enabling them to achieve in literature without writing, in situations where there is no right and no wrong. Peter (1998a) argues that the arts are essentially,

> concerned with *making* and *sharing* meanings, and stimulate a process of personal growth. Arguably they give form and expression to an inner drive to externalise images; perhaps we all have some inner need to communicate, to find forms of expression and to symbolise or encapsulate our experiences; ways in which we may all find a sense of personal validation. In schools we need to ensure that they are achievable by ensuring that children of *all abilities* develop confidence and appropriate skills.
>
> (p. 171; author's emphasis)

In a similar vein: 'The capacity for all art forms to motivate, to encourage self esteem, to stimulate the imagination, curiosity, and encourage children generally to investigate, are major outcomes of any learning experience for a child with severe learning difficulties' (Carpenter and Hills, 2002, p. 22).

Peter (1998b) suggests that the arts are capable of promoting (i) fluency of thought; (ii) flexibility of thought; (iii) originality of thought; and (iv) elaboration of thought. She goes on to argue that pupils tend to find the arts inherently motivating perhaps because there is a 'strong notion of empowering pupils to take control and responsibility in the learning process'.

On the benefits to self-esteem derived from performing in the Shakespeare Schools' Festival, Andrew Cowries, from James Rennie School in Carlisle, England, stated that 'the knock-on effect was profound. To be part of a national event, performing in a real theatre, in front of an unknown audience gave them a powerful sense of certainty and purpose' (quoted in Lancaster, 2006). And again from Melanie Peter:

> Potentially the arts offer all children the opportunity to *integrate* their knowledge, skills and understanding. A child will paint or draw what he or she has experienced, but will also experience what he or she paints, thus prompting further responses and making connections. The arts offer the potential to work in a multi-layered way, in contexts that are motivating, meaningful and energising. It is possible to capitalise on their inherent playfulness (the natural way all children learn).
>
> (Peter, 1998a, p. 171; author's emphasis)

Balshaw (2004) describes the often startling effects of entering into a 'creative partnership' experience with various (professional) artists from various disciplines over an extended period of time. At Mayfield School, a SLD/PMLD special school for three to nineteen year olds in Birmingham, England, she noted that:

- creativity and the arts offer multiple points of entry to learning especially for young people with learning disabilities;
- working in partnership with creative practitioners can start from a level playing field – unlike many learning experiences in school. Creative exploration starts from a position of ability, not disability, working with ideas generated by young people wherever they are starting from;
- school staff gain high levels of satisfaction and significant professional development opportunities through working in partnership with artists, especially where this takes staff into new skills areas;
- developing networks of learning, between groups of schools and between schools and creative individuals and organisations, offers multiple benefits in terms of support, critical debate and dissemination;
- projects which engage young people in shaping the form and content of their learning are highly effective in improving learning experiences and outcomes – we see repeated staff observation of young people's extended concentration, motivation, imagination and achievement – especially amongst pupils with special educational needs (SEN);
- providing a forum for risk-taking and giving 'permission' for alternative modes of pedagogic practice is consistently cited (by schools and the creative sector) as one of the most significant aspects of Creative Partnerships work.

(Balshaw, 2004, p. 73)

The practical challenge: Teaching the arts to those with profound learning difficulties

Most of the elements within this chapter relate directly to the education of those with SLD, but a Creative Curriculum is equally necessary for those with PMLD and we strongly advocate that they be directly involved within it. It is, however, not so easy to assess whether those with PMLD will benefit in the same way, simply because the cognitive functioning levels of those with profound learning difficulties may preclude a number of the elements of learning that we might aim for with those with SLD. The arts are, however, process based, and careful observation of the small and subtle changes in those with PMLD will indicate learning taking place over time. At the very least, the arts offer real opportunities for joint ventures, an inclusive curriculum and an addressing of the issues raised in the Quality of Life debate (Lyons and Cassebohm, 2010).

The practical challenge: Teaching the arts to those with severe learning difficulties

Part 1 – Thinking about learning

Despite the fact that the creative arts are best viewed as process-based learning, where pre-defined SMART individual targets may not be the best method of teasing out the creativity of pupils with severe learning difficulties, it is probably always best to put structure in place in the first instance in order to establish a firm foundation for learning.

Teaching the arts is not easy and may not be a skill (or a passion) given to everyone. There is a real case for saying the arts are best taught by specialists and perhaps (apart from ICT) may be the only area where specialist knowledge *in addition* to the specialist knowledge required to teach those with PMLD and SLD is required. For example, the idea that one doesn't have to be a musician to teach music is a nonsense, because it relegates the whole subject as worthless. One might as well say one doesn't have to be a bricklayer to build walls or a teacher to teach. There are of course elements of truth to this; one doesn't, but the person teaching must have *sufficient* knowledge of the theoretical background to music, art, drama or dance (or building walls). At the very least, school leaders might consider only giving the job to enthusiastic, skilled and *knowledgeable* amateurs, and they are certainly not posts that can be designated in the way that UK schools used to arbitrarily dole out positions of curriculum responsibility such as science, geography or RE.

Those willing to be 'volunteered' (whether teachers or TAs) should work with one of the arts – music, art, drama, dance – they feel most comfortable with. Start from a position of setting up routine, order, structure and certainty in your class so you can find your own and your class's comfort zone. Start with an introductory episode, either sung/played, painted/collaged/modelled, acted (perhaps one of Keith Park's call and response introductions) or danced, which you keep right throughout the year. Start small with two or three short activities and finish with a plenary where all can celebrate achievement. For some of your pupils that might mean just staying in the session, or staying in there for x minutes. Build up their ability to concentrate and stay with the activities over the year or until you feel they're in a comfort zone and ready to be stretched. Stay there for as long as you need to, but not for too long! Peter (1998a) reflects on the need to aim for a position where you can temper structure with creativity, and the desirability of teachers guiding pupils into a tripartite relationship with artistic learning. That is, promoting pupils' knowledge, understanding and skills in:

1   making the arts – developing their skills;
2   presenting the arts – realising a work of art, choreographing a dance, composing a piece of music, scripting a play;
3   appraising their own work and that of others both discriminately and constructively.

One of the greatest advantages of the arts from a curriculum perspective is that they present excellent opportunities for collaborative teaching and collaborative learning. Teachers and TAs who are specialists in (or who have become specialists in) art, drama, dance and music can work together and learn from each other. While TAs often move around classes and experience a wide variety of teaching approaches, teachers are too often isolated in their classrooms and do not maximise opportunities to learn from each other. Such an approach allows less experienced teachers to broaden their development and encourages more experienced teachers to open their minds to new ideas. It encourages both to think 'outside of the box'. For pupils and students also, there is an opportunity to stretch peer interactions into larger groups, and into a process that challenges perceived limitations and the exclusive small-group learning scenario. The authors have experience of teaching groups as large as forty (secondary-aged) students all with severe or profound learning difficulties, and while this may be too large to maximise teaching and learning opportunities, twenty or so pupils/students in a group should definitely be regarded as a practical proposition, provided there is time set aside to break off into smaller groups for a period (or periods) of the whole lesson. Peter (1998a) also suggests teachers should take a sideways step and present themselves as enthusiastic co-learners alongside their pupils and collaborators in a creative venture. Children's *genuine* self esteem will grow through their developing awareness of their own personal powers, and their being able to make real choices, decisions and changes.

(p. 170; author's emphasis)

The key elements of the individual arts might be:

For art – pattern and texture; colour, line and tone; shape, form and space.
For music – timbre, texture, duration (pulse and rhythm), dynamics, tempo, pitch and structure.
For dance – the body, actions, space, dynamics, relationships.
For drama – focus, tension, space, mood, contrast, symbol, role.

It should be noted that these elements will have very different meanings for those with severe learning difficulties than they might have for neuro-typical learners. This is not to lessen their importance, merely to recognise that because those with SLD learn differently, we need to be teaching them differently. There can be a tendency, especially in the hands of non-specialist art, music, dance and drama teachers (which is often the case in special schools) to assume that we should be following early years curriculum models. Thus art becomes telling the difference between colours, looking at how colours mix, keeping the painting on the paper, making marks. Drama becomes walking on to and exiting from the stage on cue, behaving appropriately to the action, following scripted movements, saying a few scripted lines for those who can speak. This basic skills approach may well be initial appropriate objectives for a few but they do not equate to teaching creativity. When working within the comfort zone, art, music, drama and dance can become teaching a series of skills that are seen as necessary to acquire before one can achieve. For real creativity to take place, however, the action, the art, drama, dance or music, has to be controlled (created) by the learner at as many levels as possible, and this must be the end aim of all creative arts teaching.

Part 2 – Ideas

Drama

Keith Park, Nicola Grove, Melanie Peter and Viv Hinchcliffe have published extensively on drama and all or any of their writings will be relevant. Readers should cross reference to Chapters 5 and 9 on 'Communication' and 'Literacy' since there is a fine line (or possibly no line at all) between literacy, communication and drama. All of the writers noted are interested in stretching pupils beyond the pre-scripted, very structured and teacher-led 'Christmas Show' kind of production and all of their writings give practical hands-on ideas about how you might do this. Keith Park particularly has produced an absolute mine of easy-to-replicate resources (most of which are referenced here) and working through his call-and-response method can produce instant drama teachers of enthusiastic amateurs. Thought will then want to be given to extending and stretching learners to think and problem solve issues that drama naturally throws up. Park (2002) notes a number of aims for drama, namely:

- initiation, especially for those who might seldom do it, by leading the call or pressing a switch to start the call;
- awareness of the sights and sounds involved;
- anticipation, especially of hook lines in the drama for example;
- turn–taking, especially through call and response;
- showing self (or showing off) and demonstrating a 'this is me' behaviour as, for example, when it's the pupil's turn in the name game;
- showing objects, perhaps those used as props, as an attention sharing behaviour;
- giving objects, again a shared behaviour;
- seeking physical proximity;
- gaze alternation, by looking from an object to someone else or vice versa, as a means of sharing attention;
- joint attention, as when two or more people are intentionally looking at the same thing or person at the same time;
- declarative pointing, by pointing at an object (or person) and looking at another person to indicate 'look at that'.

Sherrat and Peter (2002) have sought to establish drama firmly within the conventions of play through their 'Play-Drama Intervention' (PDI), which mirrors the play-based learning processes experienced by neuro-typical children. It recognises, however, that children with severe and complex learning difficulties might well (will probably) struggle with play because they are 'socially challenged'. Working on the imagination, exploration of make-believe and narrative, opens up opportunities to enhance the 'triad of competencies' of communication, social interaction and creative, flexible thinking: 'The assumption is that if children are challenged in their ability to engage in play and consequent social competence, then they need more of it not less!' (Peter, 2002, p. 6).

Peter (2003) assumes that the route to social competence taken by neuro-typical children is through engagement in spontaneous, generative pretend play, and seeks to recreate these conditions within a drama context.

> At the heart of all drama . . . is the opportunity for self–other imagining through the processes of role-taking; imagining oneself as the other; trying to find and finding oneself in the other, and in so doing to recognise the other in oneself.
>
> (Neelands, 2002, p. 7)

Drama of course, includes both storytelling (narrative) and poetry on the grounds that 'for most of human history, "literature" both fiction and poetry has been narrated not written – heard, not read' (Carter, 1991, p. ix) and poetry gives an automatic age-appropriate slant for secondary-age students (Park, 1999b). Readers are strongly advised to seek out the writings of Nicola Grove and her work on narrative and learning difficulties (Grove 2005, 2010, 2012), which are as extensive as they are thought provoking. The importance of drama games must also not be underestimated, since this provides an excellent way into drama for reluctant visitors. Several works by Nicola Grove and Keith Park, both together and separately, are classics of the form, particularly for example *Odyssey Now* (Grove and Park, 1996), *Macbeth in Mind* (Grove and Park, 2001) and *Dickens for All* (Park, 1998c). Park is a serial writer of both articles and books, all of which are accessible and entirely practical (Park 1998a, 1998b, 1998c, 1999a, 1999b, 2002, 2003, 2004, 2006, 2009a, 2009b, 2010,

2011 are just some examples). An ex-student of Keith's, P. J. Pilcher, has taken up the mantle and besides being a stunning 'caller' (and ad-libber) on the stage has also produced some excellent scripts (Pilcher, 2009, 2012). *Odyssey Now* is a brilliant introduction and springboard to the creative arts process and teachers and TAs unused to working in a creative arts, holistic setting, would be well advised to use this as a kind of starter pack. It has enough scenes for one scene per half-term (and so represents a whole year's work if you want it to), is self contained, offers a welter of different ideas and options, is an excellent vehicle for all pupils and students above the age of eight or so and could easily be taken on as a sixth-form project, can be performed if you want it to (although that's not Grove and Park's objective) and is an excellent vehicle for inclusive work from PMLD to mainstream.

If the key elements of drama are considered to be focus, tension, space, mood, contrast, symbol and role, what might these elements mean to those who have severe learning difficulties?

Focus – the very nature of the ability to focus demands motivation; that is, children initially learn to focus by being motivated by what they're focusing on, whether that be a person's face, a bright shiny mobile or a teat. Drama's ability to be intrinsically motivating provides an ideal vehicle to practise focus and extend the pupil's ability to focus for longer periods of time and over a wider range of activities.

Tension – all drama has tension at its core, that is, the dramatic elements are derived from contradiction, confounding expectation, creating an emotional content. Such tensions are problematic because they take us out of the comfortable and known; they demand that we think!

Space – drama is not a static art, but is constantly moving and reshaping itself across the stage. The space within the stage, the space around the actors, is very much part of the dramatic take on a practical mathematical dimension in shape and space.

Mood – drama is a key vehicle (possibly even the key vehicle) for teaching and learning emotional intelligence, because the role-playing process of taking on the characteristics of a person who is lazy, jealous, angry, anxious, takes such words out of the abstract and into the real. We cannot expect people with learning difficulties to have an automatic understanding of such 'mental state' words in the same way neuro-typical learners of the same age might, because so many of the base meanings of these words have been 'taught' and 'learned' during the process of play. And, of course, those with learning difficulties will not have learned to play co-operatively in the same way; many indeed, will not have learned to play co-operatively at all. Hinchcliffe (1996b, 1999) describes using playlets, drama, fairy stories and even storylines of TV soaps for older learners with severe learning difficulties to provide pupils with an interactive, participatory medium in which to draw their attention to people's internal states (desires, beliefs, feelings and intentions). Using techniques common in drama and theatre, e.g., 'split briefing' and 'debriefing', Hinchcliffe explores children's understanding of the inferred states of mind of story protagonists and finds this a rich medium in which children can learn about their own and other people's psychological states and feelings, areas the author says are critical to social understanding.

Contrast – is a key area of need for those with severe learning difficulties, because so much of our efforts as teachers are naturally about repetition, working within the known, providing order and structure, ensuring consistency of approach. Because it is natural (even essential) for teachers to work in this way, the element of contrast is often lost. Drama allows us to explore the contrasting natures of security and fear (*The Bear Hunt*), love and jealousy (*Othello*), avarice and altruism (*A Christmas Carol*). Just exploring understandings of what such contrasting words really mean may form a perfectly acceptable long-term and overarching goal for a year-long piece of drama.

Symbol – Vygotsky (1978) speaks tellingly of the way play is central to symbolic thought and internalised understanding, and we have already spoken of how drama can be used as a medium for teaching those with learning difficulties what might otherwise have been learned through play. As children get older, their reliance on pivots and symbols such as toys diminishes. They have internalised these pivots as imagination and abstract concepts through which they can understand the world: 'The old adage that 'children's play is imagination in action' can be reversed: we can say that imagination in adolescents and schoolchildren is play without action' (Vygotsky, 1978).

- You can explore symbolic understanding by relating a particular dramatic element to 'what does this mean to me?'
- Who loves me? What scares me? Who trusts me? Who do I trust? What makes me angry? Who makes me angry?
- You can develop symbolic understanding by asking 'what does this mean to . . .?'

Role – is an ideal opportunity to teach concrete understandings of emotional states and mental state words. The key is to make the word, words, phrase or concepts accessible to children, young people and adults with learning difficulties. This can range from a simple understanding of family role as outlined by 'The Farmer's in the Den' to the much more complex questions asked in *Hamlet*. There are myriad opportunities to practise and experience different roles and the way others see the world that can really bring to life the practical teaching of theory of mind and emotional intelligence.

Additional material on drama and the arts in general is due to by published by Equals under the title of *Understanding the Arts/Creativity*. This aims to

- provide guidance on the Creative Arts to classroom teachers and school curriculum managers;
- create a 'Learning Community' with best practice schools, via the website and experts in the field; and
- create a basis for future best practice workshops.

Information can be obtained from the Equals website at www.equals.co.uk.

Dance

It is notable that the reason why dance is held within the curriculum area of PE (in the UK at least) appears to be related to the nature of the mind directing the movement in physical exercise. While this is undoubtedly useful,

> open-ended creative movement can contribute another dimension: it implies something more than physical activity. It involves the integration of intellectual, emotional and intuitive aspects of a person; in other words movement *stimulating* the activity of the mind. This, in itself, ought to provide justification for movement and dance education as holding a central place in the curriculum!
>
> (Peter, 1997, p. 5; author's emphasis)

Technically, the basic elements of dance will focus on:

The body – which bits of the body are moving; what is emphasised; what shape does the body make; with what symmetry or asymmetry?

Actions – what is moving, what actions are being performed?

Space – where is it going; what is the size of the movement; is the movement personal or general; along what pathway?

Dynamics – how is it moving; what is the quality of the movement; how long does the movement take; what is the flow in space; how is the tension of the movement reflected?

Relationships – with whom or what is the dancer moving; what is the relationship with other people, objects, the accompaniment or the space itself?

Dance, as a curriculum area in its own right, therefore offers unparalleled opportunities for exploring the whole issue of relational touch, which sometimes bedevils education, especially secondary (post-11) education. This is especially pertinent for those with severe or profound learning difficulties since the early physical movement relationships experienced by NT conventionally developing children (for example in rough and tumble) may well have not been developed as well as they could have been, or indeed not have been developed at all. In the absence of many works on dance, education and special educational needs post Sherborne, what has been written takes on seminal importance, and Melanie Peter's *Making Dance Special* certainly comes into this category. She recommends that adults working with pupils and students take on the role of trusted carer.

> The quality of the contact offered by the carer is crucial: much is transmitted through the sense of touch. This requires a degree of social maturity and responsibility; however, it is also possible for this to be *fostered* through the movement experiences themselves – again 'learning how to do it whilst doing it'!
>
> (Peter, 1997, p. 29; author's emphasis)

Dance is another process-based teaching and learning opportunity (*learning how to do it while doing it*) where for those with learning difficulties the teaching of set skills, either in movement itself or as part of a performance activity, should be regarded as a by-product rather than the main aim. Hen and Walter (2012) are insistent that movement experiences need to be presented in an environment that is 'open to personal response, non-judgemental and firmly rooted within the concepts of achievement and success' (p. 11). This should not be about making pupils better dancers, any more than drama, art or music is necessarily about making pupils better actors, artists or musicians. Dance should not even be about making pupils better movers, or more co-ordinated, or more supple, or more fit, though these things are very likely to happen and will probably be inevitable. They are, and indeed must be looked upon as being, by-products. Dance, like the other creative arts, is a real opportunity to get to the core of the person and to develop the central theme of self-confidence in individuals and, equally importantly, to gain the confidence of supporting adults that the pupil/student can succeed.

Dance and movement with children, young people and adults with severe learning difficulties still rightly tends to take its lead from the pioneering work of the late Veronica Sherborne (Sherborne, 1990), who in turn adapted the ideas of Laban (1948), and The

Sherborne Developmental Movement (SDM) programme is still actively taught as a philosophy. Those interested in pursuing training in this should go to www.sherbornemovementuk.org. We should, however, spend some time tackling the language used as there is a strong inclination among writers discussing the merits of SDM (Hill, 2006; Filer, 2006; Hen and Walter, 2012) towards using terms such as therapeutic, psychotherapeutic and psychodynamic, which can often confuse teachers and educational leaders alike. Is this education or therapy? Does one cancel out the other or can the two be compatible?

There is often an underlying suspicion of therapy within education circles and certain educationalists and academics are vehemently opposed to the concept appearing anywhere near a curriculum document.[3] However, such views tend to be related almost entirely to an academic curriculum and are based more on the propensity of governments and local education authorities to promote such concepts as emotional intelligence as cheaper and easier 'solutions' to the myriad social problems that constantly bedevil most Western societies (Ecclestone and Hayes, 2009). It is not, they argue, the job of education to prop up failed social policies.

Within the education of those with PMLD and SLD, however, there is perhaps a more open view of the benefits of therapeutic work, no doubt derived initially from the very close and long historical association with the three medical therapies, namely Speech and Language Therapy, Occupational Therapy and Physiotherapy. Indeed, it is probably true to say that the psychodynamic therapies such as Dance and Movement Therapy, Art Therapy and Music Therapy are more suspicious of education, seeing teachers as merely purveyors of facts and instructors of skills. We have already made a case for removing the barriers between the medical therapies and education, and we would certainly claim that this chapter, at least, makes an equally strong argument for the pedagogies of both PMLD and SLD education rejecting a purely didactic approach to teaching.

Veronica Sherborne herself claimed profound gains for those participating in the SDM programme in terms of both movement vocabulary and social development. Confidence and self-confidence, self-image and awareness constitute central concepts, and are granted the same importance as body mastery and the building of relationships through movement (Sherborne, 1990). Awareness of self is gained through movement experiences that help the person physically concentrate on what is happening to their body, 'listening via touch' and by 'feelings of inner physical sensation' rather than by our usual way of looking and thinking. This helps lessen self-criticism and allows those with learning difficulties to grow in terms of self-esteem and confidence at both a physical and emotional level. The next step (she argues) is to develop an awareness of others by learning to move around and interact with others in ways that encourage the further development of trust and the building of positive relationships. These movement experiences enable the person to be appropriately supported while being encouraged to explore their unique creativity through shared movement activities, and a wide range of basic movements are suggested in the programme that effectively constitute direct practical strategies.

The emphasis is, however, 'doing with' rather than 'teaching'. Teaching, especially for those with severe (and profound) learning difficulties within the creative arts, can too easily become a didactic process, with the teacher instructing learners in the correct way to move. The teacher is the choreographer, following ideas around normative development, which are demonstrated to the learner, who copies as best he or she can. These movements (often taught in small, easily memorable pieces) are practised and re-practised and then chained together to produce performance dance. The reason we tend to teach in this way is much more to do with what is measurable in the individual lesson than what is desirable. How do we measure a reduction in self-criticism, a growth in self-esteem, a widening of the circle of supporting adults who have belief in the learners' potential and, as Hen and Walter (2012) phrase it, a 'furthering of his or her emotional, cognitive, physical and social integration'? (p. 11). Even if we could measure these things, how are we sure that the effects have come about because of the excellent dance teaching? And are these 'objectives' the stuff of education or should they be filed under the therapy section?

Once again, we come back to the central questions of SLD and PMLD curriculum development – why are we teaching this; what are we trying to achieve; are we making a difference? Of course, teaching an extension and variety of movement is important, but education surely must also tackle the big issues of emotional intelligence and empathy, self-confidence and self-esteem, encouraging the individual to value themselves as equal members of whichever community they're in. Surely this is even more fundamental to the education of those with profound and severe learning difficulties because of the very real dangers of secondary handicaps[4] being suffered by those with learning difficulties (Sinason, 1994). It is worth considering what 'ability' in any field is worth if one doesn't have the self-confidence to use it.

Finally, the inclusion of emotional education in the curriculum is based on the rationale of enabling and empowering pupils to come face to face with situations that may be highly emotionally charged, not just in dance, but in drama, art and music as well. These are opportunities to engage directly with feelings in an entirely safe and secure setting; these are opportunities to learn of consequences and options without such consequences and options being debilitating. The underlying premise is that being able to deal capably with their own feelings is the first step to being able to deal with those of others confidently, competently and safely (Hinchcliffe, 1996a). These issues are addressed more completely within Chapter 15 ('A Citizenship Curriculum').

Art

One wonders if 'art' were to be renamed 'mathematics' whether there would be any school that did not employ a specialist 'mathist' to teach its pupils and whether the subject would carry a significantly greater status than it probably currently does? Mathists would, after all, be responsible for teaching pattern, texture, colour, line, tone, shape, form and space.

However, art is not just maths, it is also language and communication, movement and physicality, geography, history, science and technology, and epitomises the principle that the arts do not work in isolation, but must be approached as an holistic experience. Most of all it forms part of the necessary aesthetic of education (Taylor, 1992) and offers a counterbalance to the potential anaesthetic that a surfeit of SMART targets would undoubtedly engender.

Pattern – is something that probably needs to be discovered by trial and error, but we can offer many opportunities to discover it through, for example, building hand looms for making carpets or designing and making wallpaper in the style of William Morris. Pattern is open to setting up co-operative working through a Henry Ford style division of labour, so that although the production-line system produces the finished article, the pattern can be seen to develop as the group progresses. Those on the autistic spectrum will take to this very readily, but be sure to change the roles on the production every four or five weeks so individuals get a chance to see their small patterns within the whole pattern.

Texture – natural and man-made textures need to be focused upon, felt and described. They may be rubbed, copied and integrated into other pieces of artwork. The study of texture offers a real opportunity for contextualising language so the words rough, smooth, hairy, shiny, pebbly and sandy carry meaning through the multi-sensory experience. As with differences of form, the widest distinctions will be perceived first, with gradual progress towards finer discrimination. The subject matter needs to include familiar situations taken from home, school, pets, play and leisure activities, holidays and recent joint outings. These can also aid 'stretching' activities (Lyons *et al.*, 2011), to extend the pleasurable and anticipatory elements of particular favourite activities and events.

Colour – always carries huge problems for many of those with SLD and is possibly a concept (like number) that one either gets or doesn't get. Whatever you do, it's probably best to avoid too much colour work with paint for those who don't get it, since it will automatically become brown after a very short time. Try working on iPads and tablets instead. George (1985) suggests that:

> The four perceptually significant colours are red, blue, yellow and green and it would be logical to start with the identification of the four and to focus on the characteristics of each colour individually. For example, red objects could be spotted on visits and collected for the classroom; red could be selected for printing, collage, patterns and shapes, and the redness enhanced by mounting the work on a green background. Redness could be emphasised through tomatoes, post boxes, fire, Father Christmas and hot cheeks. Brown, pink and grey could logically be introduced next, then the mixtures of the pigmental primaries, purple and orange. It is worth noting that pigmental primaries red, blue, yellow and the optical or light primaries red, blue, green react differently when mixed.
>
> (pp. 163–164)

Line – takes in all sorts of areas, not just those that are straight or rhythmic, but also those made by fingers in the steam on the window, in sand and mud and with water on the ground. Lines can be made by gross motor movements and are susceptible to capture through video art, so pupils can view their own movements holding red lights in delayed time. Pupils with SLD are nearly always motivated by seeing themselves on film and in photos and video art is perfect for display as a permanent loop on the TV screen in the school lobby. Focus on lines in the environment – railways, roads, rivers canals, hedgerows, telegraph wires, hair, rain running down a window pain – and express them with string, wool, torn or cut paper, trickled sand in collage and simple prints, as well as drawn lines. Make light lines on dark paper and scratch lines in plasticine or clay. Let each child choose his or her own scale of work but encourage the 'free' to control their work and the 'tight' to loosen.

Tone – can be worked on in sensory rooms and dark rooms where light and dark contrasts can be used for focus. Light against dark, dark against light, light and dark on a middle tone are features emphasised in all aspects of art work. To do this, we can work in blacks, whites and greys, as well as in light and dark tones of the colours.

Shape – needs to try to avoid the cliché of the two-dimensional circle, square, triangle and rectangle featured so often in maths lessons for those with SLD, and instead concentrate on discriminating between large and small, fat and thin, tall and short. Draw really big fat round people and really thin Lowry stick-like people; do the same with giants and dwarfs. Make a balloon collage, a fruit collage or print round shapes with lids, carrots or cut card shapes, but make the comparisons very, very obvious. This is another area that's open to the production line/co-operative working strategy so pupils have only to concentrate on one thing at a time and can make the comparisons as a group when the whole piece is put together. Production line roles can be reversed every half-term.

Form – can be made concrete (rather than abstract) by handling clay and plasticine – rolling, pushing and pulling it, making holes and changing its shape, breaking it down as well as building up, and again it is important to make the contrasts large and obvious. Encourage two or three pupils to work together to make a giant clay snowman, or go more abstract by working on a Henry Moore with papier mâché around a wire frame. Get the pupils to think big, the bigger the better. This could be a whole year's project!

Space in art refers to distances or areas around, between or within components of a piece. Space can be open or closed, shallow or deep, two-dimensional or three-dimensional. As with all areas of art (and indeed the arts in general) there are no rights or wrongs; this is a process of discovery. Pupils may lay an installation out in a corner of the school's reception area or playground area (or perhaps in the school's inclusion partner's school if you're worried about wreckage!) with many pieces of work of various descriptions 'spaced' together to form a whole. Pupils could work together in twos or threes to decide on the layout that will change every week when the next two or three create the whole. For those who might find this too conceptually challenging, you could have a session of co-operative play with them actually in the display area, and leave the items as they leave them to make the piece of art. This piece then changes after every play session, but becomes commenting and thinking points for others.

In concluding this short section on art, it is worth stating that there seems to be a singular paucity of written material advising on approaches suitable for pupils and students with SLD or PMLD apart from Rod Taylor's and Melanie Peter's contributions to adaptations of the UK National Curriculum (Taylor, 1992; Peter, 1996; Peter, 2001). There's not much in the other Creative Arts, but art seems exceptionally lacking. One must assume that this is indicative of the low esteem in which art is held by school leaders. It is a minor subject; it is not as important as maths, English or science; real learning does not take place in art; we can all tell the difference between colours, we can all roll out plasticine or clay, so anyone can teach it. Because so few schools employ specialist art teachers (or drama teachers, music teachers or dance teachers for that matter) very few schools get to discover the depth of learning that can actually take place and there are therefore very few teachers around who can write of their experiences. Artists (and dancers, actors and musicians) who are also skilled in SLD and/or PMLD pedagogy, please take note!

Music

Adam Ockleford's work on music with those with severe and profound learning difficulties in general (Ockleford, 1998, 2000, 2006; Ockleford, Welch and Zimmerman, 2002) and *Sounds of Intent* in particular (Ockleford, 2008) offers a small sample of his extensive output and will be of considerable interest to all those working (or indeed thinking of working) in this field. Originally designed to enable those with PMLD to access music, this has now developed a wider scope and includes those with severe and complex learning difficulties. *Sounds of Intent* 'maps' musical behaviour and development in children and young people with complex needs. It divides musical expression into the three areas of reactive, proactive and interactive that are distinct but interdependent, and seeks to offer a developmental map

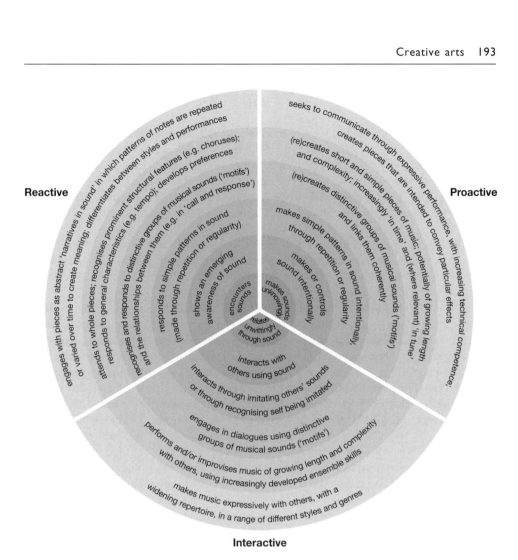

Reactive

Proactive

seeks to communicate through expressive performance, with increasing technical competence;

(re)creates short and simple pieces of music; potentially of growing length and complexity; increasingly 'in time' and (where relevant) 'in tune'

(re)creates distinctive groups of musical sounds ('motifs') and links them coherently

makes simple patterns in sound intentionally, through repetition or regularity

makes or controls sound intentionally

makes sounds unknowingly

relates unwittingly through sound

encounters sounds

shows an emerging awareness of sound

responds to simple patterns in sound (made through repetition or regularity)

recognises and responds to distinctive groups of musical sounds ('motifs') and the relationships between them (e.g. in 'call and response')

attends to whole pieces; recognises prominent structural features (e.g. tempo); develops preferences

engages with pieces as abstract 'narratives in sound' in which patterns of notes are repeated or varied over time to create meaning; differentiates between styles and performances

responds to general characteristics (e.g. choruses);

interacts with others using sound

interacts through imitating others' sounds or through recognising self being imitated

engages in dialogues using distinctive groups of musical sounds ('motifs')

performs and/or improvises music of growing length and complexity with others, using increasingly developed ensemble skills

makes music expressively with others, with a widening repertoire, in a range of different styles and genres

Interactive

Figure 12.1 The *Sounds of Intent* structure

that is both non-linear and non-hierarchical. *Sounds of Intent* is freely available through the website at www.soundsofintent.org

As in other areas of the arts (except perhaps for drama) as indeed for many of the curriculum areas covered in this book, Ockleford (2008) notes the paucity of research and general advice available to teachers in relation to music for those with severe and profound learning difficulties. There is much published for the conventionally developing NT child, but little specific for those who fall outside of the norm. What little there is has tended to fall under the music therapy umbrella. Both Lacey (1996) and Peter (1998a) caution against music in education being treated as therapy, preferring instead to regard it as 'therapeutic', with the arts in education as complementary to, not competing with, the arts as therapy. Ockleford (2008) notes the fact that very few pupils with SLD or PMLD have any opportunity to receive regular music therapy from a trained therapist. It is not so much that there is a tension between therapy and education, just that as far as music goes there is little of either from those who have the appropriate musical and special needs training. Ockleford makes a persuasive case for insisting that it should not be a case of one or the other – both are essential if we are to do justice to the subject and maximise the learning potential of our pupils and students.

It seems fairly certain that a level of musical understanding is apparent well within the first year of life (Trehub, 1990; Lecanuet, 1996; H. Papousek, 1996; M. Papousek, 1996), but whether those with SLD and PMLD follow the same musical pathways (albeit at a slower rate) is a matter of debate. Interestingly, and largely matching the basic premise of assessment schemes such as *Routes for Learning* (WAG, 2006) and the developmentally based UK P Scales (QCA, 2001) for English and maths, Ockleford (2008) argues that it does (broadly):

> [The] musical development of children and young people with complex needs follows broadly the same course as that taken by most other people [and] is supported by the 'Sounds of Intent' developmental framework, which is both internally coherent and fits the data gathered to date.
>
> The model is unlike others that have been formulated up to this point in that it focuses *only* on the development of musical interests, abilities, and preferences (while acknowledging that all auditory processing has common roots). The intention has been to avoid some of the pitfalls to which other current models have been susceptible (including QCA's 'P-levels' for music), in which musical and non-musical elements are conflated. It appears that this conceptual blending has arisen from an ignorance of what *musical* development actually comprises, and, paradoxically, has tended to limit an appreciation of music's true capacity to inform wider learning and development.
>
> (Ockleford, 2008, p. 111; author's emphasis)

Ockleford argues that music can be an extremely effective conduit through which movement, learning, communication and socialisation can be filtered and argues that particular individual abilities need specialised fostering. While for many the ability to utilise sophisticated musical strategies may be entirely intuitive, such abilities will remain hidden if formal and discrete musical education is denied. Further, even where skilled music teaching has been available, the pedagogy (or rather pedagogies) have been idiosyncratic and there has been no concerted attempt to develop a workable alternative to a mainstream National Curriculum model, which does not address the needs of those with severe and profound learning difficulties:

> Ultimately, we should remember that the value of a young person's musicality resides not in where it stands in relation to that of others, but in the extent to which it is harnessed to enhance the quality of life of the individual concerned and the wider circle with which he or she may be engaged.
>
> (Ockleford, 2008, p. 264)

Musical Interaction

As previously noted in Chapter 6 an interesting musical variation of Intensive Interaction has been developed through the work of Wendy Prevezer (2000) and especially Margaret Corke (2002, 2011) in the form of 'Musical Interaction'. This is strongly based on the principles of Intensive Interaction with its exponents arguing that it allows and encourages valid musical experiences; allows and encourages personal interactions; is a motivational communicative tool; is suitable for all learners (PMLD, SLD or ASC) who are at the earlier stages of communicative development; does not require musical ability on the part of the teacher (try using a microphone as a musical instrument, for example); and is a lot of fun. Musical Interaction, Corke (2002) suggests requires:

- *Interactors* – through face, body language and voice;
- *Social interaction games* – such as burst-pause; anticipation games; rough and tumble; give and take; physical activities (clapping, tickling, rocking, rowing, peek-a-boo, hide and seek, throwing things backward and forward);
- *Music* – although not necessarily what we might consider to be conventional music with recognisable tunes; anything that makes sounds, including voices is sufficient;
- *Structure to the lesson* – all round in a circle; a musical introduction; an (age appropriate) hello song; time for small group and peer interactions; time for one-to-one interactions; an (age appropriate) goodbye song.

Corke posits that a voluntary, active input from the learner is absolutely essential for growth and learning to take place. She argues for a move away from the traditional music sessions where only conventional tunes are played and a move towards sessions where we use music to teach interactive and communicative skills. Musical Interaction then becomes a means of allowing and encouraging valid musical experiences; a means of allowing and encouraging personal interactions; and a motivational communicative tool. Musical ability on the part of the teacher helps but is NOT essential as long as all parties are enjoying the experience.

In relation to what might be considered 'conventional' music teaching for those with severe, profound and complex learning difficulties, Pat Lloyd has written and arranged a number of songs for use in interactive group work (Lloyd, 2008) and Crosby (2002) gives some very useful 'fundamental principles' for using music as a communicative learning opportunity, which could be equally well be applied to any of the arts:

1 Keep it fun and playful.
2 Wait for a response, and wait before you jump in to help. Give the opportunity to respond.
3 Remember there is a difference between co-active playing and coercive playing. Banging the pupil's hand against a drum is not the pupil being creative, it is the adult controlling the pupil. Be sensitive in your prompting.
4 Start from the pupil's lead and develop activities accordingly.
5 Accept any response as intentional and worthwhile. Use it creatively within the music.
6 Read the pupil's non-verbal signals carefully.
7 Make the music fit the pupil, not the other way round.

Listening to music as a leisure activity

The other issue related to the arts, and one not much mentioned in regard to those with learning difficulties (apart from Ockleford's (2008) concentration on the 'reactive' element as one of the three areas within the *Sounds of Intent* framework), is their real importance as the basis of leisure activities. We must remember that all of the arts, but music and art especially, are of tremendous value as means of both exploring 'what it means to be me', and productively using time 'to do what I want', that is, self-engaging. It is very likely that many with severe and profound learning difficulties will have a considerable amount of spare time both before but especially after they leave school, and it is essential that we (as teachers) teach them the ability to make personal choices regarding likes and dislikes. That means they have to be exposed to as wide a variety of art forms as possible on a very regular basis. If we are to ensure that the twenty year old with severe learning difficulties wants to listen to more than 'Wheels on the Bus' then we must ensure that she has experienced as wide a variety of musical forms and genres as possible. This takes time, and time (class time) should be spent on just listening.

Part 3 – Creative arts essentials

Creative arts essentials might be considered to be essentials for all forms of teaching those with severe and profound learning difficulties, but work especially well in the arts. These are:

1   Observe the pupil(s)
2   Find the motivators
3   Adopt a careful approach
4   Create structure.

1 Observing the pupil(s)

See what interests the pupil has and what activities she is interested in, or for more group-based work you might write a 'strengths/needs' chart based on the group dynamics and elements that are strong or need working on. Try working on this in a multidisciplinary way so that you employ the ideas of support staff, SaLTs, physios and occupational therapists (OTs) (the latter two especially if movement and space is involved). With group work it is important to get a collective feel as much as you can and look for pupils to feed off each other. Remember, with the arts, perhaps more than any other teaching, it is not about you as the teacher, it's about them as explorers.

It may well be that there will be some more able pupils who will appear to dominate ideas and exchanges, especially if they are verbal and reasonable communicators, but this position can be a strength for the group, as those less able (and probably less confident) can take their own time to increase their involvement levels. It is interesting to note that experienced practitioners such as Keith Park quite deliberately use their more able learners to model what is possible (Pilcher, 2009; Park and Pilcher, 2010).

Penny Lacey suggests writing a 'strengths/needs' chart with the 'needs' being divided into needs 'right now' and needs 'next' (Lacey, 2010). These might be considered to be learning intentions (or in her terms 'SCRUFFY targets') so you have a loose idea of the learner's direction of travel. Be prepared for that direction to change, however, and if the learner decides to take their learning east instead of west, you need to be co-active in going with that. Carpenter *et al.*'s (2010) Engagement Scales may also be helpful here as a means of finding the optimum levels of engagement for the pupil.

Karkou and Glasman (2004) suggest that teachers need to have a flexible approach to what might be considered to be music, art, dance or drama. It is really important that teachers afford as much opportunity as they can for pupils to use the arts as forms of expression and communication.

Know where the pupil is functioning. Don't expect sharing if she is functioning at the profoundly egocentric level, but be prepared to stretch learners as much as possible. Establish the comfortable, but don't stay there indefinitely. Work at the child's developmental level not at their chronological age – but there is no reason to use childish resources when working with those who are no longer children. A fourteen year old may well want to sing 'Wheels on the Bus' in an open mic session and this free expression should continue to be encouraged, but perhaps she can also be encouraged to take the familiar and make it into something else – how about a rap version? This is after all, generalising a particular skill.

2 Find the motivators

The creative arts are often the most pertinent areas for teachers to use what already interests, since this is likely to be an existing strength of the pupil or student. It may be that a pupil: has a favourite 'flapper' that can be used as a base for a class's dance sequence; prefers particular musical instruments; prefers particular genres of music that might be used in rotation for music or dance. Learners will probably prefer particular art media that interest them but may well shy away from others, especially if there are sensory difficulties. Both Hinchcliffe (1991, 1996b) and Peter (2009) urge the use of 'real life' situations in drama, so learners can make sense of scenes and have an understanding of context.

In any event, there is a common consensus that most learners find the arts intrinsically and inherently motivating, perhaps because there is 'strong notion of empowering pupils to take control and responsibility in the learning process' (Peter, 1998b) but also because the arts are so much fun to do. They are, as we have noted with Sherrat and Peter (2002) earlier, an extension of play.

3 Adopt a careful approach

It may well be, especially if learners are new to the artistic experience and especially if there are sensory issues around proximity and noise, for example, that you will need to minimise the possible anxiety experienced. Set up a repeatable routine as an introduction and have a clear and repeatable structure for each session. Adults must be prepared to model first, whether that be a movement, or a scenario, or a rhythm or an art form.

Using repetition minimises anxiety. Don't change wholesale from week to week, session to session, but change only small parts and build these changes up around the familiar until they too become familiar.

Using the familiar minimises anxiety. Adopt settings, scenarios, materials, instruments, movements that have a context for the learners, and keep that context going from week to week and session to session.

Think about your language so the learners can become familiar with the words and phrases used to indicate different parts of the structured sessions.

4 Create structure

The arts are excellent opportunities to work on problem solving and thinking, but it is probably necessary to create structure *before* we can think how to be creative with it: 'Children may require precise boundaries within which to create – paradoxically, inventiveness, originality in creating actually happens within *constraints*' (Peter, 1997, p. 93; author's emphasis).

The presentation of opportunities to be creative and be inventive will, nonetheless, almost inevitably involve making choices, which will in turn produce consequences. We must recognise that this is potentially stressful. If you can offer 'irresistible invitations' to be involved in the arts by stressing the fun element and giving as much control as you can to learners both individually and collectively, creativity may be achieved. You must, however, progress *slowly* and only bring in one or two changes per week around your planned, consistent, repetitive, familiar structure.

Conclusion

Working through the arts is a very effective way of building a symbolic world that is both understandable and comfortable for the learner, yet at the same time challenging and thought provoking. The goal is to learn that we may substitute reality through symbols, since symbolic play provides distance from real life and both allows and encourages us to:

- experiment with all sorts of communicative forms, both expressive and receptive;
- experiment with socialisation;
- experiment with space and movement;
- discover ourselves;
- discover others;
- learn in safety;
- make mistakes;
- take risks;
- think and problem solve;
- repeat the learning process;
- have fun and enjoy life.

Notes

1   These can be found in Chapter 7 ('A Sensory Curriculum').
2   Some might argue that for drama it *mustn't* be told following the pictures and words in a big book as that's 'reading', but we maybe need to a have more open view of what drama may be and may become.
3   The title of the Ecclestone and Hayes (2009) book *The Dangerous Rise of Therapeutic Education* says it all!
4   Valerie Sinason talks of the distinct possibility (and for many, probability) of those with learning difficulties and/or physical disabilites as seeing themselves as less than others, so a 'second' handicap is imposed upon them.

Chapter 13

A problem-solving and thinking curriculum for pupils with severe learning difficulties

> Mentally retarded children are not capable of abstract thinking, but a teaching system based solely on concrete principles means that they are never exposed to this higher-level thinking. Teaching concrete principles is necessary but should be considered a stepping stone to higher more abstract principles without which their cognitive development will not have a chance of ever moving towards this higher processing.
>
> (Vygotsky, 1978, p. 89)

In a conventional mainstream curriculum model, cognition (thinking and understanding), problem solving (acting upon understanding) and even metacognition (thinking about thinking) would be placed within the general framework and context of everyday lessons. In good and outstanding schools much thought is put into strategies such as Bloom's Taxonomy (of learning objectives) (Bloom *et al.*, 1956) so the pupil is constantly steered towards deep and meaningful learning, as opposed to a shallow and superficial memory for facts.

In a history lesson on the Norman Conquest, for example, much may learned. The Battle of Hastings occurred in 1066; William's army from Normandy defeated Harold's army defending the Saxon monarchy; Harold was killed by an arrow through the eye; the battle was commemorated by the Bayeux Tapestry. These facts are well known, but do not convey any understanding of the significance of the events and a number of questions may be asked. What did it mean for the English people? How did their lives change over time? What would have happened if William hadn't invaded? What would have happened had Harold won?

The purpose of these questions is to extend learning from memory to understanding to application, and then on to the higher orders of learning that are to be found in the abilities to analyse, evaluate and create. For those with SLD we are often stuck within memory, since (i) it may take many hundreds of opportunities to repeat a skill before it is lodged in the long-term memory; (ii) those with SLD tend to find generalisation extremely difficult (Lacey, 2009); and (iii) we often get enticed by the need to provide order, structure, routine and certainty for our learners. SLD schools – and this is especially so where there may be a dual diagnosis of SLD/ASC – are usually excellent at routine, order, structure and certainty.

There are whole pedagogies based upon these principles (TEACCH and ABA, for example) and routines are a major opportunity for learning, especially with those who are functioning at the earliest stages of intellectual development. It is tempting, because it can be thought of as being less stressful, and therefore better for the pupil, to maintain routine, order, structure and certainty to such a degree that learners become reliant upon them and experience considerable distress when such certainties are taken away. This is perfectly understandable – if you're not in control of your own life, as so many with learning difficulties are not, there is some security in knowing that someone else is. This means that routine, order, structure and certainty become essentials, not options.

By accepting this, however, we may be restricting opportunities for learning because we are not expecting our pupils to think and to problem solve. When faced with problems and difficulties, as inevitably they will be, pupils who have learned to rely on routine, order, structure and certainty will have no skills or strategies to fall back upon. In these circumstances it may well be that their distress will be even greater. This chapter proposes that teaching children with SLD to think and problem solve as independently as they possibly can is not an option, it is a necessity.

Penny Lacey has been at the forefront of a growing campaign to bring thinking and problem solving back into the heart of the SLD curriculum, and she will be referenced continually in this section. Here is an extended quote that gets right to the heart of the issue:

> Children's [with severe learning difficulties] likely lack of interest in the world generally can be a challenge but providing exciting activities can help to provoke interest. We need to introduce children to different kinds of animals, let them experience the weather first hand, work with artists, make films, visit unusual places, people and things and experience a range of physical movements from abseiling to horse-riding to sailing to ice skating. Just erecting a tent and eating home-made popcorn in it can provoke many thinking skills. There is a big wide world to be discovered beyond the routine, although we must be careful not to provide a catalogue of unconnected experiences. The connection is *thinking* and *problem solving* and we need to make that very explicit or the children may not notice.
>
> (Lacey, 2009, p. 22; author's emphasis)

The theory of thinking and problem solving in children, young people and adults with SLD

Task 1

- You have planned to deliver a storytelling lesson that involves the use of four Step-by-Step VOCAs (Voice Output Communication Aid).
- The lesson is due to start at 10.00.
- At 9.55 you go to get out the machines from a cupboard in your class where you put them after their last use, but can only find one.
- It does not work.
- What do you do?

While in the normal course of events teachers would have ensured resources were adequately prepared, fully working and present ready for use, there may be occasions in a busy classroom when this is not possible. This (as an exercise in problem solving) is just one of those occasions!

Task 2

Can you analyse and write down the steps you went through to resolve your dilemma? **Problem solving** basically involves four key mental processes:

1   Perception
2   Thinking
3   Action
4   Evaluation

Perception involves (i) recognising and identifying problems, (ii) recognising opportunities.

Thinking involves (i) breaking down a problem into elements, (ii) thinking through the relevant features of the problem, (iii) planning ways to solve the problem.

Action involves remembering how to solve a problem and bringing this memory to the fore.

Evaluation involves (i) evaluating how a plan worked, (ii) recognising when existing plans and strategies need changing. Intrinsic within this is the recognition that one needs to improve one's own learning performance through:

- recognising why a task is carried out, what it involves and when it is complete;
- communicating preference and choice;
- recognising personal strengths and weaknesses;
- learning from mistakes and setting targets;
- developing attention and concentration.

Lacey (2009) points out that thinking and problem solving is almost always going to be more difficult for those with SLD because of the likelihood of a very small working memory, poor attention skills and difficulties with language and communication. Hulme and Mackenzie (1992) regard memory difficulties as placing additional strains on other cognitive skills, particularly reading and mathematics. For Collis and Lacey (1996) thinking and problem solving, and teaching about thinking and problem solving, are inextricably linked:

> Teaching becomes not only a process of ensuring that students possess a range of possible responses to a given practical problem, but also that they are aware of this repertoire and the need for its practical use. They must come to understand which learned strategy is appropriate for which situation.
>
> (p. 10)

Lacey (2009) also points to research conducted by Wishart (1988) and Jarrold *et al.* (2008) with Down's Syndrome children and adults, through which we might reasonably safely draw the conclusion that those with severe learning difficulties will learn better when they can see and touch things related to their learning. In other words, we can expect more learning to take place when we teach in a concrete manner, through real actual experience, rather than in an abstract manner through (for example) language, either written or spoken. This means that learning is likely to be enhanced if we can actually practise thinking and problem solving in real situations in real time.

The dangers of learned helplessness[1]

Teachers will be familiar with the concept of the 'zone of proximal development'. This can be simply described as the distance between the actual developmental level as determined by independent problem solving and the level of potential development as determined through problem solving under adult guidance, or in collaboration with more capable peers (Vygotsky, 1978). The adult ladders and scaffolds (lays down supports for the learner), which are gradually taken away as the learner 'learns' to be more independent and solve problems on their own. The difficulty with those with severe learning difficulties is, unfortunately, that we often forget to take these props away.

This is sometimes about the need to control and protect learners – occasionally perhaps to stop them making a mess which we have then got to clear up – and sometimes because we do not want learners to fail or because we believe that learners are unable to do things on their own; it is perhaps 'easier' (for us) if we do it ourselves and we've probably all been there with children of our own! Even if we can overcome this tendency, and all good teachers of children with SLD should strive to do this, one of the key reasons for learned helplessness continuing is time. Or perhaps, to give it proper emphasis, this should be written as TIME.

Teachers, managers of teachers and inspectors can become obsessed with time, and there is a tendency to cram all the elements of a prescribed curriculum into a weekly schedule or timetable to ensure curriculum coverage (breadth and balance). The adoption of a subject-based curriculum model has resulted in a tendency towards teaching facts rather than the ability to think and act independently. We have become a short-term, 'results'-driven industry. As a consequence, we may find ourselves rushing to finish English, maths or history so geography, RE or science can have its allotted time. For those with severe learning difficulties, this can militate against learning not only in terms of personalised learning opportunities but also opportunities to problem solve and attain deep, rather than surface, learning. For learners with SLD, deep learning takes time, and often a considerable amount of time.

It really cannot be overstated that the perceived lack of time is one of the major reasons for so many instances of learned helplessness. A term originally devised by Martin Seligman (Seligman, 1975), learned helplessness should not be looked at as merely a benign result of adults doing things for children that they might well be able to do for themselves. Seligman clearly regarded the phenomenon as extremely pernicious, in that those convinced of their inability to do things for themselves are very likely to become over-dependent on their 'controllers' and unable to express any initiative, even when it is clearly within their abilities to do so. This in turn can, and according to Seligman often does, lead to the development of a state of general ennui and even deep-rooted depression. In the light of this we might also question whether learned helplessness is a major contributory factor to the high prevalence of mental health problems among those with complex learning difficulties and disabilities (Carpenter, 2011).

We can, however, reduce learned helplessness by adopting a number of clear and unambiguous strategies that are regularly discussed and agreed by whole class and whole-school teams.

1   **Building healthy attachments that allow for independent development**, or put even more simply, recognising that any working and/or social relationship that does not actively encourage independent development is axiomatically unhealthy.
2   **Having high expectations**. This does not mean they have to be unrealistic, but having the high expectation that a learner might do an action on their own (for example, getting out their own equipment for painting and tidying up again afterwards) will mean giving extra time and may well result in additional work for the adult in, for example, (discretely) cleaning up the mess created by the learner tidying up. This is especially so

since we cannot expect learners to do things 'correctly' at the first time of asking. We may not expect them to do things 'correctly' at the fifty-first time of asking! What we can expect is that they get better with more practice.

3 **Recognising the desirability of failure**. There is nothing wrong with failing, it is how we all learn, through our mistakes. We do, however, often try to shield our most fragile learners from failure and 'pretend' they've succeeded when they haven't, much as we might let a small child win a race. Encouraging persistence means we are giving learners the opportunity to succeed on their own. It is imperative that staff work with learners to ensure there is a deep and abiding understanding that making mistakes is perfectly normal. We shouldn't, of course, applaud failure, but we must applaud trying, even if the result is failure.

4 **Providing predictable environments**. Those with SLD, especially if the additional difficulties are related to autism or ADHD, will probably not be able to learn if they are worried, anxious or fretful about what is happening, with whom and for how long, etc. For these learners especially, it is vital that we provide routine, order, structure and certainty *before* we can look to stretch learners into new ways of working and risk taking.

5 **Rewarding independent behaviours** with positive and entirely encouraging responses, and with immediate and successive opportunities to repeat the behaviour(s) in question and, indeed, extend them.

6 **Communicating with learners at their level**, not just physically by working with learners on the floor or kneeling down if they're seated, but also remembering that language can be a means of control (by those who have it and against those who don't) if we use it too much and without thought and out of context.

7 **Recognising, responding to and reinforcing learners' initiations** requires a major area of detailed thought for each individual learner. What is their favoured method of communication? What are they interested in? Are we sure we always respond positively? Are learners' initiations being channelled through challenging behaviours? If so why, and what can we do to make those initiations positive ones?

8 **Fading prompting** as early as you can will allow the learner the opportunity to try doing things on their own. It may well (will probably) result in failure, but this is merely another opportunity to learn. Supporting adults need to think about the amount of assistance given to learners every day, and every part of every day, and look to pause before the assistance is given just to see if the learner takes the initiative. Sometimes the pauses may need to be quite long, and we may need to provide a series of (carefully thought out) prompts and questions to challenge the learner to act independently.

9 **Providing real choices** (as opposed to superficial choices), which includes the power to say 'no' and be listened to when they say 'no'. This is discussed in considerable detail for PMLD within Chapter 8 ('A Care Curriculum'); the principles apply equally to those with severe learning difficulties.

10 **Identifying what the learner is interested in and using that as a basis for working with them**, since we can now bring in a motivation to learn and extend independent behaviours. Those interested in learning more about how best to engage learners should look at Barry Carpenter's Engagement Scales (Carpenter, 2010) and spend some time on each learner with their class teams.

11 **Taking risks** and encouraging learners to not be frightened of new experiences. This means adults will need to build in lots of order, structure, routine and certainty within the existing way of working *before* introducing something new. Staff will need to build

in considerable caution and take things very slowly if learners are to be encouraged to take risks. A long-term approach with many opportunities to experiment, especially when it is centred around teaching through having fun and individually motivating activities may well be the best option. This may also involve teachers and TAs being prepared to take risks themselves, for example encouraging learners to make their own decision about when it is safe to cross a road. Gradually, over what might become an extended period of time, staff may encourage more open and adventurous responses.

12   **Giving the learner time to succeed** is paramount in all of the strategies noted above. This is not only in terms of the lesson or session itself, but in recognising that learning timescales for those with SLD may be vastly different to that of the mainstream population. Some things may take many weeks, months and possibly years of constant practice to achieve. And of course, once you've given the learner time to succeed you then have to get used to the idea of *giving the learner more time!*

In practical terms, we (staff, parents, carers) need to think about:

* how often and how easily we do things for our learners;
* how often and how easily we give them cues;
* how much they expect us to help them;
* whether this constitutes a 'healthy attachment'?

The practice of thinking and problem solving in those with SLD

In a study related to neuro-typical children, Taggart *et al.* (2005) point out the importance of words related to meta-cognition if thinking is to be encouraged; they recommend practising using words such as *think, know, guess, remember, forget, mean, if, because, why* on a regular basis. Children who are at very early levels of language development need to relate the words they use to a meaningful context (Hinchcliffe, 1991) and for those with learning difficulties this will mean practising using the words inside phrases such as, 'I *know* that it is assembly next', or '*If* I go out without a coat, I'll be very cold'.

Hinchcliffe and Roberts (1987) used a similar approach, but concentrated on using the words in games, story scenarios and dramas. The authors' research with children with SLD and non-learning-disabled children indicated that language relating to intentions, desires, beliefs and feeling states (internal states) was significant in children's developing problem-solving abilities and self-advocacy skills. Hinchcliffe and Roberts analysed parental reports of the spontaneous language of a group of Down's Syndrome children aged between two and eleven years. The authors found a paucity of mental-state language used by the sample. Preliminary findings from Hinchcliffe's follow-up study (1995) investigating the frequency and type of internal state language (words that refer to intentions, cognitions and feeling states) among children with SLD showed a similar poverty of internal-state language. Hinchcliffe (1994, 1995, 1996b, 1999) found certain teaching strategies to be effective in teaching 'target' words, which were used to develop children's conscious awareness of mental events and feelings, as well as the ability to talk about them. Collis and Lacey (1996) reflect upon similar themes in their *Interactive Approaches to Teaching*.

In Chapter 10 ('A Mathematical Thinking Curriculum') we looked at the maths involved in everything around us, and of course the same principle applies to the opportunities to think and problem solve that are also all around us. We also looked at the mathematical learning that takes place when learners are baking a cake. Now list the opportunities for thinking and problem solving we can create within the same process.

- Is there a recipe and where can I find it?
- Where are the ingredients?
- What do I do if I can't reach them?
- Are there sufficient ingredients to make the cake?
- What can I do if there's not?
- Are there sufficient ingredients to make the next cake?
- Where are the cooking utensils?
- What will I need for the job?
- Where do I put the ingredients once I've measured out how much I need?
- What do I do if I put too much of one ingredient in the mix?
- How much time do I need to make and bake?
- How do I assess the time?
- Who's going to turn the oven off?
- Is there enough time to wash and tidy up?
- What can I do if there's not?
- What do I do with the cake once it's baked?

In Chapter 14 ('A Play Curriculum') we look specifically at the power of games to engender fun and motivation to learn, and specifically talk about devising new games and adapting existing games to suit our learners. Now list the opportunities for thinking and problem solving that we can create in the process of playing a game.

- How do we decide what game to play?
- Where are the resources for the game kept in order to start?
- What do I do if one (or more) of the resources is missing?
- Do I know the rules?
- How many players are needed?
- What do we do if we have too few players?
- What do we do if we have too many players?
- Do we need to split into teams?
- How do we decide who is on what team?
- What if I need help?
- Does anyone else need help and what can I do about it?
- Do we have a big enough space for the game to be played?
- Where can we go if not?
- What time do we need to finish?
- Where are the resources for the game kept in order to tidy away?

We must remember that it is often us (teachers, TAs, parents, carers) who are the providers of thinking and problem-solving opportunities. We can provide and we can also deny. We *must* strive to be providers. Teachers will be aware that the Developmental Approach tends to:

- adopt 'traditional good practice' for SLD/PMLD teaching;
- teach to a curriculum;
- focus on a specific objective;
- teach one small step at a time with lots of opportunities for practice;
- use the same equipment to avoid confusion;
- utilise rote learning.

Unfortunately this can also lead us, and the children and young people who we teach, into the 'comfort trap'. Here, as we've established, routine, order, structure and certainty are absolutely vital for effective learning to take place; *but* if we always apply routine, order, structure and certainty, learning will be neither maximised nor deep.

How then can we reconcile these two approaches to make them work for the child, that is, provide them with security routine order and structure and *at the same time* build in elements of unpredictability and problem solving? Some answers:

- Build up the routine, order, structure and certainty so it is second nature for your learners to follow the routine. Then change it. You must not change it all the time since that would be chaos, and the change must always (or at least mostly) be as planned as possible. Remember we are *teaching* learners to think and problem solve.
- In any event, take being 'comfortable' as a real danger sign.
- Occasionally have different starts to lessons, different endings, different middles. Set up difficulties that are outside of your control. 'The whiteboard is broken today. How can we do our morning greeting?'
- Learners will look to you, the teacher, as being the font of all wisdom so you must make it absolutely clear to them that you have absolutely no idea what to do. Recognising that teachers also have problems will give pupils confidence to accept their own.
- Swap rooms with equipment in different places for pupils to find.
- Don't label cupboards with symbols; expect learners have to look in each cupboard and then remember where things are. It is after all, what we all do in our own houses (and other people's).
- When you're sure they've remembered where things are, change everything around. It's what supermarkets do, so they've got to get used to it!
- Swap staff or ensure staff 'play ignorant' as well and act as if they don't know. In any event, don't do things for your pupils.
- Use different parks, walks, shops, cafés, supermarkets.
- Go somewhere different when travel training and ask a learner to find the way back.
- Use backward chaining.
- Don't tell them they're wrong – give them a chance to find out for themselves. For example, give them a fork for soup, provide only small bricks when they'll need big bricks, start your dance lesson in too small a classroom. Ask the learner(s) if anything is wrong. Ask the learner(s) if anything could be better.
- Allow them to fail.
- Praise for trying.
- Ensure low-level sabotage whenever you can.
- Asking for help is good and should be encouraged. Making mistakes is fine – getting something wrong or having a go/goes is positive – it's how we learn and extend our thinking.

- Never use the word 'wrong' unless with the very able.
- Pupils need to get *unused* to failure.
- Everything we do is somehow related to problem solving but to someone without a learning disability it just appears to be natural and normal and everyday. We spend most of our lives subconsciously thinking ahead, planning, organising, trying to ensure that problems are kept to a minimum. That's why we have to concentrate *very hard* to deliberately create problems. It doesn't come naturally.
- Questioning (ourselves) builds self-confidence.
- Ask if this is an orange ball (when red is presented).
- Ask for a *Yes* or *No* to avoid the learned echolalia of repeating the last thing they've heard.
- When a skill is established we should ask *No* or *Yes* – because we want them to think.
- The last part of building self-confidence is to question the answer, 'Are you sure that's red?' This applies to all learning, for example, 'Are you sure this is the right way back to school?'
- We need to get into the habit of questioning what pupils are doing.
- Check the answers they give to questions (even when correct) to develop their self-belief and confidence to make choices and decisions.
- Give practice at making mistakes – give a two-pence piece rather than two-pound coin when going shopping and see what happens. You have to be brave and take risks or learning may not happen.
- For the more able, encourage the ability to justify their decisions and question ours – we aren't always right just because we're the grown ups!
- Concentrate on teaching affective and effective communication skills. A pupil with SLD may know how to complete a task or do something but may not have the communication skills or physical skills to do it without help. Being able to communicate that is often vital.
- Learning *must* be generalised in order for problem solving to be most effective.
- Skills *must* be mastered before we can ask learners to generalise. So, for example, within making toast, pupils must know how to plug in and unplug the toaster safely, and these skills may need to be practised repetitively. Problem solving becomes difficult if the core (base) skills are sketchy.
- Build in 'thinking and practice time'. Where's my coat? What do I need? How much money? Where am I keeping it? What am I buying? Do I have a bag? In the first instance, such times could take most or possibly all of the lesson, so that you don't have any time left to do whatever it is you'd planned. We must have the courage to go with this. Things will speed up, but only with practice.
- We need to teach learners how to ask for help and we need to teach learners how to ask for help from each other. Teamwork and group decision making should be encouraged, because you (the teacher) are not always going to be there, and we (the adults) are not always the wise ones, and they (the learners) will be adults them-selves soon enough. If someone cannot do it, point out the problem to the group and ask someone in the group to solve it. The more able will of course get there first and will appear to dominate the learning. Go with this – it's called co-operative learning and modelling.
- Present a cooking task with three packets of mince to six students – what do we do?
- Move tables collectively. Share a book, a packet of crisps, a box of raisins, etc.

- Remember the importance of time, motivation, failure and success.
- Problem solving and thinking *always* work best when pupils are motivated to find the solution. Make it fun!
- Do the above with activities they *really* enjoy.
- Give *lots* of time to succeed.
- There is no such thing as failure – it is merely another opportunity to succeed.

Note

1   Observant readers will note that this issue has already been addressed in Chapter 4 ('A Cognition Curriculum'), and although we have tried to avoid repetition, there are a number of subtle differences of approach for those with SLD; the whole issue of learned helplessness is so vital to the education of both those with PMLD and SLD that we've put this in again.

Chapter 14

A play curriculum for pupils with severe learning difficulties

Imagine you see before you two young children on a beach. They have spades in their hands and there are small buckets in the immediate vicinity. They have built a sandcastle with two outer walls, the first of which is gradually disappearing under the oncoming tide. There is much consternation and many shrieks from one child, although the other seems much more stoical, even relishing the situation. What do you think they're doing? They could be doing a number of things, including witnessing the imminent collapse of civilisation as we know it, but whatever it is, it has probably involved imaginary and co-operative play.

In 1977, reporting on a playgroup of children with physical disabilities, Christine Simons noticed that the

> children seem unaware of the advantages of playing together in a group where they can exchange ideas and roles because they have not been shown how. Mostly they are accustomed to a one to one relationship with an adult and find it difficult to relate to and to cooperate with their peers.
>
> (Simons, 1977, p. 17)

That this might still be the picture in quite a few special school playgrounds up and down the UK at least, indicates how little the 'subject' of play is taken seriously as an area to be taught and learned for those with severe and profound learning difficulties. That play is of major benefit to all children cannot be seriously in doubt and we will not waste precious words justifying it as an activity to be indulged. This does not mean, however, that sufficient, or often any, thought or time has gone into measuring the importance of play for those with SLD and PMLD, and ensuring that adequate time is given to *teaching* it throughout their school lives. It is to the teaching of play to those with SLD (and to a degree those with PMLD) that we therefore address our thoughts in this chapter.

If we have bemoaned the absence of research within the other areas of learning that might be deemed to be important for those with SLD (as outlined in this book), play plumbs new depths. We must assume that it has not been thought about because it is something small children do in playgroups before they get to school, when of course, they then concentrate on the serious business of education. In the UK at least, maths and English and science are much more important. If play does happen, and we're sure it does, it happens in the playground in children's free time, or out of school in children's free time. Children learn to play as they've always learned to play, on their own and with each other, with as little help from adults as possible. The problem is, this is exactly what those with SLD do not do, since, as we have noted previously, children with SLD tend not to learn incidentally.

There are a number of reasons for this:

- They are unlikely to learn spontaneously and to be able to generalise (one piece of play into another).
- They will have difficulties remembering what they played last time and with whom and exactly what the rules were last time (and the time before that).
- They will have poor communication skills, both expressive and receptive. It is challenging to take children with you to play new and different games if you can't communicate, and equally difficult to follow the rapid changes that are likely to occur when other children take the lead.
- They will have difficulties in repairing communicative breakdowns. Play that ends in squabbles will stay ended.
- They will have poor concentration and may not be able to follow the 'rules', which themselves may be changed from minute to minute. They may wander off to some other attraction within a very short time.
- They will have difficulties with abstract concepts – making games up, conceptualising different scenarios.
- Their language may be hard to interpret or understand, and language (or at least easily understood communications) are essential to co-operative play.
- The play might end too soon, when those with SLD may need hundreds (and those with PMLD may need thousands) of opportunities to learn.
- They will lack a sense of narrative which often drives play. Narrative is extremely complex, very challenging and may take many years for those with SLD to learn.
- They may have difficulty in understanding directions given by another child and be confused by the demands placed upon them in what is often, even with quite young children, a rapidly developing free-flow scenario.
- Inevitably children with SLD will be delayed in their understanding of representation, which is critical to symbolic play.

We may add to the above the even more socially debilitating conditions of an additional diagnosis of autism, in which case they may:

- have problems with flexibility of thought, perhaps engaging in rigid routines or rituals which prevent the development of play skills;
- lack social reciprocity;
- exhibit behaviours which may be circular, with repeating patterns;
- naturally incline to preferring solitude and therefore lack the motivation to communicate socially;
- lack social and emotional directedness;
- have a high level of compulsions and rituals;
- have only a limited ability to communicate in unstructured situations;
- have a limited ability to communicate beyond simple requests;
- use inappropriate language and have difficulties mapping language to the task;
- have difficulties understanding non-verbal communications;
- lack a 'folk psychology' of others making it hard for them to understand what 'makes people tick';
- have difficulty with emotional involvement with people;

- have a limited appreciation of the feelings of others;
- lack an awareness of the motives of other people their intentions and internal states.

Why play needs to be a core feature of a curriculum for those with SLD

Hussein (2010) contends that play should be recognised alongside education as a vital part of children's healthy and happy development; for Booth *et al.* (2006) play is at the heart of early education; Adams *et al.* (2000) note that a sound theoretical understanding (of play) aids reflection and effective teaching. Seach (2007) argues that children's

> playful engagement with objects and activities enables them to establish a dialogue with all that they encounter, creating experiences that promote their emotional well-being, transforming their knowledge and establishing a sense of belonging to a particular social and cultural group.
>
> (p. 1)

Jennings (2012) notes the importance of play in the development of healthy attachments and Aitken *et al.* (2000) point to the practice afforded to gross body movements achieved through rhymes, rhythms and songs as in, for example, 'Ring-a-ring o' roses, we all fall down'. We, as teachers of those with learning difficulties, spend a long time trying to inculcate the rules of the class and the school (of appropriate behaviour, of relationships with one another) and tend to forget that NT conventionally developing children often learn these essential elements through play. Vygotsky (1978) notes, for example, that children might play house and adopt the roles of different family members, and rather poignantly, he cites an example of two sisters actually playing at being sisters. The rules of their relationship that largely go unnoticed in daily life are consciously acquired through play.

Lewis *et al.* (2000) found that pretend play was significantly correlated with both expressive and receptive language. A study by McCune (1995) tested three hypotheses on the relationship between pretend play and language development. These relationships included: an increasing depth of vocabulary (lexicon) with the onset of pretending; combinations in language with the onset of symbolic play combinations; and the beginning of rule-governed language being associated with hierarchical combinations in play. The study found that children made language gains at the same time as equivalent play developments (McCune, 1995). It is not clear, however, which comes first, and while this may well remain an impossible chicken and egg conundrum, it is clear that the ability to co-operatively play is bound to be seriously compromised if the ability to effectively (and affectively) communicate is absent or significantly impaired.

Vygotsky (1978) also noted that as well as the social rules children acquire through play, such as those of the sisters noted above, they gain what we now understand as self-regulation. When a child stands at the starting line of a running race, for example, she may well want to run immediately so as to reach the finish line first, but her knowledge of the social rules surrounding the game and her desire to enjoy the race enable her to regulate her initial impulse and wait for the start signal. Play is a powerful medium for developing such essential attributes as emotional regulation (Seja and Russ, 1999), social competence (McAloney and Stagnitti, 2009), problem solving (Russ, 1998) and understanding narrative (Peter, 2003).

Children with disabilities are at risk of not developing complex play skills that underpin the ability to participate in [such activities] as interacting with friends, conversing with others and engaging as a play partner. Facilitating these skills in children is of paramount importance . . . so that children can engage in their school communities, at home and with friends.

(Stagnitti *et al.*, 2012, p. 302)

Play as a dynamic process

McConkey (2006) is clear about how we ought to regard play as an educational activity: 'Play is better thought of as a process rather than a product; as actions rather than an activity; as a verb rather than a noun' (McConkey, 2006, p. 8). He goes on to point out that play is a dynamic continuum that starts with adult/baby interactions, so 'we can see how it is possible for parents to play with new-born babies even though their only contribution may be a stare, a gurgle or a yawn' (McConkey, 2006, p. 8).

Play is at the heart of Intensive Interaction (Nind and Hewett, 1994; 2001; 2006; Hewett and Nind, 1998) and this must form the starting point and indeed the cornerstone for all pupils and students, of whatever age, who struggle with the basics of communication and the ability to form and maintain relationships with others. While the basics of Intensive Interaction are fairly simple, and indeed often intuitive, the ability to keep McConkey's dynamic going are not, and it is essential this is not an area that is allowed to stagnate and wither away for want of that dynamic. With those with PMLD, the dynamic is largely in the hands of the interactors whether they be teachers, TAs, family, friends, bus escort or peers, and it is vital that schools set up a regenerative process with regular training opportunities for all involved, especially for interactors who are new to the process. Playing the same old games with the same old people can get very boring for all of us, and while there is much to be said for the familiar, particularly for those with PMLD, the dynamic requires regular regeneration.

Playing with non-learning-disabled peers

Although Roeyers (1995) and Trevarthen *et al.* (1998) have pointed out that children generally make for better playmates than adults, it is extremely problematic for children with SLD to play co-operatively with each other because of all of the reasons noted above. It's difficult enough when one child finds co-operative play challenging, but when both/all do the likelihood of it taking place is bleak. Logically, a mediator who is skilled in the art of play and has sufficient communication skills is required, and equally logically we might therefore turn to other (non-learning-disabled) children. On the face of it, such options will open up all sorts of inclusive opportunities and we would not want to deny these, but they must be approached with caution. Not only will the non-learning-disabled children need considerable training, supporting adults will still need to take an active observational, as well as modeling and re-modeling role. Their role in supporting play is not just to ensure safety or other considerations that might go with the job of a playground supervisor, this is to ensure that we are actively *teaching* play to those with SLD. The training needed for non-learning-disabled peers is to ensure that they do not slip into paternalisitic roles and interact with their peers with SLD as they would a younger sibling, or worse, a toddler. The dire consequences of learned helplessness are just as ever present in play as they are in work!

Play deficits or different ways of learning?

Before this takes place, however, children with SLD will themselves need some considerable work in building up experience of the processes required to play co-operatively. In an interesting study looking at the conditions that might be needed to support play in an inclusive setting, Fani Theodorou and Melanie Nind looked at a single child with an autism diagnosis but without learning difficulties. They argue that teachers need to operate in the triple (but not mutually exclusive) roles of supporters of play, mediators of play and active play partners (Theodorou and Nind, 2010).

In making their points about the need to actively support play opportunities between those with autism and their peers without, Theodorou and Nind take exception to what they consider to be overly structured play theories that concentrate on deficit-led, medical models. They point out that there may be misunderstandings and confusions about the actual ability of children with autism to play because of the multiple categorisations of play. For example, Trevarthen *et al.* (1998) argue that 'careful observations have often come to the conclusion that many kinds of play are less affected in autistic children than was expected' (p. 109). For Theodorou and Nind (2010) it is

> not only the types of research that have fed the focus on play deficits; theoretical and environmental factors have also contributed. The domination of cognitive developmental theories in the play literature has placed a stress on play deficits in children with developmental impairments (Seach, 2007). Simultaneously, and interconnected, these children have had fewer play opportunities as adults intervene with programmes based on a more structured, adult-led philosophy (Greenspan and Wieder, 2003). Many widely used autism-specific techniques actually reduce peer interaction, which may in turn delay the development of play.
>
> (p. 103)

There is a case for arguing that Theodorou and Nind are overly harsh on what is effectively an interactive methodology within Greenspan and Wieder's *Floortime*, ascribing a greater degree of adult-led (as opposed to adult-interactive) philosophy than seems intended in the literature, and some might detect an element of political correctness (or at least political leanings towards an inclusive model of education) in their insistence that deficit models are intrinsically dangerous. They do, however, counter that potential charge in arguing that their agenda

> is not to deny the 'facts' regarding difficulties children with autism face but to challenge the helpfulness of normative benchmarks and the remedial intervention pathways they lead to. It is helpful, we argue, to examine in detail the actions and interactions that underpin the inclusion of children with autism in play.
>
> (p. 103)

This notion of 'normative benchmarks' echoes the points made in the opening chapters of this book in relation to the dilemmas of difference arguments. It is not our role to opine on whether those with autism learn differently (and therefore should be taught differently), although Jordan (2005) for one seems clear that they do and should be. But in relation to those with SLD (and PMLD) in play, we once again find an example of the fact that those with SLD (and PMLD) do learn differently. If this is so, the whole pedagogy in relation to play needs to be fundamentally different. We would concur with Theodorou and Nind that deficit models tend to point to what children (with autism, with SLD, with PMLD) cannot (apparently) do. We cannot change the autism, the SLD or the PMLD; they are for life. A number of educators may take this as a reason not to teach play, since children with SLD and PMLD and ASC cannot (apparently) do it. We do not hold this view. But it is nonetheless vital that we understand and acknowledge what children do not understand in order to arrive at a different point of entry. It is not that children with SLD and PMLD (or ASC for that matter) cannot play co-operatively, it is that they learn to do it differently and we must therefore teach them differently.

Types and stages of play

Wolff (1979) categorised play into six types as follows:

1   *Solitary play* is defined as an activity that a child plays alone without interaction with others. This type of play offers no social skills but a sense of privacy.
2   *Parallel play* is when a child engages with a similar activity to his or her peers without interacting with them, verbally or physically.
3   *Positive interaction with peers* is a play behaviour between a child and another that sometimes involves verbal communication. This play category affords social skills, such as sharing: for example, climbing or sliding down the slope together while talking, etc.
4   *Negative interaction with peers* is a type of play that involves aggressive behaviour, such as fighting, refusing to share any play features, unwillingness to help or work together with a peer, etc.
5   *Positive interaction with adults* is when a child is willing to work together with an adult by offering or receiving help. This play behaviour affords social skills, such as communication.
6   *Negative interaction with adults* is when a child is being non-co-operative with an adult, for example resisting interaction, kicking, screaming, etc.

Sherratt and Peter (2002), in discussing the nature of teaching play and drama to those on the autistic spectrum (and not necessarily with severe or profound learning difficulties), describe both the levels and the social dimensions of play. They argue that the levels of play can be described as:

*   Sensorimotor play – primarily exploratory, where the properties of objects are felt, squeezed, shaken, smelled and mouthed, etc. These are very early cognitive functioning explorations, although of course we do not outgrow these skills and will still use them if we need to, even as adults.
*   Relational play – the exploration of the object reveals its properties, so we discover that it bounces, or makes a noise when squeezed, or fits nicely into this big box.
*   Functional play – where specific toys are used as designed, for a specified purpose. These might be cars, dolls, tea sets, etc. Notice that although the child's relationship with the toy is functional, pretence may still come into play as the cars are raced or crashed, and the dolls are fed or need changing.
*   Symbolic play – where pretence comes into play in terms of the object, which comes to stand for something else, such as a stick becoming a sword.

- Socio-dramatic play – which now involves acting situations out with roles. Even here, however, it should be noted that other play participants, either children or adults, are not required. It is perfectly feasible to have a multi-cast five act playlet with just one actor taking all the roles.

With regard to the social dimensions of play, Sherratt and Peter (2002) regard them as being:

- solitary;
- parallel – not necessarily playing with but playing alongside, and there may be no acknowledgment or even recognition of the other's presence;
- shared – in the sense that the resources or group of objects are shared, and though there may be an acknowledgment of the other's presence it is fleeting rather than sustained;
- turn-taking – the first stirrings of co-operative play in the clear acknowledgment of the other's involvement in the activity;
- co-operative.

At this stage it is really important to note that though both the levels and social dimensions of play are broadly developmental indicators, that is they will broadly apply to the play development of NT conventionally developing learners, they are not linear and 'progress' is not dependent on achievement within the previous level.

Getting stuck

The thing about these steps and those with severe learning difficulties is that while we do often make attempts to engage young children with SLD in play, the dominance of the normative benchmarks noted by Theodorou and Nind above ensures that (in the UK at least) we tend not to carry this on in, any formal teaching sense, beyond the age of five or six, whether the children have got it or not. Because largely, those without learning difficulties have got it by then, and enter school (comparatively) fully formed social beings, the normative model has no need for formal educational refinement beyond the age of five or six. In the UK, the Early Years Foundation Stage (EYFS) curriculum is suffused with play; play runs through the very centre and is clearly held in high esteem. The National Curriculum on the other hand mentions it only in passing in terms of role play in drama, games children might be involved in to learn various other things such as number and formal games (such as football, basketball or hockey) in terms of PE. The NT conventionally developing curriculum assumes, rightly, that children will have learned to play by the time they get to the age of five or six. Play – the learning of play, the practice of play – then reverts to what NT conventionally developing children do; they play on their own and with others in relatively self-governing situations. Adults' roles are much more about ensuring safety and conflict resolution, as in Wolff's negative interaction with peers play, noted above.

Those with SLD will, however, largely get stuck somewhere along the developmental line in much the same way as they get stuck with conventional understandings of maths or literacy. The answer is not to give them more of what they get stuck at, because the problem is likely to lie in the cognitive difficulties experienced, that is, the deficits. What we therefore need to do is jump stages, and we can still come back if it's appropriate to the individual.

Rather like teaching money by starting with high value coins and low value notes and working our way backwards, so we might need to start with a level of play that our learners can achieve at and work our way backwards.

In a small-group case study conducted by the one of the authors (Imray, 1996) a version of heuristic play was set up with three students with PMLD. Heuristic play is a term originally coined by Goldschmeid and Jackson (1994) and derives from the root of the Greek word eureka, meaning 'I have found (it)'. Goldschmeid and Jackson made considerable claims for the process of allowing young infants from six months or so up to the age of three to discover 'play' through interaction with everyday household objects made of natural materials. There are now a number of commercial variations on this such as 'Treasure Baskets' (Gascoyne, 2012) and the principles of such play techniques for NT conventionally developing young children are well established. The new UK curriculum for children up to the age of five, the Early Years Foundation Stage, has play in general and specific variations of play such as heuristic play at its core, more of which later.

This particular group of students with PMLD consisted of three ambulant, fairly able (in PMLD terms) students, one boy and two girls, who would have been classified today as working at around P2 to P4 in UK P Scale terms, aged eleven to thirteen. Two of them were excellent at Intensive Interaction (these were the two P4 students who were certainly able to consistently take the initiative and understand that the adult was following their lead) and one of these had quite good interpersonal skills, although only with adults. All had good gross and fine motor movement. The three were deliberately chosen because of their physical abilities and because they rarely had time off school, and as this was intended to be an extended experiment lasting the whole academic year; this was key. Before every session lasting about forty-five minutes, held on the same morning in the same classroom, the room was cleared of chairs and furniture as much as was possible with sufficient space allowed in the central area for the students to move around the room and interact with the objects. These were such things as tennis balls, metal chains, pieces of coloured cloth, balls of wool, wooden clothes pegs, kitchen implements such as spatulas and spirtles, etc., and lots of boxes and tins of various sizes. The first author observed every session, but did not intervene, being there merely to ensure the students didn't injure themselves or each other. There was occasionally one other staff member present, who was under strict instructions to remain as silent and as unobtrusive as possible. There were thirty-three sessions in total over the year.

The students didn't injure themselves or each other, but they didn't do anything else either. One of the girls walked around the room self-engaging with her hands, the other girl sat on the floor, gently rocking and quietly singing to herself, while the boy sat on the floor for most of the time, went to one of the adults in the room at fairly regular intervals to seek a short reassurance, and very occasionally picked up a tennis ball and let it drop. Apart from this latter (very occasional) activity, these were all things that all three did as a matter of course when left on their own in any environment (Imray, 1996).

Assuming that the cognitive disabilities of the students precluded them from making the leap towards self-engaging and playful discovery, another group was set up the following year of four boys with SLD aged eleven and twelve, all functioning between P5 and P7 in UK P Scale terms. To allow the play to work on a cognitive functioning level, it was decided to purchase an indoor play tent, and place various household items in it and in other parts of the room. Other conventional toys, such as large trucks and play kitchen equipment, were also provided and halfway through the year a dressing-up box was added. The same principles of non-adult intervention were applied. There were twenty-seven sessions of forty-five minutes in all, across the academic year, and again, the first author was present for each session.

In some ways this second, more cognitively able group did interact with the play materials and indeed each other. The natural heuristic play materials were totally ignored by all, but the tent/house was used considerably and the conventional toys occasionally. Once the boys had got used to the set up and recognised that the adults were not going to organise anything (which took several weeks to establish) a pattern of play started to emerge. One of the boys (Keith) had extremely good linguistic skills, much more so than the others, although his cognitive level was on a par, and he took on the role of parent/teacher/adult. Two of the other boys (Alan and Ian) quickly became subservient to him while he told them what to do, although the fourth (Faisal) usually absented himself from the play and stared out of the window. There was occasional aggression as Keith got angry that the others weren't doing what he wanted, or Ian took his frustration at being told off by Keith out on Alan although, interestingly, rarely on Keith. As the sessions went on over the year, the roles became set and established, getting into patterns of behaviour that none of the participants seemed either able or willing to alter (Imray, 1997).

The point about both of these examples is that there was an expectation on the first author's part that, given time and opportunity, some or all of both sets of students would make the cognitive leap. The fact that these expectations were confounded, however, points not just to the absence of adults in Theodorou and Nind's roles of supporters of play, mediators of play, and active play partners, but also to the extreme difficulties that those with PMLD and SLD will have in playing when structure is absent. Just as in teaching problem solving and thinking, in play we might have to put the structure into place *before* we can take it away.

Teaching play skills: The 'doing' of play

Stagnitti (2010) suggests that the act of play involves the 'doing' of play (the development of play skills), the 'being' of play (the expression of who they are) and the 'role' of player (engaging with others in meaningful interactions) and it is this doing that we would suggest is a necessary pre-condition before play can be extended out to co-operative play for those with SLD. With NT conventionally developing learners, these abilities tend to come together and develop alongside the communicative skills necessary to play co-operatively. For those with SLD, such communicative skills may never arrive, or at least take an awfully long time to evolve.

Psychotherapeutic play-based programmes such as PALS (Positive Attachments and Learning to Succeed) (Chaloner, 2001) and EPIC (Everyone Playing in Class) (Woolf, 2008, 2011) are features of both mainstream and special school teaching programmes in the US and the UK with children with ESBD (Emotional, Social and Behavioural Difficulties). A central feature of their application is a sound working knowledge of Attachment Theory, on the basis that a strong bond needs to be established between teacher and pupil that mirrors that of a primary caregiver. Although such considerations do not normally apply for those with SLD[1], the play elements of such programmes might be detached and used with those with SLD.

Similarly, Stagnitti et al. (2012) describe a study involving an occupational therapy-derived programme entitled 'Learn to Play', a child-led play-based intervention aimed at developing self-initiated pretend-play skills in children. This programme divides learning to play into set levels (Stagnitti, 2009), which mirrors play of conventionally developing children at set periods, namely level 1 (eighteen months to two-and-a-half years old), level 2 (three years old) and level 3 (four to five years old). From this chapter's perspective, levels 1 and 2 seem particularly interesting because they involve basing the play on set known scenarios such as putting teddy to bed, taking dolly for a walk in the park, etc., moving the child from observer to active participant, with repetition being a key factor and involving, initially at least, the distinct possibility that the supporting adult will do all of the playing while the child watches.

Of the 2012 study, the authors concluded, after sessions lasting one hour twice per week, over six months:

> typical indicators of play accounted for an increase of 47.3% in shared variance with social interaction and an increase of 36% in shared variance for social connection. For language, object substitution ability accounted for 50% of the shared variance, which was an increase of 27% from baseline.
>
> (Stagnitti *et al.*, 2012, p. 302)

Like Theodorou and Nind's intervention techniques, 'Learn to Play'[2], PALS and EPIC are not based on theories around how those with SLD might learn to play, but based almost entirely around free play. In all four techniques there is a strong link to research on children with autism. While a certain amount of adult modeling takes place initially, especially with 'Learn to Play', it may be that there are expectations of moving children on to free play that might move too fast for those with SLD. Play theories for those with SLD and PMLD don't really exist other than through strategies such as Intensive Interaction, and this should certainly form a base for relational play. What we might need, however, is a bridge between the two, so children are first taught about relationships through, for example, Intensive Interaction, then taught about playing and *then* let loose on imaginative play schemes such as 'Learn to Play'. The middle part, the 'playing bridge', might be taken up by games: 'games are not time out from real work; they are the most intensive developmental work you can do' (Nind and Hewett, 2001, p. 66).

There are many considerable advantages of teaching play through games for those SLD:

- Games have structure and clear rules and allow all to play the game as long as the participants have the cognitive ability to understand the rules. Many games exist with very simple rules.
- Games allow for endless repetition and such a repetitive structure gives more opportunities to remember, follow and build upon from week to week.
- Pupils with SLD do not tend to get bored by a high level of repetition because it affords them time to understand and therefore be directly involved with what's going on.
- The general excitement that can be generated is likely to sweep all before it while they get to know and practise the rules, and the chances of engagement are considerably enhanced.
- There is constant contact with other children in an atmosphere of expectation and fun.
- Games teach children to relate to both object and person (rather than just one or the other).
- Games reinforce the pleasure of shared experiences.

- They involve the constant practice and learning of fundamental skills such as turn-taking, sequencing, anticipation, and linking words and actions together.
- Games afford the chance to actively, and in context, explore 'mental state' words such as 'excitement', 'feeling', 'risk', 'chance', 'disappointment', 'elation', 'jealousy', 'envy', etc.
- Games give early experiences of co-operative play as concepts of the 'team around me' evolve.
- Games get children used to the concepts of winning and losing.
- Games accept failure and defeat as everyday occurrences. The concept of trying and 'having a go' is elevated above the fear of failure.
- Games spread the failure among the team rather than concentrating on a single individual. Success is elevated by carrying a shared group elation, and failure to win carries a reduced significance because the individual is not at fault.
- Games carry considerable opportunities for collective practising of problem-solving and thinking skills.
- Games are entirely open to changes in the rules as long as these are clear and agreed. In this way they can re-enforce teaching about change and flexibility and generalisation.
- The ability to play games makes children look more attractive to other children and increases the opportunities for contact in both special and inclusive settings.
- Games have the potential to be continued at breaks and lunchtimes by the children themselves.

And when we get to this last stage we know for sure that children are ready for child-led free co-operative play.

What games might we play?

One to one or small group games with young learners such as tickle monster; 'row, row, row your boat'; rolling a ball or throwing and catching; peek-a-boo; Mr Potato Head; round and round the garden; blow bubbles and trying to pop them before they hit the ground.

'Activity' games that can quickly develop into free play for those pupils who might be at that developmental level, such as ordinary playgrounds with swings and round a bouts and especially adventure playgrounds. There are numerous games such as 'Shark Attack' for playing in the swimming pool, as well beachball catch and water polo.

Games in the ball pool, which are especially good for rough and tumble and 'king of the castle'. Teachers are often wary of such games as they can sometimes quickly get out of hand, and there is a risk of children getting hurt; but there is no chance of children learning what is an appropriate amount of rough if they don't have practice. Sessions can start off being very short, perhaps a minute or two several times during the day, and build up from there. Such activities might go some way towards the physical curriculum as well as allowing pupils opportunities to let off steam.

Sand and water play, with lots of buckets, spades, spoons, jugs, bowls, cups, etc., for pouring and digging, especially if the size of the sand pit and the amount of water allow for several adults and children to play at once. Flowing water fed round by a pump down long shutes with little holding pools along the way is particularly attractive to children of all ages and might even be considered as a justifiable item of big expense ahead of the soft play room. It is certainly likely to get used a lot (especially if you can place it indoors), is much less likely to break down and is not complex to switch on!

Small group or one-to-one games for any age such as hide and seek; pin the tail on the donkey; pass the parcel; musical chairs; blind man's bluff; musical statues; Simon says; sleeping lions; what's the time Mr Wolf; balloon and spoon relay race; barrel relay race; three-armed relay race (tie children's arms together rather than their legs); skittles; flap the kipper; treasure hunts; prize walk number game (musical chairs only with numbers in big circles drawn onto the floor). When the music stops, children have to run to a circle and stand on it. A big die gets thrown and those standing on that number are the winners. This can be easily transferred to a team game so points are added up and the team with the most points wins – group hug! Beanbag-toss game – into different sized holes for different scores; hopscotch; 'ring-a-ring o' roses'; 'The Farmer's in the Den'. Games like 'The Farmer's in the Den' are excellent for working on 'Theory of Mind' (Baron-Cohen, 1997) where children have the opportunity to be the farmer, the wife, the child, the dog. There are, no doubt, numerous variations of this game around the world that will carry different cultural significances. Duck, duck, goose; Hokey-Cokey (as in the song 'You do the Hokey-Cokey and you turn around, that's what it's all about'). Well-practised hands at this will pause for children to take the lead as to what the next action might be. Songs such as 'Hokey-Cokey' are also excellent for gathering children back into concentration mode when games (as they sometimes do) get a bit rowdy; tag and variations of it such as Shark Attack where pupils have to run from one end of the hall or the playground to the other without being caught (and disgustingly eaten) by the shark. Children become sharks when they themselves get eaten. For older children this might become Zombie Attack.

Board games for older pupils: lotto/bingo; ludo; Kim's game; snakes and ladders.

Card games: snap; pelmanism.

There are a number of published books on games, listed below, although only one of this list has been written specifically with those with learning difficulties in mind (Barratt *et al.*, 2000). Even this will need some adaptation to be suitable for those with severe learning difficulties, but such adaptations can be the stuff of staff meetings where many heads can make lights work!

Suggested books for games

Barratt, P., Border, J., Joy, H., Parkinson, A., Potter, M. and Thomas, G. (2000) *Developing Pupils' Social Communication Skills*. London: David Fulton.

Barron, P. (2008) *Classroom Gems: Practical Ideas, Games and Activities for the Primary Classroom*. Harlow: Pearson Education.

Barron, P. (2009) *Classroom Gems: Outdoor Learning: Games, Ideas and Activities for Learning Outside the Primary Classroom*. Harlow: Pearson Education.

Delmain, C. and Spring, J. (2003) *Speaking, Listening and Understanding: Games for Young Children*. Bicester: Speechmark.

Leach, B. J. (2000) *10-Minute Games*. Witney, Oxfordshire: Scholastic.

Ludwig, A. and Swan, A. (2007) *101 Great Classroom Games*. New York: Mcgraw-Hill.

Extending play on

While the purpose of elevating games is to bring an initial structure to play, perhaps so necessary for those with severe learning difficulties (with or without an additional autistic diagnosis), it is vitally important that we build in progression towards supported free play, perhaps using semi-structured schemes such as Karen Stagnitti's 'Learn to Play' noted above.

More work would need to be done with this to ensure it is accessible for those with severe learning difficulties, but it most definitely seems to have promise.

What is also vitally important is that we adopt play as being as necessary a part of the pedagogy and curriculum for those with SLD as formal maths might be for NT conventionally developing learners. For those with SLD, the subject of 'Play' needs to be given a capital letter. The fundamental principles must be that Play is not relegated to something that's just done in the playground, and it is not left to pupils and students to find their own level in their own time. Nor should we stop thinking about Play when children move into the main part of the school from the early years. Learning to play, for those with SLD, does not stop at the age of six, and for many it may go on right through the secondary phase. Play may well metamorphose into drama and the other areas of the Creative Curriculum, and there is a very strong case for suggesting that Play should be set within the Creative Curriculum, perhaps forming the primary beginnings of a wider and differently specialised secondary curriculum. Play is a subject to be taught and we must give it serious consideration. This chapter is, we hope, a start on that road.

Notes

1   We're not saying that Attachment Theory is not an issue for some pupils and students with SLD (or PMLD), just it is not an issue that might be part of the norm, as it might well be for those with ESBD.
2   The 'Learn to Play' study involved nineteen children aged five to eight, seventeen of whom had mild or moderate learning difficulties, eleven had autism and two of whom were defined as having severe learning difficulties.

Chapter 15

A citizenship curriculum for pupils with severe learning difficulties and profound and multiple learning difficulties

This chapter is probably as close to a common chapter with the PMLD section of this book as we're likely to get. It is divided into four distinct, but very interrelated sections dealing with, in turn (i) choice, democracy and community participation, (ii) behaviour, (iii) sex and relationships education (SRE), and (iv) the world of work. This last is less applicable to those with PMLD and presents much more of a polemic, but it is an issue that needs to be aired, and air it we will.

Citizenship and community participation

Citizenship, if it is to mean anything, must involve at its core the notion that all citizens are a part of, rather than being apart from (Cole, 1989), all of the various communities around them, unless of course the individual, or group of individuals, specifically chooses to absent him/herself or themselves, from the whole. It may be that some of those with PMLD or SLD (especially if they have an additional ASC) will choose to absent themselves and this position must be respected, but generally, we believe this not to be the case.

This may be perceived to be part of the individual's general quality of life, and perhaps a fundamental constituent of happiness. Certainly, for most of us, happiness will very much depend upon us being an active and equal part of the communities around us. We, as educators, will need to make special efforts to ensure those with PMLD are part of the communities around them, without necessarily expecting any additional educational benefits; that is, community participation must be an aim in itself if we are to enable those with PMLD to be full citizens. This will mean curriculum time and regular, probably weekly, curriculum time being spent outside of the school. This will in turn mean organising volunteers and helpers and students from the local mainstream school to support access to the local communities for those with PMLD. This involves having regular relationships with the people and places around us, whether they be shops, cafés, libraries, schools, museums, farms or factories and of course all of the people who inhabit such places; whatever you can organise on a regular basis. Persuading others that inclusion is a positive benefit to all in society, not just those with PMLD, becomes a central tenet of such a philosophy and practice.

Citizenship and choice, democracy and happiness

For those with SLD, participation in the communities around them will come more naturally as part of the curriculum, as they shop and travel for example, and less conscious effort needs to be expended. For both groups, however, the concept of citizenship will need to generate more than just interaction with wider communities; it needs to take place in school and within the education they receive. That is, their introduction to the concept of living in a democratic society should start with schools' abilities and willingness to personalise the curriculum, so that active and real choices are being enacted all the time, as a matter of course. Education needs to be something done with pupils, not something done to pupils. Concepts such as schools councils must be treated with the greatest possible caution lest they be purely window dressing.

The idea that someone with SLD (let alone someone with PMLD) can be an active and independent voice on a school council without a huge amount of prior learning within a Problem-Solving and Thinking Curriculum (see Chapter 13) is frankly questionable. The fact that those with SLD and PMLD are 'consulted' on a school's council does not automatically equal either choice or democracy, and there is a real danger that such bodies will be entirely tokenistic. Choice, democracy and citizenship need to be everyday occurrences for those with PMLD and SLD as they undertake the *process* of learning through the personalisation of learning.

Armando DeFinizio, who prior to writing *Personalising learning in a 21st-century context* (DeFinizio, 2011) was Principal of Bristol Brunel Academy (a large mainstream secondary state-funded school in England), posits five main criteria for effective personalisation.

1   *Accept that students are children who are still developing,*[1] and that they will come with their own problems and difficulties. Why for example *is there a need for . . . exclusions? Surely, if we want to personalise the education of all our students, we should be educating the student who has needs around, for example, anger management?*

2   *As educators, it is our role to educate the whole child* as opposed to compartmentalising learning and assuming we are only teaching maths in a maths lesson or communication in an English lesson. Educating the whole child includes educating her to think, and problem solve, and make choices, and say 'no', and be as independent as she can be, and lead as full and active a sex life as she wants to have.

3   *The teacher's expertise lies in their understanding of pedagogy. They no longer have a monopoly on information.* Knowledge of how children, young people and adults with SLD and PMLD learn and how teachers can most effectively teach them will allow pupils and students to grow at their own pace in their own time. For those with SLD and PMLD, most education and learning are processes, not products that can be predefined.

4   *Hierarchies stifle independence, creativity and decision making* and just as an overbearing and over controlling headteacher will stifle the initiative of school staff, so over-controlling teachers will stifle the initiative of schoolchildren. We need to step back from assuming we know everything and children know nothing unless we provide the answers. This, however, means taking risks!

5   *A sense of belonging will encourage growth* and being an essential part of the educational process is key. Pupils need to know that they can opt out as well as in; that they don't have to adopt challenging behaviours to get their point across; that they will be listened to and that they do have a voice.

We have already referred to the Quality of Life (QOL) arguments put forward by Gordon Lyons and Michael Cassebohm (see Chapter 2) but it might be worth going back to the concept of happiness as something a civilised society might wish for its citizens with SLD and PMLD. Citizenship is, after all, a two-way process of individual and societal interaction.

Lu and Shih (1997) regard happiness as composed of three related components: (i) positive affect; (ii) absence of negative affect; and (iii) satisfaction with life as a whole. Bearing this in mind, might we relate this directly to notions of inclusion, personalisation and democracy? As quoted in Davis and Florian, 2004:

> As Florian and Hegarty (2004) note: 'the term SEN covers an array of problems from those arising from particular impairments to those related to learning and behavioural difficulties experienced by some learners some of the time . . . Many people are disabled by an impairment but they may or may not be handicapped by the condition . . . However, there are some conditions and impairments that are known to create barriers to learning unless accommodations are made. A person with a visual impairment, for example, may need *some kind of support or accommodation* to achieve the same functioning as the person without the visual impairment . . . The term special education is often used to refer to the process of making such accommodations.
>
> (p. 34; emphasis their)

Is it feasible for an education system to include happiness here, so that with 'some kind of support or accommodation' the same functioning (in terms of happiness) can be achieved for the person with the learning difficulty as the person without the learning difficulty? Andrew Colley has written of the centrality of happiness in the education of those with PMLD:

> If I were teaching Maths to a class of mainstream students, I would want them to enjoy my class. I know they will learn better if they are happy. But I also want them to be able to do the maths. This will take hard work. So in trying to get them to a certain level in Maths, my commitment to their happiness might slip a little and be replaced by a desire for them to learn and achieve. As an exam approaches I might find myself not caring very much at all about their happiness.
>
> In a PMLD classroom, it's kind of the other way round. The happiness, the well-being of the students should be right up there, all the time. Because when Ramzi, or Sammy, or Usha laugh – which they do quite a lot – their laughter, their happiness is just as valid, just as all embracing, just as real as anybody else's. Like all of us, it probably means they are happy, it usually means they are comfortable. It might just mean they are at ease with themselves. Which when you have spent your whole life being observed, followed, toileted, strapped into cars and chairs, lifted, fed and told 'no', is a pretty precious thing.
>
> Can happiness be taught? Probably not, but it can be modelled and encouraged. External circumstances can be arranged to make it likely. A student is far more likely to feel comfortable and happy if their personal care is dealt with professionally and sensitively for instance. We can also create environments using space, colour and sound which prioritise the comfort, calmness and well being of our students.
>
> (Colley, 2013, p. 91)

Although they are not specifically arguing for those with PMLD (or SLD), being primarily concerned with education of the mainstream student, Ecclestone and Hayes (2009) regard education as being fundamentally about the imparting of knowledge, and one doesn't have to be happy to receive it or, for that matter, to deliver it: 'Knowledge can be taught passionately or indifferently by and to people who may be distraught, upset, happy or content.

It does not matter. Knowledge, as it were, conquers all' (Ecclestone and Hayes, 2009, p. 153). This conjures up the somewhat disconcerting mental picture of a miserable teacher teaching miserable children as in Dickens' wonderfully named Wackford Squeers in the equally apposite Dotheboys Hall or Thomas Gradgrind issuing forth in *Hard Times*:

> Now, what I want is, Facts. Teach these boys and girls nothing but Facts. Facts alone are wanted in life. Plant nothing else, and root out everything else. You can only form the minds of reasoning animals upon Facts: nothing else will ever be of any service to them. This is the principle on which I bring up my own children, and this is the principle on which I bring up these children. Stick to Facts, sir!
>
> (Dickens, 1854)

It may be that the indifferent teaching of knowledge will and does work when teaching NT conventionally developing children (although we have our considerable doubts on this), but it will not work for those with SLD and PMLD and we should not (must not) tolerate the contemplation; good teaching works best when you have the pupils working with you. We may adopt a utilitarian view of happiness (the greatest good for the greatest number) for society as a whole, but it seems reasonable to suggest that pupils' happiness is something to aim for as far as we are able. Whether it is the only thing to aim for, as Lyons and Cassebohm (2010) seem to be suggesting, is another matter entirely.

Citizenship and behaviour

It is self-evident that issues of challenging behaviour (CB) presented by those who have severe or profound learning difficulties need to be addressed. There is a considerably higher than average chance of those with SLD and PMLD having attendant challenging behaviours (Allen *et al.*, 2006) with Harris (1995) estimating a figure of between ten and fifteen per cent of the SLD school population regularly exhibiting CB. Emerson (1995) suggests a figure of between one in six and one in eight (between 12.5 per cent and 16.5 per cent), while Male notes the figure as nearer twenty-five per cent (Male, 1996). Indeed the Dawn Male study also reflects that some UK SLD schools report their figures as approaching fifty per cent of their population exhibiting some form of challenging behaviour at various times in their school lives, a figure supported by a similar study conducted by Porter and Lacey (1999).

In the UK at least, there has been a clear perception for some time that CB problems are increasing in both number and complexity (Ofsted, 2006). Although exclusions, both temporary and permanent, used to be commonplace as schools sought to achieve in a results-centred teaching environment (Waddell, 1998; Hanko, 2003), there has recently been a move towards challenging permanent exclusions (Ofsted, 2010), though this may in turn have placed additional strains on schools and may have led to disaffected school staff (Lloyd Bennet, 2006), particularly in the mainstream sector (Axup and Gersch, 2008; Derrington, 2009).

The generally punitive policies adopted by many UK mainstream schools, especially the secondary sector, means, however, that habitual challenging behaviours are often not dealt with; they are merely exported to another school, or another agency, or of course, back to parents, through the policy of fixed-term and permanent exclusions. It may be that most UK (secondary) mainstream schools don't even recognise they have a problem, so keen are they to ensure that the whole responsibility for change lies with the student. We must assume they pursue the medical model of disability, where mistakenly problems are seen to lie within the child rather than with those who are in a position of power and who have a clear responsibility to address the needs of those with difficulties and disabilities. The views espoused by DeFinizio (2011) noted above are, unfortunately, both extremely rare and very contentious, and mainstream schools might do well to reflect on more positive approaches to supporting those of their students who do exhibit habitual challenging behaviours (Imray, 2012).

There are a number of factors in relation to habitual challenging behaviour that have been noted to particularly apply to those with SLD and PMLD. Chadwick, Kusel and Cuddy (2008) found that,

> family factors such as a history of interrupted/disrupted maternal care, parental criticism of the child and aggressive parental disciplinary practices were also associated with behaviour problems (with those with severe intellectual disabilities), although the direction of causation was unclear.
>
> (p. 864)

Chadwick *et al.* also found that factors such as gender, social disadvantage and epilepsy (well established as risk factors in the population at large) were not significant factors with this group. This supported an earlier longitudinal study of fifty children with CB and SLD by Chadwick, Walker, Bernard and Taylor (2000), which found that limitations in daily living skills and the ability to exercise independence were significant predictors of behaviour problems in adults with SLD. A study conducted by Janssen, Schuengel and Stolk (2002) found that those with severe intellectual disabilities are more prone to stress than the general population, a finding made worse by the fact that this group had ineffective strategies for dealing with such stress.

For Colley (2013) CB is more about the person being challenged than the person doing the challenging, a point of view that reminds us of the fact that CBs rarely happen in an empty room[2]; that is, challenging behaviour is a relational concept and we (the challenged) need to think about why they (the challengers) are challenging. We have deliberately put the point this way because it inevitably leads us to the conclusion that CBs are communications; we may consider them to be poor communications, but they are communications nonetheless. When we remember that one of the major defining characteristics of both SLD and PMLD is difficulties (and often extreme difficulties) in both receptive and expressive communications it is hardly surprising that Hewett (1998b) could opine that 'challenging behaviour is normal'!

Imray (2008) is of the firm opinion that the vast majority of CBs displayed by those with SLD and PMLD are resolvable, and suggests we approach such issues through adopting set fundamental principles:

- Effectively tackling a behaviour that challenges demands an identification of the degree of learning difficulty.
- The resolution to the problems of the challenging behaviour will vary depending on the nature of that learning difficulty. The more intellectually impaired a pupil is, the less likely they are to understand the effect their actions might have upon others. Many pupils and students with SLD and all those with PMLD will probably

not understand how their actions affect others. Asking somebody at a very low developmental level to stop pinching, biting, scratching, etc., is a bit like asking a twelve-month-old baby to stop crying – a fairly pointless exercise! It is also really important that we establish whether the pupil has an additional ASC. As a general rule, for those with SLD/ASC, the person's autism is the key[3]; for those with PMLD/ASC the person's profound learning difficulty is the key.

- Changing behaviour is not just about the child changing – it is very much about us changing.
- There is no such thing as behaviour without a reason; all behaviours have a reason behind them and that reason always has a meaning for the person with CB.
- We cannot hope to change the behaviour unless we're prepared to both try to understand and try to accept the meaning behind the behaviour.
- The fact that the behaviour continues usually means that either we haven't been able to teach a better way of communicating, or that we are not listening to the communicative behaviours of the person with CB.
- It is really important to recognise the contribution of having learning difficulties in the formation of challenging behaviour. For most children with learning difficulties, behaviours that challenge staff are not premeditated or intended to have any particular outcome, other than in the broadest sense of 'give me attention' or 'take me away from this', they are, rather, reflections of the students' difficulties in understanding how they can fit in with the many complex routines that make up ordinary life.

Imray (2008) has put together the 'magnificent seven'; words that he feels hold the key to working with those with habitual challenging behaviours and learning difficulties. These are

- why
- consistency
- positive
- reward
- control
- success
- time.

Let us take these one at a time.

Why is always the first question to ask, and the question to come back to again and again. It is probably, however, also the question that causes most uncertainty. Perhaps the key to 'why' is to simplify the possible reasons because otherwise we are in danger of being overwhelmed, especially if the reasons for the behaviours are hidden within a cloud of problems. We might initially find out why the behaviour is happening by observation, checking files and records to see what other people think, discussing the issues with other professionals, discussing the issues with parents.

An effective shortcut, for pupils and students with SLD at least, is to take the line that behaviours are likely to surface in one of two ways, through either (or both) of (i) task avoidance and/or (ii) attention seeking (Carr and Durand, 1985). Imray (2008) suggests that the resolution to both of these types of behaviour is also simple; if a child, young person or adult is habitually exhibiting CB in order to gain attention, we need to give the amount of attention the person needs; if a child, young person or adult is habitually exhibiting CB in order to avoid a task, we need to take the task away.

While attention-seeking behaviours may well have their roots in Attachment Theory (Bowlby, 1988; Ainsworth *et al.*, 1978), very little has been written about this area with regard to those with SLD and PMLD. Nonetheless, Raaska *et al.* (2012) found attachment disorders to be more common among internationally adopted children with learning disabilities than in the general population and both Sterkenberg *et al.* (2008) and Schuengel *et al.* (2013) see it as a highly relevant area for future research. We would also particularly point to studies conducted by De Schipper *et al.* (2006) and De Schipper and Schuengel (2010) as clearly indicating the significant probability that attachment disorders can be addressed through close bonding with known close professionals such as TAs. In many ways here we are revisiting earlier ideas on *Gentle Teaching* put forward by McGee *et al.* (1987), and Nind and Hewett's various writings on *Intensive Interaction*. That is, love is a key component in the education of all those with learning difficulties and challenging behaviour, and for some love needs to be taught.

No doubt many will see 'love' as being as much as about education as the psychological theories of attachment disorder, that is, nothing. Such issues, they will argue, are more to do with therapy and therapeutic models and have no place in the classroom (Ecclestone and Hayes, 2009). This rather blinkered view, however, takes no account of the enormous influence school, and those who work in schools, can have in providing, solidity, consistency, warmth, affection, positive feedback, positive role models and the host of other basic human needs that some families and communities may not be able to offer. We wish to make it clear we are not 'blaming' families for challenging behaviour, far from it; there may a welter of reasons for families being unable to provide sufficient support and sanctuary. It is more a question of what we regard education to be. That is, the wholesale adoption of what Cornwall and Walter (2006) describe as a 'target driven economy' in education, where academic progress is seen as the primary (and often the only) concern, automatically denies many children, and especially those who display habitual challenging behaviours, the opportunities afforded to others. Cornwall and Walter (2006) go further in arguing that 'it is foolish, short-sighted and downright dangerous to ignore the broader holistic nature of the learning and teaching relationship and the ecology of the learner's situation' (p. 9).

This is, however, by no means an easy or cheap option, although it is probably the only option that will work in the long term. Some pupils and students with extreme attention-seeking behaviours will need dedicated one-to-one support in school. This person, usually a TA, might need to work with this one pupil and no one else, and suffer the slings and arrows of outrageous challenging behaviour for some considerable time (years rather than months). Make no mistake, however, such pupils and students will steal the time anyway, because class teams cannot leave the pupil to their own devices for fear of these very same challenging behaviours.

The idea that task-avoiding behaviours will be resolved if we take the task away is simple, but the role of the educator clearly demands that we educate. As such, the challenge for us is to re-introduce the activity so assiduously avoided, and this can probably only be done exceedingly cautiously and slowly. The classic way to achieve this is to offer a very small task for a very big reward, and this must be something, or a choice of somethings, that the learner really likes to do. Class teams often fall foul of this fairly simple strategy by pushing too hard too fast, and for some, on the extreme end of the CB continuum, a few seconds of 'work' for twenty minutes reward really can be appropriate. With task-avoiding behaviours, the pupil needs to be absolutely certain she can be successful and we will only achieve this if we go at her pace. Once the pattern has been established we can start to push a bit harder, but always be mindful that the learner will have bad days as well as good, and we might have to temporarily revert back to a very safe target on those bad days.

Consistency of approach is not necessarily about consistency in every setting, although this is obviously advantageous. We (as educators) might need to think about what we can effect and, as within any school, any behaviour policy has very little chance of working if everyone is doing their own thing. The best way of achieving consistency is to have collective ownership of any plan, and that means meetings of the whole group are really important.

Positive responses to habitual challenging behaviours are always more effective than negative responses. We therefore need to be very careful about using negative language (including saying the word 'no'), punishments, threats or consequences when dealing with habitual challenging behaviours in those with SLD or PMLD. There are a number of very good reasons for this, which are explored more fully in Imray (2012), but they are essentially that:

- Punishment automatically brings out the negative in us (and the child!).
- It is open to abuse because it has fear at its centre.
- Not everybody is able to command the same degree of fear.
- It is likely to breed resentment and a behaviour spiral.
- If we use punishment as a core factor, the behaviour will always surface, because we are waiting for it to happen before we act.
- Using negatives teaches what a person should not do, not what a person should do, so saying 'no' or 'don't do that' makes us believe that we're doing something, when in fact, we're doing nothing.[4]
- Punishment is a short-term solution that may suppress the behaviour but does not resolve it.
- Punishment is often confused with establishing boundaries. They are not the same at all and it is perfectly possible to establish boundaries through the use of a reward system that ensures an entirely positive response.
- Punishment does not encourage the person to take individual responsibility for their actions.
- A civilised society should perhaps, be marked by its degree of investment in positive rewards over negative punishments.

We must remember the challenging behaviour would probably not exist without the learning difficulty. Punishing a child with a learning difficulty for his challenging behaviour is the same as punishing a child for his learning difficulty. Rewarding good behaviour is a much more effective policy than punishing bad behaviour. It means we have a considerably greater long-term chance of extinguishing the behaviour.

Reward recognises that challenging behaviour can be an extremely powerful tool for the learner in that it can often bring instant pay-offs, such as greater attention or immediate withdrawal of problem activities or situations. If we look to using the learner's strengths, interests and obsessions as a basis for rewarding the promotion of more positive behaviours we will effectively be making the new behaviour much more worthwhile than the old one.

Success is clearly key because there is absolutely no point in bringing in a Behaviour Support Programme (BSP) that is going to fail. We have to make it as easy for the pupil to succeed as possible, since success breeds success and failure breeds failure. We need to remember the importance of the learning difficulty itself in establishing the behaviour in the first place. Whatever you decide to do it is probably best if you don't try to change everything at once; perfection is a lifelong project! Pick one behaviour to work on at a time (the one-rule rule) and remember that behaviour is just like any other subject and should be taught to the pupil like any other subject – that is with her learning difficulty in mind. Sometimes it is the most important subject to teach; sometimes it is the only subject to teach!

Control is something that many pupils and students with CB lack and seek. It is vitally important that any programme's long-term target is for the learner to take control of their own behaviour, but pupils with SLD and PMLD are likely to spend a very large percentage of their life being controlled by others. Not much wonder some seek to exercise control in the only way they can. It helps to bear in mind some basic human rights: everyone has the right to say 'no', and even more importantly, everyone has the right to be listened to when they say 'no'. Taking away that right is not the answer, but teaching a better way of saying 'no' might be; a way that is both positive and rewarding for the learner is far more likely to have both short-term and long-term benefits for everyone.

Time as a concept is fundamental in both the short-term and the long-term. If using basic behavioural techniques for those with SLD (rewarding positive behaviours) you should see a significant change within four weeks at the most, if you've got it right. If there is no change, stop the programme, check all of the words in the magnificent seven, and try something else. The long-term strategy must always be for the learner to take control of their own behaviour. Of course working with those with PMLD, as well as those who might be seeking attention, will probably take much longer because they will involve relational changes – they are long-term solutions.

Writing a behaviour support plan

So often with children, young people and adults with CB we naturally concentrate on what challenges us and, as such, thoughts about, and relationships with, such persons can become excessively negative. This is not surprising if we're being hurt on a daily basis. To counter this, as well as to provide a solid platform for a behaviour support plan (BSP), it is really useful to write a Behaviour Strength and Needs Chart.

Draw a vertical line down the middle of a sheet of A4 paper and, with others who know the person with CB well, write a list on the left side of the paper of all the positive things you can think of about the person. Concentrate especially on things she really likes to do, however inconsequential these may seem. You should have a list of at least ten things. Use these positive things as a basis for rewards that can be granted to the pupil for giving up her behaviours.

On the right side write a list of all the behaviours you feel the person needs help in changing if she is to become an active and interactive citizen. As Jordan (2001) notes, these may:

- be dangerous – to self, others or property;
- interfere and restrict – especially in the rate of the behaviour;
- affect others;
- be criminal or socially unacceptable behaviours.

Once you've written the list, set them in order of priority; if you could only change one thing, what would that be? Having a 'one-rule rule' is a useful way of remembering that, for those with habitual challenging behaviours, breaking the plethora of rules that we set is a daily and probably an hourly occurrence. They're always breaking them, which means of course they're always failing. If we only have one rule and we just concentrate on this one rule, we have much greater chance of success. This means we have to 'allow' the breaking of the other rules, but once the one rule is worked on and established, we can move on to the next. If we don't help the pupil to succeed, the pupil will always fail; we will always fail.

Despite our insistence that SMART targets are generally inappropriate vehicles for other areas of learning noted in this book, for both individuals and groups who have SLD or PMLD, the exception to the rule is CB. This is, however, more to do with staff perceptions than pupil perceptions, since there is often a tendency towards 'slippage'; and especially so when the BSP is going well. If you're expecting the pupil to work for ten minutes, that ten minutes has to be kept to. You could, on a bad day, change the ten minutes into six, but you cannot on a good day make the ten minutes into twenty[5]. The pupil must be secure in the knowledge that you are keeping your part of the bargain. She agrees not to exhibit the CB; you agree to stick to the timings she can manage and reward her for doing so. Having SMART targets also allows us to be consistent in approach, irrespective of whoever is working with the pupil.

The essential principles behind this approach are therefore:

- **Behaviours are communications** and we need to listen to the behaviours because they are telling us why.
- **Be aware of the developmental levels that your pupils are working at**. As a general working rule, using rewards will probably not be effective for those with PMLD and we need to take a much longer-term approach using relational bonding approaches that will centre on Intensive Interaction (Nind and Hewett, 1998; 2001).
- **Be aware if your pupils have an additional ASC diagnosis**. Again as a general rule, the key is deep knowledge of the individual's autism, and we certainly cannot fall back on attention seeking as being a reason why.
- **Always approach the problem from a positive perspective**. This means we're working with the pupil rather than against her.
- **Involve as many people both inside and outside your setting as possible**. The more people who are working within the same approach, the more consistent your BSP will be.
- **Use rewards that are essentially motivating and personal to the learner**. Using a reward system based on the pupil's own interests and motivators makes the new approach even more effective, because not only does the pupil gain the same effect in not doing the task and/or gaining attention, but she also gets rewarded as well!
- **Give control back to the learner**. Recognise that the CBs of most pupils who have SLD or PMLD are desperate attempts to wrest some control back into a life that may be totally out of their own control. We lose no face by giving pupils and students a chance to gain control.
- **Make targets time bound** using such simple devices as sand-timers or alarm clocks. This is likely to take much of the stress and anxiety away from learners who don't know what it is that is expected from them and may be very frightened that it is much too much.

- **Success is key**. We need to recognise that habitual challenging behaviours are usually fairly effective methods of task avoiding and/or gaining attention. If we want to change these behaviours to ones that will allow the pupil to be an active part of all the communities around her, we have to teach, in a very real and concrete manner, what the pupil should be doing instead of the CB in order to gain the same effect.
- **Behaviour (for some) is just as much a learning process as any other subject**. We need to celebrate the fact that we are teaching behaviour and we need to record our successes. Knowing that Jacinta has gone from twenty pinches an hour to five an hour needs to be shouted across the school and blared from the rooftops with trumpets and drums. Now we need to work with Jacinta on reducing that to two pinches an hour and then two pinches a day. The learning process must continue, but always at a pace that the pupil can manage.

Finally, with regard to CB, the above approaches are not merely the wishful thinking of theoreticians; they do actually work. The Bridge School in Islington, north London, an all-age (two to nineteen) school for 160 children, young people and adults with SLD, PMLD and ASC, has been working on these approaches since the mid-1990s. Ofsted[6] currently rates it as an 'outstanding' school and school staff, all school staff, do actually buy into a philosophy that is entirely positive and rejects the use of sanctions and punishments as a means of controlling behaviour. The Bridge School, like the vast majority of state-funded special schools, does not decide on its intake and has its share of those who exhibit extremes of challenging behaviour. Nonetheless, The Bridge School did not exclude a single pupil between 1996 and the date of this publication, either permanently or temporarily, for any time or any reason (Barratt, 2013). It can be done and it should be done.

Citizenship and sex and relationships education

In covering this particular part of the curriculum we want to explore three particular, distinct, yet related aspects. First, we want to touch upon the difficulties involved in teaching Sex and Relationships Education (SRE) to that very small percentage of the whole school population with severe or profound learning difficulties. Second, we want to reflect on the importance and centrality of SRE within the curriculum as a whole, especially for secondary-age students, and third, we want to ask some questions that all societies should be reflecting upon. There are not necessarily either right or wrong answers to these questions, but that doesn't alter our need to ask them. Much of this section builds on the writings of Dixon (1988); Craft (1994); Downs and Craft (1996); Crissey (2005); Kerr-Edwards and Scott (2005); Tissot (2009) and Imray and Andrews (2012). Certainly we cannot underestimate the centrality of Anne Craft, Caroline Downs and Hilary Dixon to our understanding of this extremely complex and often controversial topic.

We need also to make it absolutely clear that we are tackling this from a liberal, Western societal perspective. As such we have made certain assumptions about what is normal, acceptable and desirable. It may well be that a number of societies outside of the Western liberal tradition, or indeed individuals or groups within liberal, Western societies, do not hold these views. We are therefore apologising if we offend, but make no apology for expressing the views.

The UK background

On 23 October, 2008 the UK's Labour Government published its response to the Report by the SRE Review Steering Group, in which it announced its intention to make SRE statutory. In April 2010 these plans were dropped in order to get various urgent legislation through before the May election of that year, which of course the Labour Government lost. As at March 2013, it is unclear what the Coalition Government's policy on SRE is and what (if anything) it intends to change, other than notice of a general re writing of the National Curriculum. Schools still, however, need to make provision for *sufficient* SRE curriculum time. Given that both the Conservative and Liberal Democrats (the parties that make up the current UK coalition government) opposed the making of SRE compulsory, and although nothing is certain in politics, it can probably safely be assumed that not much will change.

Successive UK governments have generally been advised by a number of bodies with regard to SRE, to the fore being the Sex Education Forum, a charity established in 1987, which has now expanded its focus from schools to include home, care, health, community, youth and secure settings. The Forum believes SRE should be (i) an integral part of lifelong learning, (ii) an entitlement for boys, girls; those who are heterosexual, lesbian, gay or bisexual; those with physical, learning or emotional difficulties; those with a religious or faith tradition and (iii) provided within an holistic context of emotional and social development (Sex Education Forum, 2005). The Forum goes on to suggest that there are three key elements to SRE: (i) acquiring information; (ii) developing skills; and (iii) exploring attitudes and values, and warns that *information about sex alone can never be enough*. This is especially so for those with learning difficulties and forms a major part of the thinking behind this section.

Some philosophical questions to answer

Is it an inclusive entitlement for special needs pupils to be taught the same as their mainstream peers, or at least 'as close to the functioning of their mainstream peers as possible'? (Maddison, 2002, p. 21). What should pupils with SLD be capable of understanding about SRE by the time they leave school? Can an SLD SRE curriculum reflect both? Should an SLD SRE curriculum reflect both?

Shared sexual knowledge

One of the key areas of teaching SRE to those with severe and complex needs, including autism, is that they are very likely to have missed out on a shared sexual knowledge. Although, 'socially' shared sexual knowledge probably plateaus around the age of puberty, it does form a major part of young people's inherent understanding of both sex and sexual relationships. Those with severe or profound learning difficulties, however, will probably not have attained the social maturity of an average young adult, will probably not have developed effective peer relationships and are highly unlikely to have had the same experiences. They may, indeed, be the victims of social asexualisation where their sexuality is not recognised, as if their learning difficulties had eliminated the possibility of sexuality. Parents, other adults and peers may be uncomfortable with the subject of sexuality, which can lead to further isolation in social situations. Such teenagers may well have 'sexual needs' that they attempt to express, but when they do (often in ways or at times that are considered inappropriate) their behaviours may well be 'punished'. The conflict that ensues may then lead to further inappropriate behaviours and so the spiral continues. The 'oversexualisation' observed in some young people with SLD or PMLD may, however, be viewed as a result of a lack of understanding of both social conventions and the notion of consent, and it is these areas particularly that need to be addressed within an SRE school programme.

Case Study 1

David is eighteen. He has SLD and ASC and is functioning at around Level 1/2 of the NC, that is, at the level of a conventionally developing five or six year old. He has been telling you (as his teacher) that he is having constant thoughts about women, and often masturbates in the shower at home, although he always makes sure the door is locked. He has also told his parents, but they have reacted very aversely and have told him he will be punished severely if he continues. Naturally, he is very worried about this.

There are, understandably, occasional cultural and religious differences between schools and parents that those with SLD or PMLD might find quite problematic. Technically, David is doing the right thing in locking the bathroom door, and his natural honesty, so common in those with ASC, is an endearing quality. His parents, however, clearly have a problem with his sexuality and school staff need to assure him that masturbation at his age is perfectly normal. The school might also look to inform parents (in a very low-key and non-judgmental way) of what they have advised David.

Privacy

As noted above, the key areas to be considered when formulating an SRE policy and practice for those with SLD are probably (i) teaching a social understanding of both privacy and consent and (ii) teaching that these two areas are strongly interdependent.

The issue of privacy falls into two main areas: first, where on my body and other people's bodies is private, and second, where can I go to be private and to have privacy. For those with SLD it is always much better to specifically and correctly name the body parts we consider to be private. We may spend time recognising that these parts may be called different things, but clearly labelling, for example, the penis as the penis and always referring to it as such in future, is an important first step. We must also recognise that for those with sensory issues – especially for some on the autistic spectrum – all parts of the body may be considered as entirely private. We have learned a great deal in the last twenty years or so from writers who are themselves autistic such as Temple Grandin, who talks eloquently about the extreme difficulties she has in accepting touch from anyone on any part of her body (Grandin and Scariano, 1986).

The second area of privacy relates to 'where I can go to be private'. It is extremely important for both schools and parents/carers to recognise the need for some with SLD to have time on their own in private, when doors can be at least shut if not locked on the inside, with perhaps a 'Do Not Enter' sign being hung up. There are some who consider toilets to be inappropriate areas for privacy (because of the potential vulnerability in public toilets), but taking these away in schools at least is likely to relegate the young person to nil private space, and it might therefore be better to concentrate on teaching the golden rule, that privacy equals a locked door.

Case Study 2

Sean is 13 years old, he has Down's Syndrome and is operating at Level 1 of the NC, that is at around the level expected of a NT conventionally developing five year old. Lately, Sean has been caught in the toilets watching students from other tutor groups changing their pads, and has been discovered in other classrooms taking pads out of cupboards. He has been found at the urinal in the boys' toilet with another student, both with their pants down touching their own penises. Recently, while in a public swimming pool, Sean disappeared for five minutes only to be discovered in a cubicle with another boy (from his tutor group) who was naked. Staff have also observed Sean in the toilet, with the cubicle door wide open playing with his penis on more than one occasion.

There is of course a considerable danger of overreaction here, and one would hope that the necessary call to Social Services, and indeed their response, would be quietly stated and low key. The situation with Sean highlights the need for continual revision and maintenance of a number of 'understandings', which Sean had previously established. The power of the sexual urge can, however, be exceedingly strong, and obviously in this case much more individual work is needed with Sean to ensure he understands the boundaries that must be observed.

Teaching young people with SLD the difference between public and private places is a matter of clearly naming where these might be in school, at home and in the local community and spending at least half a term or so initially ensuring that students understand and can identify where they are. This is an area of such extreme importance that this work will probably need to be repeated on an annual basis, although you might not need a whole half-term each year.

Consent

Ensuring that others do not touch me in private bodily places without my consent is also relatively straightforward, with lots of opportunities to practise saying 'no' in structured classroom and role-play situations. This is another area that will need to be constantly revisited in some depth at regular (say yearly intervals) to ensure that understanding has been maintained and that students have been able to generalise their understanding to real situations.

The issue of consent, however, makes the matter slightly complicated with regard to those who might need to touch pupils' private body parts (parents, doctors, nurses and occasionally school staff) and extremely complicated with regard to the possibility that those with SLD – just like every other member of society – may want someone to touch them in 'private' places; in other words, may want to enter into sexual relations with another person.

In the field of severe and profound learning difficulties particularly, there is a real danger of effectively desexualising (and perhaps even dehumanising) individuals by teaching young people to say 'NO' very clearly, without addressing the issue of saying 'yes'. This is not just an issue of sexual relations but is very much an issue of sexual relationships, and here we may be getting into much more complicated territory. In any event, we as a society should be asking ourselves some searching questions.

Do those with severe or profound learning difficulties have the right to have sex? According to Life Site News, both Australia's and Denmark's Social Services Departments can link up and pay for sex workers for disabled people as part of their social care package.

www.lifesitenews.com/news/archive/ldn/1950/93/5093003 (accessed on 13 November, 2011). We make no comment on this, other than to note that other agencies need to come to the fore here, particularly in providing access to an effective and functional advocacy system for those who might have no formal means of communication and decision making. There is currently, in the UK, no guarantee that any such access will be supplied at any time of a disabled person's life and we need to consider, as a society, whether that is equitable.

Case Study 3

Julie and Nazim are both sixteen and have been close for some time. They both have severe learning difficulties, but are verbal, know what they like and dislike and are capable of making decisions. They've recently taken to holding hands and kissing each other hello and goodbye when they meet in the playground. They both say they're in love and want to get married. They both say they want to have sex with each other.

Do those with severe learning difficulties have the right to make choices about sexual partners over the age of sixteen? We tend these days to accept sexual experimentation in youth as being a normal part of growing up; we may argue about the increasingly early age that this seems to happen, but the general principle of freedom of expression and association for the young is fairly well established. Does this also apply to those with learning difficulties? For young men (and young women) with severe learning difficulties, for example, same-sex sexual relationships do not seem to offer up the same automatic social barriers as for their neuro-typical peers. That is, young men and women with SLD seem generally much more willing to experiment sexually with their same-sex peers without any concept of being labelled as being either gay or bisexual; they are just being themselves.

When, however, do they have the freedom and privacy to form such relationships? Certainly not at school; certainly not at after-school clubs; probably not at home. It is all very well to teach learners about public and private, but if you are *never* allowed to be in private with someone else the idea of saying 'yes' becomes largely academic. Worse still, we might effectively be teaching a lie; you can say 'yes' but, unlike the rest of society, you cannot enact that 'yes'. Again, this is iniquitous. The greater the degree of learning difficulty the more likely we are (as a society) to withdraw freedoms accorded to everyone else. As long ago as 1994, Hilary Brown questioned whether people with learning disabilities were really free to be sexual beings (Brown, 1994) and it may be that we, as a society, have not made that much progress over the intervening years. Balancing protection of the most vulnerable with our desire for inclusion by granting them equality of opportunity is not easy.

As at the early part of 2013, the legislative position of teaching SRE in the UK is held in the *Sex and Relationship Guidance* issued by the Department for Education and Science in 2000. This states that all schools must provide an up-to-date policy that describes the content and organisation of any SRE provided outside NC science, given that the science curriculum is likely to include biological facts as they relate to humans and other forms of life. This policy is essentially the responsibility of the school governors and they must ensure it is developed and made available to parents/carers for inspection. Clearly, this will involve considerable guidance from headteachers and senior leadership teams. Secondary schools are required to provide an SRE programme, which includes (as a minimum) information about sexually transmitted infections and HIV/AIDS, although special schools may need to make separate arrangements (DfES, 2000). Under the Education Act of 1993, any parent may at any time, exercise their statutory right to withdraw their child from all or part of the sex education programme, except for the teaching of the biological aspects of human growth and reproduction necessary under National Curriculum Science as noted above. In the UK at least, it seems likely that only a very few secondary-aged students with SLD will attend such science classes and, by definition, the complexity of the information imparted would probably make understanding in any detail quite challenging to all but the most cognitively able.

The essential role of adults

A number of years ago, Ann Craft, one of the pioneers of teaching sexual matters to students with SLD, noted that staff carried certain key roles (Craft, 1994) as teachers, counsellors, protectors, interveners, and last but by no means least, empowerers. Let us look at these one at a time, bearing in mind that in the best schools the staff referred to by Craft are not just those who are qualified teachers. For many children, young people and adults with SLD and PMLD the 'teachers' who have the most effect will be the ones who know them best.

Staff as teachers

Staff need to be competent in, and feel comfortable with, setting up and running structured programmes covering SRE. They will of course have the distinct advantage of knowing the group they are going to teach as well as having clear understandings of their individual needs. It may be that your school makes a conscious decision to teach SRE in separate gender groups, and for some things this may be the best approach, although the authors do not see it as an essential. Decisions on this will very much depend on the nature of the group being taught and there can be no hard-and-fast rule. You will certainly need to look at the cognitive ability of the group and the key may very much depend on the likelihood of the student entering into a sexual relationship within the next year or so, but more of that later.

Staff as counsellors

Irrespective of the structured programme on personal relationships, some individuals with learning difficulties will need individual or pair counselling about aspects of their lives and we will need to identify who these might be rather than leave it to chance. As always, early intervention is advised.

Staff as protectors

As a group, young people with learning difficulties are likely to have increased vulnerability to sexual abuse and sexual exploitation, especially by those they know well. The chances of being abused or exploited by a stranger is naturally limited, especially for the less able since they are very unlikely to be left on their own for any length of time, and in any event the prospect of effectively teaching 'stranger danger' to someone with SLD is fraught with difficulties, because the concept of being a stranger is so abstract. If two people have never met before and introduce themselves to each other, perhaps touching each other in the process (by shaking hands for example) are they still strangers? At what point in the relationship do strangers become not strangers? At what point in the relationship is a new friend to be trusted? Clearly, staff have a responsibility towards the personal integrity and safety of individuals with complex needs within their own institution, but there may be a danger, in a risk-averse environment, of stifling potential social relations for fear of them developing into something sexual. Two questions therefore need to be asked: is there a real danger and are we being too protective?

Staff as interveners

Where a particular sexual behaviour brings a person with a learning difficulty into conflict with legal boundaries and/or societal boundaries, it may be necessary for staff to intervene and redirect the student away from a potentially complex situation. This clearly needs to be done with tact, understanding and patience.

Staff as empowerers

Staff are clearly key in the process of enabling students through encouragement, facilitation and the imparting of skills, to exercise power over their own lives and to make their own choices at their own pace.

The key features may therefore be seen to be:

- a recognition of the vital role played by staff;
- that self-realisation, self-expression and self-confidence are at the centre of any formal or informal SRE programme;
- that progress must be at each individual student's pace and must bear in mind their individual cognitive abilities;
- that any educational programme might be formed around the premise of 'guided' decision making.

Case Study 4

Kerwin is twelve years old, has SLD and in UK terms is functioning around P5, that is he will see the world much as a conventionally developing two or three year old might. Kerwin masturbates obsessively throughout the day, and often becomes confused and disorientated when stopped, when he can exhibit quite challenging and occasionally aggressive behaviours. He will sometimes attach himself physically to a person – using them to masturbate with. At home Kerwin sleeps with his mother in her bed and masturbates in the bed at night; he also masturbates in front of his sisters. When asked what strategies they use at home to deal with this behaviour Mum has said, 'I smack him on the hand – very hard.'

Does Kerwin have the right to masturbate and, if so, when and where? Can we teach him what and where is appropriate? He will probably need to gain some control over his environment, timetable and rights to privacy. Further, the role of parents and other family members is clearly critical in the successful ability to generalise skills learned in school and there is no doubt that parents' involvement and contributions over time will directly shape their children's education. As such they need to be involved and be an essential and active part of a tripartite educational experience involving pupil, family and school. It may be that some parents and families will not want this role, but that mustn't stop us from trying to maximise their involvement.

A core curriculum

Up until this point in this book, we have avoided being prescriptive about what might constitute an actual working curriculum document. We have quite deliberately spoken in generalities, because a prescriptive curriculum which follows a clear developmental pathway may suit some of your pupils and students but by no means all. We recognise that while we may have ideas, we don't necessarily have all the answers; the more you know about your individual pupils and students, and your groups of pupils and students, the more answers you will have. The key to many curriculum documents for those with SLD and PMLD will therefore be the ability to offer a fairly flexible array of options.

With regard to an SRE Curriculum, however, your school may need to make certain philosophical decisions that will be related to what is likely. That is, how many students with SLD have formed a sexual relationship with others in the past? How many have formed platonic relations in the past? How many are likely to enter into sexual relations in the immediate future, say one or two years from now, or after leaving school? What we might need is a core curriculum document that is:

- flexible enough to teach according to individual need at any particular time;
- capable of being revisited at regular intervals and thereby strengthening previous learning;
- capable of building on previous learning.

A *Base SRE Curriculum* might be divided into the key sections of:

1   Knowing my body
2   Knowing me
3   Private and public
4   Touching others and allowing others to touch me
5   Forming relationships
6   Sexual intimacy

Let's take these one at a time:

Knowing my body might naturally be subdivided into knowing the body parts; knowing their functions (what the parts of the body do); understanding age differences and gender differences; exploring my clothes, both on top and underneath; and looking at issues of personal hygiene, especially as the body starts to change with puberty. We might also begin the process of tackling menstruation, sexual feelings and masturbation. These latter two points are always fraught because of the abstract and individual nature of sexual feelings and the extreme difficulties of teaching masturbation. It is not an issue that we have the space to explore fully here, but we certainly need to consider the possibility of actively teaching it rather than just letting those with SLD find their own way, because a number will never find their own way and may easily adopt bizarre and/or unsafe practices in the absence of knowledge. Equally certainly, this needs to be an issue for multi-agency discussion and parents/carers must be involved, and it may be the specifically trained sex workers need to be employed for this purpose. This may well be another area where Florian and Hegarty's (2004) observations on inclusion that '*some kind of support or accommodation* to achieve the same functioning' as the person without the learning difficulty, might be needed. It is unfortunately, however, not within the bounds of possibility that individual schools take this on. Central allowing legislation will undoubtedly be needed and we hope that at least one UK member of parliament with a reforming zeal reads this book. At the very least, it is a matter that should and must be openly debated.

Knowing me might be sub-divided into reflecting on what I like and what I don't like; who I like and who I don't like; what I can do and what I can't do; trusting somebody and thinking about who I can trust; me, you and us; types of people in my life, especially friends, family, teachers (in the broadest sense) and people in the community, etc.; developing a positive self-image and high self-esteem.

Private and public will section off into where on my body is private; where on my body is not private; when can I be by myself; where can I go to be private; where do I spend time with other people; my room. This last point touches on a delicate issue that many families might find difficult, not just from a philosophical perspective (what are the risks involved in allowing a person with learning difficulties to be on their own) but purely from a practical position of space in the home. In households where it is just not physically possible for someone with learning difficulties to have a room of their own, parents, carers and families might need to think about operating a bedroom rota system so the person can have at least some pre-arranged and regular, weekly, private time.

Touching and allowing others to touch me, where we can explore public and private places as well as the issues of where on my body I can touch in public; where is it inappropriate to touch myself in public; where on the body can I touch others; gaining permission to touch; resisting pressure and saying 'no'; saying 'yes'; making choices. This whole area of touching and allowing others to touch me forms the cornerstone of the thinking behind an effective SRE policy and practice. That is, we must avoid the dilemma of being so concerned with ensuring the protection of individual learners by teaching them to say 'no', that 'no' becomes all they can ever say. There are probably bound to be times when an individual wants to say 'yes' and we must not deny him or her that right. The answer probably lies in ensuring that permission to touch and be touched is as firmly entrenched within the individual and group consciousness as it can be. Touching really is OK, as long as we have permission to do so. Intimate touching is also OK, as long as we have permission to do so and as long as it's done in private. There will still be problems relating to the age of the people involved, but that is probably the least of our concerns because those under the age of consent are very likely to be heavily supervised for most of the time wherever they are.

Forming relationships will again lead to a number of questions and explorations, particularly around what a relationship means; the difference between liking somebody and loving somebody; the difference between loving a close relation and a boyfriend or girlfriend; dating; having a girlfriend or boyfriend; same-sex relationships; giving and receiving compliments; sharing a special time or event.

Sexual intimacy, the final part of the base curriculum, may not be applicable to all and may only be taught to those who have demonstrated a sexual persona already or are close to demonstrating a sexual persona. It will therefore involve explanations of what might constitute a sexual act with another person; the recognition that tenderness, care and empathy are key components of any sexual act with another; safe sex; the possible consequences of unsafe sex, especially related to pregnancy and possible sexually transmitted diseases. It is perhaps a rather sad contemplation of the freedoms within Western liberal democracies that pornographic images (and especially violent and dominating depictions of the sexual act) are so openly and freely available to today's youth, at a time when they are themselves searching for their own sexual identity. It is to be hoped that such images do not skew the learning and understanding of those with learning difficulties.

Catherine Tissot (2009), writing eloquently of issues that might stop us from teaching SRE effectively to those with autism, notes a number of difficulties that will equally apply to those with SLD and PMLD, namely:

- the nature of the learning difficulty;
- parents' religious and cultural beliefs;
- the difficulties in teaching a concrete concept of privacy;
- the views and personal beliefs of the staff;
- the law, especially in relation to the difficulties of teaching masturbation;
- the challenges that *will* emerge by actually enabling sexual identity;
- the beliefs of society.

Tissot (2009) also suggests that we need to:

- get parents on board;
- adopt a multi-disciplinary, holistic approach;
- develop a curriculum in partnership with all staff;
- audit resources across all key stages;
- appoint a key person to manage curriculum development and delivery.

SRE for those with PMLD

If it is possible to have a more contentious area than SRE for those with SLD, it might be the question of what exactly is SRE for those with PMLD? Clearly the whole nature of consent will be hugely problematic, but that really shouldn't prevent us from discussing the subject and it may be that we have to approach this issue on a person-by-person basis, with the view of a very skilled and entirely objective advocate to the fore. Again, these are issues that are directly related to the inclusive 'rights' of all citizens and it may be that we have to think very creatively about offering choices to each individual in their adult years. It may not be an issue for schools, but education does not stop at eighteen or nineteen, and it is not the intention of this book that reference to learning should be limited by age. We do not know the answer, but that shouldn't stop us searching for lots of possibilities.

SRE resources

- The Bridge School in Islington, north London offers training in SRE to any and all working in the field of profound learning difficulties, severe learning difficulties and/or autistic spectrum disorders. Bespoke tailored courses can also be offered to schools and other organisations at their place of work. Go to www.thebridgelondon.co.uk and follow the training links or email training@thebridge.islington.sch.uk.

- Equals, a charity committed to improving the lives of children and young people with learning difficulties and disabilities through supporting high-quality education, publishes an adapted PSHE and Citizenship curriculum document which includes SRE. This is obtainable at **www.equals.co.uk**.
- www.growingandlearning.co.uk offers guidance, tips and support for parents and carers in:
  - the importance of teaching children and young people with a learning disability about sexuality and sexual health issues;
  - information and support about working with young people with communication difficulties;
  - advice about using communication symbols and visual learning methods;
  - information for parents and carers of young people with an autism spectrum diagnosis.
- Excellent and clear DVD resources for those teaching SRE can be obtained from www.lifesupportproductions.co.uk. The *Jason and Kylie DVDs* are especially recommended.
- www.starsinthesky.co.uk is a dating website for people with special educational needs.
- www.imageinaction.org has a number of SRE drama and games books and resources.
- Two books that are still very relevant and very well written, both giving a number of practical lesson plans and ideas are (i) Ann Craft (ed) (1994) *Practice Issues in Sexuality and Learning Disabilities.* London. Routledge, and (ii) Caroline Downs and Ann Craft (1996) *Sex in Context.* Pavilion.

Citizenship and the world of work

As noted in the introduction to this chapter, our observations on the world of work are probably more in the nature of a polemic, but opinions are for airing, and here are ours. It seems to us extraordinary the vast amount of energy and comment given over to the inclusion of those with SLD and PMLD into the education system, from governments, government agencies, academics and the media, compared to the virtually non-existent commitment displayed by successive UK governments and all the other bodies mentioned to ensuring the inclusion in the right to work for all those who can. There are, in our opinion, very many school leavers with SLD, perhaps not a majority but close to, who are perfectly capable of working for some or all of what might be considered a normal working week. The jobs they do would of necessity need to be low-skilled and repetitive and would probably be jobs currently performed by machines of various kinds. This is not to demean the nature of the work, since over the last 300 or 400 years of the UK's economic history very many of the jobs previously undertaken by people are now undertaken by machines. Opening up the world of work to those with SLD will need conscious effort on the part of central governments to organise such manufacturing enterprises that would replace machines with people. The philosophy of such enterprises should be to make a profit like any other business and to be self-sustaining, like any other business, since charity might be short-lived in economic downturns. The wages need not be high, since all of those employed would be in receipt of considerable state-funded benefits, but the social consequences, in terms of self-esteem, camaraderie, gainful employment of time, citizenship and lifelong learning could be immeasurable. This might be an additional dilemma, 'The Dilemma of Rights', that we need to discuss and it may involve a considerably higher proportion of the working population than just those with SLD!

Notes

1   In these five headings, the italicised phrases are direct quotes from DeFinizio (2011, p. 216), while the explanations of these are our take on what they might mean for the education of those with SLD and PMLD.

2   The obvious exception to this is Self Injurious Behaviour (SIB). Unfortunately, there is not the space in this book to do this subject justice, but those interested in further reading might refer to *Turning the Tables on Challenging Behaviour* (Imray, 2008).

3   As far as the authors are aware there is very little written with regard to autism and severe learning difficulties, apart from Rita Jordan's *Autism With Severe Learning Difficulties* (2001). Fortunately it is an excellent book and those interested in behaviour are strongly advised to read Chapter 8 at least.

4   Even when using positive language, we must be very careful of talking in riddles. Phrases such as 'hands down' or 'gentle hands' might mean something to us but very little to the person we are apparently communicating with. If you're trying to teach an alternative behaviour, be clear and be specific, as in 'hands on lap' or 'clap three times'.

5   You could of course get the pupil's permission to extend the time, by offering a choice board at the end of the allotted time (say ten minutes), which includes a 'carry on working' symbol. If the pupil picks this, she can do another ten minutes before being offered the choice board again.

6   Ofsted is the Office for Standards in Education, a UK centrally funded independent body that judges schools' performance against set criteria. 'Outstanding' is the highest judgment it can make.

References

Abbott C. and Lucey H. (2005) 'Symbol communication in special schools in England: The current position and some key issues', *British Journal of Special Education*, 32(4): 196–201.

Abbott D. and Marriot A. (2012) 'Money, finance and the personalisation agenda for people with learning disabilities in the UK: Some emerging issues', *British Journal of Learning Disabilities*. Early View (Online Version of Record published before inclusion in an issue).

Adams S., Medland P. and Moyles J. (2000) 'Supporting play-based teaching through collaborative practice-based research', *Support for Learning*, 15(4): 159–164.

Ainscow M. (2006) *Responding to the challenge of learner diversity: A briefing paper for the teaching and learning in 2020 review*. Manchester: University of Manchester Faculty of Education.

Ainsworth M., Blehar M., Waters E. and Wall S. (1978) *Patterns of attachment: A psychological study of the strange situation*. New Jersey: Lawrence Erlbaum.

Aird R. (2001) *The Education and Care of Children with Profound and Multiple Learning Difficulties*. London: David Fulton.

Aird R. (2009) 'A commentary on the National Strategies DCSF Special Educational Needs/Learning Difficulties and Disabilities (SEN/LDD) progression Guidance Project 2008–09', *The SLD Experience*, 53: 10–14.

Aitken S., Buultjens M., Clark C., Eyre J. T. and Pease L. (2000) *Teaching children who are deafblind*. London: David Fulton.

Allen D., Lowe K., Jones E., James W., Doyle T., Andrew J., Davies D., Moore K. and Brophy S. (2006) 'Changing the face of challenging behaviour services: The special projects team', *British Journal of Learning Disabilities*, 34(4): 237–242.

Arthur M. (1994) *Communicative instruction in the 1990's: An overview of future directions*, in K. Linfoot (ed) *Communication strategies for people with developmental disabilities: Issues from theory and practice*. Artarmon: MacLennan & Petty. pp. 177–197.

Arthur-Kelly M., Foreman P., Bennett D. and Pascoe S. (2008) 'Interaction, inclusion and students with profound and multiple disabilities: Towards an agenda for research and practice', *Journal of Research in Special Educational Needs*, 8(3): 161–166.

ASCET (1984) *Advice: Teacher training and special educational needs*. London: Advisory Committee on the Supply and Education of Teachers.

Ashcroft E. (2002) 'Communication passports: Towards person-centred planning', *Living Well*, 2(4): 11–13.

Axup T. and Gersch I. (2008) 'The impact of challenging student behaviour upon teachers' lives in a secondary school: Teachers' perceptions', *British Journal of Special Education*, 35(3): 144–151.

Ayers H. (2006) *An A to Z Practical Guide to Learning Difficulties*. London: David Fulton.

Balshaw M. (2004) 'Risking creativity: building the creative context', *Support for Learning*, 19(2): 71–76.

Bannerman-Haig S. (1997) 'Facilitating change', *Dance and the Child International (UK)*, Journal Four: 14–18.

Bannerman-Haig S. (2006) *Stretching, tensing and kicking: Aspects of infantile movement in dance movement therapy with children and adolescents in special education*, in H. Payne (ed) *Dance movement therapy: Theory, research and practice*. London: Routledge.

Barber M. (1994) *Contingency awareness: Putting research into the classroom*, in J. Coupe O'Kane B. and Smith (eds), *Taking control*. London: David Fulton.

Barber M. and Goldbart J. (1998) 'Accounting for learning and failure to learn in people with profound and multiple learning disabilities', in P. Lacey and C. Ouvry (eds) *People with profound and multiple learning disabilities*. London: David Fulton. pp. 102–116.

Barnes C. (2010) *Proposal to introduce and develop AfL using Routes for Learning and video evidence for students working at P Levels 1–3 in KS1 at Willow Dene School*. London: Willow Dene School.

Baron-Cohen S. (1997) *Mindblindness. An essay on autism and theory of mind*. Massachusetts: MIT Press.

Barr O. (2009) *Development of services for children*, in M. Jukes (ed) *Learning Disability Nursing Practice*. London: Quay Books. pp. 399–423.

Barratt P. (2013) *Headteacher's report to governors*. London: The Bridge School.

Barratt P., Border J., Joy H., Parkinson A., Potter M. and Thomas G. (2000) *Developing pupils' social communication skills*. London: David Fulton.

Barron P. (2008) *Classroom gems: Practical ideas, games and activities for the primary classroom*. Harlow: Pearson Education.

Barron P. (2009) *Classroom gems: Outdoor learning: Games, ideas and activities for learning outside the primary classroom*. Harlow: Pearson Education.

Bates E., Camaioni L. and Volterra V. (1975) 'The acquisition of performatives prior to speech', *Merrill-Palmer Quarterly*, 21: 205–216.

Beckerleg T. (2009) *Fun with messy play. Ideas and activities for children with special needs*. London: Jessica Kingsley.

Bennett N. (1999) *Research on teaching-learning processes. Theory into practice: practice into theory. Eighteenth Vernon-Wall Lecture*. British Psychological Society.

Biederman G. B., Davey V. A., Ryder C. and Franchi A. S. (1994) 'The negative effects of positive reinforcement in teaching children with developmental delay', *Exceptional Children*, 60: 458–465.

Blanchard J. (1999) 'Using targets for school improvement in a school for pupils with severe, profound, multiple or complex learning difficulties', *The SLD Experience*, 24: 18–19.

Bloom B. S., Engelhart M. D., Furst E. J., Hill W. H. and Krathwohl D. R. (1956) *Taxonomy of educational objectives: the classification of educational goals: Handbook 1: Cognitive domain*. New York: Longmans.

Bluestone J. (2002) *The Churkendoose anthology*. Seattle: Handle Institute.

Bogdashina O. (2003) *Sensory perceptual issues in autism and Asperger syndrome*. London: Jessica Kingsley.

Bond L., Van Wyck I. and Gasquez Navarro D. (2011) *PMLD planning, recording and assessment*. London: The Bridge School.

Bondy A. and Frost L. (2001) 'The Picture Exchange Communication System', *Behavior Modifcation*, 25: 725–744.

Booth T., Ainscow M. and Kingston D. (2006) *Index for inclusion: Developing play, learning and participation in early years and childcare*. Bristol. Centre for Studies on Inclusive Education (CSIE).

Bottos M., Feliciangeli A., Scutio L., Gericke C. and Vianello A. (2001) 'Functional status of adults with cerebral palsy and implications for treatment of children', *Developmental Medicine and Child Neurology*, 43: 516–528.

Bovair K., Carpenter B. and Upton G. (eds) (1992) *Special curricula needs*. London: David Fulton and NASEN.

Bower E., Mitchell D., Burnett M., Campbell M. J. and McLellan D. L. (2001) 'Randomised controlled trial of physiotherapy in 56 children with cerebral palsy followed for 18 months', *Developmental Medicine and Child Neurology*, 43: 4–15.

Bowlby J. (1988) *A secure base: Clinical applications of attachment theory*. London: Routledge.

Brennan K. A., Wu S. and Love J. (1998) 'Adult romantic attachment and individual differences in attitudes toward physical contact in the context of adult romantic relationships', in Rholes W. S. and Simpson J. A. (eds) *Attachment theory and close relationships*. New York: Guilford Press.

Browder D. M., Trela K., Gibbs S. L., Wakeman S. and Harris A. A. (2009) 'Academic skills', in Odom S. L., Horner R. H., Snell M. E. and Blacher J. (eds) *Handbook of developmental disabilities*. New York: Guildford Press.

Brown E. (1996) *Religious education for all*. London: David Fulton.

Brown H. (1994) 'An ordinary sexual life?: A review of the normalisation principle as it applies to the sexual options of people with learning disabilities', *Disability & Society*, 9(2): 123–144.

Brown N., McLinden M. and Porter J. (1998) 'Sensory Needs', in P. Lacey and C. Ouvrey (eds) *People with profound and multiple learning disabilities*. London: David Fulton.

Bullowa M. (1979) 'Introduction: Prelinguistic communication: a field for scientific research', in M. Bullowa (ed) *Before speech*. Cambridge: Cambridge University Press.

Bunning K. (1996) 'Development of an "individualised sensory environment" for adults with learning disabilities and an evaluation of its effects on their interactive behaviours'. Unpublished thesis. London: City University.

Bunning K. (1998) 'To engage or not to engage? Affecting the interactions of learning disabled adults', *International Language and Communication Disorders*, 33: 386–391.

Bunning K. (2009) 'Making sense of communication', in J. Palwyn and S. Carrnaby (eds) *Profound intellectual multiple disabilities: Nursing complex needs*. Oxford: Wiley-Blackwell.

Burden R. (1990) '"Process" in cross-curricular work', in Smith B. (ed) *Interactive approaches to teaching the core subjects*. Bristol: Lame Duck Publishing.

Byers R. (1994) 'Teaching as dialogue: Teaching approaches and learning styles in schools for pupils with learning difficulties', in J. Coupe-O'Kane and B. Smyth (eds) *Taking control*. London: David Fulton.

Byers R. and Rose R. (1994) 'Schools should decide . . .', in R. Rose, A. Fergusson, C. Coles, R. Byers and D. Banes (eds) *Implementing the whole curriculum for pupils with learning difficulties*. London: David Fulton.

Cahill M. (1992) 'The arts and special educational needs', *Arts Education*, December Issue: 12–15.

Caldwell P. (2005) *Finding you finding me. Using Intensive Interaction to get in touch with people whose severe learning disabilities are combined with autistic spectrum disorder*. London: Jessica Kingsley.

Caldwell P. (2007) *From isolation to intimacy: Making friends without words*. London: Jessica Kingsley.

Camaioni L. (1993) 'The development of intentional communication: A re-analysis', in J. Nadel and L. Camaioni, *New perspective in early communicative development*. London: Routledge.

Campbell F. K. (2001) 'Inciting legal fictions: Disability's date with ontology and the ableist body of the law', *Griffith Law Review*, 10: 42–62.

Carman S. N. and Chapparo C. J. (2012) 'Children who experience difficulties with learning: Mother and child perceptions of social competence', *Australian Occupational Therapy Journal*, 59(5): 339–346.

Carpenter B. (2010) *Curriculum reconciliation and children with complex learning difficulties and disabilities*. London: Specialist Schools and Academies Trust.

Carpenter B. (2011) 'Pedagogically bereft! Improving learning outcomes for children with foetal alcohol spectrum disorders', *British Journal of Special Education*, 38(1): 37–43.

Carpenter B., Cockbill B., Egerton J. and English J. (2010) 'Children with complex learning difficulties and disabilities: Developing meaningful pathways to personalised learning', *The SLD Experience*, 58: 3–10.

Carpenter B., Egerton J., Brooks T., Cockbill B., Fotheringham J. and Rawson H. (2011) *Complex learning difficulties and disabilities research project final report*. Wolverhampton: Specialist Schools and Academies Trust.

Carpenter B. and Hills P. (2002) 'Rescuing the arts: The sunmoves project', *The SLD Experience*, 32: 22–24.

Carr D. and Felce J. (2007) 'The effects of PECS teaching to phase III on the communicative interactions between children with autism and their teachers', *Journal of Autism and Developmental Disorders*, 37: 724–737.

Carr E. G. and Durand V. M. (1985) 'Reducing behavior problems through functional communication and training', *Journal of Applied Behavior Analysis*, 18(2): 111–126.

Carter A. (ed) (1991) *The Virago book of fairy tales*. London: Virago Press.

CCEA (2006) *Quest for learning: Guidance and assessment materials: Profound and multiple learning difficulties*. Belfast: The Council for Curriculum, Examinations and Assessment (Northern Ireland).

Chad K. E., Bailey D., MacKay H., Zello G. and Snyder R. (1999) 'The effect of weight bearing physical activity on bone mineral content and estimated volumetric density in children with spastic cerebral palsy', *Journal of Paediatrics*, 135: 115–117.

Chadwick O., Walker N., Bernard S. and Taylor E. (2000) 'Factors affecting the risk of behaviour problems in children with severe intellectual disability', *Journal of Intellectual Disability Research*, 44(2): 108–123.

Chadwick O., Kusel Y. and Cuddy M. (2008) 'Factors associated with the risk of behaviour problems in adolescents with severe intellectual disabilities', *Journal of Intellectual Disability Research*, 52(10): 864–876.

Chaloner W. B. (2001) 'Counselors coaching teachers to use play therapy in classrooms: the Play and Language to Succeed (PALS) early, school-based intervention for behaviorally at-risk children', in A. A. Drewes, L. J. Carey and C. E. Schaefer (eds) *School-based play therapy*. New York: John Wiley & Sons.

Cole T. (1989) *Apart or a Part? Integration and the growth of British special education*. Milton Keynes: Open University Press.

Colley A. (2013) *Personalised learning for young people with profound and multiple learning difficulties*. London: Jessica Kingsley.

Collis M. and Lacey P. (1996) *Interactive approaches to teaching*. London: David Fulton.

Corke M. (2002) *Approaches to communication through music*. London: David Fulton.

Corke M. (2011) *Using playful practice to communicate with special children*. London: David Fulton/Nasen.

Cornwall J. and Walter C. (2006) *Therapeutic education. Working alongside troubled and troublesome children*. London: Routledge.

Coupe O'Kane J. and Goldbart J. (1998) *Communication before speech*. London: David Fulton.

Cox M. (1991) *The child's point of view*. London: The Guilford Press.

Craft A. (ed) (1994) *Practice issues in sexuality and learning disabilities*. London: Routledge.

Crissey P. (2005) *Personal hygiene? What's it got to do with me?* London: Jessica Kingsley.

Crosby K. (2002) 'Communication through music for pupils with profound and multiple learning difficulties', *The SLD Experience*, 32: 19–21.

Cutler I. (2000) 'Down the numeracy strategy road', *The SLD Experience*, 26: 7–8.

Davis P. and Florian L. (2004) *Teaching Strategies and Approaches for Pupils with Special Educational Needs: a scoping study*. Research Report 516. London: DfES.

DCSF (2009) *Personalised learning – A practical guide*. Nottingham: Department for Children, Schools and Families Publications.

De Bildt A., Sytema S., Kraijer D., Sparrow S. and Minderaa R. (2005) 'Adaptive functioning and behaviour problems in relation to level of education in children and adolescents with intellectual disability', *Journal of Intellectual Disability Research*, *49*(9): 672–681.

Dee L., Lawson H., Porter J. and Robertson C. (2008) 'Personalising the curriculum for 14–25s with learning difficulties', *The SLD Experience*, 51: 25–32.

DeFinizio A. (2011) 'Personalising learning in a 21st-century context' (pp. 214–219) in J. Sebba, A. Peacock, A. DiFinizio and M. Johnson 'Personalisation and special educational needs', *Journal of Research in Special Educational Needs*, *11*(3): 203–224.

Delmain C. and Spring J. (2003) *Speaking, listening and understanding: Games for young children*. Bicester: Speechmark.

Department of Health (2004) *The chief nursing officer's review of the nursing, midwifery and health visiting contribution to vulnerable children and young people*. London: Department of Health.

Derrington C (2009) *Behaviour in primary schools: Final report*. London: Channel 4.

DES (1978) *Special educational needs: Report of the committee of enquiry into the education of handicapped children and young people*. London: HMSO.

DES (1982) *Mathematics counts (The Cockfroft Report)*. London: HMSO.

De Schipper J. C., Stolk J. and Schuengel C. (2006) 'Professional caretakers as attachment figures in day care centers for children with intellectual disability and behavior problems', *Research in Developmental Disabilities*, 27: 203–216.

De Schipper J. C. and Schuengel C. (2010) 'Attachment behaviour towards support staff in young people with intellectual disabilities: Associations with challenging behaviour', *Journal of Intellectual Disability Research*, 54: 584–596.

Dewart E. and Summers H. (1995) *The pragmatics profile of everyday communication skills in children*. Windsor: NFER–Nelson.

DfE (2009) *Progression guidance 2009/10. Improving data to raise attainment and maximise the progress of learners with special educational needs, learning difficulties and disabilities*. Nottingham: Department for Education Publications.

DfE (2010) *Progression 2010–11: Advice on improving data to raise attainment and maximise the progress of learners with special educational needs*. Nottingham: Department for Education Publications.

DfE (2012) *Statutory framework for Early Years Foundation Stage: Setting the standards for learning, development and care for children from birth to five*. Runcorn: Department for Education Publications.

DfEE (1998) *The National Literacy Strategy: Framework for teaching*. London: Department for Education and Employment Publications.

DfEE (1999) *The National Numeracy Strategy: Framework for teaching mathematics*. Sudbury: Department for Education and Employment Publications.

DfEE (2000). *Sex and relationship education guidance*. Department for Education Publications. 0016/2000.

DfES (2003) *Data collection by type of special educational needs*. London: Department for Education Publications.

Dickens C. (1854*) Hard times*. London: Chapman Hall.

Dixon H. (1988) *Sexuality and mental handicap*. London: LDA.

Donaghy M. (1993) *Errata*. Oxford University Press.

Donaldson M. (1978) *Children's minds*. London: Fontana.

Donaldson M. (1989) *Sense and sensibility*. University of Reading: Reading and Language Information Centre.

Donaldson M. and Reid J. (1982) 'Language skills and reading: A developmental perspective', in A. Hendry (ed) *Teaching reading: The key issues*. United Kingdom Reading Association: Heinemann.

Downing J. and Siegel-Causey E. (1988) 'Enhancing the non-symbolic communication behaviour of children with multiple impairments', *Language, Speech and Hearing Services in Schools*, 19: 33–48.

Downs C. and Craft A. (1996) *Sex in context.* Pavilion.

Dunst C. (1980) *A clinical and educational manual for use with the Uzgiris and Hunt Scales of infant psychological development.* Austin, Texas: Pro-Ed.

Durkin K. and Conti-Ramsden G. (2007) 'Language, social behavior, and the quality of friendships in adolescents with and without a history of specific language impairment', *Child Development*, 78(5): 1441–1457.

Dyson A. (2001) 'Special needs in the twenty-first century: Where we've been and where we're going', *British Journal of Special Education*, 28(1): 24–29.

Ecclestone K. and Hayes D. (2009) *The dangerous rise of therapeutic education.* London: Routledge.

Emerson E. (1995) *Challenging behaviour: Analysis and intervention in people with learning disabilities.* Cambridge: Cambridge University Press.

Emerson E., Hatton C., Robertson J., Roberts H., Baines S. and Glover G. (2010) *People with learning disabilities in England 2010.* London: Department of Health.

Ephraim G. W. E. (1979) 'Developmental processes in mental handicap: A generative structure approach', Unpublished PhD thesis. Uxbridge: Brunel University Department of Psychology.

Evans P. (1997) 'Structuring the curriculum for pupils with learning difficulties', in S. J. Pijl, C. J. W. Meijer and S. Hegarty (eds), *Inclusive education: A global agenda.* London: Routledge.

Evans P. and Ware J. (1987) *Special care provision: The education of children with profound and multiple learning difficulties.* Windsor: NFER-Nelson.

Farrell M. (2005) *Inclusion at the crossroads: Special education concepts and values,* London: David Fulton.

Farrell M. (2006) *Celebrating the special school.* London: David Fulton.

Felce D. (1997) 'Defining and applying the concept of quality of life', *Journal of Intellectual Disability Research*, 41(2): 126–135.

Filer J. (2006) 'SDM and its role in family therapy', in C. Hill (ed) *Communicating through movement.* Clent: Sunfield Publications.

Florian L. (1998) 'Inclusive practice: What, why and how?' in C. Tilstone, L. Florian and R. Rose (eds) *Promoting inclusive practice.* London: Routledge.

Florian L. (2008) 'Special or inclusive education: Future trends', *British Journal of Special Education*, 35(4): 202–208.

Florian L. and Hegarty J. (2004) *ICT and special educational needs: A tool for inclusion.* Buckingham: Open University Press.

Foreman P., Arthur-Kelly M., Pasco S. and Smyth King B. (2004) 'Evaluating the educational experiences of students with profound and multiple disabilities in inclusive and segregated classroom settings: An Australian perspective', *Research and Practice for Persons with Severe Disabilities*, 29(3): 183–193.

Frost L. and Bondy A. (1994) *The picture exchange communication system training manual.* Newark: Pyramid Education.

Fujiura G. T. (2003) 'Continuum of intellectual disability: Demographic evidence for "forgotten generation"', *Mental Retardation*, 41: 420–429.

Gascoyne S. (2012) *Treasure baskets and beyond: Realizing the potential of sensory-rich play.* Maidenhead: Open University Press.

Gelman R. and Gallistel C. R. (1978) *The child's understanding of number.* Cambridge, MA: Harvard University Press.

George S. (1985) 'Art from six to sixteen', *British Journal of Special Education*, 12(4): 163–165.

Gibson L. (1989) *Literacy learning in the early years: Through children's eyes.* London: Cassell.

Gillespie and Roberts M. (1987) 'Developmental core curriculum: Motor-sensory level'. Unpublished Paper: Rectory Paddock School.

Goddard A. (1997) 'The role of individual educational plans/programmes in special education: A critique', *Support for Learning*, *12*(4): 170–174.

Goldbart J. (1994) 'Opening the communication curriculum to students with PMLDs', in J. Ware (ed) *Educating children with profound and multiple learning difficulties*. London: David Fulton.

Goldbart J. and Caton S. (2010) *Communication and people with the most complex needs: What works and why this is essential*. London: Mencap.

Goldschmeid E. and Jackson S. (1994) *People under three: Young children in day care*. London: Routledge.

Goldsmith J. and Goldsmith L. (1998) 'Physical Management', in P. Lacey and C. Ouvry (eds) *People with profound and multiple learning disabilities*. London: David Fulton.

Gough P. B. and Tunmer W. (1986) 'Decoding, reading and reading disability', *Remedial and Special Education*, 7: 6–10.

Gough P. B., Hoover W. A. and Peterson C. L. (1996) 'Some observations on a simple view of reading', in C. Cornoldi and J. Oakhill (eds) *Reading comprehension difficulties: Processes and intervention*. Mahwah, NJ: Lawrence Erlbaum Associates.

Grandin T. (2006) *Thinking in pictures*. New York: Vintage Press.

Grandin T. and Scariano M. (1986) *Emergence labelled autistic*. New York: Warner.

Greenspan S. I. and Weider S. (2003) *Engaging autism: The Floortime approach to helping children relate, communicate and think*. Reading, MA: Perseus Books.

Grosse G., Behne T., Carpenter M. and Tomasello M. (2010) 'Infants communicate in order to be understood', *Developmental Psychology*, *46*(6): 1710–1722.

Grossman H. J. (ed) (1973) *Manual on terminology in mental retardation*. Washington, DC: AAMR.

Grove N. (2005) *Ways into literature: Stories, plays and poems*. London: David Fulton.

Grove N. (2010) *The big book of storysharing*. London: Senjit.

Grove N. (ed) (2012) *Using storytelling to support children and adults with special needs*. London: Routledge.

Grove N., Bunning K., Porter J. and Olsson C. (1999) 'See what I mean: Interpreting the meaning of communication by people with severe and profound intellectual disabilities', *Journal of Applied Research in Intellectual Disabilities*, *12*(3): 190–203.

Grove N. and Park K. (1996) *Odyssey now*. London: Jessica Kingsley.

Grove N. and Park K. (1999) *Romeo and Juliet: A multi-sensory approach*. London: Bag Books.

Grove N. and Park K. (2001) *Developing social cognition through literature for people with learning disabilities: Macbeth in mind*. London: Jessica Kingsley.

Guess D., Seigal-Causey E., Roberts S., Rues J., Thompson B. and Seigal-Causey D. (1990) 'Assessment and analysis of behavior state and related variables among students with profoundly handicapping conditions', *Journal of the Association for Persons with Severe Handicaps*, 15: 211–230.

Guppy P. and Hughes M. (1999) *The development of independent reading*. Buckingham: Open University Press.

Hanko G. (2003) 'Towards an inclusive school culture – but what happened to Elton's affective curriculum?', *British Journal of Special Education*, *30*(3): 125–131.

Harris J. (1995) 'Responding to pupils with SLD who present challenging behaviour', *British Journal of Special Education*, *22*(3): 109–115.

Harris J. (2006) 'Time to make up your mind: why choosing is difficult', *British Journal of Learning Disabilities*, *31*(1): 3–8.

Harris J., Cook M. and Upton G. (1996) *Pupils with severe learning disabilities who present challenging behaviour*. Kidderminster: BILD.

Harris J., Hewett D. and Hogg J. (2001) *Positive approaches to challenging behaviour.* Kidderminster: BILD.

Hastings R., Sonuga-Burke E. J. S. and Remington B. (1993) 'Connotations of labels for mental handicap and challenging behaviour: A review and research evaluation', *Mental Handicap Research*, 6(3): 237–249.

Hen M. and Walter O. P. (2012) 'The Sherborne Developmental Movement (SDM) teaching model for pre-service teachers', *Support for Learning*, 27(1): 11–19.

Hewett D. (ed) (1998a) *Challenging behaviour: Principles and practices.* London: David Fulton.

Hewett D. (1998b) 'Challenging behaviour is normal', in P. Lacey and C. Ouvry (eds) *People with profound and multiple learning difficulties.* London: David Fulton.

Hewett D. (2006) *The most important and complicated learning: That's what play is for!* ICAN. *Talking Point*, March (www.talkingpoint.org.uk, accessed 6 February 2009).

Hewett D. (2007) 'Do touch: Physical contact and people who have severe, profound and multiple learning difficulties', *Support for Learning*, 22(3): 116–123.

Hewett D. (ed) (2011) *Intensive interaction: Theoretical perspectives.* London: Sage.

Hewett D. and Nind M. (eds) (1998) *Interaction in action: Reflections on the use of intensive interaction.* London: David Fulton.

Higginson W. (1999) 'Glimpses of the past, images of the future: Moving from 20th to 21st century mathematics education', in C. Hoyles, C. Morgan and G. Woodhouse (eds) *Rethinking the mathematics curriculum.* London: Falmer Press.

Hill C. (2006) *Communicating through movement.* Clent: Sunfield Publications.

Hinchcliffe V. (1991) 'Two stages in the process of learning to read: Implications for children with severe learning difficulties', in B. Smith (ed) *Teaching the core subjects through interactive approaches.* Bristol: Lame Duck Publishing.

Hinchcliffe V. (1994) 'A special special need: Self-advocacy, curriculum and the needs of children with severe learning difficulties', in S. Sandow (ed) *Whose special need?* London: Paul Chapman.

Hinchcliffe V. (1995) 'The social-cognitive development of children with severe learning difficulties'. Unpublished PhD thesis: Brunel University.

Hinchcliffe V. (1996a) 'English', in B. Carpenter, K. Bovair and R. Ashdown (eds), *Enabling access: Effective teaching and learning for pupils with learning difficulties.* London: David Fulton.

Hinchcliffe V. (1996b) 'Fairy stories and children's developing theories of mind', *International Journal of Early Years Education*, 4(1) 35–46.

Hinchcliffe V. (1997) 'A Bermuda Triangle for training: The case of severe learning difficulties', in J. Davies and P. Garner (eds) *At the crossroads: SEN and teacher education.* London: David Fulton.

Hinchcliffe V. (1999) 'It all comes out in the wash: Using TV 'soaps' with pupils with learning disabilities', in S. Fawkes, S. Hurrell and N. Peacey (eds) *Using television and video to support learning.* London: David Fulton.

Hinchcliffe V. (2001) 'Tailoring literacy to pupils with special needs: Bespoke or 'off the peg' strategies?', *The SLD Experience*, 31: 6–9.

Hinchcliffe V. (2012) 'Personalisation and learning: Spending time on the things that matter', Unpublished presentation to Bromley Special and Mainstream Headteachers, Bromley: Riverside School.

Hinchcliffe V. and Roberts M. (1987) 'Developing social cognition and metacognition', in B. Smith (ed) *Interactive approaches to the education of children with severe learning difficulties.* Birmingham: Westhill College.

Ho A. (2004) 'To be labelled or not to be labelled: That is the question', *British Journal of Learning Disabilities*, 32: 86–92.

Hobbs N. (1975) *The futures of children: Categories, labels, and their consequences (report of the project on classification of exceptional children).* San Francisco, CA: Jossey-Bass.

Hodkinson A., (2012) 'Illusionary inclusino – what went wrong with New Labour's landmark educational policy', *British Journal of Specail Education*, 39(1): 4–11.

Hogg J. (1991) 'Developments in further education for adults with profound intellectual and multiple disabilities', in J. Watson (ed) *Innovatory practice and severe learning difficulties.* Edinburgh: Moray House Publications.

Hogg J., Reeves D., Roberts J. and Mudford O. C. (2001) 'Consistency, context and confidence in judgements of affective communication in adults with profound intellectual and multiple disabilities', *Journal of Intellectual Disability Research*, 45(1): 18–29.

Hoover W. A. and Gough P. B. (1990) 'The simple view of reading', *Reading and Writing*, 2: 127–160.

Hulme C. and Mackenzie S. (1992) *Working memory and severe learning difficulties.* Hove: Lawrence Erlbaum Associates.

Hussein H. (2010) 'Using the sensory garden as a tool to enhance the educational development and social interaction of children with special needs', *Support for Learning*, 25(1): 25–31.

Imray P. (1996) 'Heuristic play: Report on secondary PMLD group'. Unpublished paper, London: Rosemary School.

Imray P. (1997) 'Heuristic play: Report on secondary SLD group', unpublished paper, London: Rosemary School.

Imray P. (2005) 'Moving towards simple, understandable and workable definitions of SLD and PMLD', *The SLD Experience*, 42: 33–37.

Imray P. (2008) *Turning the tables on challenging behaviour.* London: Routledge.

Imray P. (2012) 'Saying NO to 'no'!', *The SLD Experience*, 64: 17–20.

Imray P. and Andrews T. (2012) 'Sex and relationships education (SRE) and learning difficulties', *Insight 37. Curriculum Bitesize*: 8–12.

Imray P., Gasquez Navarro D. and Bond L. (2010) 'A PMLD curriculum for the 21st century', *The SLD Experience*, 58: 11–17.

Imray P. and Hinchcliffe V. (2012) 'Not fit for purpose: A call for separate and distinct pedagogies as part of a national framework for those with severe and profound learning difficulties', *Support for Learning*, 27(4): 150–157.

Janssen C. G. C., Schuengel C. and Stolk J. (2002) 'Understanding challenging behaviour in people with severe and profound intellectual disability: A stress-attachment model', *Journal of Intellectual Disability Research*, 46(6): 445–453.

Jarrold C., Nadel L. and Vicari S. (2008) 'Down Syndrome research and practice', cited in P. Lacey (2009) 'Teaching thinking in SLD schools', *The SLD Experience*, 54: 19–24.

Jennings S. (2012) 'Healing stories with children at risk: The StoryBuilding approach', in N. Grove (ed) *Using storytelling to support children and adults with special needs.* London: Routledge.

Johnson M. and Parkinson G. (2002). *Epilepsy: A practical guide.* London: David Fulton.

Jones F., Pring T. and Grove N. (2002) 'Developing communication in adults with profound and multiple learning difficulties using objects of reference', *International Journal of Language and Communication Disorders*, 37(2): 173–184.

Jordan R. (2001) *Autism with severe learning difficulties.* London: Souvenir Press.

Jordan R. (2005) 'Autistic spectrum disorders', in A. Lewis and B. Norwich (eds) *Special teaching for special teaching? Pedagogies for inclusion.* Maidenhead: Open University Press.

Kahn J. V. (1976) 'Utility of the Uzgiris and Hunt Scales with severely and profoundly retarded children', *American Journal of Mental Deficiency*, 80: 663–665.

Karkou V. and Glasman J. (2004) 'Arts, education and society: the role of the arts in promoting the emotional wellbeing and social inclusion of young people', *Support for Learning*, 19(2): 57–65.

Kaufman B. N. (1994) *Son rise: The miracle continues.* Tiburon, CA: H. J. Kramer.

Kaufman R. K. (2003) 'Building the bridges: Strategies for reaching our children', in G. Jones (ed) *Autism early intervention: A supplement for good autism practice journal.* Kidderminster: BILD.

Kellet M. (2000) 'Sam's story: Evaluating Intensive Interaction in terms of its effect on the social and communicative ability of a young child with severe learning difficulties', *Support for Learning*, 15(4): 65–71.

Kellett M. and Nind M. (2003) *Implementing Intensive Interaction in schools: Guidance for practitioners, managers and coordinators*. London: David Fulton.

Kerr-Edwards L. and Scott L. (2005) *Talking together: Books one and two*. London: FPA.

Kiernan C. and Kiernan D. (1994) 'Challenging behaviour in schools for pupils with severe learning difficulties', *Mental Handicap Research*, 7(1): 17–20.

Knill C. (1992) *Touch and communication*. Cambridge: LDA.

Kossyvaki L., Jones G. and Guldberg K. (2012) 'The effect of adult interactive style on the spontaneous communication of young children with autism at school', *British Journal of Special Education*, 39(4): 173–184.

Laban R. (1948) *Modern educational dance*. Plymouth: MacDonald and Evans.

Lacey P. (1996) 'Music', in B. Carpenter, R. Ashdown and K. Bovair (eds) *Enabling access: Effective teaching and learning for pupils with learning difficulties*. London: David Fulton.

Lacey P. (2006) 'What is inclusive literacy?' *The SLD Experience*, 46: 3–7.

Lacey P. (2009) 'Teaching thinking in SLD schools', *The SLD Experience*, 54: 19–24.

Lacey P. (2010) 'Smart and scruffy targets', *The SLD Experience*, 57: 16–21.

Lacey P. (2011) 'Developing a curriculum for pupils with PMLD', *The SLD Experience* 61: 4–7.

Lacey P., Layton L., Miller C., Goldbart J. and Lawson H. (2007) 'What is literacy for students with severe learning difficulties? Exploring conventional and inclusive literacy', *Journal of Research in Special Educational Needs*, 7(3): 149–160.

Laevers F. (ed) (1994) *Defining and assessing quality in early childhood education. Studia Paedagogica*. Leuven: Leuven University Press.

Lamond I. (2010) 'Evaluating the impact of incorporating dance into the curriculum of children encountering profound and multiple learning difficulties', *Body, Movement and Dance in Psychotherapy*, 5(2): 141–149.

Lancaster K. (2006) 'Shakespeare – "In other words"', *The SLD Experience*, 44: 3–4.

Lancioni G., O'Reilly M., Singh N., Oliva D., Baccani S., Severini L. and Groeneweg, J. (2006) 'Micro-switch programmes for students with multiple disabilities and minimal motor behaviour: Assessing response acquisition and choice', *Developmental Neurorehabilitation*, 9(2): 137–143.

Lancioni G., O'Reilly M., Singh N., Sigafoos J., Didden R. and Doretta O. (2009) 'Persons with multiple disabilities accessing stimulation and requesting social contact via microswitch and VOCA devices: New research evaluation and social validation', *Research in Developmental Disabilities*, 30(5): 1084–1094.

Latham C. (2005) *Developing and using a communication book*. Oxford: ACE Centre Advisory Trust.

Leach, B. J. (2000) *10-Minute Games*. Witney, Oxfordshire: Scholastic.

Leadbeater C. (2005) *The shape of things to come: Personalised learning through collaboration*. London: The Innovation Unit.

Leaning B. and Watson T. (2006) 'From the inside looking out – An Intensive Interaction group for people with profound and multiple learning difficulties', *British Journal of Learning Disabilities*, 34(2): 103–109.

Lecanuet J.-P. (1996) 'Prenatal auditory experience', in I. Deliege and J. A. Sloboda, *Musical beginnings*. Oxford: Oxford University Press. pp. 3–34.

Leinhardt G. and Pallay A. (1982) 'Restrictive educational settings: Exile or haven?', *Review of Educational Research*, 52: 557–578.

Lewis A. and Norwich B. (2000) 'Is there a distinctive special educational needs pedagogy?', in *Specialist teaching for special educational needs*. Tamworth: NASEN.

Lewis J. (2000) 'Let's remember the 'education' in inclusive education', *British Journal of Special Education*, 27(4): 202.

Lewis V., Boucher J., Lupton L. and Watson S. (2000) 'Relationships between symbolic play, functional play, verbal and non-verbal ability in young children', *International Journal of Language and Communication Disorders*, 35(1): 117–127.

Lima M., Silva K., Amaral I., Magalhaes A. and De Sousa L. (2011) 'Beyond behavioural observations: A deeper view through the sensory reactions of children with profound intellectual and multiple disabilities', *Child: Care, Health and Development*. doi: 10.1111/j.1365–2214.2011.01334.x

Lima M., Silva K., Magalhaes A., Amaral I., Pestana H. and De Sousa L. (2012) 'Can you know me better? An exploratory study combining behavioural and physiological measurements for an objective assessment of sensory responsiveness in a child with profound intellectual and multiple disabilities', *Journal of Applied Research in Intellectual Disabilities*, 25(6): 522–530.

Lindsay G. (2007) 'Educational psychology and the effectiveness of inclusive education/mainstreaming', *British Journal of Educational Psychology*, 77(1): 1–24.

Lloyd Bennet P. (2006) 'Helpful and unhelpful practices in meeting the needs of pupils with emotional and behavioural difficulties: A pilot survey of staff views in one local authority', *British Journal of Special Education*, 33(4): 188–195.

Lloyd P. (2008) *Let's all listen. Songs for group work in settings that include students with learning difficulties and autism*. London: Jessica Kingsley.

Lock A. (1999) 'Why not to teach the literacy hour', *The SLD Experience*, 24: 2–4.

Locke J., Ishijima E. H., Kasari C. and London N. (2010) 'Loneliness, friendship quality and the social networks of adolescents with high-functioning autism in an inclusive school setting', *Journal of Research in Special Educational Needs*, 10(2): 74–81.

Longhorn F. (1988) *A sensory curriculum for very special people*. London: Souvenir.

Longhorn F. (1993) *Planning a multi-sensory massage programme for very special people*. London: Catalyst.

Longhorn F. (2000) *Numeracy for very special people*. Bedfordshire: Catalyst Education.

Low, S. (2004) 'Effects of Mobility Opportunities Via Education (MOVE) Curriculum on range of motion, motor skills, and functional mobility of children with severe multiple disabilities: A pilot programme', *Developmental Medicine and Child Neurology AACPDM*, abstract Vol. 46.

Lu L. and Shih J. B. (1997) 'Personality and happiness: Is mental health a mediator?', *Personality and Individual Differences*, 22(2): 249–256.

Ludwig A. and Swan A. (2007) *101 great classroom games*. New York: Mcgraw-Hill.

Lyons G. and Cassebohm M. (2010) 'Life satisfaction for children with profound intellectual and multiple disabilities', in R. Kober (ed) *Enhancing the quality of life of people with intellectual disabilities*. Social Indicators Research Series 41, DOI 10.1007/978-90-481-9650-0-12: 183–204.

Lyons, G. and Cassebohm, M. (2011) 'Curriculum development for students with profound intellectual and multiple disabilities: How about a quality of life focus?', *Special Education Perspectives*, 12(2): 24–39.

Lyons G. and Cassebohm M. (2012) 'The education of Australian school students with the most severe intellectual disabilities: Where have we been and where could we go? A discussion primer', *Australasian Journal of Special Education*, 36(1): 79–95.

Lyons G., Cassebohm M. and Mundy-Taylor J. (2011) '"Stretching": A simple strategy for improving the quality of life of children and young people with profound and multiple learning difficulties', *The SLD Experience*, 61: 8–12.

Ndaji F. and Tymms P. (2009) *The P Scales: Assessing the progress of children with special educational needs*. London: Wiley-Blackwell.

Maddison A. (2002) 'A study of curriculum development in a new special school', *British Journal of Special Education*, 29(1): 20–28.

Magiati and Howlin (2003) 'A pilot evaluation study of the Picture Exchange Communication System (PECS) for children with autistic spectrum disorders', *Autism*, 7(3): 297–320.

Male D. B. (1996) 'Who goes to SLD schools?', *Journal of Applied Research in Intellectual Disabilities*, 9(4): 307–323.

Male D. B. (2000) 'Target setting in schools for children with severe learning difficulties: Headteacher's perceptions', *British Journal of Special Education*, 27(1): 6–12.

Male D. B. (2001) 'Inclusion opportunities for pupils with severe and profound and multiple learning difficulties', *The SLD Experience*, 30: 6–10.

Male D. B. (2008) 'Recent research', *The SLD Experience*, 50: 39–40.

Male D. B. and Rayner M. (2009) 'Who goes to special schools?', *Educational and Child Psychology*, 26(4): 19–30.

Manolson A. (1992) *It takes two to talk: A parent's guide to helping children communicate*. Toronto: Hanen Centre.

Marlow N., Wolke D., Bracewell M. and Samara M. (2005) 'Neurologic and developmental disability at 6 years of age following extremely preterm birth', *New England Journal of Medicine*, 352(1): 9–19.

Maslow A. H. (1973) *The further reaches of human nature*. London: Penguin.

Mayston M. (2000) 'The Bobath concept today'. Talk given at the CSP Congress, (October 2000) (accessed at www.bobath.org.uk/concepttoday.php on 20 August 2011).

McAloney K. and Stagnitti K. (2009) 'Pretend play and social play: The concurrent validity of the child-initiated pretend play assessment', *International Journal of Play Therapy*, 18(2): 99–113.

McConkey R. (2006) 'Realising the potential of play for ALL children', *PMLD Link*, 18(3): 8–10.

McConkey R. and McEvoy J. (1986) 'Games for learning to count', *British Journal of Special Education*, 13(2): 59–62.

McCune L. (1995) 'A normative study of representational play at the transition to language', *Developmental Psychology*, 31(2): 198–206.

McGee J. J., Menolascino F., Hobbs D. and Menousek P. (1987) *Gentle teaching: A non-aversive approach to helping persons with mental retardation*. New York: Human Science Press.

McLeskey J. and Waldron A. L. (2011) 'Educational programs for elementary students with learning disabilities: Can they be both effective and inclusive?', *Learning Disabilities Research and Practice*, 26(1): 48–57.

McLinden M. and McCall S. (2002) *Learning through touch*. London: David Fulton.

McNicholas J. (2000) 'The assessment of pupils with profound and multiple learning difficulties', *British Journal of Special Education*, 27(3): 150–153.

Mednick M. (2002) *Supporting children with multiple disabilities*. Birmingham: Question Publishing.

Miliband D. (2004) 'Personalised learning: building a new relationship with schools'. Speech to the North of England Education Conference, Belfast 8 January 2004. www.standards.dfes.gov.uk/innovationunit/personalisatin/

Millar S. (2009) 'Meaningful technology for early level learners', *The SLD Experience*, 53: 15–22.

Millar S. and Aitken S. (2003) *Personal communication passports: Guidelines for good practice*. Edinburgh: Call Centre.

Miller J. (1998) 'Personal needs and independence', in P. Lacey and C. Ouvry, *People with profound and multiple learning disabilities*. London: David Fulton.

Minow M. (1990) *Making all the difference: Inclusion, exclusion and American Law*. Ithica, NY: Cornell University Press.

Mittler P. (1979) *People not patients: Problems and policies in mental handicap*. London: Routledge.

Mittler P. (2000) *Working towards inclusive education: Social contexts.* London: David Fulton.

Mittler P. (1996) 'Training for the 21st century', *The SLD Experience*, 15: 2–3.

Mix K. S., Huttenlocher J. and Cohen Levine S. (2002) *Quantitative development in infancy and early childhood.* Oxford: Oxford University Press.

Montagu A. (1986) *Touching: Human significance of the skin.* New York: Harper and Row.

Montgomery L. M. (1985) *Anne of Green Gables.* New York: Avenel Books.

Murray L. and Trevarthen C. (1986) 'The infant's role in mother–infant communication', *Journal of Child Language*, 13: 15–29.

Musselwhite C. R. and Burkhart L. J. (2001) *Can we chat? Co-planned sequenced social scripts: A make it/take it book of ideas and adaptations.* www.lburkhart.com/product (accessed on 18 November 2010).

Ndaji F. and Tymms P. (2009) *The P scales. Assessing the progress of children with special educational needs.* London: Wiley-Blackwell.

Neelands J. (2002) '11/09: The space in our hearts', *Drama Magazine*, 9(4): 4–10.

Nind M. and Hewett D. (1988) 'Interaction as curriculum', *British Journal of Special Education*, 15(2): 55–57.

Nind M. and Hewett D. (1994) *Access to communication: Developing the basics of communication with people with severe learning difficulties through Intensive Interaction.* London: David Fulton.

Nind M. and Hewett D. (2001) *A practical guide to Intensive Interaction.* Kidderminster: British Institute of Learning Disabilities.

Nind M. and Hewett D. (2006) *Access to communication* (2nd edition). London: David Fulton.

Norwich B. (2008) *Dilemmas of difference, inclusion and disability: International perspectives and future directions.* London: Routledge.

Norwich B. (2010) 'A response to "Special educational needs: A new look"', in M. Warnock and B. Norwich, *Special educational needs: A new look.* London: Continuum.

Norwich B. and Gray P. (2007) 'Special schools in the new era: Conceptual and strategic perspectives in special schools in a new era: How do we go beyond generalities?' Special Educational Needs Policy Options Paper 2, series 6: 28–34 (www.nasen.org.uk) (accessed 4 January 2013).

Norwich B. and Lewis A. (2005) 'How specialized is teaching pupils with disabilities and difficulties?', in A. Lewis and B. Norwich (eds) *Special teaching for special children?* Maidenhead: Open University Press.

Norwich B. and Nash T. (2011) 'Preparing teachers to teach children with special educational needs and disabilities: The significance of a national PGCE development and evaluation project for inclusive teacher education', *Journal of Research in Special Educational Needs*, 11(1): 2–11.

Nye J., Fluck M. and Buckley S. J. (2001) 'Counting and cardinal understanding in children with Down Syndrome and typically developing children', *Down Syndrome Research and Practice*, 7(2): 68–78.

Ockleford A. (1998) *Music moves: Music in the education of children and young people who are visually impaired and have learning disabilities.* London. RNIB.

Ockleford A. (2000) 'Music in the education of children with severe or profound learning difficulties: Issues in current UK provision, a new conceptual framework, and proposals for research', *Psychology of Music*, 28(2): 197–217.

Ockleford A. (2002) *Objects of reference: Promoting early symbolic communication.* London: RNIB.

Ockleford A. (2006) 'Using a musical-theoretical approach to interrogate musical development and social interaction', in N. Lerner and J. Strauss (eds) *Sounding off: Theorizing disability in music.* New York: Routledge. pp. 137–155.

Ockleford A. (2008) *Music for children and young people with complex needs.* Oxford: Oxford University Press.

Ockleford A., Welch G. F. and Zimmerman S. (2002) 'Music education for pupils with severe or profound learning difficulties', *British Journal of Special Education*, 29(4): 178–182.

OECD (2006) 'PISA 2003 sample questions', quoted in T. Clausen-May (2007) 'International mathematics tests and pupils with special educational needs', *British Journal of Special Education, 34*(3): 154–161.

Ofsted (2004) *Setting targets for pupils with special educational needs.* HMI 751. London: Ofsted.

Ofsted (2006). *Inclusion: Does it matter where pupils are taught?* HMI 2535.

Ofsted (2010) *The special educational needs and disabilities review.* London: HMSO.

Orr R. (2003) *My right to play. A child with complex needs.* Maidenhead: Open University Press.

Pagliano P. (1998) 'The multi sensory environment: An open-minded space', *British Journal of Visual Impairment, 16*(3): 105–109.

Pagliano P. (2001) *Using a multisensory environment: A practical guide for teachers.* London: David Fulton.

Papousek H. (1996) 'Musicality in infancy research: Biological and cultural origins of early musicality', in I. Deliege and J. A. Sloboda (eds) *Musical beginnings.* Oxford: Oxford University Press. pp. 37–55.

Papousek M. (1996) 'Intuitive parenting: A hidden source of musical stimulation in infancy', in I. Deliege and J. A. Sloboda (eds) *Musical beginnings.* Oxford: Oxford University Press. pp. 88–112.

Park K. (1998a) 'Form and function in early communication', *The SLD Experience*, 21: 2–5.

Park K. (1998b) 'Theory of mind and drama games', *The SLD Experience*, 22: 2–5.

Park K. (1998c) 'Dickens for all: Inclusive approaches to literature and communication with people with severe and profound learning disabilities', *British Journal of Special Education, 25*(3): 114–118.

Park K. (1999a) 'Storytelling with people with sensory impairments and additional difficulties', *The SLD Experience*, 23: 17–20.

Park K. (1999b) 'Riverrun and pricking thumbs: The use of poetry', *The SLD Experience*, 25: 11–13.

Park K. (2002) '"The Tempest" on stage at Shakespeare's Globe Theatre', *PMLD Link.* Spring Issue.

Park K. (2003) 'Shakespeare's "Twelfth Night" on stage at the Globe Theatre', *The SLD Experience*, 37: 3–7.

Park K. (2004) 'Interactive storytelling: From the Book of Genesis', *British Journal of Special Education, 31*(1): 16–23.

Park K. (2006) 'A funny thing happened on the way to the Globe', *The SLD Experience*, 46: 29–33.

Park K. (2009a) 'Mother Goose: developing language and communication skills through drama', *The SLD Experience*, 53: 7–9.

Park K. (2009b) *Bible stories in Cockney rhyming slang.* London: Jessica Kingsley.

Park K. (2010) *Interactive storytelling: Developing inclusive stories for children and adults.* Bicester: Speechmark.

Park K. (2011) 'Plant stories', *The SLD Experience*, 60: 23–27.

Park K. and Pilcher P. J. (2010) 'Bible stories in Cockney rhyming slang', *The SLD Experience*, 57: 12–15.

Paterson S. J., Girelli L., Butterworth B. and Karmiloff-Smith A. (2006) 'Are numerical impairments syndrome specific? Evidence from Williams syndrome and Down's syndrome', *Journal of Child Psychology and Psychiatry, 47*(2): 190–204.

Peter M. (1996) 'Art', in B. Carpenter, R. Ashdown and K. Bovair (eds) *Enabling access: Effective teaching and learning for pupils with learning difficulties.* London: David Fulton.

Peter M. (1997) *Making dance special.* London: David Fulton.

Peter M. (1998a) '"Good for them, or what?" The arts and pupils with SEN', *British Journal of Special Education, 25*(4): 168–172.

Peter M. (1998b) 'Accessing the curriculum through the arts for pupils with special educational needs', *Support for Learning, 13*(4): 153–156.

Peter M. (2001) 'Art' in B. Carpenter, R. Ashdown and K. Bovair (eds) *Enabling access: Effective teaching and learning for pupils with learning difficulties.* (Revised Edition) London: David Fulton.

Peter M. (2002) 'Play-drama intervention: An approach for autism and hard-to-reach children', *The SLD Experience*, 34: 6–10.

Peter M. (2003) 'Drama, narrative and early learning', *British Journal of Special Education*, 30(1): 21–27.

Peter M. (2009) 'Drama: Narrative pedagogy and socially challenged children', *British Journal of Special Education*, 36(1): 9–17.

Piaget J. (1952) *The origins of intelligence in children.* New York: International Press.

Pilcher P. J. (2009) 'Pinochio by Carlo Collodi, adapted by P. J. Pilcher', *The SLD Experience*, 54: 13–18.

Pilcher P. J. (2012) '"Oliver Twist" – an illustrated script', *The SLD Experience*, 63: 28–37.

Pollitt C. and Grant S. (2008) 'PMLD: finding the answers?', *The SLD Experience*, 51: 19–24.

Porter J. (1993) 'What do pupils with severe learning difficulties understand about counting?', *British Journal of Special Education*, 20(2): 72–75.

Porter J. (2000) 'The importance of creating a mathematical environment', *The SLD Experience*, 26: 16–17.

Porter J. (2005a) 'Awareness of number in children with severe and profound learning difficulties: Three exploratory case studies', *British Journal of Learning Disabilities*, 33(3): 97–101.

Porter J. (2005b) 'Severe learning difficulties', in A. Lewis and B. Norwich (eds) *Special teaching for special teaching? Pedagogies for inclusion.* Maidenhead: Open University Press.

Porter J. (2010) 'Developing number awareness and children with severe and profound learning difficulties', *The SLD Experience*, 57: 3–7.

Porter J. and Lacey P. (1999) 'What provision for pupils with challenging behaviour? A report of a survey of provision and curriculum provided for pupils with learning difficulties and challenging behaviour', *British Journal of Special Education*, 26(1): 23–28.

Porter J., Ouvry C., Morgan M. and Downs C. (2001) 'Interpreting the communication of people with profound and multiple learning difficulties', *British Journal of Learning Disabilities*, 29(1): 12–16.

Prevezer W. (2000) 'Musical interaction and children with autism', in S. Powell (ed) *Helping children with autism to learn.* London: David Fulton.

Pring T. (2004) 'Ask a silly question: Two decades of troublesome trials', *International Journal of Language and Communication Disorders*, 39(3): 285–302.

Prizant B., Wetherby A., Rubin E., Laurent A. and Rydell P. (2006) *The SCERTS Model: A comprehensive educational approach for children with autism spectrum disorders. Volume I: Assessment.* Baltimore, MD: Paul H. Brookes Publishing.

QCA (2001a) *Planning, teaching and assessing the curriculum for pupils with learning difficulties.* London: Qualifications and Curriculum Authority.

QCA (2001b) *Planning, teaching and assessing the curriculum for pupils with learning difficulties. Mathematics.* QCA/01/739.

QCA (2004a) *Planning, teaching and assessing the curriculum for pupils with learning difficulties.* London: Qualifications and Curriculum Authority.

QCA (2004b) *Using the P scales.* London: Qualifications and Curriculum Authority.

QCA (2009) *The P scales: Level descriptors P1 to P8.* London: Qualifications and Curriculum Authority.

QCAA, Wales (2003) 'Personal, health and social education for pupils with PMLD', as reported in J. Ware (2005) 'Profound and multiple learning difficulties', in A. Lewis and B. Norwich (eds) *Special teaching for special teaching? Pedagogies for inclusion.* Maidenhead: Open University Press.

QCDA (2009) *Planning, teaching and assessing the curriculum for pupils with learning difficulties. General guidance.* London: Qualifications and Curriculum Authority.

Raaska H., Elovainio M., Sinkkonen J., Matomäki J., Mäkipää S. and Lapinleimu H. (2012) 'Internationally adopted children in Finland: Parental evaluations of symptoms of reactive attachment disorder and learning difficulties – FINADO study', *Child: Care, Health and Development*, *38*(5): 697–705.

Rawlings M., Dowse L., and Shaddock A. (1995) 'Increasing the involvement of people with an intellectual disability in choice making situations: A practical approach', *International Journal of Disability and Developmental Education*, 42: 137–153.

Remington B. (1996) 'Assessing the occurrence of learning in children with profound intellectual disability: A conditioning approach', *International Journal of Disability, Development and Education*, 43: 101–118.

Rieber R. W. and Carlton A. S. (1993) *The collected works of L. S. Vygotsky, Volume 2: Fundamentals of defectology (abnormal psychology and learning disabilities)*. New York: Plenum Press.

Robbins B. (1991) 'Mathematics for all', in R. Ashdown, B. Carpenter and K. Bovair (eds) *The curriculum challenge*. London: Falmer Press.

Robbins B. (1996) 'Mathematics', in B. Carpenter, R. Ashdown and K. Bovair (eds) *Enabling access: Effective teaching and learning for pupils with learning difficulties*. London: David Fulton.

Robbins B. (2000) 'Does teaching numeracy lead to mathematical learning?', *The SLD Experience*, 26: 9–12.

Roch M. and Levorato M. C. (2009) 'Simple view of reading in Down's syndrome: The role of listening comprehension and reading skills', *International Journal of Communication Disorders*, 2: 206–223.

Roch M., Florit E. and Levorato C. (2011) 'Follow-up study on reading comprehension in Down's syndrome: The role of reading skills and listening comprehension', *International Journal of Language and Communication Disorders*, *46*(2): 231–242.

Roeyers H. (1995) 'Peer mediated proximity intervention to facilitate the social interactions of children with a pervasive developmental disorder', *British Journal of Special Education*, *22*(4): 161–163.

Rose R. (1998) 'The curriculum. A vehicle for inclusion or a lever for exclusion?', in C. Tilstone, L. Florian and R. Rose (eds) *Promoting inclusive practice*. London: Routledge.

Rose R., Fergusson A., Coles C., Byers R. and Banes D. (eds) (1994) *Implementing the whole curriculum for pupils with learning difficulties*. London: David Fulton.

Rosenbaum P. L., Walter S. D., Hanna S. E., Palisano R. J., Russell D. J., Raina P., Wood E., Bartlett D. J. and Galuppi B. E. (2002) 'Prognosis for gross motor function in cerebral palsy', *Journal of the American Medical Association*, *88*(11): 1357–1363.

Rotheram-Fuller E., Kasari C., Chamberlain B. and Locke J. (2010) 'Social involvement of children with autism spectrum disorders in elementary school classrooms', *Journal of Child Psychology and Psychiatry*, *51*(11): 1227–1234.

Runswick-Cole K. (2011) 'Time to end the bias towards inclusive education?', *British Journal of Special Education*, *38*(3): 112–119.

Russ S. (1998) 'Play, creativity and adaptive functioning: Implications for play interventions', *Journal of Clinical Child Psychology*, *27*(4): 469–480.

Russell G. (2002) 'Communication passports', *Eye Contact*, 32: 15–17.

Sacks S. Z. (1998) 'Educating students who have visual impairments with other disabilities', in S. Z. Sacks and R. K. Silberman (eds) *Educating students who have visual impairments with other disabilities*. Baltimore: Brookes.

St Margaret's School (2009) *The profound education curriculum*. Tadworth: Profound Education.

Samuel J., Nind M., Volans A. and Scriven I. (2008) 'An evaluation of Intensive Interaction in community living settings for adults with profound intellectual disabilities', *Journal of Intellectual Disabilities*, *12*(2): 111–126.

Savage R. (2001) 'The "Simple view" of reading: Some evidence and possible implications', *Educational Psychology in Practice*, 17: 17–33.

SCAA (1996) *Planning the curriculum for pupils with profound and multiple learning difficulties.* London: SCAA.

Schalock R., Luckasson R. and Shogren K. (2007) 'The renaming of mental retardation: Understanding the change to the term intellectual disability', *Intellectual and Developmental Disabilities*, 45: 116–124.

Schuengel C., Clasien de Schipper J., Sterkenburg P. S. and Kef S. (2013) 'Attachment, intellectual disabilities and mental health: Research, assessment and intervention', *Journal of Applied Research in Intellectual Disabilities*, 26: 34–46.

Schweigert P. (1989) 'Use of microswitch technology to facilitate social contingency awareness as a basis for early communication skills', *Augmentative and Alternative Communication*, 5: 192–198.

Schweigert P. and Rowland C. (1992) 'Early communication and microtechnology: Instructional sequence and case studies of children with severe multiple disabilities', *Augmentative and Alternative Communication*, 8: 273–284.

Scrutton D. (1984) *Management of the motor disorders of children with cerebral palsy.* London: Spastics International Medical Publishers.

Seach D. (2007) *Interactive play for children with autism.* London: Routledge.

Sebba J. (2011) 'Personalisation, individualisation and inclusion', in J. Sebba, A. Peacock, A. DiFinizio and M. Johnson, 'Personalisation and special educational needs', *Journal of Research in Special Educational Needs*, *11*(3): 203–224.

Sebba J., Byers R. and Rose R. (1993) *Redefining the whole curriculum for pupils with learning difficulties.* London: David Fulton.

Sebba J. and Sachdev D. (1997) *What works in inclusive education?* Ilford: Barnardos.

Seja A. L. and Russ S. W. (1999) 'Children's fantasy play and emotional understanding', *Journal of Clinical Child Psychology*, 28: 269–277.

Seligman M. (1975) *Helplessness: On depression, development and death.* San Francisco, CA: W. H. Freeman.

Sen A. (2001) 'Social exclusion: Concepts, application and scrutiny', Social Development Papers No. 1. Manila. Office of Environment and Social Development. Asian Development Bank.

Sex Education Forum (2005) *Sex and relationships education framework, Factsheet 30.* London: National Children's Bureau.

Sheehy K. and Howe M. (2001) 'Teaching non-readers with severe learning difficulties to recognise words: The effective use of symbols in a new technique', *Westminster Studies in Education*, *24*(1): 61–71.

Sherborne V. (1990) *Developmental movement for children.* Cambridge: Cambridge University Press.

Sherrat D. and Peter M. (2002) *Developing play and drama in children with autistic spectrum disorders.* London: David Fulton.

Simmons B. and Bayliss P. (2007) 'The role of special schools for children with profound and multiple learning difficulties: Is segregation always best?', *British Journal of Special Education*, *34*(1): 19–24.

Simons C. (1977) 'Learning to play together', *British Journal of Special Education*, *4*(2) 17–19.

Sinason V. (1994) *Mental handicap and the human condition.* London: Free Association Books.

Sissons M. (2010) *MAPP: Mapping and Assessing Personal Progress.* North Allerton: The Dales School.

Smith B. (1994) 'Handing over control to people with learning difficulties', in J. Coupe-O'Kane and B. Smith (eds) *Taking control: Enabling people with learning difficulties.* London: David Fulton.

Smith F. (1985) *Reading.* Cambridge: Cambridge University Press.

Smith F. (2011) *Understanding reading: A psycholinguistic analysis of reading and learning to read.* (6th Edition). London: Routledge.

Smith Myles B., Tapscott Cook K., Miller N., Rinner L., and Robbins L. (2000) *Asperger syndrome and sensory issues: Practical solutions for making sense of the world.* Kansas: Autism Asperger Publishing Company.

Smyth C. M. and Bell D. (2006) 'From biscuits to boyfriends: The ramifications of choice for people with learning disabilities', *British Journal of Learning Disabilities*, 34(4): 227–236.

Spargo D. and Northway R. (2011) 'Meeting the health needs of children and young people with severe and profound learning disabilities: The contribution of the school nurse and community learning disability nurse', *The SLD Experience*, 61: 19–24.

Spiker D., Boyce G. C., and Boyce L. K. (2002) 'Parent–child interactions when young children have disabilities', in L. M. Glidden (ed) *International review of research in mental retardation*. San Diego, CA: Academic Press.

Staff of Rectory Paddock School (1983) *In search of a curriculum*. (2nd edition) Sidcup: Robin Wren Publications.

Stagnitti K. (2009) 'Play intervention – The learn to play program', in K. Stagnitti and R. Cooper, *Play as therapy. Assessment and therapeutic interventions*. London: Jessica Kingsley. pp. 176–186.

Stagnitti K. (2010) 'Play', in M. Curtin, M. Molineux and J. Supyk-Mellson (eds) *Occupational therapy and physical dysfunction enabling occupation*. (6th edition) London: Elsevier. pp. 371–387.

Stagnitti K., O'Connor C. and Sheppard L. (2012) 'Impact of the Learn to Play program on play, social competence and language for children aged 5–8 years who attend a specialist school', *Australian Occupational Therapy Journal*, 59(4): 302–311.

Staves L. (2001) *Mathematics for children with severe and profound learning difficulties*. London: David Fulton.

Sterkenberg P. S., Janssen C. G. C. and Schuengel C. (2008) 'The effect of an attachment-based behaviour therapy for children with visual and severe intellectual disabilities', *Journal of Applied Research in Intellectual Disabilities*, 21(2): 126–135.

Stewart D. S., Mallet A., Koltonowska G., Pembleton S., Baldwin C. and Evans P. (2000) 'Mathematics for life long learning', *The SLD Experience*, 26: 18–19.

Stoneman Z. (2009) 'Disability research methodology: Current issues and future challenges', in S. L. Odom, R. H. Horner, M. E. Snell and J. Blacher (eds) *Handbook of developmental disabilities*. New York: Guildford Press.

Tadema A. C., Vlaskamp C. and Ruijssenaars A. J. J. M. (2005) 'The development of a questionnaire of child characteristics for assessment purposes', *European Journal of Special Needs Education*, 20: 325–339.

Taggart G., Ridley K., Rudd P. and Benefield P. (2005) *Thinking skills in the Early Years: A literature review*. Slough: National Foundation for Educational Research.

Tartaglia N. R., Hansen R. L. and Hagerman R. J. (2009) 'Advances in genetics', in S. L. Odom, R. H. Horner, M. E. Snell and J. Blacher (eds) *Handbook of developmental disabilities*. New York: Guildford Press.

Taylor R. (1992) 'Art', in K. Bovair, B. Carpenter and G. Upton (eds) *Special curricula needs*. London: David Fulton and Nasen.

Taylor S. and Park K. (2001) 'Watergate goes Lycra', *The SLD Experience*, 30: 20–21.

Terzi L. (2010) 'Afterword: Difference, equality and the ideal of inclusion in education', in M. Warnock and B. Norwich, *Special educational needs: A new look*. London: Continuum.

Theodorou F. and Nind M. (2010) 'Inclusion in play: A case study of a child with autism in an inclusive nursery', *Journal of Research in Special Educational Needs*, 10(2): 99–106.

Thomas G. and O'Hanlon C. (2005) 'Series editors' preface', in A. Lewis and B. Norwich (eds) *Special teaching for special children*. Maidenhead: Open University Press.

Tilstone C. (1999) '"Networking": effective inset for the Literacy Hour', *The SLD Experience*, 23: 7–9.

Tissot C. (2009) 'Establishing a sexual identity. Case studies of learners with autism and learning difficulties', *Autism*, 13(6): 551–556.

Trehub S. E. (1990) 'The perception of musical patterns by human infants: The provision of similar patterns by their parents', in M. A. Berkley and W. C. Stebbins (eds) *Comparative perception, Vol. 1: Mechanisms*. New York: Wiley. pp. 429–459.

Trevarthen C. and Aitken K. (2001) 'Infant intersubjectivity: Research, theory and clinical application', *Journal Child Psychology and Psychiatry*, 42(1): 3–48.

Trevarthen C., Aitken K., Papoudi D. and Robarts J. (1998) *Children with autism: Diagnosis and intervention to meet their needs*. London: Jessica Kingsley.

Uzgiris I. and Hunt J. (1975) *Assessment in infancy: Ordinal scales of psychological development*. Urbana: University of Illinois Press.

van der Putten A., Vlaskamp C. and Schuivens E. (2011) 'The use of a multisensory environment for assessment of sensory abilities and preferences in children with profound intellectual and multiple disabilities: A pilot study', *Journal of Applied Research in Intellectual Disabilities*, 24(3): 280–284.

Van Walwyk L. (2011) 'Measuring progress in children with profound and multiple learning difficulties', *The SLD Experience*, 60: 9–16.

Vlaskamp C. and Cuppen-Fonteine H. (2007) 'Reliability of assessing the sensory perception of children with profound intellectual and multiple disabilities: A case study', *Child: Care, Health and Development*, 33(5): 547–551.

Vygotsky l. L. S. (1978) *Mind in society: The development of higher psychological processes*. Edited and translated by M. Cole *et al.* MA Harvard University Press.

Waddell M. (1998) *Inside lives: Psychoanalysis and the growth of personality*. London: Tavistock.

WAG (2006) *Routes for learning: Assessment materials for learners with profound learning difficulties and additional disabilities*. Cardiff: Welsh Assembly Government.

Ware J. (1987) 'Providing education for children with profound and multiple learning difficulties: A survey of resources and an analysis of staff–pupil interactions in special care units'. Unpublished PhD thesis. University of London Institute of Education.

Ware J. (2003) *Creating a responsive environment for people with profound and multiple learning difficulties*. London: David Fulton.

Ware J. (2005) 'Profound and multiple learning difficulties', in A. Lewis and B. Norwich (eds) *Special teaching for special teaching? Pedagogies for inclusion*. Maidenhead: Open University Press.

Ware J. (2011) 'Developing communication skills for all learners', *The SLD Experience*, 61: 25–31.

Warnock M. (2010) 'Response to Brahm Norwich', in M. Warnock and B. Norwich, *Special educational needs: A new look* (edited by L. Terzi). London: Continuum Books.

Wedell K. (1992) 'Assessment', in K. Bovair, B. Carpenter and G. Upton (eds) *Special curricula needs*. London: David Fulton.

Weeks Z. (2012) 'Counting and the use of resources, *The SLD Experience*, 62: 7–11.

Weinberg W. A. and Brumback R. A. (1992) 'The myth of ADHD: Symptoms resulting from multiple causes', *Journal of Child Neurology*, 7(4): 431–445.

Wendelborg C. and Kvello O. (2010) 'Perceived social acceptance and peer intimacy among children with disabilities in regular schools in Norway', *Journal of Applied Research in Intellectual Disabilities*, 23: 143–153.

Wetherby A. and Prizant B. (2000) 'Introduction to autism spectrum disorders', in A. Wetherby and B. Prizant (eds) *Autism spectrum disorders: A transactional developmental perspective, Vol. 9*. London: Paul Brookes Publishing.

Wilcox M. J., Kouri T. A., and Caswell S. (1990) 'Partner sensitivity to communication behaviour of young children with developmental disabilities', *Journal of Speech and Hearing Disorders*, 55: 679–693.

Wilkinson C. (1994) 'Teaching pupils with profound and multiple learning difficulties to exert control', in J. Coupe O'Kane and B. Smith (eds) *Taking control: Enabling people with learning difficulties*. London: David Fulton.

Winstock A. (1994) *The Practical Management of Eating and Drinking Difficulties in Children*. Bicester: Winslow Press.

Wishart J. (1988) 'Cognitive development in young children with Down syndrome: Developmental strengths, developmental weaknesses', cited in P. Lacey (2009) 'Teaching thinking in SLD schools', *The SLD Experience*, 54: 19–24.

Wishart J. (2005) 'Children with Down's syndrome', in A. Lewis and B. Norwich (eds) *Special teaching for special teaching? Pedagogies for inclusion*. Maidenhead: Open University Press.

Wolff P. (1979) 'The adventure playground as a therapeutic environment', in D. Canter and C. Sandra (eds) *Designing for therapeutic environments: A review of research*. New York: John Wiley & Sons. pp. 87–117.

Woolf A. (2008) 'Better playtimes training: Theory and practice in an EBD primary school', *Emotional and Behavioural Difficulties*, 13(1): 49–62.

Woolf A. (2011) 'Everyone playing in class: A group play provision for enhancing the emotional well-being of children in school', *British Journal of Special Education*, 38(4): 178–190.

Yesseldyke J. E. (1987) 'Classification of handicapped students', in M. C. Wang, M. C. Reynolds and H. J. Walberg (eds) *Handbook of special education: Research and practice. Volume 1: Learner characteristics and adaptive education*. Oxford: Pergamon Press.

Zijlstra H. P. and Vlaskamp C. (2005) 'The impact of medical conditions on the support of children and profound intellectual disabilities and multiple disabilities', *Journal of Applied Research in Intellectual Disabilities*, 18(2): 151–161.

Index